Why Do You Need This New Edition?

If you're wondering why you should buy this new edition of *Everyday Use,* here are five good reasons!

❶ Separate chapters on invention and memory (ch. 2) and arrangement, style, and delivery (ch. 3) **show you how to generate ideas for writing and then how to organize and present your ideas.**

❷ More than two dozen annotated readings have been added in a new anthology at the end of the book to give you **numerous samples and guidance for your own writing.**

❸ An increased emphasis on visual literacy throughout the text **highlights the connection between the visual and the written and helps you understand how to read images rhetorically.**

❹ Advice is offered throughout to help you **apply rhetorical concepts not only to written essays, but also to oral presentations.**

❺ A new appendix, A Guide to Avoiding Plagiarism, provides concrete suggestions for quoting, summarizing, and paraphrasing to give you **the information you need to avoid unintentionally plagiarizing.**

PEARSON
Longman

Everyday Use

Rhetoric at Work in Reading and Writing

Second Edition

Hephzibah Roskelly
University of North Carolina at Greensboro

David A. Jolliffe
University of Arkansas

New York   San Francisco   Boston
London   Toronto   Sydney   Tokyo   Singapore   Madrid
Mexico City   Munich   Paris   Cape Town   Hong Kong   Montreal

For James Kinneavy and Joseph Comprone
rhetoricians, teachers, mentors

Senior Acquisitions Editor: Katherine Meisenheimer
Development Editor: Francine Weinberg
Senior Marketing Manager: Sandra McGuire
Senior Supplements Editor: Donna Campion
Production Manager: Stacey Kulig
Project Coordination, Text Design, and Electronic Page Makeup: S4Carlisle
Cover Design Manager: Wendy Ann Fredericks
Cover Designer: Kay Petronio
Cover Photos: istockphoto
Photo Researcher: Chris Pullo
Senior Manufacturing Buyer: Roy Pickering
Printer and Binder: R.R. Donnelley and Sons
Cover Printer: Coral Graphics Services, Inc.

For permission to use copyrighted material, grateful acknowledgment is made to the copyright holders on pp. 353–355, which are hereby made part of this copyright page.

Library of Congress Cataloging-in-Publication Data
Roskelly, Hephzibah.
    Everyday use : rhetoric at work in reading and writing : college version / Hephzibah
Roskelly, David A. Jolliffe. — 2nd ed.
        p. cm.
    Includes bibliographical references and index.
    ISBN 978-0-205-59097-1 (pbk. : College Edition) — ISBN 978-0-13-135528-6 (AP Edition) — ISBN
978-0-13-135529-3 (AP Teacher's Annotated Edition)   1.   English language—Rhetoric—Study and
teaching.   2.   Report writing-Study and teaching.   3.   English language—Rhetoric.   4.   Report
writing.   I. Jolliffe, David A.   II. Title.
    PE1404.R668 2008
    808′ .042071—dc22
                                                                              2007051144

Please visit us at www.ablongman.com

ISBN 13: 978-0-131-35528-6 (AP* Edition)
ISBN 10: 0-131-35528-7 (AP* Edition)
ISBN 13: 978-0-131-35529-3 (AP* Teacher's Annotated Edition)
ISBN 10: 0-131-35529-5 (AP* Teacher's Annotated Edition)
ISBN 13: 978-0-205-59097-1 (College Edition)
ISBN 10: 0-205-59097-7 (College Edition)

1 2 3 4 5 6 7 8 9 10—DOC—10 09 08

Contents

Preface   *xii*

1   Everyday Use: Rhetoric in Our Lives   1

Rescuing Rhetoric from Its Bad Reputation: Definitions
     and Examples   3

What Does "Being Skilled at Rhetoric" Mean?   5

Developing Skill with Rhetoric: The Rhetorical Triangle   6
     Key #1: Understanding Persona   8
     Key #2: Understanding Appeals to the Audience   11
     Key #3: Understanding Subject Matter and Its Treatment   13

Modifying the Basic Rhetorical Triangle:
     Rhetoric Occurs in a Context   15
     Key #4: Understanding Context   16
     Key #5: Understanding Intention   18
     Key #6: Understanding Genre   19

Rhetoric in Everyday Life: *Your* Life, *Your* Community   21
     Rhetoric and Citizenship   22
     Rhetoric and Community   24
     Rhetoric and Conscientious Consumption   26

Interchapter 1   29

2   Understanding the Traditional Canons of Rhetoric:
Invention and Memory   33

Rhetoric at Work: Context and the Three Appeals   34

Invention   36

Systematic Invention Strategy I: The Journalist's
     Questions   36

Systematic Invention Strategy II: Kenneth Burke's
     Pentad   39

Systematic Invention Strategy III: The Enthymeme   42

Systematic Invention Strategy IV: The Topics   46
   The Basic Topics   46
   The Common Topics   48

Intuitive Invention Strategies: A Preview   51

Memory   52

Interchapter 2   55

3   Using the Traditional Canons of Rhetoric: Arrangement, Style, and Delivery   57

Arrangement   58
   Genres   58
   Functional Parts   60
   Questions About the Parts   61

Style   63
   Style and Situation   64
   Style and Jargon   65
   Are *You* and *I* Okay?   65
   Style and Contractions   66
   Style and the Passive Voice   66
   Dimensions of the Study of Style: Sentences,
      Words, and Figures   67
   Sentences   67
   Parallel Structure   70
   Words   73
   General Versus Specific Words   74
   Formal Versus Informal Words   74
   Latinate Versus Anglo-Saxon Words   76
   Common Terms Versus Slang or Jargon   78
   Denotation Versus Connotation   79
   Figures of Rhetoric: Schemes and Tropes   79
   Schemes Involving Balance   80
   Schemes Involving Interruption   81

Schemes Involving Omission   82

Schemes Involving Repetition   82

Tropes Involving Comparisons   83

Tropes Involving Word Play   84

Tropes Involving Overstatement or Understatement   85

Tropes Involving the Management of Meaning   85

Delivery   86

Rhetorical Analysis   87

Interchapter 3   91

4   Rhetoric and the Writer   93

Writing as Process: Making the Right Moves for Context   94

Writing as a Rhetorical Process   95

Inventing   95

Investigating   96

Planning   96

Drafting   97

Consulting   98

Revising   99

Editing   99

**Real Writers at Work: Cases for Studying Writing
and Rhetoric**   100

Erica: Slow Starter   100

Erica's Intention and Invention   103

Apply Erica's Solution   104

Chan: Confused About Context   106

Chan, Context, and Notes   109

Apply Chan's Solution   111

Tasha, Lewis, and Susan: A Group at Work on
Writing   112

Nell: The Rhetorical Reviser   114

You Pull It All Together   116

Using What You Read   118

Revising Your First Effort   118

Revising for Persona   119

Revising for Audience   120

Revising Subject   120

Revising Evidence   121

Interchapter 4   123

5   Rhetoric and the Reader   125

Predicting What's Next   126
Understanding How Readers Predict   129

Rosenblatt and Interaction: Two Kinds of Reading   130
Rosenblatt, Reading, and Rhetoric   133
Rhetorical Analysis of *Chaos*   134

Matching Experience and Intention   135

Rhetorical Analysis: You Try It   139

Building the Reader's Repertoire   143

Reading Your Own Writing   145

Interchapter 5   151

6   Readers as Writers, Writers as Readers:
Making Connections   153

Reading and Writing: Different? Similar?   154

The Literacy Memory   156

The Process of Making Meaning: Readers as
Writers   157

More About Prediction and Revision in Reading   161

Prediction and Revision in Writing: Writers as Readers   163

More About Prediction and Revision in Writing   164

Voice and Rhetoric   165

What We Hear When We Read and Write   166
The Logical Appeal: Logos   166
The Ethical Appeal: Ethos   169
The Emotional Appeal: Pathos   171
The Appeals Combined   173

Reading, Writing, and Synthesis: The Researched
   Argument   176
   Tackling the Rhetorical Argument   177
   Assessing a Researched Argument   178

Interchapter 6   189

7   Rhetoric in Narrative   191

Character   194
   Rhetorical Choices for Character   195
   Flat and Round, Static and Dynamic   196
   Character and the Pentad   198

Setting   200
   Summary and Scenic Narration   202

Conflict and Plot   204
   Tragedy Versus Comedy   205
   Conflict in Decision Making   206
   Conflict in Relationships   206
   Conflict with the Elements   206
   Conflict and the Pentad   207
   Protagonist, Antagonist   209

Narrator: Point of View   209
   First-Person Narration   210
   Third-Person Narration   211
   Second-Person Narration   212
   Reliable and Unreliable Narrators   213
   Narrators in Poems   214

Theme   215
   Theme and the Pentad   215
   Symbols   216
   Images   216
   Diction   217
   Syntax   217

A Final Word About Narrative—and About
   Rhetoric   218

Interchapter 7   219

READINGS   221

Henry David Thoreau, "On the Duty of Civil
    Disobedience"   222

Eavan Boland, "It's a Woman's World"   238

Alice Walker, "Everyday Use"   240

ADDITIONAL READINGS   247

Civil Rights and Responsibilities   247

Bob Dylan, "The Times They Are a-Changin'"   248

Rock the Vote Web Pages   249

Jonathan Swift, "A Modest Proposal"   251

John Donne, "Meditation 17"   257

Toni Morrison, Nobel Lecture   259

Dominic Behan, "Patriot Game"   265

Jane Addams, "The Settlement as a Factor in the Labor
    Movement"   266

Mohandas K. Gandhi, "Seven Social Sins"   274

Sitting for Justice: Woolworth's Lunch Counter   275

Feminism and Women's Issues   277

Sojourner Truth, "Ain't I a Woman?"   277

Emily Dickinson, "The Soul Selects Her Own Society"   280

Kate Chopin, "The Story of an Hour"   280

Susan Glaspell, "Trifles"   283

Mike Baldwin, "Our Standards . . ."   295

John Everett Millais, *Ophelia*   296

Virginia Woolf, "Shakespeare's Sister"   297

Katha Pollitt, "Girls Against Boys"?   299

Catherine Haun, "A Woman's Trip Across the Plains
    in 1849"   301

Ethnicity and Culture   316

William Shakespeare, "Shylock's Defense"   317

James Baldwin, "Stranger in the Village"   318

Gabriel García Márquez, "A Very Old Man with
    Enormous Wings"   327

Louise Erdrich, "Indian Boarding School:
    The Runaways"   332

Amy Wu for the U.S. Department of Homeland Security,
    "Border Apprehensions: 2005"   333

Jacob Riis, *Lodgers in a Crowded Bayard Street Tenement: Five
    Cents a Spot*   336

Art Spiegelman, from *Maus II: A Survivor's Tale (And Here
    My Troubles Began)*   337

Leonard Pitts Jr., "The Game of Justice Is Rigged"   339

Glossary of Rhetorical Terms   341

Credits   353

Index   367

Preface

To prepare students to succeed as students and citizens, college writing courses need to achieve several goals. First, they need to teach students to read carefully and critically, interacting with texts of all kinds and actively constructing their meanings, not simply decoding them or believing a text has only one meaning. Second, they need to teach students to conceive good, compelling ideas to write about; to elaborate those ideas in full, effective papers; and to produce them in correct, standard English. Third, they need to teach students to comprehend the structures of language—whole texts, paragraphs, sentences, words, punctuation marks, mechanical conventions, and so on—and to understand both how writers put these structures to work in texts and how readers use them to make sense of texts. One term is inherent in all these goals: *rhetoric*, the art of crafting effective texts for specific audiences. One ultimately rhetorical idea unifies these goals: Writing, whether "literary" or "ordinary," is a purposeful art and craft, and the central aims of a college writing course ought to be to teach students to *read* texts to see how their purpose is made manifest and to *produce* texts that accomplish the purposes that students and their teachers aim to have them accomplish.

Everyday Use: Rhetoric at Work in Reading and Writing is designed specifically for use in English courses that try to achieve these goals. In seven chapters, a series of interchapters, and an anthology of readings, this book offers the foundations for an English course that would teach students how to understand the argument and artistry of texts they read and how to produce their own texts that are rich, purposeful, and effectively crafted.

New To This Edition

We have made numerous updates and added new elements throughout this edition of *Everyday Use* to give instructors and students new pedagogical tools and options. In particular, we draw your attention to the following:

- We have created separate chapters on invention and memory (Chapter 2) and arrangement, style, and delivery (Chapter 3), allowing for a fuller discussion of the five canons of rhetoric.
- We have added a new anthology of readings at the end of the text. These Additional Readings—including more than two dozen essays, poems, songs, and stories—highlight three enduring themes: Civil Rights and Responsibilities, Feminism and Women's Issues, and Ethnicity and Culture.

- In recognition of the increasingly important role visual rhetoric plays in many courses, we have strengthened our emphasis on visual literacy throughout the text. This edition more clearly highlights the connection between the visual and the written and provides additional guidance on how to read images rhetorically.

The Book's Plan

Chapter 1 raises the seemingly simple, yet ultimately complex, question, "What is rhetoric?" In unpacking this question, the chapter addresses three common misperceptions, all of which impede educators' efforts to help students become responsible and effective readers and writers. The first is that rhetoric is something that public figures—notably, politicians—and academics display but not something that students can develop expertise in. The second is that the term *rhetoric* connotes uses of language that are in some way inauthentic. In this misguided view, rhetoric is language that is overly embellished, so thoroughly "dressed up" that it disguises either a lack of substance in a text or a covert, potentially unethical attempt to sway an audience. The third misperception is that rhetoric comprises only the visible features of style and organization in a text. To counter these views, the chapter generates a robust definition of rhetoric that students can understand: Rhetoric is the ability to discover all the things a writer might do in a situation to lead his or her readers to think or act in a certain way, and to use those things—techniques for generating effective ideas and arguments, methods of organizing a text, strategies of sentence structure and diction, and so on—to achieve a desired goal. The chapter explains that rhetoric represents a set of activities—reading, writing, speaking, listening, and discussing—that all intellectually engaged people—students, teachers, and public figures alike—participate in every day. It makes clear that comprehending what rhetoric is and how it works is vitally important to understanding how written texts influence thought and action, in school and in the community, for good or ill.

Chapters 2 and 3 introduce students to a tradition of rhetorical concepts and terms, a tradition with roots in antiquity but applications in our own time. Offering clear, useful activities along the way, these chapters teach students about the five major canons of rhetoric—invention, arrangement, style, memory, and delivery—in terms they can understand and use in their courses and in their lives outside the classroom.

Chapter 4 focuses on the relation between rhetoric and writing and accomplishes two goals. First, it reviews for students the major tenets of writing as a process and shows students how much richer a process it becomes when one looks at the many facets of writing rhetorically. Second, it offers a series of case studies of real student writers who put into practice a great many of the concepts and principles introduced in the first two chapters.

Chapter 5 turns its attention to a subject rarely examined in discussions of rhetoric but one that is central to helping students become more critical, careful users and critics of language. The subject is reading. This chapter explains what it means to read a text rhetorically and to analyze the "landscape" of the text, those things an author does to achieve his or her purposes with readers. By taking up the hands-on activities in this chapter, students come to understand that reading itself is a kind of writing—that they must actively construct a text they read, not simply decode it passively or wait to have its one and only meaning handed down to them.

Chapter 6 builds on the earlier chapters by showing students how reading and writing are connected. The chapter demonstrates, again with challenging, useful activities, how reading with a rhetorically sensitive perspective can help a student become a better, more capable writer, and how writing with an eye to rhetorical effectiveness can lead a student to become a more observant and critical reader.

Chapter 7 takes many of the principles that have been developed in the previous chapters and shows students how to apply them in reading and writing critically about literature—particularly, short stories, novels, and plays. By working with activities in this chapter, students come to understand that literature is not some rarefied corpus that they must approach with passive reverence but is instead a body of work that represents real writers' responses to the world they lived in and helped to shape.

Following each chapter is an interchapter. All seven of the interchapters focus on the same three works: "On the Duty of Civil Disobedience," the famous essay by Henry David Thoreau; "It's a Woman's World," a wonderfully challenging poem by the contemporary Irish poet Eavan Boland; and "Everyday Use," the marvelous short story (whose title we gratefully borrowed for the title of this book) by Alice Walker. These three works appear in their entirety in the "Readings" section, pages 221–246.

The interchapters invite students to know these three works in detail and to apply to them the principles and concepts developed in each chapter. The authors of this book hope that by reading the Thoreau, Boland, and Walker works intensely, students will learn to see all the texts they read and write, both in school and beyond it, through a productive and eye-opening rhetorical lens.

Then beginning on page 247, "Additional Readings" extends and helps students apply the rhetorical insights they gathered as they read and reread "On the Duty of Civil Disobedience," "It's a Woman's World," and "Everyday Use." Loosely grouped in three categories—Civil Rights and Responsibilities, Feminism and Women's Issues, and Ethnicity and Culture—these readings invite students to consider further the dimensions of ideas raised by Thoreau, Boland, and Walker.

Additional Resources

The Additional Resources to accompany *Everyday Use: Rhetoric at Work in Reading and Writing*, written by the authors, presents a wealth of materials to help instructors, including chapter highlights, teaching suggestions, classroom activities, collaborative activities, and answers to chapter activities. The Manual provides sample syllabi showing how the text can be used in conjunction with readings and explains methods for connecting assessment to instruction.

MyCompLab

MyCompLab is a Web site that offers comprehensive online writing resources in one dynamic, accessible place. At MyCompLab, students can use interactive tutorials and exercises for grammar, writing, and research; do peer review; and see instructors' comments. Go to *mycomplab.com* to register for these premiere writing tools and much more.

Acknowledgments

We're grateful to many colleagues across the country for their encouragement and support, and especially the following:

Ann Berthoff, University of Massachusetts, Boston
Elizabeth Chiseri-Strater, University of North Carolina at Greensboro
William Covino, Florida Atlantic University
Peter Elbow, University of Massachusetts, Amherst
Marilyn Elkins, University of California, Los Angeles
Dawn L. Elmore-McCrary, San Antonio College
Ronald R. Hulewicz, Broward Community College
Jeraldine Kraver, University of Northern Colorado
Linda Macri, University of Maryland, College Park
Karen Nulton, Educational Testing Service
Kate Ronald, Miami University
Dale Ross, Iowa State University
Renee Shea, Bowie State University
Bonnie S. Sunstein, University of Iowa
Ed Uehling, Valparaiso University

We'd like to thank Fran Weinberg, our creative and patient editor; Allison Harl for her assistance in finding additional readings for the second edition; Eben Ludlow, our original guru for the first edition; and Katherine Meisenheimer, our new sponsor at Pearson Longman.

Our loving thanks go to Gwynne Gertz, Michael Roskelly, and Natchez, Claire, Charlie, Levi, Hank, and Daisy for their loyal support.

H.R.

D.A.J.

Everyday Use
Rhetoric in Our Lives

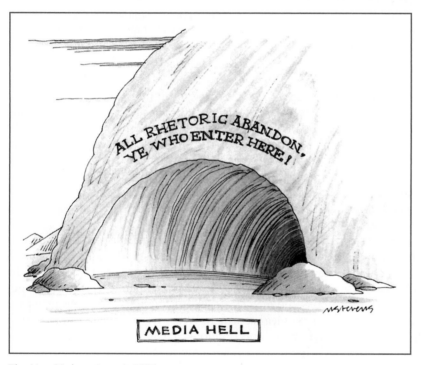

The New Yorker, *June 4, 1990.*

Late night on Route 66, somewhere in Arizona.

Nick checks the speedometer, slows. He looks over at Kate quickly, then focuses on the road. He clears his throat.

Kate stares out her window. The corner of her mouth twitches.

NICK: So, do you think there are many cops on the road?

KATE: This time of night?

NICK (SPEEDING UP): Well . . . guess not.

Kate reaches for the radio buttons. He reaches at the same time. Their fingers touch.

NICK AND KATE (AT ONCE):   Sorry.

NICK: I mean . . . for the radio.

KATE: Me too.

Kate looks out the window again. She begins to hum with the radio. Nick looks over at her again, longer this time. He begins to hum too. She turns to him now. He slows the car.

NICK: So, do you still want to go to the Grand Canyon?

What do you think is going on in this movie snippet? If you were to explain it, your analysis might go something like this: These two people have had an argument. He wants the fight to be over, but he doesn't want to be the first to apologize. She wants it to be over too, but she doesn't want to give in. They're looking for a way to say they're sorry without saying it. They're going to be back together before they get to the Grand Canyon. The writer of the script has used gestures, actions, and sounds, as well as words, to convey the message that these two people want to make up, and the reader of the scene gets the message, probably without any difficulty.

How this communication between the writer and the reader happens is the subject of this book. Readers and writers can understand one another so well because every day they use **rhetoric,** which might be defined initially as the art that humans use to process all the messages we send and receive. Messages are all around us—in books and magazines, in our conversation, in the news, in music and art, and in the movies we watch. When we produce messages, rhetoric helps us get ideas, emotions, and opinions across to others. When we receive messages, rhetoric helps us understand the ideas, emotions, and opinions of those around us.

The writer of the movie scene above uses what he knows from experience, reading, or observation to write the descriptions of how each **character** moves and acts. The reader also uses experience, reading, or observation to understand the characters' actions and to understand what the writer is suggesting. As the writer writes and the reader reads, they negotiate through the **rhetorical choices** they have made, and they begin to anticipate, making decisions about what's happening and what will happen next.

Reader and writer decide these things, moreover, based on how they perceive the scene and how they understand the scene in context. If the movie is billed as a horror film, the last line of the scene might take on a sinister implication. If the main characters are played by comedians, readers wait for a punchline.

We all use rhetoric every day, whether we use it deliberately or not, and we all respond to rhetoric every day, whether we're conscious of it or not. Since the world around us carries messages that get received or lost or translated or transformed, to understand rhetoric is to understand the world better and to participate in it more fully.

Rescuing Rhetoric from Its Bad Reputation: Definitions and Examples

It's sometimes difficult to overlook the unsavory (and undeserved) reputation that the term *rhetoric* has. Many people are most familiar with the word only in its negative sense, describing something that has style but no substance: "His speech was mere rhetoric." Or, even worse, the term *rhetoric* sometimes refers to a speaker's lack of sincerity or deliberate falseness in order to coerce an **audience** to follow a wrongheaded or evil course of action. To be an effective rhetorician, in this ill-considered definition, means to hoodwink the audience, to get them to believe that what is false is actually true, and to manipulate facts or emotions to serve the speakers' unscrupulous ends. In this sense, someone might claim that Hitler was a good rhetorician because he could, through his language and skillful manipulation of events, encourage people to believe the worse cause was the better one.

When someone defines *rhetoric* in this way, he or she is making a negative assumption about the ethics of the person who's speaking. To call a **speaker** "full of rhetoric" is to suggest that he or she doesn't have much to say or is using false and misleading language. Indeed, for many historical reasons, people also tend to think that rhetoric is the opposite of clear communication, exists in contrast to reality, and acts as a roadblock to making progress on important issues. Consider, for example, the following sentence from a newspaper article about parental involvement in schools.

> After all of these years and all of this rhetoric, the infrastructure to help families know what to do to support this [school–parent] partnership that everybody talks about is still not there.
>
> —Washington Post, *January 16, 2001*

The writer of this sentence obviously thinks that, at best, the discussions of parental involvement in the media, in school boards, and in parent–teacher associations—what the writer refers to as "all of this rhetoric"—have not helped such involvement to take place. At worst, the writer apparently believes, "all of this rhetoric" has impeded progress toward parental involvement in schools.

These definitions about the misleading, cloudy, potentially evil nature of rhetoric are, quite frankly, wrong. They are legacies of several moments in history when some influential philosophers misunderstood rhetoric.

A better definition of rhetoric, one that explains how and why communication works, presumes that a speaker or writer (or **rhetor [REH-tor],** to use an ancient Greek term that encompasses both speakers and writers, *a term we will use throughout this book when we are referring to someone who may be a writer, speaker, reader, or listener*) is searching for methods to persuade hearers or readers *because* he or she has something valuable to say, something that arises from his or her position as an honest, inquiring, ethical person. The *rhetor* in classical times referred to the speaker, to "the good person speaking well," as Roman rhetorician Quintilian defined the speaker.

Here, then, is a useful definition of rhetoric. Rhetoric refers to two things:

- The art of analyzing all the language choices that writer, speaker, reader, or listener might make in a given situation so that the text becomes meaningful, purposeful, and effective
- The specific features of texts, written or spoken, that cause them to be meaningful, purposeful, and effective for readers or listeners in a given situation

Activity

What follows is a situation that might be quite common where you go to school. Read the scenario carefully. Then, in a group, discuss the choices involving language that Randall Leigh makes in order to be persuasive. Evaluate the specific features of his requests to his classmates.

Randall Leigh is a bright but rather forgetful person, and because of the latter, he is a compulsive calendar keeper. Nearly every day, he gets up, looks at his day planner, figures out what he needs to do when, and then heads out, either to school or to his part-time job at Computers 4 U, where he works 20 hours a week. Randall lives close enough to school so that he can walk to his classes, but he has to rely on the city bus system to get to work since he does not own a car.

One day, Randall slips up. He neglects to check his day planner until after he gets to school. He thinks he is not scheduled to work that afternoon, but, alas, he is wrong. He is due at work exactly 30 minutes after his last class—just enough time to get there on the city bus. But here is the problem: Randall has come to school flat broke—he doesn't even have the $1.50 bus fare it costs to get to work. He is pretty sure he can borrow the money from someone at work that will enable him to get home, but getting to work is another matter.

He decides he needs to appeal to his classmates for the $1.50 bus fare. Seeing his buddy Brandon approach in the hallway, Randall tries his first maneuver.

"Hey, Brandon, you have to help me out," he says. "I just realized that I have to be at work this afternoon, and I'm completely broke. I can't call in sick, man—you've been there, you know how important I am to the store. I have to answer all the customers' technical questions that the manager can't answer, and that's most of them. So, is there any way you can stand me $1.50 for bus fare?"

"Sorry, dude," Brandon replies, "I'm really short myself, and I have to take Louanne out for a burger after school today and patch some things up between us. Wish I could help out, but I just can't."

"Sheesh," Randall thinks to himself, "I lose out to Brandon's temperamental girlfriend." But then Randall sees the object of his own affections, Kim, walking his way.

"Hey, Kim, how's my best friend in the whole world doing today?"

"What do you want, Randall?"

"Now, what makes you think I want anything? It's always just such a joy to see you, that's all. You light up my life, and all that—you bring me bliss, love, companionship. Why, just to be seen with you makes me the envy of most of the guys in the school."

"Uh-huh."

"But since you mention it," Randall goes on, "there would be something you can do that would make me very, very happy. You see, like the fool I am, I came to school today without any money, and I have to get to work right after class today. I don't suppose you could spare a buck fifty for bus fare, could you?"

"Oh, Randall, all that buttering up for just bus fare?" Just then, a gaggle of Kim's friends ambles by, and she joins them. "Ta ta, Randy," she says. "Good luck getting to work!"

Randall is beside himself—how is he going to get the bus fare? He spies Nate walking his way. He doesn't know Nate very well—they were partners in a bio lab once, and they got along pretty well. Randall decides to try a long shot.

"Hi there, Nate—long time no see."

"Oh, hi, Randall. What's up?"

"Nate, I'm in a really tight spot. You know me to be an honest, dependable guy, don't you? Remember when we worked on the lab report together? I held up my end of the project, didn't I?"

"Of course, you did," Nate says. "You were the best lab partner I've ever had."

"Well," Randall proceeds, "since you know you can trust me, and you know I'm good for it, how about lending me $1.50, just till I see you again? See, I have to get to work right after class today, and I absentmindedly left home without any money for bus fare, and, well, if there's anybody you can count on to pay you back, you know I'm the guy."

"Hmmm, let me check to see if I can help you out," Nate replies. "I might have an extra $1.50 that I can front you."

What Does "Being Skilled at Rhetoric" Mean?

Once you accept the broader, more inclusive definition of rhetoric, you begin to understand that becoming skilled at rhetoric is a valuable part of your education, one that you will work on throughout your school years and beyond. Consider the following:

- Being skilled at rhetoric means being able to make good speeches and write good papers, but it also means having the ability to read other people's compositions and listen to their spoken words with a discerning eye and a critical ear.

- Being skilled at rhetoric means reading not only to understand the main and supporting points of what someone writes but also to analyze the decisions the rhetor makes as he or she works to accomplish a purpose for a specific audience.

- Being skilled at rhetoric means being able to *plan and write* compositions, not just write them.
- Being skilled at rhetoric means being able to examine a situation—in school, in your community, in society as a whole—and determine what has already been said and written, what remains unresolved, and what you might say or write to continue the conversation or persuade readers to take action.

What all these statements add up to is that a person skilled at rhetoric needs to develop a very full menu of reading and writing techniques, strategies, and skills, and needs to be judicious in how he or she uses them. There is so much you can do when you write a paper to make it effective for readers. For example, you might open your paper with a surprising question or quotation. You might challenge your readers' assumptions about a topic. You might write a long, complicated sentence followed by a short, abrupt one. You might rely on complex, carefully selected vocabulary that will show your reader you have an in-depth knowledge of the subject you're writing about. Being skilled at rhetoric does not mean that you have to *use* everything you know in every composition you write. It means that you are able to take an inventory of what you *might* do to make a paper impressive and select the options that work most effectively with your readers.

Developing Skill with Rhetoric: The Rhetorical Triangle

The best way to begin developing skill with rhetoric is to envision the basic rhetorical activity—creating a text that you hope will be meaningful, purposeful, and effective for a reader, or reading a text so that it becomes meaningful, purposeful, and effective for you—as a triangle. The **rhetorical triangle** has its roots in the work of Aristotle, a fourth-century B.C.E. Greek philosopher who wrote extensively about rhetoric. The rhetorical triangle (or **Aristotelian triad,** as some people call it) suggests that a person creating or analyzing a text must consider three elements:

- The subject and the kinds of **evidence** used to develop it
- The audience—their knowledge, ideas, attitudes, and beliefs
- The character of the rhetor—in particular, how the rhetor might use his or her personal character effectively in the text

A diagram of the basic rhetorical triangle is shown on page 7.

Notice that the triangle has arrows from one point to another and that the arrows go both ways. These arrows show the dynamic nature of the rhetorical act. The rhetor understands something about the audience—who they are, what they know—and that understanding makes the rhetor highlight certain elements of character and personality and downplay others. The rhetor creates a **persona**—literally a "mask" but figuratively the character that the audience perceives behind the text—based in part on who the rhetor presumes the audience

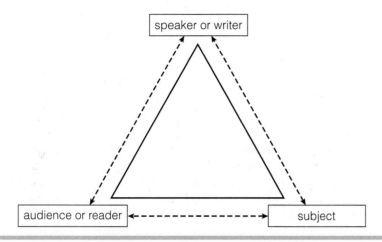

Rhetorical Triangle

to be and in part on what he or she knows and believes about the subject of the text: that is, on what bits of evidence or proof he or she finds most compelling and persuasive. Members of the audience, in turn, hold some beliefs, based on knowledge and past experience, about the rhetor and about the subject, and they tap into these beliefs as they listen or read. Also, members of the audience use their ability to reason—to put together evidence logically—and they are persuaded by the strength of the evidence presented about the subject.

Throughout the remainder of this chapter, we will use the diagram of the rhetorical triangle, initially in its basic form and later in a slightly modified form, to introduce six keys to developing skill with rhetoric. The first three keys—understanding persona, understanding appeals to an audience, and understanding subjects—emerge from the basic triangle. The last three keys—understanding context, understanding intention, and understanding genre—grow out of the triangle in its modified form.

Activity

Reread the scenario about Randall Leigh and the bus fare in the previous activity (pages 4–5). Then, in a group, discuss the following questions:

- What kind of persona did Randall try to present to each of his three audiences—Brandon, Kim, and Nate?
- What assumptions do you think Randall made about each of the three audiences—Brandon, Kim, and Nate—that led him to make decisions about how to present his case?
- What kinds of plea, evidence, or proof did Randall employ with each of the audiences to try to persuade Brandon, Kim, and Nate to lend him the bus fare?

- What do you think Brandon, Kim, and Nate knew about Randall—his personality, his job, and so on—that led them to react the way they did to his entreaties?

Key #1: Understanding Persona

A rhetor who understands persona is able to do two things: first, speak or write so that the audience members perceive a distinct character, usually one who is educated, considerate, trustworthy, and well intentioned; second, make **inferences** and judgments about the character and personality of another writer or speaker, analyzing how that writer appeals to the audience, invites the audience to interact with current or historical events, and wants the audience to act after they have finished reading or listening to the text.

Listen to this **voice** from an editorial in the *Sports Illustrated* of August 5, 2002:

Subjects we're tired of hearing about, because nothing-is-ever-going-to-change-anyhow:

1. Does the Second Amendment mean just the militia?
2. Did Shakespeare really write Shakespeare?
3. Yes, but what about the Grassy Knoll?
4. Is Oprah going to marry Stedman?
5. Should Pete Rose go into the Hall of Fame?

What can you tell so far about the position the writer is developing? How do you know it? Have you ever asked yourself any of the questions the writer poses? They vary in seriousness, but the writer has linked them together because they're all seemingly irresolvable. The writer seems to be humorous and a little mocking, as though there's no point in writing about any of the questions he's posed. Here's the next word:

Still.

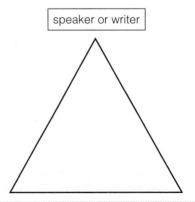

So the writer, Frank Deford, is going to write about something that he already believes to be irresolvable. "Still," he just can't help it. He's going to write. About Pete Rose, which you've probably guessed because the piece appears in *Sports Illustrated*. You've also guessed it for a rhetorical reason—it appears last in the group of questions. The next paragraph suggests reasons that Rose belongs in baseball's Hall of Fame.

> It is Hall of Fame induction time again (Ozzie Smith went in on Sunday), so we ought to at least mention the lunacy of baseball's freezing Charlie Hustle out of Casa Immortality. First of all, it is irrational to deny the man who made the most hits in history a place in Ye Olde Shrine. Second, it is stupid. Third, it is not working: the only person the ban benefits is Pete himself.

What strikes you here? Deford sets the situation for his piece—"It is Hall of Fame induction time again"—to suggest that Rose's failure to be inducted should at least be mentioned. Deford appears reasonable, listing three reasons that Rose should be admitted. What about Deford's **tone,** his **attitude** toward the subject he's writing about? Given that one of the three reasons is "It is stupid," we might see Deford continuing the tone of light mockery that his questions at the beginning suggest. The **diction** of the paragraph—"Charlie Hustle" (a nickname for Rose?), "Casa Immortality," "Ye Olde Shrine"—is informal and at the same time specialized. Baseball fans would know whether Rose was called Charlie Hustle or not, and they'd know who Ozzie Smith was.

As you might predict from the last sentence of Deford's paragraph, the writer goes on to develop his case about how Rose has benefited from being the "Official Pariah of Baseball," selling his image and his case in products, on talk shows, and on Main Street in Cooperstown, New York, the home of the Hall of Fame itself. Deford develops his case with anecdotes about baseball fans, with the history of baseball commissioners' unfair exclusion of other figures like Shoeless Joe Jackson in the early twentieth century, and finally with this admission:

> Of course Pete Rose is guilty of betting on baseball. He's as guilty as, well, Paul Hornung, who bet on NFL games while playing in the NFL but is properly plaqued in Canton. He's as guilty as all sorts of putative baseball immortals who stoke up on steroids. But Rose was guilty only when he was a manager. Even if he bet on baseball, even if he disobeyed the infield fly rule or shot Cock Robin, there is not a scintilla of evidence that he did anything untoward when he was playing the game. Even if you fervently believe that Manager Rose soiled the National Pastime, how unfair, how Un-American, is it that the glories of his youth should be censored by the sins of male menopause? That's just not right.

Comparing Rose with other rule violators in sports who have nonetheless been honored for their accomplishments, Deford makes his logical point: there is no **logic** in denying Rose. The final paragraph slams baseball by noting that in the matter of Pete Rose, "Baseball has long had a trust exemption." The surface logic and the light tone are both obvious as you read. You might have to read it again to hear the **irony** and underlying displeasure, even anger, at those who are responsible for making decisions about the national pastime. This is a writer who loves baseball and who believes unjust punishments sully the game.

Writers usually want the persona they develop and the voice they use to be genuine, to reflect who they really are. Occasionally, however, writers use the mask of another voice for comic **effect** or to underscore the seriousness of a position they believe in. You might be familiar with Jonathan Swift's famous essay "A Modest Proposal" (1729), in which he mock-seriously suggests that a good solution to the economic woes of Ireland would be to begin eating Ireland's children.

> I have been assured by a very knowing American of my acquaintance in London, that a young healthy child well nursed is at a year old the most delicious, nourishing and wholesome food, whether stewed, roasted, baked, or broiled; and I make no doubt that it will equally serve in a fricassee or a ragout.

Swift's tone sounds reasonable, in contrast to the outrageousness of his proposal. Readers are led to understand the tragic plight of the Irish by reading the details of suffering and deprivation in the supposedly dispassionate voice of the speaker. As readers, we do more than sympathize. We are moved to anger and to a desire to change the situation we read about.

Writers thus use their voices—indeed, they create and sustain a tone with those voices—to affect readers' understanding and belief. Using the term *persona*, Aristotle referred to the character that readers could discern from the writer's or speaker's use of words, arrangement of ideas, and choice of details. The persona was the mask that Greek actors wore when they performed, either the exaggerated smile or frown mask of comedy and tragedy that you're familiar with as a **symbol** of theater. The word persona today is used to show the artfulness of the speaker's creation of voice, how deliberately the speaker selects words, tells a story, and repeats phrases in order to help listeners hear the voice that the speaker has decided will be most effective. Swift wore a mask of high good humor and reasonableness that served to underscore his appalling suggestions and reinforce the horror of poverty in Ireland. The mask you wear as a writer doesn't hide you from your readers—it meets them head on and interacts with them purposefully and effectively.

Activity

In his novel *The Adventures of Tom Sawyer,* Mark Twain creates a scene in which a student reads the following composition to the class. Read the composition carefully, and then in your group discuss how Twain wants us, his readers, to characterize the persona of the speaker. Be sure to point out specific parts of the composition that support your **claims.**

IS THIS, THEN, LIFE?

In the common walks of life, with what delightful emotions does the youthful mind look forward to some anticipated scene of festivity! Imagination is busy sketching rose-tinted pictures of joy. In fancy, the voluptuous votary of fashion sees herself amid the festive throng, "the observed of all observers." Her graceful form, arrayed in snowy robes, is whirling through the mazes of the joyous dance; her eye is brightest, her step is lightest in the gay assembly.

In such delicious fancies time quickly glides by, and the welcome hour arrives for her entrance into the elysian world, of which she has had such bright dreams. How fairylike does everything appear to her enchanted vision! Each new scene is more charming than the last. But after a while she finds that beneath this goodly exterior, all is vanity: the flattery which once charmed her soul now grates harshly upon her ear; the ballroom has lost its charms; and with wasted health and embittered heart she turns away with the conviction that earthly pleasures cannot satisfy the longings of the soul!

Key #2: Understanding Appeals to the Audience

A text becomes rhetorical only when an audience reads or hears it and responds to it. A key to developing skill with rhetoric, therefore, is understanding *how* a text appeals to an audience. Once again, Aristotle's ideas are influential. In ancient Athens, as Aristotle taught his students to discuss and create speeches about important issues, he developed a system that explained to his students how to locate the "available means of persuasion" as they developed their **personae** (the plural of *persona*), understood the needs and the knowledge and experience of their hearers, and researched and developed their topics. Rhetoric, he argued, could help students accomplish their aims as they spoke, primarily to persuade hearers to a course of action based on a common search for truth.

This persuasion happens, Aristotle taught, because a rhetor makes three kinds of closely related **appeals** to an audience through a spoken or written text.

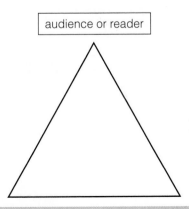

- A rhetor employs **logos** by offering a clear, reasoned central idea (or ideas) and developing it (or them) with appropriate evidence to appeal to an audience's sense of logic.
- A rhetor appeals to **ethos** by offering evidence that he or she is credible—knows important and relevant information about the topic at hand and is a good, believable person who has the readers' best interests in mind.
- A rhetor appeals to **pathos** by drawing on the emotions and interests of the audience so that they will be sympathetically inclined to accept and buy into central ideas and arguments.

The rhetor does not necessarily make these appeals in separate sections of a text. A single sentence can appeal to logos, the audience's interest in a clear, cogent idea; ethos, the audience's belief in the credibility and good character of the writer; and pathos, the audience's emotions or interests in regard to the topic at hand. And a rhetor seldom uses one of the appeals to the exclusion of all others. Think about Deford's piece (pages 9–10). He uses logic, or reasonableness, to argue for Rose's induction into the Hall of Fame. But he connects his logical explanations to emotion as he comments on "the glories of his youth" and to ethics as he calls baseball authorities to task for their less than even-handed dealing with Rose's case: "That's just not right."

Aristotle believed that speakers and hearers really did want to know the truth or the best course of action. He said that rhetoric is useful because "things that are true and things that are just have a natural tendency to prevail over their opposite," which makes rhetors and audience members mutually responsible as they communicate their best thoughts about a subject. The "good person speaking well," as Quintilian put it, wants to persuade to the better course, not the worse one; Deford wants to convince his readers that inducting Pete Rose is only fair, the best course of action to take in a case that is complicated by other ethical considerations. Rhetoric works because speakers and writers and listeners and readers engage together in the process of making meaning and coming to understanding.

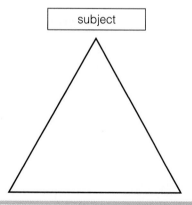

subject

Key #3: Understanding Subject Matter and Its Treatment

To become a successful rhetor—that is, to be a "good person speaking well"—you must develop skill in treating the subject matter fairly, fully, and effectively in a text. Some people might contend that the treatment of subject matter goes beyond the realm of rhetorical skill—in other words, that generating material for a text and producing the text itself are separable activities. We disagree. It is vital for a successful rhetor to comprehend that *what* one decides to include in a composition is intimately connected to *why* one is speaking or writing, *whom* one is speaking or writing to, and *what kind* of text one is composing.

To develop skill with treating subjects, a rhetor needs to understand four essential concepts. First, he or she needs to recognize that any topic, proposition, question, or issue that might generate the subject of a text must offer at least two paths of interpretation, analysis, or argument—the subject must be an "open" one. A text can never be effective rhetorically if it covers subject matter about which everybody already agrees. So, for example, if you were taking a class on the works of William Shakespeare and you wrote a paper claiming that Shakespeare was a famous late-sixteenth- and early-seventeenth-century English playwright, your audience might say, "Well, of course. We already know that." But if you wrote a paper claiming that William Shakespeare was a famous late-sixteenth- and early-seventeenth-century English playwright whose plays demonstrate remarkable insights into European history and politics, even though Shakespeare himself never traveled or studied in Europe, then members of your audience would probably perk up and say to themselves, "Hmmm, that's an interesting angle. Let's see what this writer can do to flesh out that claim."

Your audience's response to the fuller, more debatable topic illustrates the second concept about subject matter treatment that a budding rhetor needs to understand: A successful speaker or writer generates effective material by capitalizing on what audience members already know, making them curious to know more about the topic, and then satisfying their curiosity by providing facts, ideas, and interpretations that build on what they already know. To continue our earlier example: The audience members for your paper about Shakespeare already know that he was a famous late-sixteenth- and early-seventeenth-century English playwright, and they may even know (as you do, once you've learned it in class) that there is some dispute about whether Shakespeare himself actually wrote the 34 plays that bear his name. Such an audience would find your topic compelling because it would speak to their curiosity about how a young man with only a grammar school education in a rural town in England could write such historically, politically, and socially rich plays. In your Shakespeare paper—indeed, in all effective compositions that you produce—your audience will look for believable material that supports a point that you are making about a topic that they either are curious about already or become curious about because your title and the opening of your composition have made them so.

This desire for believable material in support of a general point illustrates the third and fourth concepts that a person developing skill with rhetoric needs to understand about subject matter treatment: The basic move of all effective rhetorical texts is claim-plus-support, and the central responsibility of a rhetor developing a subject is to generate ample, substantial material to support the points he or she wants to make. A budding rhetor can use the phrase *claim-plus-support* as a shorthand reminder of this fact: All successful texts, written or spoken, are made up of a series of points the rhetor wants to make. One of these points may be the main point of the text, sometimes called the **thesis statement.** To develop this main point, the rhetor generates a series of subsidiary, supporting points, and to flesh out these points, the rhetor comes up with facts, details, examples, illustrations, and reasons—all those things that cause a reader or listener to think, "Ah, I see *why* and *how* the point is being made." And this ability to create appropriate, effective points and supporting material must be active and robust. As we will explain in Chapter 2, the first of the ancient **canons** of rhetoric was **invention,** the craft of generating material to flesh out the topic of a text. A good rhetor will often produce *more* material—more general points and supporting material—than he or she actually needs in a text, in order to *choose* the points and material that will be most effective with the audience.

Activity

Read the following editorial that was published February 1, 2001, by the nationally syndicated columnists Jack Anderson and Douglas Cohn. Then, in your group, discuss the following questions:

- Who might be the audience for this column?
- How do Anderson and Cohn appeal to this audience (or these audiences)?
- Select one audience that you think might pay attention to this column, and describe how the column addresses or alludes to what the members of this audience probably feel, think, believe, and know about the subject matter.
- What is the principal claim that Anderson and Cohn make? How do they support that claim? Can you detect one or more claims besides the principal one? If so, how is that claim (or how are those claims) supported?
- If you were working as an assistant to Anderson and Cohn and had to generate *more* material for additional columns on this subject, what kinds of questions would you raise or what kind of issues would you address?

HOW ABOUT ONE STUDY AT A TIME?

Prompted by first lady Laura Bush, education is the front-burner issue for the Bush administration, but the arguments are centering around the wrong issues: vouchers and accountability.

The real issue is the structure of education. Vouchers are generally being discounted because they would divert badly needed funds from the public school system. Accountability is a problem only in the remedy; schools whose students do not meet the standards are to be penalized when they should be counseled and assisted.

The solution is to change the system. Socrates educated his students in very small numbers, one subject at a time. It was a good method—a method we could use today.

True, we cannot provide one instructor for every five to 10 students, but we can teach one subject at a time. It is well known that students do better in summer school than during the regular school year, and the reason is that they are immersed in one subject for a short period of time. They can focus, they can concentrate, they can explore, they can question—and they cannot be ignored.

The idea of trying to have students simultaneously learn six or seven subjects forces unwanted choices upon them, because they must choose how they will allocate their time. And there are educators who defend this system, claiming that time management is an important element of education. Baloney. Is it more important than learning the subjects?

The primary goal of education is to graduate students who have actually learned the subject matter. Why impose extraneous forces and decisions upon them? Why complicate their lives? Why increase rather than decrease the pressures?

Instead, imagine an educational system that mirrors summer school. The school year would be divided into six or seven units. Each unit, lasting five or six weeks, would be devoted to the study of a single subject. Students who hate mathematics, language, history or science would be able to devote all of their scholastic energies to those subjects, one at a time. And teachers, keenly aware that not all of their students love the particular subject as much as they do, would have enough time to provide individual attention to each of them.

Next comes the curriculum. There was a time in our history when Latin was mandatory. Today, the study of a foreign language is mandatory for most college-bound students. However, since virtually none of them can expect to graduate from high school or college fluent or even conversant in the language, the study of foreign languages should be elective.

Mathematics has a similar problem. A study of algebra, geometry and trigonometry is fine, but what possible purpose is served by forcing students in their last years of high school or first years of college to study calculus if they are not planning to major in math or science?

While some of these suggestions may be controversial, the objective of graduating students who have learned the subjects is not.

—United Feature Syndicate, *Jack Anderson and Douglas Cohn*

Modifying the Basic Rhetorical Triangle: Rhetoric Occurs in a Context

While the basic rhetorical triangle sets out the three initial keys to developing skill with rhetoric, the triangle needs to be modified so that it reflects three vital facts. First, rhetorical transactions always take place in a **context**—a convergence of time, place, people, events, and motivating forces—that influences how the rhetor understands, analyzes, and generates the persona, the appeals, and

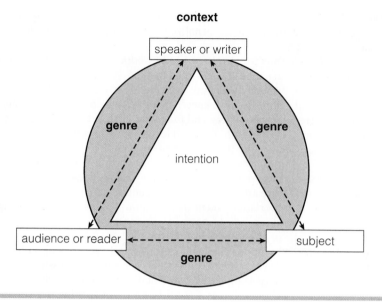

Revised Rhetorical Triangle

the subject matter material. Second, every rhetorical transaction is designed to achieve an **aim,** a **purpose,** or an **intention.** Third, when rhetors consider what aim they hope to accomplish in a particular context, they select an appropriate type of text, or **genre,** to achieve that purpose. These three facts thus lead to three additional keys to developing skill with rhetoric.

Key #4: Understanding Context

Just as the seventeenth-century poet John Donne argued in his famous Meditation 17, "No man is an island, entire of itself," so budding rhetors need to understand that no text they create or analyze is an island, separate unto itself. Every speech or written composition arises from a context: the convergence of the immediate situation calling forth the text, any pertinent historical background information about the topic, the persona and identity of the rhetor, and the knowledge and beliefs of the audience. The context of a speech or written composition strongly shapes how rhetors argue their positions or explore their ideas. An effective speaker or writer knows how to allude to the context in a work; a careful reader understands how context affects a text under analysis.

Let's say it's April 2007, and a writer is analyzing the cult of celebrity in American society in the wake of the death of celebrity icon Anna Nicole Smith in January 2007. The writer would likely be remiss not to acknowledge Smith's death and the media frenzy surrounding it, since they would have been so much in the public consciousness. The barrage of media attention, the details of Smith's rise to fame, and her mysterious death become part of the context the writer should address in discussing celebrity, whatever the writer's position on the issue might be.

context

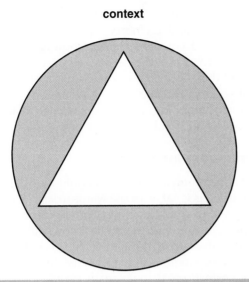

Rhetors can refer to topical events—that is, time-bound moments like the Columbine high school shooting, the O. J. Simpson trial, the voting problem in Florida in the 2000 presidential election, the Teapot Dome scandal, the McCarthy hearings, the Watergate break-in, or the Chicago Seven—as they consider how to approach subjects, how to provide evidence, and how to connect with audiences. One problem with using current events, of course, is that their currency fades quickly. Some of the events just mentioned, for example, may be so far in the past that readers don't recognize them. (The Teapot Dome scandal was a corporate double-dealing scandal during the administration of Warren Harding in the 1920s, the McCarthy hearings were a congressional inquiry prompted by fears of communism in the 1950s, the Watergate break-in happened in 1974 and led to the resignation of President Richard Nixon, and the Chicago Seven was a group of antiwar activists tried in court for their protests during the Democratic National Convention in 1968.) Still, even though they lose force quickly, topical events serve the important purpose of locating time and space for an audience and in explaining and exploring the contexts that lead rhetors to conclusions.

Rhetors also use wider cultural contexts as they make decisions about their texts. The writer on celebrity cults might allude to this country's passion for heroes and fascination with wealth, exemplified by a host of figures past and present, best-selling books, and blockbuster movies. Are the rich really different from us, as F. Scott Fitzgerald famously said? Using a broad cultural lens allows the rhetor to understand the complexity of issues and to use cultural context to generate evidence as well as to create an effective writer's persona.

Context, then, can be immediate or distant, bound by current events or historical patterns. You might stop to consider how you would work with context if you were writing about celebrity culture. Is there an event that has happened in your school or community that would provide evidence and help persuade or interest readers if you used it? In Greensboro, North Carolina, many residents remember the homecoming and fan frenzy surrounding the return of hometown boy Chris Daughtry, a finalist on the television show *American Idol.* Local stories abound about both the thrill and the peril of sudden fame or wealth for community residents, and these local stories sometimes add both weight and interest to the argument you might make.

In short, effective rhetors know how to use context to help an audience understand and respond positively to the text's message.

Key #5: Understanding Intention

A fifth element that a rhetor must understand is intention, also called aim or purpose. A rhetor's intention is what he or she wants to *happen* as a result of the text, what he or she wants the audience to *believe* or *do* after hearing or reading the text. In some **rhetorical situations**, the rhetor knows his or her intention right from the start; in other situations, the intention becomes clear as the text evolves.

Consider the first situation. You may begin with an intention, saying to yourself: "I want to write an essay to persuade people to use public transportation." Often when you begin with an aim, you already have strong feelings and opinions about the issue, maybe because you've read a lot about it already or because you have personal experiences that have convinced you of the rightness of your position. Your task in this case is to find enough evidence and to present it fairly enough to justify the aim you begin with.

In other situations, you begin with a topic you're interested in but don't yet carry strong opinions about: "I want to write about using public transportation." Or you're assigned that topic by a teacher: "Write about the advantages and disadvantages of public transportation." When you begin with a topic, you discover your aim as you write. Part of the mark of a successful **writing process** and a successful writing product is the ability to take a topic and discover an aim through the exploration of ideas and evidence.

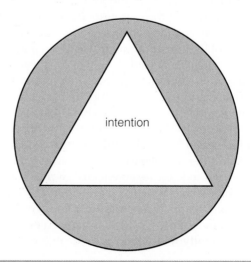

intention

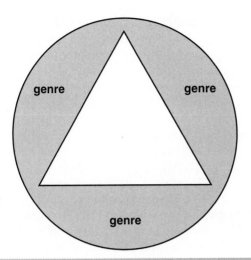

As a reader, you discover intention in the process of reading much as a writer discovers intention in the process of writing. In one text, the writer may announce a purpose—in this case, a persuasive one—at the beginning of an essay: "We need to take the bus to work. And here's why." In that case, you the reader understand immediately what the writer has in mind, and you make a decision quickly about what your disposition is with regard to that aim. You the reader might think about what you know and believe about pollution, buses, and city problems. (Notice how you are drawing on context as you interpret?) And you will think about how the writer sounds, and whether you like the voice that states its aim so quickly and assertively.

In another text, the writer might begin with a story and wait to announce the aim, or use the story to imply the aim. The writer might marshal facts and figures to prove the case and end the essay with a sentence that generalizes about the purpose. You, the reader, comprehend the reason for the story or the use of figures as you begin to understand the aim. And you decide whether or not the evidence or the stories have effectively conveyed the aim. You analyze the rhetoric of the piece, in other words, to decide on its success.

Activity

Choose an issue or subject that relates to some event at your school. Draw your own illustration of it. Keep in mind the triangle. Share your drawings with your group, and see if your "readers" understand the context, your aim, and your persona.

Key #6: Understanding Genre

A sixth key to developing skill with rhetoric also emerges from the modified rhetorical triangle. Because every act of writing and reading is embedded in a context, and because every writer writes to accomplish an aim and every reader reads to discover that intention, every rhetor chooses to produce a certain *type* of text—a genre appropriate for the intention and in the particular context. A rhetor needs to recognize the rich variety of kinds of texts—genres—that he or she can choose from as a writer and respond to as a reader.

Let's look at a scenario that might make this context-intention-genre connection clearer. Suppose that your advisor tells you that a local service organization, the Retired Senior Volunteer Program (RSVP), is inviting students to apply for a partial scholarship in psychology or social work, two fields you're considering as majors. Immediately, you understand part of the context—you have a motivation to write a letter of application, and you have an incentive to produce a text. You do a bit of research on the program, and you discover that RSVP places a strong emphasis on what it calls "intergenerational volunteer" work—projects that involve both senior citizens and younger citizens in community improvement. This is right down your alley; just last year, in fact, you and your grandmother volunteered to work together at a drop-in food pantry sponsored by a church in your neighborhood. Voilà, you understand a little more about the context—you know something about one of the areas stressed by RSVP. Since you know that RSVP has money to support college students and because you think you might need some financial assistance for college, you also have an intention: You need to persuade the scholarship committee at the local RSVP chapter that you are an extremely deserving candidate for the scholarship. So, in this context with this intention, what type of composition do you write? Do you write a poem that shows your creativity with words and images? No. Do you write a scientific laboratory report about some aspect of aging and psychology? No. You write a courteous, convincing letter, detailing your credentials as a student, your interest in the fields that the organization wants to support, and your experiences with your grandmother that show how much you have already learned from intergenerational research and how much you think you can continue to learn. Context plus intention lead to genre.

Students who are just beginning to develop their rhetorical skills sometimes have difficulty thinking creatively about genre. Many students have been taught that every paper they write for their courses needs to be the same type: It needs to have an opening paragraph that "hooks" the reader and ends with a **thesis** statement; then it needs to have three "body" paragraphs, each of which begins with a topic sentence and develops some aspect of the thesis statement; and then it needs to conclude with a paragraph that restates the thesis. This type of writing, commonly called the five-paragraph essay, is taught in many American high schools. (Curiously, almost no other system of secondary education in the world puts so much emphasis on this particular genre.) There is absolutely nothing wrong with knowing how to write a five-paragraph essay. It is a genre that students ought to master because it is especially useful when students have to write a timed, impromptu essay for a test. But it is not the only genre writers should learn to produce. A rhetor needs to look at the particular context that's calling forth the writing, consider his or her intention in this context, and then ask, "Is the five-paragraph essay *appropriate* for this context and this intention?" It may be the case that some assignments would be better served with a paper that ranged beyond five paragraphs; that offered a more provisional, tentative thesis that the writer would want to qualify or rethink part of the way through the paper; or that provided subheadings or employed narrative. As valuable as the five-paragraph essay is, it remains a relatively "closed" genre, one that suggests that a writer has drawn all of his or her conclusions before writing and put them "in the can," rather than thinking deeply about the topic at hand and reflecting that complex thinking in a more complicated genre.

Think of all the genres you could write by tapping into this connection between context and intention. For example, let's say that you, a part-time worker yourself, have just read two or three really interesting magazine articles about the effects on students of holding a part-time job. Given that so many students you know work while they are in school, you know that the context is a rich one, and you would like to write something that would combine the insights you gained from the articles with your own thoughts about the benefits and drawbacks of part-time employment. Given this context and this intention, you decide to write a feature article that might be published in your school newspaper. Or, to consider another example, let's say that you, along with other people who live in your neighborhood, are concerned about the potential traffic congestion (and danger) that might come about if a large hardware store opens near a very busy intersection, as has been proposed. The city development commission has announced a public hearing on the proposed construction. So you and your neighbors might go to the intersection, conduct a study of the current rate of traffic, speculate based on your best estimates about how traffic will increase if the hardware store opens, and then write a documented, scientific study, complete with an introduction, methods of investigation, findings, and implications, and present it with a cover letter opposing the construction of the store to the development commission. Both of these examples illustrate the kind of thinking a skillful rhetor does about genre. He or she asks, "What is the context for this writing? Who needs to know what I intend to write about? Therefore, what is the *best*, most *appropriate* genre to produce?"

Rhetoric in Everyday Life: *Your* Life, *Your* Community

You are using this book in a course. But the study and practice of rhetoric apply to far more than academic projects. When you develop skill in reading, writing, and speaking clearly and effectively in school, you are at the same time learning how to negotiate the complexities of communication in your life outside the school walls.

As a citizen and a consumer, you are constantly a reader of messages—in ads or promotions, on the Internet, in the print media, and in cultural, community, and family traditions and ideals. Understanding rhetoric can help make you aware of how and why those messages influence you. Understanding rhetoric, you can contribute to the civic conversation more effectively and conscientiously in what you buy, what you vote for, and how you speak in your community.

The following section and activities are designed to show how being skilled in rhetoric can help make you a more active citizen and discerning consumer of all the many texts you confront and analyze in everyday life.

Rhetoric and Citizenship

What does it mean to be a good citizen? One way to answer this complicated question is to use a metaphor: Citizenship is a two-way street, and being skilled at rhetoric gives you the ability to travel in both directions successfully. Here's what we mean.

When you are a citizen, you look to a series of governing units that you expect certain things from. In turn, they expect certain things from you. Let's say you are a citizen of the United States, the state of Illinois, and the city of Downers Grove. (This describes the citizenship of one of the authors of this book!) Among other things, you expect the United States to provide a strong and stable set of armed forces—the Army, Navy, Air Force, Marines, and Coast Guard—that can protect the country from attacks by individuals or groups who oppose our nation. In turn, the U.S. government expects 18-year-old men (but, for now, not women—more on this issue in following paragraphs) to register with the Selective Service System and in times of national crisis to be willing, within the limits of their conscience, to be drafted into the armed forces. Among other things, you expect the state of Illinois to establish and enforce regulations by which the public schools operate. In turn, the state of Illinois expects students to study a prescribed set of subjects in secondary school in order to receive a high school diploma. (Do you recall the activity, earlier in this chapter, that asked you to examine Jack Anderson and Douglas Cohn's argument for "one-subject-at-a-time" schooling?) You also expect Downers Grove to maintain large, open, wooded areas as parks where residents can relax and enjoy nature. In turn, Downers Grove expects you to respect the cleanliness and safety of the parks by not littering, not chopping down trees, and not allowing pets to run wild in them.

Good citizens generally understand a lot about these mutual expectation—how their community, state, or country will behave toward them and how they behave within their community, state, or country. Whether they're aware of it or not, citizens use rhetoric to consider what citizenship provides and expects. Rights and responsibilities are conveyed directly from government, indirectly from schools and the media—as propositions or suppositions. Good citizens learn to examine these texts critically, deciding how and if they meet citizens' expectations or responsibilities. As citizens we learn to read, listen, weigh alternatives, and engage in conversation as we work to understand issues and arguments, as well as the language used to embody them. The process of engaging in civic issues, of becoming a good citizen, is a process of using rhetoric effectively.

Let's consider an example of how being skilled at rhetoric can help you be a well-informed citizen. While women serve in all the armed forces of the United States, they have neither been required to register for the Selective Service System nor been drafted. The federal government came close to drafting women in World War II because there was a shortage of military nurses, but a surge of volunteerism made the draft of women unnecessary. Three decades later, the draft of men was deemed unnecessary as well. As the Vietnam War ended, so did the drafting of young men in 1973, and from 1975 to 1980 18-year-old males were not required to register with the Selective Service. But when the Soviet Union invaded Afghanistan in 1980, there was concern about America's ability to deploy its armed forces quickly, and President Jimmy Carter asked Congress to reinstate the law requiring young men to register for the draft. Congress complied but only after debating the question of whether young women should also be required to register and, in times of crisis, be drafted. Since at that time it was the policy of the Department of Defense not to involve women soldiers in combat, Congress decided not to require 18-year-old women to register. This decision, however, was challenged. A district court in Pennsylvania, responding to a lawsuit brought by several young men, ruled that the exclusion of women from the draft violated a clause in the Fifth Amendment to the U.S. Constitution, which states that no citizen may "be deprived of his life, liberty, or property without due process of law." The case, *Rostker v. Goldberg*, was later appealed to the U.S. Supreme Court, which ruled that the exclusion of women was not unconstitutional. The question of whether 18-year-old women should be required to register for the draft has resurfaced regularly since then. Bodies ranging from the U.S. Senate to a Presidential Commission on the Assignment of Women in the Armed Forces to the General Accounting Office have debated the question, with decisions reached in 1992, 1994, and 1998 not to require women to register and not to subject them to the draft.

Activity

The issue of women in the armed services came to the fore again in early 2003, just as the United States and its coalition partners were planning to take military action against Iraq. Read the following editorial, which appeared later that year, on June 20, 2003, in the *Daily Illini*, the student newspaper at the University of Illinois at Urbana-Champaign. Then do two things: First, in your group, analyze how the anonymous author of this editorial creates a persona, appeals to the audience, and addresses the subject matter. Second, write your own response to the editorial. Pay attention to how you incorporate the context, determine an aim, and decide on the appropriate genre to frame your response.

INCLUDING WOMEN IN THE DRAFT

Uncle Sam wants you. Be an army of one. Commercials, posters and pamphlets bearing these slogans—and others like them—encourage many to enlist in the military. But even more people are available to the armed forces.

In addition to all the men and women who enlist on their own, men must register for the draft. Men ages 18 to 25 are eligible to be drafted into the military during times of war. Only men.

The idea of conscription is distasteful to many, but the draft is an unfortunate necessity. While many people do become more patriotic in times of war, not all feel obligated to enlist. Running out of manpower at a crucial point in a war would be disastrous.

Critics of mandatory enlistment say it's wrong to force anyone to register for the draft. But when it comes down to the wire, the draft pool is a needed resource. Fighting wars without soldiers is impossible.

Historically, only men have had to register for the draft. But society is different now, and equality is a closer goal.

Women are able to enlist in the military voluntarily, and female soldiers are considered an asset. If women are able to enlist by choice, it should also be made mandatory for them to register to be drafted. It's unfair that only men are forced into combat. America is one nation, with one society. It's unfair that one sex can be forced to fight the battles of both.

Women in other countries are drafted into the military. Every Israeli citizen must serve in the Israeli army. Other countries have considered or implemented conscription for women already, and the United States should follow suit.

Opponents of women being in the military might argue that women may have to leave a family behind or become pregnant while on active duty. But health concerns that would distract from duty would need to be addressed and details would need to be hammered out for maternity leave.

Others argue that women shouldn't have to register because they won't be able to physically handle a combat situation.

This is a moot point because the military provides training and decides where each person will be placed, including less physical jobs. It's unlikely that a women who lacked the physical skills for combat would be placed in that situation. Nor would a man.

The military wants to win wars, and it would be detrimental to place people in positions they are not qualified for or lack an affinity for. But with a bigger pool of help to choose from, the military could only better itself.

Rhetoric and Community

When you are skilled at rhetoric, you are not only in a position to make good decisions about national political questions, such as whether all 18-year-olds should be required to register for the draft; you are also in a better position to understand and respond to important issues and concerns in your local community.

Consider the following scenario. In Downers Grove, a wooded suburb about 20 miles west of Chicago, drivers used to see interesting signs over and over as they traveled south on Belmont Avenue, a busy road. Planted in several front yards were large white placards, with a simple message in bold, black, all-capital letters: NO MEANS NO. The average motorist driving past these signs might not have known exactly what they meant, but passersby certainly perked up and paid attention to them.

Here's the story behind the signs: Along the western edge of Belmont Avenue was a substantial parcel of undeveloped park land, owned by the city. A proposal was made that the Downers Grove Park District build a large, state-of-the-art water theme park on this site. Proponents of this plan said the theme park would draw both visitors and new residents to Downers Grove, provide an excellent venue for family recreation, and generate considerable income for the city. The opponents—including the homeowners who put the signs in their yards—conceded this last point: The theme park would indeed generate revenue. But the opponents believed that the theme park would also attract to Belmont Avenue hordes of people who didn't care about keeping the area clean and safe and regular traffic jams on the street in front of their homes. They worried that the theme park would become a site for loitering and potential vandalism.

Sensing that they would need community support, city officials who hoped to see the water theme park succeed put the question to a vote. In a referendum, voters were asked whether they supported the construction of the park on Belmont. They overwhelmingly voted no. But much to the voters' surprise, city officials appeared at the next council meeting after the election and, claiming the election was not a *binding* referendum, announced their intention to go ahead with the water theme park development. That's when the signs went up in people's yards: NO MEANS NO.

Why are these signs so effective? There are no fancy words—just three monosyllables making up one simple sentence. The graphics are not all that impressive: plain black capital letters on a white background. Yet the signs caught people's attention and motivated them to find out the story behind them. Why? At the level of literal meaning, the sentence was a **tautology,** a direct (and perhaps needless) repetition of an idea. But on a deeper level, the message was very strong. NO MEANS NO sounded like a strong, forceful parent disciplining an unruly child who was trying to get away with something forbidden. NO MEANS NO had an air of finality to it, suggesting that this was really the final word on the issue. And the appearance of so many signs in people's yards, all of which said NO MEANS NO, suggested that people in this neighborhood were unified, bonded, together.

Of course, not all the signs and public displays one might see in a community are as negative as NO MEANS NO. Throughout Downers Grove, for example, there are signs on posts that say *Downtown Downers Grove: Catch the Spirit,* a message that suggests the residents can find plenty to do in the small downtown area. Outside many of the schools, one sees signs that proclaim *Excellence in Education.* And not all of the rhetoric that defines and binds together a community can be found inscribed on signs in yards and on lampposts. In addition to signs, communities—like Downers Grove and, perhaps, the city, town, or village where you live—call upon their residents to identify with the municipality, to support and take part in events it sponsors through brochures, newsletters, and town meetings. All of these materials together constitute the rhetoric of the community, the statements that the community makes about itself and that it wants its residents to believe and support.

signs banner = message

newsletter

HW

4 para per both

Activity

With one or two classmates take a walk or drive through the community where you live. First of all, notice any signs and banners that are posted. How do these signs and banners suggest the community wants to portray itself? What points are they trying to convey? How effectively do the language and the graphics on the signs and banners contribute to conveying the message? Second, find a brochure or newsletter that is published by the town, city, or county where you live. Ask the same questions about it.

When you've finished examining signs, banners, and a brochure or newsletter (or perhaps two or three of them), discuss the community's rhetoric. Here are some questions you can ask:

- Do the artifacts you find—the signs, banners, brochures, or newsletters—create a persona? If so, how would you describe and characterize it?

- How do the artifacts appeal to you as an audience?

- What aspects of the "subject matter" of the city, town, village, or community do the artifacts emphasize? How do they do so?

- Are you able to see an overall aim or intention in the artifacts? If so, what is it?

Rhetoric and Conscientious Consumption

One message should be clear by now: Being skilled at rhetoric is one of the most important abilities you can develop in your life in and out of school. If you can read materials with a discerning eye; if you can scope out a situation and understand what is at issue in spoken and written documents and discussions; and if you can speak and write clearly, fluently, and correctly, then you are going to be in a much stronger position to succeed in whatever intellectual task you tackle. Think about this: You are surrounded by, and often immersed in, language—from the books, magazines, and newspapers you read to the conversations you have, the television you watch, the music you listen to, and the Internet you surf. A great deal of this language is trying, either openly or subliminally, to get you to do something: Vote for this candidate, buy that product, support this cause, oppose that movement. How do you know what to do, which advice to heed, which path to follow? To a certain extent, of course, you can follow a "gut instinct" in these matters. But certainly you don't want to rely solely on what your emotions tell you to do when an important decision faces you. You want to be able to survey the situation at hand—read, listen, consult, and think. You want to be able to consider the benefits and drawbacks of all the possible courses of action. You want to decide wisely. You want, in other words, to use your rhetorical skills.

One of the most important decisions citizens make these days is how they might respond to the growing environmental crisis in this country and in the world. From transportation to food to clothing to lightbulbs, consumers are suddenly bombarded with information—sometimes conflicting—about which choices make sound environmental sense.

Consider the following ads. Notice, as you read them, the kinds of information presented, the kinds of appeals, what is said, and what's implied. Take a look too at the way each ad presents itself—its format, its print size, and any other factors you notice.

How does a good reader evaluate the claims of the ads?

How does each ad attempt to persuade its audience?

What is each ad attempting to persuade the reader to do?

As you analyze the ads, compare and contrast the rhetoric of the two. You might decide which of the two is more persuasive to you and why.

Since 1969, it has been our mission to be a leader in the furniture industry.
Having kept this promise, we are proud to announce, naturalLEE. All the style and
comfort of LEE with environmentally-conscious fabrics, finishes, and frames.

It's time to act responsib•LEE

800.892.7150

naturalLEE.com

Interchapter

After each chapter in this book, you will find an interchapter, which summarizes the preceding material and then raises questions about three pieces of writing. Those pieces of writing, which appear in their entirety later in this book, are

- the 1849 essay "On the Duty of Civil Disobedience" by Henry David Thoreau (pages 221–237).
- the 1982 poem "It's a Woman's World" by Eavan Boland (pages 237–239).
- the 1973 short story "Everyday Use" by Alice Walker (pages 239–246).

You'll notice that we've borrowed Alice Walker's title as the title for this book.

By asking you to apply to the three works the concepts about rhetoric raised in the preceding chapter, each interchapter expects you to look at the essay, the poem, and the story from a different angle; together, the interchapters will cause you to become intimately familiar with what the authors had to say and how they said it. You'll apply the concepts about rhetoric raised in each chapter to the three works we include. Each interchapter asks you to look at the texts from different angles; together, the interchapters help you become deeply knowledgeable about the authors' intentions and strategies.

We hope that you'll read these pieces of literature several times as you proceed through the interchapters. It's always a good idea to read each one fairly quickly to get a sense of the whole piece and then begin to read in a more focused way as you engage in the activities and respond to the questions we present in the interchapter.

Overview of the Major Points in Chapter 1

- Rhetoric is not some complex art that only scholars and specialists know how to use. Rhetoric is a technique and a set of practices—which *you* can acquire, experiment with, and master. Then in a situation that calls for you to speak or write, you will be able to find all the available means to shape people's thinking, change their minds, or influence their actions.

- *Rhetoric* also refers to the actual features of a written or spoken text—its central ideas; its organization, emphases, and focus; and its syntax, diction, and imagery—that lead listeners or readers to pay attention to it and to take up the writer's or speaker's purpose.

- A rhetorical situation, one that calls for speaking or writing, contains six elements you can analyze, either in isolation or in relation to one another: the writer or speaker; the reader or listener (sometimes referred to as the audience); the subject matter, or content; the aim, or intention, of the document created; the context (the time, the place, and the community or forum) in which the written document or spoken text is operating; and the genre (the type of composition, its structure, and its organization).

- You can analyze each of these elements by looking at specific features of texts and asking yourself these questions:
  1. What kind of person does the writer or speaker seem to be?
  2. Who is the audience for this text—in other words, whom does the speaker or writer seem to be addressing?
  3. What seems to be the relationship between the speaker or writer and the audience?
  4. What is the central idea that this text develops?
  5. How is the text developed—through examples? descriptions? stories?
  6. How is the text organized? How are its parts arranged? How are the parts connected? How does this arrangement of parts help the development of the text?
  7. What is the context for the text? In what community, or forum, is this text operating?
  8. How does the context influence the writer or speaker or the relationship of the writer or speaker with the audience?

Activities and Discussion Questions for Chapter 1   Use these questions and comments as guides for your own discussion and writing about these works.

Henry David Thoreau, "On the Duty of Civil Disobedience" (published 1849)

The text appears on pages 221–237. In a discussion with a group of your classmates, or in a well-developed, well-organized essay, address one or more of the following questions.

1. Based on your reading of "Civil Disobedience," what kind of person does Henry David Thoreau seem to be? How would you characterize his state of mind and emotion as he composed "Civil Disobedience"? Cite specific examples from "Civil Disobedience" to support your claims about Thoreau's voice and persona.
2. What does Thoreau do in "Civil Disobedience" to urge his readers to believe in him as a trustworthy, credible person? Point out specific passages where you felt Thoreau was (or was not) particularly believable.

3. One device a writer can use to get a point across is **metaphor,** a comparison of two dissimilar objects or ideas that does not use the words *like* or *as*. Thoreau uses metaphor extensively in "Civil Disobedience." Notice, for example, what he compares *machinery* to, or how he uses *gaming* metaphorically. Select one or two metaphors and explain, citing specific examples from the text, how they help Thoreau's central idea become more vivid for his readers.

4. How do you think Thoreau wanted his readers to react to "Civil Disobedience"? What did he want them to feel? think? believe? do? How do you know? Again, point to specific places in the essay that help you determine Thoreau's purpose.

Eavan Boland, "It's a Woman's World" (published 1982)

The text appears on pages 237–239. Discuss the following ideas in your small group, or choose one and write a well-developed essay of your own. Remember that poetry depends so much on sound for its message that you should listen to someone read "It's a Woman's World" aloud or read it aloud yourself.

1. Create a character description for the speaker in the poem. What might she look like? What kind of work does she do? What are some words in the poem that suggest how she feels about women and their roles? What clue does the title give you about her attitude?

2. Consider the speaker's ethos. How does she make herself believable? Find specific places in the poem where you hear the speaker establishing her own right to speak. Notice especially how she uses pronouns. Why is it important that she uses first-person plural?

3. One striking feature of this poem is the way that the speaker uses details. Pick a few of the details she uses, and comment on how they contribute to the meaning of the poem and to the attitude of the speaker toward her subject. Pay attention to the way she uses verbs and the way she makes verbs out of nouns—for example, in "milestone our lives"—as she creates these details.

4. Repetition is an especially useful strategy for poets, since it aids both in stressing meaning and in creating rhythm. Find places where repetition helps reinforce the speaker's purpose or create effect.

5. Explore how the speaker makes connections to her readers. What does she want readers to feel at the end of the poem? Are there particular words in the text that suggest how she wants readers to react?

Alice Walker, "Everyday Use" (published 1973)

The text appears on pages 239–246. In a discussion with a group of your classmates, or in a well-organized essay, address one or more of the following questions.

1. "Everyday Use" was written in the 1970s, a time when civil-rights issues had begun to focus on matters of ethnic pride and heritage. How does knowing that context help you to comment on the **conflict** this story presents as well as on its message?

2. Which character do you feel the most sympathy for? Explain why, using lines from the story to illustrate your position.

3. Although there are no white people who are obvious characters in the story, racial difference and racism are subtly made part of the story's context. How do you see that racial context in the story, and how does it contribute to the meaning?

4. As you think about the writer's intention, consider why this story begins with the dedication "for your grandmama."

Understanding the Traditional Canons of Rhetoric: Invention and Memory

2

"*Write about dogs!*"

One clear message in the first chapter is that rhetoric is something you do every day. When you decide to read something challenging—one of your lessons for school, an editorial column in a magazine you subscribe to, or an informative site on the Internet—you don't say to yourself, "Okay, now I have to be a rhetorician." You simply say, "Okay, now I'm going to read," and then you *use* skills and strategies to guide and assist your reading. Similarly, when you begin to write something—a paper for one of your classes, a letter applying for an award, or an e-mail to a friend—you don't say, "Now, I must be a rhetorician." You simply write (knowing what a complex process that is!), and you employ the skills and strategies that have worked for you in the past.

The goal of this chapter and the next is to help you understand *how* you do these things. In these chapters, we explain a set of traditional rhetorical concepts and examine strategies for using those concepts as you read and write. The concepts are what classical rhetoricians called the **canons**—invention, arrangement, style, memory, and delivery. As you learn about each of the five canons, you will understand how valuable they are for shaping your thoughts as a rhetorically sensitive reader and for guiding your actions as a rhetorically effective writer. You will also see how the canons are **heuristic** devices, points of reference that you can return to regularly and systematically as you analyze texts and write compositions of your own.

Most people who study rhetoric explain the canons in the order listed above and here again: invention, arrangement, style, memory, and delivery. Moreover, most people who study rhetoric understand that the canons are related: How you go about inventing, for example, is influenced by how you intend to arrange your material. But for the sake of simplicity, we will separate our consideration of the canons into two groups. In this chapter, we will explain the two canons that guide the generation of material: invention and memory. In Chapter 3, we will explain the three canons that are involved with transmitting material to a reader or listener: arrangement, style, and delivery.

Like the angles on the rhetorical triangle, the canons are useful perspectives from which to see rhetoric at work in everyday life. We'll review quickly two concepts that come from Chapter 1 to show how they're related to the canons: context and appeals.

Rhetoric at Work: Context and the Three Appeals

Chapter 1 explains two truths about every piece of writing. First, a piece of writing always exists in **context**. A situation prompts the writer to write about a certain subject, members of an audience read the piece, and a purpose determines how the writer approaches both the situation and the audience. Second, a piece of writing works in three closely related ways—to convey its information and points to readers, to influence their thinking, and perhaps even to change their actions. We call these ways **appeals**.

- Writing appeals to readers by making a clear, coherent statement of ideas and a central argument. Teachers of rhetoric refer to this appeal as **logos**, a Greek term that is best translated into English as "embodied thought."
- Writing appeals to readers by offering **evidence** that the writer is a trustworthy, well-educated, believable person who has done his or her homework and has the best interests of the readers in mind. Teachers of rhetoric refer to this appeal as **ethos**, which translates roughly as "good-willed credibility."
- And writing appeals to readers by relating to, and sometimes even speaking directly to, their emotions and interests. Teachers of rhetoric refer to this appeal as **pathos**, which translates roughly as "feeling." The English cognate words *sympathy* and *empathy* are directly related to this appeal. A good writer wants his or her readers to empathize with—or, literally, to feel—his or her ideas and arguments.

While there is some value in examining how a piece of writing accomplishes each of these appeals separately, it's important to remember that the appeals are closely related. In other words, when you are analyzing the rhetorical effectiveness of a piece of writing, you need to examine how its statement and development of central ideas and larger **claims** both establish the credibility of its writer and tap into the emotions and interests of the reader. When you are planning your own writing, you need to analyze the same intertwined appeals in your own work.

Each of the five canons of rhetoric explained in this chapter and the next suggests strategies you can use to make these appeals—to logos, ethos, and pathos—for your readers.

- **Invention** strategies help you to generate material that is clear, forceful, convincing, and emotionally appealing.
- Techniques of **arrangement, style,** and **delivery** help you to put your material into structures, patterns, and formats that will be understandable to your readers and help them to see you as a credible, sympathetic, even impressive person.
- Methods of tapping into your readers' **memories** and cultural associations will assist your efforts to clarify your ideas and arguments for readers and will help them to see you as a person who is on their side, who is one of them.

Activity

Picture the following magazine ad. The advertisement is for *Stone Soup: The Magazine for Young Writers and Artists.* The ad lists two quotations: "The *New Yorker* of the 8 to 13 set," from *Ms.* magazine, and "Blessings on the adult advisers of this enterprise," from the *New Yorker.* The copy then reads: "Christmas, Hanukkah, birthdays—*Stone Soup* is a gift that brings hours of enjoyment, not just on the day it is received but throughout the year. *Stone Soup*'s stories, poems, and illustrations are all by children. It's the perfect gift for creative 8- to 13-year-olds."

In a small group, discuss the central argument of this ad and decide its primary appeal—to logos, pathos, or ethos. Rewrite the ad with another primary appeal.

Invention

Most people think of invention as the act of creating something new—a new product, process, device, or formula. This is not exactly the meaning of invention that rhetoricians use. The term *invention* in rhetoric comes from the Latin verb *invenire,* meaning "to find." Inventing as a rhetorician is like conducting an inventory. Stores have to close every now and then to take an inventory—they need to *find* what products they have on their shelves and analyze their stock so that they can plan sales better. Similarly, rhetorically skilled readers need to take inventories, finding and analyzing what a writer did to state and develop the main ideas in a work. Rhetorically skilled writers, likewise, take inventories of what they have in their storehouses of experiences, ideas, reading background, and observations that they can effectively pull together in a composition. Invention, then, is the art of finding and developing material.

Just as some writers like to make a definite plan before they begin a writing project and others simply begin writing and see what emerges, some people find it helpful to invent using a clearly defined strategy, while others like to invent more spontaneously. We'll call the clearly defined invention strategies *systematic* and the more open and spontaneous ones *intuitive.* In this chapter, we'll describe the systematic strategies in some detail and provide a preview of the intuitive strategies. You'll learn more about the intuitive strategies by seeing them at work in a series of scenarios in Chapter 4.

Systematic Invention Strategy I: The Journalist's Questions

Perhaps the most widely known systematic invention strategy is the journalist's questions. When journalists write news stories, they ask six questions:

- Who was involved?
- What took place?
- When did it happen?
- Where did it happen?
- Why did it happen?
- How did it happen?

A skilled journalist can write a lead that answers all six of those questions, and then write the remainder of the news story simply by unpacking, or describing point by point, the details about each of those six points.

The journalist's questions are doubly useful. Not only can you use them to generate material for any composition you might write; you can also use them to help you comprehend what you read. Consider, for example, the section of "Civil Disobedience" in which Thoreau discusses spending a night in jail. Using the journalist's questions as a guide, the reader can say that Thoreau was arrested and put in jail for one night sometime prior to 1849, when he composed "Civil Disobedience." The jail was in Concord, Massachusetts. Thoreau was jailed for refusing to pay his poll tax. The arrest apparently happened without resistance from Thoreau himself. That's the simple who-what-when-where-why-and-how of the case.

This bare outline, of course, does little to explore the rich substance of Thoreau's piece. Let's work through the journalist's questions a second time and see what taking a thorough inventory with the six questions reveals about how Thoreau appeals to his audience and achieves his purpose.

- **Who was involved?** Certainly Thoreau himself, but what about the other jailed person we learn about, Thoreau's cellmate, the person whom the jailer introduced as "a first-rate fellow and a clever man"? Why do you suppose Thoreau describes him in such detail? Here is a man who is allegedly a criminal, yet he gets several months of free room and board in a neatly decorated cell and goes out every day to work at harvesting hay. Do you think Thoreau is making any comment about the American system of justice and incarceration with such a description?

- **What took place?** Clearly, on one level, the event was just a night in jail for Thoreau. But take a closer look at the paragraph that begins, "It was like traveling into a far country, such as I had never expected to behold, to lie there for one night." Thoreau clearly did more than simply sleep in the cell. What ideas do you think Thoreau is trying to suggest by seeing his "native place in the light of the Middle Ages"?

- **When did it happen?** The timing is vital, and you need to know a bit more background information to understand fully this passage from "Civil Disobedience." In 1848, the United States was involved in a war with Mexico, a war that many intellectuals, including Thoreau, thought was unwarranted and unethical. Knowing this, how do you think Thoreau capitalizes on the times he's living in?

- **Where did it happen?** The location is very important, but its significance emerges only when you know that Concord, Massachusetts, where Thoreau was jailed, was not simply some small New England town. Concord was a site of one of the major battles in the American War for Independence, fought some 70 years before Thoreau wrote "Civil Disobedience," and was during his lifetime a center for intellectual ferment in the young United States.

- **Why did it happen?** The arrest happened because Thoreau failed to pay his poll tax, but that fact as well warrants more examination. A poll tax was a tax levied against all citizens of voting age to support the activities of the government. Since Thoreau disagreed with the government's actions, particularly its waging war against Mexico, he refused to pay the required tax.

- **How did it happen?** Thoreau was arrested with little fanfare, but the quiet uneventfulness of Thoreau's arrest underscores a major point he makes in "Civil Disobedience." If a person is morally justified in objecting to the laws under which he or she lives, that person has a right—Thoreau might even say a duty—to refuse to obey those laws. But the refusal must be civil—no big protests, no violence, just refusal.

A conscientious and comprehensive application of the journalist's questions, as you can see, produces an ample inventory of the ideas introduced and developed in a text.

Activity

Consider the following lead paragraph: "For developing a concept of securing small loans to new businesses in developing countries, the Bangladeshi economist Mohammed Yunus yesterday was awarded the 2006 Nobel Peace Prize." Given this lead, what details is the news story that follows obligated to unpack for readers?

Activity

Just as the journalist's questions can be used systematically to take an inventory of what a writer does to achieve a purpose, so you can use them when you are planning to write. Think about a paper you are working on right now or will begin soon, and use the journalist's questions to come up with as much material as possible. You may have relatively little to say about some of the questions and a lot to say about others, and you may not eventually *use* everything you generate, but writers almost always have more material than actually gets into final drafts.

- In the situation you are writing about, who was involved? Who was the central person? What people were around this person in the situation, interacting with him or her? How were the central person and the other person(s) in the situation connected or related?
- What took place? What were the obvious main actions and events? What are some other actions and events that might be related to the main ones?
- When did it happen? Why was the timing important? Was there a feeling of crisis or immediacy in the situation? If so, what caused it? If not, did its absence make any difference in the situation?
- Where did it happen? Why was the location important? What persons, actions, and events surrounded the main one you are writing about?

- Why did it happen? What were the main obvious causes? Were more subtle, difficult-to-detect causes present?
- How did it happen? What means were used to achieve a result in the situation?

Systematic Invention Strategy II: Kenneth Burke's Pentad

In his influential book *A Grammar of Motives,* the twentieth-century critic and philosopher Kenneth Burke sets out a systematic invention strategy called the **dramatistic pentad,** which on the surface looks like the journalist's questions. (*Pentad* is a Greek word meaning "group of five.") But there are two differences between the journalist's questions and the pentad, and the second difference makes the pentad a good device for analyzing a text you read and for taking an inventory of what you might write.

Burke proposes the five points of the pentad as things a person could say not only about a written text but also, more broadly, about any purposeful or intentional act that communicates meaning. Here are the five points:

- **Act:**   What happened?
- **Scene:**   When and where did it happen?
- **Agent:**   Who did it?
- **Agency:**   How was it done?
- **Purpose:**   Why was it done?

Instead of the who-what-when-where-why-and-how of the journalist's questions, Burke's pentad offers a what-when-where-who-how-and-why series. It also offers a way to see these questions as potentially related to one another, with some relationships potentially more significant than others. Because it provides a way to understand relationships, it is particularly useful as a strategy for analyzing human behavior, in real life or in literature.

Burke's pentad becomes most useful for both analysis of a situation and invention of one as you consider those elements in relationships, which Burke called **ratios.** Burke makes clear that constructing these ratios can be playful. There are no "right" or "wrong" answers about them. Instead, they are what he calls **casuistries,** little mental games a reader can play when analyzing a text or a writer can play when planning a piece of writing.

Here's an example of how a writer can use a casuistry to generate different lines of an argument by creating ratios.

> *George Washington chopped down the cherry tree.*
>
> *Scene-act:*   The writer could argue that the act follows from the circumstances.
>
> *In the eighteenth century, boys chopped down trees.*

Agent-act: The writer could argue that the act follows from the character of the person.

George was a practical action-oriented fellow even as a child.

Agency-act: The writer could argue that the act follows from the available means.

The axe was sharper than George thought and sliced through the trunk.

Purpose-act: The writer could argue that something needs to be done to accomplish the act.

George was given the axe so that he could learn to chop.

Act-act: The writer could argue that the act follows from other acts.

George had chopped down many other trees before without notice.

You can see how creating ratios from situations allows you to consider possible motives or reasons for behavior. Consciously or unconsciously, writers formulate ratios as they decide which elements of stories they will highlight and which they will omit or play down. You could create other statements, and other ratios, from the sentence *George Washington chopped down the cherry tree,* and each would reveal something potentially interesting about the situation.

To see how the pentad can help you both analyze the substance of a text and take an inventory of what you might do in a successful one yourself, let's return to an issue introduced in Chapter 1, the proposal by the Downers Grove village council to build a water amusement park on Belmont Road in that suburb. As you recall, it was the village's persistence in planning this theme park that led residents to put signs in their yards that read, defiantly, NO MEANS NO. The protest came in response to the village's proposal. Here are some possibilities that might explain the situation:

Scene-act: The residents put up the sign because a theme park is not appropriate in their neighborhood.

Agent-act: Residents, feeling betrayed by their elected officials, demonstrated their frustration with the village council.

Agency-act: The signs were unambiguous and demonstrated the solidarity of the residents in their protest.

Purpose-act: Signs along the major street in the village would make officials and the media take notice.

Act-act: Other businesses that had negatively affected the neighborhood had been allowed to encroach upon property.

Activity

Work with the five points of Burke's pentad and several ratios to analyze the following editorial, which was posted on "The Scrivener," a Web site that welcomes submissions from high school writers. First of all, consider the *act* as Mike

Cameron's wearing the Pepsi shirt to school. What would you say about the other four points in the pentad? Which ratios would you emphasize in taking an inventory of what the author, Joel Caris, did in the piece? Then think of the act as Mike Cameron's suspension from Greenbrier High School, and answer the same questions. Finally, consider the act as the prize money awarded by the Coca-Cola Bottling Company.

> A somewhat disturbing event occurred in Evans, Georgia. Greenbrier High School suspended a 19 year old student, Mike Cameron, for wearing a Pepsi shirt. The shirt did not have a marijuana leaf on it, did not promote alcohol or tobacco, and implied nothing sexual. It was simply a shirt with a Pepsi logo on it. Most schools do not consider wearing a Pepsi shirt a punishable offense. Greenbrier, however, did consider it a punishable offense—at least for one day.
>
> It was Coke Day at the high school. Coca-Cola executives were visiting the school, which was competing for a $500 prize in a contest set up by the Coca-Cola Bottling Company of Augusta. Greenbrier High School was also competing nationally for a much more substantial prize of $10,000. The disturbing part of this story is not that a high school hoped to receive a little monetary assistance from a local company. The disturbing part is the implications that come with the awarding of corporate money to public schools and what that high school did in an effort to win the money.
>
> Coke Day activities included the baking of Coke cakes in home economic classes. In science classes, experiments were conducted to determine the sugar content of Coke and the day's finale was a school picture of the high school students spelling out "Coke."
>
> When Cameron and fellow classmate Dan Moxley decided to express their soft drink preference by proudly displaying Pepsi shirts during the school picture, they were both suspended for a day. Apparently, Greenbrier High School was quite upset at the boys' use of self-expression at such an inopportune time. Cameron was scolded by administration and told he might have cost the school $10,000.
>
> What is frightening about this story is the school's reaction when faced with the possibility of free money. This was a public high school, supported by taxpayer money, blatantly pandering to a big corporation. So eager was Greenbrier to cash in on the contest that they condemned a teenager for professing a personal choice and forced their students to participate in classroom activities that resembled Coke commercials more than they did educational lessons.
>
> Public schools should not be partaking in corporate sponsorship. By allowing such things to take place, we are hurting our education system—a system that has suffered too many blows as it is. Considering the funding crisis many schools are experiencing, it is understandable that they would be eager to come across a little extra cash. However, public schools can not be compromising their objectivity and true purpose—education—to appease corporations with deep pockets and a burst of generosity in the face of free advertising.
>
> —*Joel Caris, "Corporate Sponsorship of Our Schools"*

Activity

Choose one of the following:

1. Use the five points of Burke's pentad and several ratios to take an inventory of what you might write in an editorial for your local or school newspaper about one of the following topics: homelessness in America, college scholarship funding, young voters' interest in politics, the cult of celebrity, or another situation of interest.

2. Use the five points of Burke's pentad and several ratios to decide how you might research one of these historical events: the Edict of Milan in 313, the defeat of the Spanish Armada in 1588, the Cherokee Trail of Tears Removal of 1838–1839, the Women's Rights Convention in 1849, the assassination of Dr. Martin Luther King Jr. in 1968, or a relevant event that you've studied in one of your courses.

Systematic Invention Strategy III: The Enthymeme

A third systematic can come into play when you are analyzing how a writer has developed the material in a text or when you're planning your own composition, and this strategy involves an important guideline from Aristotle's *Rhetoric*: People usually write about issues, problems, and subjects that admit to at least two possible viewpoints that are open to challenge or rethinking. In other words, nearly everything people write represents an **argument,** a carefully constructed and well-supported representation of the way a writer sees an issue, problem, or subject.

An editorial calling for more flexible attendance policies for students who work full-time would clearly be an argument. So would a petition seeking stronger governmental action against real-estate development near protected forest preserves. But you don't need a controversial, public issue in order to write an argument. Many, if not most, of the papers you might write for classes are arguments. A paper for European history about railroads in eighteenth-century England would not be simply an overview of the rail system; it would instead be a carefully reasoned, well-crafted argument about the influence of the railroads on, say, commerce, urbanization, or warfare. A paper for astronomy about the United States' lunar exploration missions in the 1960s and 1970s would probably not be simply a summary of all the flights to the moon; instead, it would be a well-planned, well-supported argument about the ultimate success of the Apollo program, or about future prospects for lunar colonization. A paper for English class calling for a comparative analysis of the styles of Ernest Hemingway and F. Scott Fitzgerald would not contain a bald listing of features of one and then the other author; instead, it would be a thoughtfully constructed, well-documented argument about the similarities and differences between the two writers' styles and about their contributions to creating influ-ential American literature in the early twentieth century. Another way of putting all this is to say that when a writer decides on a topic, he or she has a reason to choose it. That reason—interest in rail systems, hope for space exploration, opinions about Fitzgerald—determines how and how much the writer will say to an audience.

Part of the invention of ideas involves the rhetorical concept of the **enthymeme** (pronounced **EN**-thuh-meem). When you read a text in order to analyze it, you unpack and describe the major and secondary enthymemes you find. When you generate material for a text you're writing, you work through the premises for the arguments in the text, and you try both to guide the readers' per-ceptions of the logical relationships among ideas and to accommodate the beliefs that underlie them. This kind of logical reasoning from beliefs and statements Aristotle called the **syllogism** (**SIH**-luh-*jih*-zəm), and the enthymeme is itself a kind of syllogistic reasoning. The pattern of the syllogism is in three parts: a **major premise,** a **minor premise,** and a **conclusion.** The major premise is always some irrefutable **generalization** about the world, the minor premise is always some particular statement that falls under the general category, and the conclusion is always the statement that follows from the major premise and the minor premise. Here is a classic syllogism, taught in logic courses for centuries:

Major premise: All humans are mortal. (irrefutable generalization)

Minor premise: Socrates is a human. (particular instance of the generalization)

Conclusion: Therefore, Socrates is mortal. (idea that logically follows)

And here is a syllogism about a more current topic.

Major premise: All U.S. citizens who are single, under 65 years old, and earn more than $7,200 a year must file a federal income tax return.

Minor premise: Jody McGillicutty is a single U.S. citizen under 65 who earned $7,300 last year.

Conclusion: Therefore, Jody McGillicutty must file a federal income tax return.

Notice that the progression from premise to conclusion in the syllogism is airtight. You can't argue with the conclusion of a syllogism structured correctly—that is, when the major premise is an irrefutable general truth and when the minor premise is a particular instance of that general truth. Now consider a set of statements that looks as though it might be a syllogism.

Major premise: Women are wise.

Minor premise: Kate is a woman.

Conclusion: Therefore, Kate is wise.

But if the major premise is arguable—perhaps all women are not wise—the syllogism breaks down.

An enthymeme resembles a syllogism in the movement of its own logic, but it differs from a syllogism in two important ways. Instead of having an irrefutable general truth for a major premise, an enthymeme has as its starting point an assumption, a statement, or a proposition that the writer *presumes* the audience accepts and that the writer can build an argument upon. And, because the writer presumes, or wants to presume, that the audience believes and accepts the assumption that holds the major-premise slot, that part of the argument frequently goes unstated. In most arguments, the writer provides the other parts of the enthymeme and assumes that the audience is going to complete for itself the unspoken major premise.

> *Unstated premise:*   [Women are wise.]
>
> *Minor premise:*   Kate's a woman.
>
> *Conclusion:*   Of course, she gave me good advice.

Consider an enthymeme that might sit at the center of the petition, briefly described earlier, that calls for stronger governmental action against excessive real-estate development near forest preserves. Let's say that the central argument in the petition is this: Because the construction of large housing developments that adjoin forest preserves upsets the ecosystem and drives wild animals out of their natural habitats, governments should limit the number and size of houses built in such developments. The enthymeme as presented here contains only a minor premise—that is, one or more observations about the situation at hand—and a conclusion.

> *Major premise:*   [Unstated]
>
> *Minor premise:*   The construction of large housing developments that adjoin forest preserves upsets the ecosystem and drives animals such as deer, raccoons, and skunks out of their natural habitats. (two particular observations about the situation at hand)
>
> *Conclusion:*   Therefore, city, county, and state governments should limit the number and size of houses built in such developments.

What is the unspoken major premise here? What does the writer of this petition assume—or want to assume—that the audience already feels, thinks, believes, or knows about the situation at hand? It is this: As creatures of the earth, animals deserve a habitat, just as humans do.

A petition like this one would probably offer substantial documentation for its minor premise, providing statistics about the number of animals hit by automobiles in developing areas and about the possible spread of disease and destruction caused by animals being driven out of their natural habitats. The petition might also provide some details of a plan, hinted at in the enthymeme's conclusion, for governments to limit developments next to forest preserves. But the petition would never actually have to state its major premise explicitly. Would it be stronger and more effective if it did? Maybe the petition is stronger *because* the readers have to do the work of filling in the major premise themselves.

What happens when a writer makes an enthymeme that an audience might *not* accept? When you analyze an argument or plan one of your own, you should consider this possibility and look for it. As a case in point, let's look at the enthymeme we've just been working with, now presented in its fully stated form.

> *Major premise:*   Animals such as deer, raccoons, and skunks, as creatures of the earth, deserve a stable ecological habitat in which to live, as do humans.
>
> *Minor premise:*   The construction of large housing developments that adjoin forest preserves upsets the ecosystem and drives animals such as deer, raccoons, and skunks out of their natural habitats.
>
> *Conclusion:*   Therefore, city, county, and state governments should limit the number and size of houses built in such developments.

What if a reader responded to the argument by saying, "Animal rights are fine, but humans are more important than animals, and humans have a right to alter ecological habitats to suit their own needs"? If a reader responded this way to the argument, whether the major premise was explicitly stated or left tacit, then the writer would be up against an instance of what ancient rhetoricians called ***petitio prinicipi,*** or **begging of the question.** When readers respond in this way to an argument, the writer must attempt to change the audience's minds. What had been the unspoken major premise, the tacit starting point, of the central enthymeme becomes the conclusion of a new enthymeme. The writer thinks about what unspoken assumption this new enthymeme rests upon and considers a new major, unstated assumption. Here, for example, is how one might argue to change the minds of anyone who initially begged the question of the first enthymeme.

> *[Major premise:]*   [unstated: All creatures of the earth play a natural role in maintaining the ecological stability of an area.]
>
> *Minor premise:*   Animals such as deer, raccoons, and skunks contribute to the ecological stability of an area near rural property by feeding on vegetation and smaller animals.
>
> *Conclusion:*   Animals such as deer, raccoons, and skunks, as creatures of the earth, deserve a stable ecological habitat in which to live, as do humans.

Readers who begged the first question have objections answered by the writer's new enthymeme.

When writers generate material for their compositions by thinking about the enthymemes they might develop, they generally focus on just the skeleton—the bare structure or shape—of their argument. As the argument gets fleshed out in writing, writers would likely provide specific details to support the premises or the conclusion, and they might draw on stylistic and organizational resources to help make the case. These might include, of course, an appeal to the credibility and character of the writer (an appeal to ethos) or to the emotions and interest of the audience (an appeal to pathos) as well as to the audience's logical ability to reason through examples and proofs toward a conclusion (an appeal to logos).

Activities

1. In his book *High and Mighty*, Keith Bradsher labels the sports utility vehicle (SUV) "the world's most dangerous vehicle." He points out that the Ford Explorer gets 14 miles to a gallon of gas, less than half what the average new automobile in Japan gets. He notes that the Chevy Suburban emits 7.5 times more air pollution than the average automobile. He reports how in traffic accidents, "SUVs . . . slide over cars' bumpers and sturdy door sills, slamming into passenger compartments" of smaller vehicles. Describe Bradsher's argument as an enthymeme. Explain the unspoken assumption that forms the major premise.
2. Find a short piece of writing from class reading or from the newspaper. Describe an enthymeme from the argument it makes.

Systematic Invention Strategy IV: The Topics

One of the most thorough devices for taking an inventory of what you might write is the set of **topics** of invention drawn form Aristotle's works. It's easy for the modern student to be confused by the term *topics* because people often use the term to mean the subject matter a writer might write about. But the topics as Aristotle described them refer not to the subjects of compositions but to the *places* a writer might go to discover strategies and methods for developing their ideas. (The word *topos* actually means "place" in Greek.) Accordingly, the topics are related to the concepts that many people refer to as the **rhetorical modes.** Each of the four basic topics and each of the common topics represents a place where writers can use particular patterns of reasoning to generate ideas and evidence.

The Basic Topics

According to Aristotle, there are four **basic topics** a writer can use to find material for writing on any subject. These four topics are such ordinary patterns of reasoning that Aristotle calls them the **konnoi topoi**—literally, the **"people's topics."** Here are the topics and examples of how they can be used to generate material for oral and written discussion.

- **Possible and impossible:** Using this topic for invention, you look for material that allows you to argue that if X is possible, then so is Y, or that if X is impossible, then so is Y.

  EXAMPLE   Suppose you are writing a letter to your congressional representatives asking that they support increased funding for cancer research. Arguing the possible, you might say that since the scientific community came up with cures for typhoid fever, diphtheria, polio, and a range of other diseases, it's possible for them to find a cure for cancer provided there is sufficient funding for research. Or say you are writing about life-supporting conditions on planets other than Earth. Arguing the impossible, you might reason that since the polar ice caps on Earth can't support much life, it's certainly impossible for life as we know it to survive on planets largely covered by ice.

- **Past fact:** This topic allows you to consider ideas suggesting that, given all the known conditions, X probably happened in the past.

  EXAMPLE   You are writing about Babe Ruth for a history of sports course, examining whether he really did "call the shot" on his famous home run at Wrigley Field. You read the inconclusive accounts of the event and, based on what you've read about Ruth's bold personality and showmanship, you argue that he did indeed point with his bat to the very place in the stands where he intended to hit the home run—just before he hit it right to that spot. Or suppose you are writing a paper about President Harry Truman's decision to order the atomic bombing of Hiroshima and Nagasaki at the end of World War II. You might argue, given all the historical facts and interpretations surrounding those events, that the United States was, as Truman maintained, simply trying to end the war more quickly than it could have without the bomb.

- **Future fact:** Using this topic, you can find ideas that allow you to argue that X will probably happen in the future.

  EXAMPLE   You are writing a paper analyzing the proposals to build a Star Wars defense system—a system of satellites that would shoot down incoming missiles and protect the United States from attack. You argue that, given the history of defense systems built ostensibly for defensive purposes being used instead to attack other countries, in all probability any Star Wars system would be used offensively rather than defensively.

- **Greater and less:** This topic allows you to argue that since X happened, so will Greater-Than-X, or if Y happened, so will Less-Than-Y.

  EXAMPLE   Imagine you are writing an analysis of whether increased standardized testing will lead to higher achievement in public schools. Arguing the greater, you could claim that if the state of Texas can show gains in student performance as a result of a rigorous program of testing in the schools, so can all the states if they simply follow the Texas model. Or suppose you are writing a paper for an education class about vertical teams, groups of teachers at different grade levels who try to sequence instruction so that one grade leads carefully to the next. Arguing the less, you could claim that if large corporations can improve their product by creating vertical teams across levels of management and labor, so can small schools.

The Common Topics

A second set of topics useful for taking an inventory of the substance of a text you might analyze or for generating material for your own compositions has its origin in Aristotle's philosophical treatise called, simply, the *Topics*. This second set, which includes the previously mentioned four basic topics as a single topic called *circumstances*, is referred to simply as the **common topics.** Again, let's look at them and examples of using them for taking an inventory of what you might write in a composition.

- **Definition:** Using this topic for invention, you generate material by defining key terms, providing for each term its genus, or the class of things it belongs to, and species, the features that distinguish the thing being defined from all other items in its class.

  EXAMPLE   Think about writing a paper arguing that students with learning disabilities ought to be exempted from taking standardized tests. You would need to demonstrate clearly what you mean by the term *learning disability* by describing as fully as possible what you mean generally by disability and then clarifying which disabilities specifically influence a person's learning.

- **Division:** Using this topic for invention, you divide some or all of your subject matter into parts.

  EXAMPLE   You are writing a paper on how to successfully perform a major role in a play. You might divide this whole topic initially into two parts: how to rehearse and how to perform. And then you might divide the rehearsal part into three additional sections: how to prepare for rehearsal, how to act during the rehearsal, and how to debrief yourself with your fellow cast members after each rehearsal.

- **Comparison and contrast:** Using this topic for invention, you generate similarities (comparisons) or differences (contrasts) about aspects of your subject matter.

  EXAMPLE   Imagine that you are writing a brochure about the best colleges for a person who is interested in community service. After consulting the catalogues and Web sites of a half dozen or so colleges with community service programs, you might show how the colleges are similar and different on these dimensions: relation of community service to students' majors, relation of community service to general education, range of community needs served by the programs, and proximity and accessibility of the community service programs to the college campus.

- **Relationships:** Using this topic for invention, you can generate material that shows different kinds of relationships between aspects of your subject matter.

  EXAMPLE   Suppose you are writing an analysis of whether increasing the number of lanes on a congested highway will actually eliminate most of the traffic jams. Arguing a **causal relationship,** or a cause-and-effect relationship, you could point out that increasing the number of lanes will actually make traffic worse because, with greater accessibility along the highway, more homes and businesses will be built, thus attracting even more cars. Or suppose you are writing a paper about the growth of women's sports in high schools and colleges. Arguing an **antecedent-consequence relationship,** you could make a case that when women's sports become as important to a school as men's, then women's teams will need the same kinds of institutional support in terms of locker rooms, travel arrangements, uniforms, cheerleaders, and so on. Or, to take another example, suppose that you are writing a paper about how slowly a bill providing funding for social programs moves through Congress. Arguing the relationship known as **contradictions,** or contraries, you could claim that since the complicated layers of governmental bureaucracy keep such programs in constant need of funding, a more streamlined procedure in Congress would keep a regular source of funds flowing to social programs.

- **Circumstances:** These topics include the (1) possible and the impossible, (2) past fact, and (3) future fact, all covered within the four basic topics outlined in Aristotle's *Rhetoric* and described earlier.

- **Testimony:** Using this topic of invention, you can generate material by investigating what authorities or people with extensive experience with your subject say about it. In addition, you can generate material by consulting any documents, laws, or precedents pertaining to your subject.

  EXAMPLE   Imagine, again, that you are writing a paper about the growth of women's sports in high schools and colleges. You could collect testimony by interviewing the athletic directors of several schools, and asking about their experiences with the growth of female participation in sports. You could read primary material from the federal government about Title IX of the Education Amendments of 1972, the law that helps to foster equal funding for men and women in all educational activities including sports, and secondary material—books, articles, and chapters about the sharp growth in women's participation in athletics.

Activity

Read the following editorial column, "The ABC's of Home Schooling," by Julia Morse. With the members of a small group, analyze how Morse uses the following topics to generate material for her column: (1) the greater, (2) the possible, (3) division, (4) cause-and-effect relationship, and (5) comparison. Once you have finished analyzing Morse's invention, generate a paragraph on Morse's issue with your group. Use at least one of the following topics: (1) definition, (2) future fact, and/or (3) testimony.

THE ABC'S OF HOME SCHOOLING

Jodie Morse

As a blissfully unattached single devoid of responsibility for anything (except my rent) and anyone (save my bevy of blissfully unattached friends), I've always found nothing more frightening than the prospect of having kids of my own to feed and shelter. Recently, though, I've been dwelling on something far scarier: educating them—myself. With an estimated two million kids from all economic classes now schooled at home, this isn't just idle worrying on my part. And considering I will surely never make enough money to pay for private schools—and fancy myself always living in hip urban centers with shoddy public schools—somewhere down the line home schooling might actually prove the most attractive option. After all, I do write articles every week on how to fix the nation's schools. How hard would it be to actually do it?

My actual knowledge of home schooling was rather limited, mainly to those geeky kids who year after year win the national spelling bee with words I can't even pronounce. To find out more I spent last weekend at a home schooling exhibition at a Denver Holiday Inn, a 5000-strong confab of parents, children and education experts who got together to purchase curriculum, take seminars and talk shop. My first lesson: these people rise with the sun. When I arrived at 7:30 am on Saturday morning, a swarm of parents had already staked out the still-shuttered exhibition hall. When they finally opened the gates and I scanned the panoply of products now geared for home schoolers, I realized why they allowed the extra time. You name it, you could buy it: day-by-day lessons from kindergarten through high school, $600 state-of-the-art microscopes, fiddle lessons, membership in home schooling bowling and sewing leagues, natural oils meant to purify young minds. "Mom, look, they have owl pellets," one boy squealed over the crowd. I followed to find a biological supply booth ready to outfit those parents who'd delved into dissection. Also on sale: preserved sharks, sheep brains and frogs.

As much as I love formaldehyde, I was more drawn to the informational seminars. They promised to enlighten home school parents on, well, the very topics just about every parent everywhere obsesses over. What to do if your kid has ADD? How to discern your child's learning style and resolve conflicts? What kinds of foods help children concentrate—and keep them from bouncing off the walls? Unsurprisingly, the "Designing a College Preparatory High School Program" was bursting at the seams with parents. They probably made a beeline there from the vendor doing brisk business selling Princeton Review and Kaplan SAT prep software.

With support systems like this in place, home schooling certainly wasn't the lonely endeavor I'd imagined it—long days chained to the kitchen table with a couple of library books and low-tech science experiments of my own making. And after an exhausting day in Denver, I'm at least willing to admit home schooling to the realm of the possible—even the doable—provided I can ditch the lesson about the sheep's brain.

—Time.com, June 29, 2001

Intuitive Invention Strategies: A Preview

The systematic invention strategies are helpful for analyzing the strategies writers use and for planning your own writing. But in addition to the systematic strategies, writers can employ a number of more intuitive techniques to generate ideas, information, and perspectives. Chapter 4 presents case studies of writers using several of these strategies to plan their compositions. As a preview, here are thumbnail descriptions of these techniques.

- **Freewriting:** When you freewrite, you simply try to write, nonstop, for a set period of time—perhaps five to ten minutes—about whatever comes to mind when you think about your subject matter. Freewriting is sometimes difficult because it requires that you turn off your internal editor, that little voice inside your head that says what you *shouldn't write* because it might not be correct. Freewriting allows you to get as much writing accomplished as possible without concerning yourself with clarity, organization, or usage. The assumption is that you will shape, revise, amplify, and correct your prose as you proceed to work on a composition. Because writers often fear error overmuch at the beginning of a writing process, freewriting can allow good ideas and interesting perceptions to emerge and not get suppressed by the pressure to be right.

- **Keeping a journal:** Many writers keep a **journal** where they record their observations, their thoughts, and their responses to their reading. They may respond to prompts from their teachers or write self-generated questions and concerns. A person who writes in a journal for 20 minutes three times a week will generate a substantial amount of material that, like freewriting, can serve to encourage the flow of ideas. Journal writing can often become the basis for more formal writing.

- **Conversations:** Just talking, either with one friend or classmate or a group, can be a productive way to generate material for a composition. The better you know your conversational partners, the more you and they can ask probing questions, offer competing or complementary insights, and suggest new avenues that you should pursue in a writing project. Listening well and speaking up are ways to nurture what a writer knows and to suggest what a writer needs to know. Good talk may be your most effective strategy for invention.

Memory

Even though students studying rhetoric usually learn about the canon of memory after they have studied principles of arrangement and style, which we cover in the next chapter, we think there's a good reason to connect memory to invention. How we go about analyzing texts is shaped in large measure by the prior knowledge about the text's subject matter, which we have stored in our memory. How we go about planning to write a text is influenced by the "cultural memory" that a writer—and, ideally, his or her readers—can tap into.

Today, most of the important work that advances the collective knowledge of the world's communities is done in writing. Scholars write books and articles; journalists write columns; government workers write white papers; and specialists in many fields write reports, case studies, feasibility analyses, and project plans. Our culture places great emphasis on getting things in writing.

In ancient Greece and Rome, when citizens were often asked to speak for themselves in public forums and writing was not so widespread in the culture, teachers included memory as one of the canons of rhetoric. Public speakers, and students learning the texts of their culture, would copy, imitate, and finally memorize texts they had heard and then produce their own texts. They "learned by heart" the texts they needed to remember. The phrase suggests how much words and ideas need to be internalized before they become part of memory. Would-be public speakers were taught various techniques (called **mnemonic devices,** derived from the Greek word for memory, *mnesis*) to memorize their speeches so that they could deliver them without notes or a script. The most commonly taught mnemonic device was the **house analogy.** Speakers were taught to associate different parts of their speech with specific locations in their houses—for example, the introduction of their speech was like the entrance way, the developmental sections of their speech became like various rooms that they could move into one after the other, until they reached the conclusion and exited from the back door of the house. In a primarily oral culture, it was as important for an effective communicator to learn the art of memory as it was to learn about the strategies of invention, arrangement, and style.

In our writing culture, the significance of memory in a person's rhetorical abilities—indeed, the way memory is actually defined in rhetoric—has shifted. Memory in contemporary thinking about rhetoric has to do in part with how much knowledge, information, and data a writer can access electronically or otherwise and then use judiciously. Memory also has to do with the cultural memory of a writer; that is, what the writer knows about history, art, science, and literature. The writer uses cultural memory to tap into deeply held beliefs, assumptions, and ideals, as a way to establish rapport with readers, build arguments through evidence, and develop the persona. A writer who begins an essay by saying, "I have been on my own yellow brick road for the year I've been in college" draws on the memory that he has and that he hopes his readers might have of Dorothy and the Wizard of Oz. In doing so, the writer makes a connection to Dorothy's desire in the movie and builds a rapport with readers who know the story so well that *yellow brick road* is enough of a clue to the memory of the entire context of the film.

To use a commonly understood phrase, *do you want fries with that?*; to employ an allusion like the yellow brick road; or to create an analogy to a current event—war in Iraq as analogous to war in Vietnam, for example—is to make use of memory for both reader and writer.

Activity

In 1986, educational theorist E. D. Hirsch published a book called *Cultural Literacy: What Every American Should Know,* which concluded with a list of terms that every "culturally literate" person should be familiar with and have in their memory. Hirsch surveyed literacy and culture experts to come up with the list. Some might say that the list reveals more about the list maker than about what constitutes American cultural literacy. Still it's an interesting test of cultural memory and of how we share it.

Here's a partial list from the *K*s.

Karachi	Kent State University
Karaktova	KGB
Kismet	Khomeni, Ayatollah
Kelvin, Lord	Kruschev, Nikita
Kentucky Derby	kill with kindness
Knesset	kinetic energy
Knock on wood	knee jerk
Kangaroo court	King, Martin Luther, Jr.
Keep the wolf from the door	kingdom come
kelvinator	kingdom was lost, For want of a nail the

Part 1. Test your cultural memory.

1. Identify all the terms you know.
2. In a small group, discuss the terms to become familiar with more of them.
3. Share your group's cultural memory with the class.

Part 2. Add to the list.

What terms would you and your group add to the list as terms everybody should know?

Interchapter

2

Overview of the Major Points in Chapter 2

- The five traditional canons of rhetoric—invention, arrangement, style, memory, and delivery—suggest strategies for creating clear, compelling texts. Such compositions appeal to logos, ethos, and pathos. You can analyze the five canons in a writer's work or plan to use them in your own.
- The canon of invention comprises strategies—both systematic and intuitive—that writers can use to generate abundant material for texts.
- The canon of memory today guides writers to try to tap into the "cultural memory" of their readers effectively.

Activities and Discussion Questions for Chapter 2   Use these questions and comments as guides for your own discussion and writing about these works.

Henry David Thoreau, "An Essay on Civil Disobedience" (published 1849)

The text appears on pages 221–237. In a discussion with a group of your classmates, or in a well-developed essay, address one or more of the following questions.

1. State and explain what you see as the central enthymeme in "Civil Disobedience." Then describe and explain what you see as one of the subsidiary or supporting enthymemes.
2. Point out and explain a way you see Thoreau using the topics as a strategy of invention.
3. Point out some ways you see Thoreau tapping into the "cultural memory" of his readers. To what does the text refer or allude with the expectation that readers will know the reference or allusion? How do these references and allusions affect the appeal of readers today?

Eavan Boland, "It's a Woman's World" (published 1982)

The text appears on pages 237–239. In a discussion with a group of your class-mates or in an essay, address the following question:

1. Is there a central argument in "It's a Woman's World"? If so, what is it? Using the structure of an enthymeme, state and analyze the argument.

Alice Walker, "Everyday Use" (published 1973)

The text appears on pages 239–246. In a discussion with a group of your class-mates, or in a well-organized essay, address one or both of the following questions:

1. Is there a central argument in "Everyday Use"? If so, what is it? Using the structure of an enthymeme, state and analyze the argument.
2. Do you see "Everyday Use" in any way as a story about cultural mem-ory? If so, explain how. How do these references and allusions affect the appeal of readers today?

Using the Traditional Canons of Rhetoric: Arrangement, Style, and Delivery

3

"*My heartfelt thanks to Kitty Lundell for writing my speeches, and to Keith Donegan for delivering them.*"

The five traditional **canons** of rhetoric—**invention, arrangement, style, memory**, and **delivery**—have formed a useful, related package of strategies for readers and writers since classical antiquity. A person recognizes a **context**—a coming together of **occasion, audience,** and **purpose**—that calls for effective speaking or writing. Motivated by this recognition, the person works to *invent* material that will be suitable for the text to produce something in which the invented material is *arranged* in an effective way, to write prose that manifests a *style* that is both appropriate and engaging, and then to *deliver* the product to readers or listeners in the very best way possible. In eras before writing became the primary mode of communicating, the person might have committed the text to *memory* in order to deliver it. Once writing became the primary mode of transmitting texts, the person would have tapped into the *cultural memory* that the context suggests.

Chapter 2 demonstrated how you can use the two canons most directly related to *generation* of texts—invention and memory—as you analyze other people' compositions and plan and execute your own. This chapter aims to accomplish the same function with the other three canons—arrangement, style, and delivery, the canons that are most directly connected to *communicating* your arguments, ideas, and perspectives to your audience. By the end of this chapter, you will be fully equipped to conduct a thorough rhetorical analysis of a text and to plan and produce your own effective composition.

Arrangement

Once a writer invents—comes up with topics, decides on a focus, plans an argumentative strategy, considers proof, and maybe writes a draft or a beginning of one—the writer begins to consider how and where to place ideas, facts, and examples to make them most effective. The second canon of rhetoric is arrangement. Just as the concepts underlying the first canon, invention, help you both to analyze the texts written by someone else and to plan your own compositions, so too can the principles of arrangement help you as both reader and writer.

The principles of arrangement help a writer plan to (1) order and structure the parts of a piece of writing and (2) support the different parts. Clearly, the principles of invention and arrangement work hand in hand. As a writer, your goal in invention is to discover ideas and to take inventory of everything you might say to make your position clear and compelling. Your goal in arrangement is to select the best and most appropriate ideas, examples, and propositions from that inventory and to decide how to order the parts of the composition most effectively to help you achieve your purpose.

Genres

An important principle that helps govern arrangement is **genre,** the type of composition writers produce. As you recall from Chapter 1, a writer decides which genre to produce based on the context at hand and the aim he or she wants to accomplish in that context. Genres usually have their own rules for arrangement. At the beginning of this book, we noted how a script writer would make decisions about the scene based on the kind of film the scene was a part of, its genre. To take another example, scholarship applications require different formats—openings, details, endings—than science reports, in which you'd include an abstract, an explanation of the research question, a description of methods and materials, a report on findings, a discussion of results, and a list of published works you referenced. And a sonnet you might write to a sweetheart would be arranged in 14 lines of iambic pentameter, perhaps divided according to traditional Shakespearean form into quatrains, with a final two lines, or couplet. All these guidelines about how to write a sonnet, a lab report, or an application letter revolve around genre and conventions of arrangement.

Since most of the genres a writer must produce have their own rules of arrangement, it doesn't do you much good to look for one pattern of arrangement that works for all genres. To put it simply, there is no single pattern, no particular format, that will work in every writing situation. To be sure, though, almost every composition you write and every text you analyze have a beginning, a middle, and an end. In general terms, we can talk about the function of those sections.

- The beginning of a composition usually sets out the central question the paper will answer or the argument the paper will develop and hints at how the development will proceed.

- The middle of a paper usually offers points in support of the answer to the central question or the argument and substantiates or explores those points with examples, illustrations, details, and reasons.

- The end of a paper usually draws together the material developed in the middle and addresses the question "So what?" That is, the end tells readers what they might consider or act upon.

This basic pattern of beginning, middle, and end, in addition to making intuitive sense, also has historical roots in the literature of ancient rhetorical theory. Aristotle, for example, wrote in his *Rhetoric* that a composition needs to have only what some people might consider the middle section: a statement of the argument, including its central and supporting points, and a proof of those points. Introductions and conclusions, according to Aristotle, are optional and should be added in situations where the audience needs to have the argument introduced in the beginning and drawn together, or synthesized, at the end. Aristotle's teacher, Plato, on the other hand, wrote that a composition should be like a body—it needs to have a head, a torso, and feet.

As rhetorical theory developed in the 500-odd years following Aristotle's death in 322 B.C.E., teachers of rhetoric described in increasingly formal terms the principles of arrangement that then guided the construction of persuasive compositions. Most teachers of rhetoric in ancient Rome, for example, taught their students to produce a six-part speech, consisting of exordium, or introduction; narration; partition; confirmation; refutation; and peroration, or conclusion.

- In the **exordium,** literally the *web* that draws listeners into the speech, the speaker would introduce the subject at hand and include material that would make the audience both attentive and receptive to the **argument**.
- The **narration** would offer background material on the case at hand.
- The **partition** would divide the case and make clear which part or parts the speaker was going to address, which parts the speaker would not take up, and what order would be followed in the development.
- The **confirmation** would offer points to substantiate the argument and provide reasons, details, illustrations, and examples in support of those points.
- The **refutation** would consider possible objections to the argument or its supporting points and try to counter these objections.
- The **peroration** would draw together the entire argument and include material designed to compel the audience to think or act in a way consonant with the central argument.

The six-part oration was never intended to be a general format, a plan of arrangement for all arguments. It was a format for a specific genre—the courtroom declamation, in which an orator would speak on behalf of himself or a client he was called upon to represent. Now, the six-part oration is a strategic resource for readers to use in analyzing the functional, as opposed to structural, arrangement of a text and for writers to use in planning "moves" of their own.

Functional Parts

What are these moves? What should you look for when you analyze arrangement? First of all, you can look at the entire text you are analyzing and try to divide it into some **functional parts,** remembering while you do so that not all texts are going to have all parts. Ask yourself these questions:

1. Is there some section that clearly lets the reader know what subject the composition is about and what the writer's purpose is? If so, where does this section begin and end? In this section, can you find an answer to the central question that the text has been written in response to, or can you find an indication of the text's central argument?
2. Is there a part that explains any background information that the reader needs to know in order to be able to understand the answer to the central question or argument that the composition offers? If so, where does this section begin and end?
3. Is there some sentence or paragraph that focuses the readers' attention on some particular issue, aspect, or **theme** that the paper will examine in contrast to others that it might?

4. Is there some section that purposefully sets out material in support of the paper's answer to the central question or its argument? If so, where does this section begin and end?

5. Is there a part that examines possible objections to the answer, argument, or supporting material? If so, where does this section begin and end?

6. Is there a sentence or section where the writer specifically answers the "So what?" question? In other words, is there a section where the writer hints at what he or she hopes readers will think and do on the basis of what they have read in the text?

By answering these questions, you can get a sense, at least provisionally, of how the parts of the text work.

Activity

Return to the column by Joel Caris, "Corporate Sponsorship of Our Schools," on page 41. Ask the six questions just listed about the editorial, and discuss your answers with the members of a small group.

Questions About the Parts

Now you can turn your attention to analyzing the effectiveness of the way the writer works within the parts. If you can find a part that lets the reader know the subject of the composition and the writer's purpose, you might ask yourself questions like these:

■ Are the subject and purpose directly stated or implied? How does the *degree* to which these elements are revealed or concealed strike you as a reader?

■ Is some angle consciously foregrounded and other material downplayed? What is the effect of this foregrounding versus backgrounding in the opening section?

■ Is there a statement that suggests to the reader the course that the remainder of the paper will take? How does the presence (or absence) of such a statement affect your reading?

If you can identify a part that explains any background information necessary for the reader to know in order to understand the paper's position, ask yourself the following questions:

■ Is there a statement about the direction that this part of the paper will take—any terms or phrases at the beginning of paragraphs or passages that help you move through the material, or words like "first," "second," or "last"? What effect do these words have on you as a reader?

- Does the writer follow any discernible order in providing this background information? Is the order chronological (arranged by time)? spatial (arranged by location)? incremental (arranged by order of importance)? What effect does the ordering of the material have on you as a reader?
- Does the writer provide transitional words or phrases that connect the sentences or paragraphs of this part? Do these words or phrases suggest that the writer is *continuing* and *adding on* to the material already presented, relating a *result* to what came earlier, or *contrasting* what comes later with what appeared earlier?

If you can identify a sentence or paragraph that focuses the readers' attention on some particular issue, aspect, or theme in contrast to others that it might, ask yourself questions like these:

- What does the writer do that *brings to the forefront* some material and consciously *puts in the background* other material? What is the effect of foregrounding versus backgrounding in this section?
- Is there a sentence that suggests the course that the remainder of the paper will take? What effect does this mapping have on you as a reader?

If you can find a part that concentrates on support of the paper's central question or its argument, ask yourself these questions:

- Are there words or sentences that map out the direction a part of the paper will take—words like "first," "second," and "last," for example? What effect do these devices have on you as a reader?
- Do you detect any of the following methods of development in this section: relating anecdotes or longer stories, describing scenes and evoking sensory images, defining terms and concepts, dividing the whole into parts, classifying the parts according to some principle, or providing cause-and-effect reasoning? What effect on you as a reader do any of these methods of development have?

If you can identify a part that examines possible objections to the answer, argument, or supporting material, ask yourself questions like these:

- Is there language that suggests the writer wants to *counter* the objections? What is this language? What effect does it have on you as a reader?
- Does some language suggest that the writer wants to *concede* the objections? What is this language, and what is its effect on you?

Finally, if you can identify a part where the writer specifically addresses the question "So what?" ask yourself the following questions:

- Is there a direct charge to readers to think or act in a new way after reading the piece, or does the writer imply new ways of thinking and acting? How does the *degree* to which these elements are revealed (or perhaps concealed) persuade you?

- What does the writer do with the words, phrases, and sentences in this part to give the composition a *sound* of finality? What effect does this language have on you as a reader?

If you can generate good answers to these questions by referring to places in the text, you will have done a thorough analysis of its arrangement. In addition, you will have given yourself ideas to ponder when you follow conventions to arrange the genre that is appropriate for your own writing situation.

Activity

In a small group or by yourself, take a careful look at one of two kinds of texts, perhaps a paper you have recently written for one of your classes and a column on the op-ed page (that is, the page opposite the editorial page) of a major daily newspaper. Use the six groups of questions on pages 60–61 to identify the functional parts of the text. Then use the questions on pages 61–62 to analyze the effectiveness of the arrangement within each part.

Style

Simply put, style, the third canon of rhetoric, consists of the choices a writer makes regarding words, phrases, and sentences. To begin thinking about style, consider this hypothetical situation (or perhaps the situation is not completely hypothetical for you): Two people you know show up in class generally looking very different. One wears bright-colored clothes, with lots of flowing scarves and elaborate accessories—pins, bracelets, and necklaces. The other dresses completely in black—top, pants, socks, and shoes—and wears no accessories. Underneath, are both people alike, or does style reflect personality? Is style governed by occasion and appropriateness? Do you think these people make conscious choices about their style?

These questions provide a good entry point for thinking about style in writing. Each of the people just described has a style of dress, and every writer and piece of writing have a style. People choose styles to reflect themselves in their writing as well as in what they wear, and the style they choose expresses meaning. A particular clothing style or writing style can be appropriate in some situations and not in others. And, for all these reasons, stylistic choice in clothes and writing is, or can be, conscious. Conscious choice about stylistic decisions in writing can help writers reflect themselves, communicate meaning, and influence readers.

Style and Situation

If you are the kind of person who likes definite answers, style can be a baffling subject. Whether you are analyzing the style of a piece of writing or planning your own composition, the answer to nearly every question you might pose about whether particular words, sentences, or figures of speech is a *good* choice is almost always the same: "It depends."

"What does it depend on?" you might ask (or "Upon what does it depend?" if you want to vary your style!). It depends on the concept of *situational appropriateness*. Remember that all writing emerges from a situation—a convergence of a need to write, a writer, an audience, a subject matter, a purpose, a genre, and a time and place. The question of whether a particular word, sentence, or figure of speech is right is a question of whether it is right *for the particular writing situation*.

Consider, for example, the situation when you are required to write an analytical paper for a history class.

1. The need to write comes from the inquiry you are engaged in. The study of history involves many documents and incidents that are open to interpretation, and people write about history in order to close gaps in knowledge and to offer a possible reading of the past that makes good sense to other people interested in the same historical period.

2. You, the historian, are the writer. As a historian, you are expected to come across as a person who is genuinely interested in history, uses the terminology that historians use, employs their methods for interpreting texts and events, and generates the kind of reasoned, supported points in your writing that they admire.

3. You may think the audience for your paper is only your history teacher, but it's wise to think about the teacher as a member of a larger intellectual community of historians, who expect you to behave like one of them when you are writing a paper for their consideration.

4. The subject matter is likely an aspect of the particular period of history you are studying—an economic, cultural, military, or social aspect—which might have some special terminology associated with it that you could be expected to use in your composition.

5. The purpose of your composition is to show you understand the history you write about enough to explain the particular piece of it you examine. Your goal is to present a clear, unified analysis of some historical material; to organize your analysis around a strong, salient thesis; and to support your thesis with a documented summary and with paraphrases, and quotations of material from primary and secondary historical texts.

6. The genre is the academic analytic paper, a composition that introduces the subject; states a thesis; provides ample points in support of the thesis; backs each point up with examples, reasons, illustrations, and details;

and then offers a conclusion that reinforces the thesis for an audience of other historians.

7. The time and place for such a project are generally an academic term in a high school, college, or university, and all varieties of academic prose follow a rich array of stylistic choices.

Each of these individual elements in the writing situation, as well as the situation as a whole, can influence the choices you make involving words, sentences, and **figurative language.** Considering these situational elements carefully can help you decide, for example, whether to employ special terminology, to use first-person singular pronouns (*I, me, my, mine*) or to refer to the reader in the second person (*you, your, yours*), to use **contractions,** and to choose active or passive voice.

Style and Jargon

Many writing communities—academic disciplines, professional organizations, and so on—demonstrate an ambivalent attitude toward the use of specialized terminology. Admonitions such as "write for the general reader" and "avoid 20-dollar words" appear regularly in professional guides to effective writing. These cautionary statements are wise—to a certain extent. Good writers usually want to develop a style that the well-educated, diligent reader will find accessible. Moreover, writers who choose to use elaborate, complicated words *for no good reason in the writing situation* can often produce baffling, even comic effects. (A true story: One of the authors had a student who wrote the following sentence in a paper for a junior English course: "When my cat expired, I waxed lachrymose." When asked what she meant, the student said, "When my cat died, I started crying." The instructor urged her to use the simpler words.)

Such guiding statements as these, however, tend to oversimplify the actual word choice practices of communities of readers and writers. It's a plain fact that many communities have specialized vocabularies that readers expect to encounter in the community's documents and that writers new to the community are expected to know and use. Outsiders to the community often refer disparagingly to these sets of terms as **jargon,** but jargon is not necessarily bad. The use of specialized, complicated terms becomes a problem only when a writer (1) does not understand what the terms mean or (2) uses the terms in a composition that will have an audience beyond the community of readers and writers who know the terminology. The latter case becomes even more troubling when writers use jargon, either purposefully or subconsciously, to establish their insider status in a community, knowing that their readers are not part of it.

Are You and I Okay?

Young writers in nearly all intellectual communities often feel confused about whether they may use first-person and second-person pronouns and whether they may use contractions in their compositions. Once again, the answer depends on the situation. For most academic papers, like the analytical paper for history just described, the use of first-person pronouns is not appropriate because the focus in this kind of writing is on the subject rather than on the person writing about the subject. Further, in such papers, it is not appropriate for writers to refer directly to their readers as *you*. On the other hand, if the situation calls on writers to offer a personal response to a piece of literature or a historical event, then it would be inappropriate for someone to tackle this task *without* writing in the first person. Similarly, if the situation calls for an open letter on a controversial issue to congressional representatives working on legislation to address it, then it would be nearly impossible for the writer to produce a successful letter that did not refer to the representatives directly as *you*.

Style and Contractions

The use of contractions is also governed by the notion of appropriateness. In most formal, academic papers, and in business-oriented letters and reports, writers generally avoid contractions like *it's, can't, wouldn't,* and *doesn't*. In informal papers and personal letters, writers should feel free to use the same kinds of words, including contractions, they would speak to their audience if they encountered them face to face. To contract or not to contract depends on the writer's intention, in terms of relationship with the reader and with the subject matter at hand.

Style and the Passive Voice

Guides to effective writing in many fields often urge writers to "write in the active voice" and "avoid the passive voice." That's good advice but limited in its applicability. Remember the difference between sentences in the active voice and those in the passive voice. An active voice sentence follows this pattern:

DOER → ACTION → RECEIVER

The lab technician filtered the solution.

A passive voice sentence follows this pattern:

RECEIVER → ACTION (BY DOER)

The solution was filtered.

The solution was filtered by the lab technician.

Notice three differences between the active and the passive. First, since the active voice emphasizes who did what, many readers think active sentences are stronger and more forceful. Second, since a passive-voice verb always consists of a helping verb and a main verb, sentences in the passive voice are often wordier than sentences in the active voice. Third, the doer of the action in a passive-voice sentence is expressed in a prepositional phrase following the verb, and passive-voice sentences are grammatically complete without this phrase—as "The solution was filtered" demonstrates. Therefore, some readers maintain that the passive voice is potentially irresponsible—that passive-voice sentences can conceal the doer of the action when the reader has a right to know who does what. Readers, teachers, and editors who make these claims are right. Active-voice sentences generally do sound stronger and more authoritative. Passive-voice sentences are often more difficult to process, and they do frequently conceal the doer of the action.

But a writer can rarely avoid using the passive voice altogether. It can't be done. (Notice the passive-voice sentence.) Once again, situational appropriateness needs to be your guide when you are analyzing or planning style. Passive-voice sentences occur frequently in scientific and technical writing, where writers are trying to emphasize not who did what but what was done. Writers also use the passive voice, consciously or subconsciously, to shift material around in a sentence. As any editor will explain, the most emphatic position in any sentence is usually at or near the end, and employing the passive voice is one of several ways a writer can emphasize a subject by moving it from beginning to end of the sentence.

Dimensions of the Study of Style: Sentences, Words, and Figures

Three broad categories of style help writers to analyze the style of a text and to make their own stylistic choices. Every choice we analyze or make in these categories potentially affects the meaning of a composition, the reader's perceptions of the credibility of the writer, and the willingness of the reader to accept the text's argument or exploration. These categories are

- **Sentences:** grammatical type, placement of details, variety
- **Words:** level of elaborateness and formality, difficulty, technicality
- **Figures:** schemes and tropes (terms defined below), figurative language

Sentences

Sentences can be classified in many ways, and it's helpful to consider the potential effect a particular type of sentence might have on a reader in a certain situation. One of the most basic ways of classifying sentences is according to the number and type of clauses in them.

- A **simple sentence** has a single independent clause.

    Abraham Lincoln struggled to save the Union.

    Within its single clause, a simple sentence can have a **compound subject,** a compound verb, or both.

    Abraham Lincoln and Andrew Johnson struggled to save the Union.

> Abraham Lincoln struggled to save the Union and persevered.
>
> Abraham Lincoln and Andrew Johnson struggled to save the Union and persevered.

- A **compound sentence** has two clauses, each of which could exist as a simple sentence if you removed the conjunction connecting them.

  > Abraham Lincoln struggled to save the Union, and Andrew Johnson assisted him.
  >
  > Abraham Lincoln and Andrew Johnson struggled to save the Union and persevered, but the leaders of the Confederacy insisted that the rights of the states were more important than the maintenance of the Union.

- A **complex sentence** has two clauses, one independent and at least one subordinate to the main clause.

  > When the leaders of the Confederacy insisted that the rights of the states were more important than the maintenance of the Union, Abraham Lincoln and Andrew Johnson struggled to save the Union and persevered.

- A **compound-complex sentence** has the defining features of both a compound sentence and a complex sentence.

  > When the leaders of the Confederacy insisted that the rights of the states were more important than the maintenance of the Union, Abraham Lincoln struggled to save the Union and persevered, and Andrew Johnson assisted him.

Why should you be concerned with whether a sentence is simple, compound, complex, or compound-complex when you are analyzing someone else's writing or planning your own? The answer is that function grows out of form. When you need to make a succinct point, often a short, simple sentence will do so effectively. A short, simple sentence can suggest to a reader that you are in control, that you *want* to make a strong point. If you're trying to show how ideas are balanced and related in terms of equal importance, a compound sentence can convey that to the reader. A single compound sentence or a series of them in a composition can suggest to your reader that you are the kind of person who takes a balanced view of challenging issues, that you want to give equal weight to more than one side of an issue. If you want to show more complicated relationships between ideas, then complex and compound-complex sentences can communicate the intricacies of your thinking. A single complex or compound-complex sentence or a series of them can cue a reader that yours is a mind that willingly takes up complicated issues and tries to make sense of them, both for yourself and for your readers.

A second method of analyzing sentences looks at them in terms of another important structural distinction—as **loose sentences** or **periodic sentences.** Just as writers can vary the number and type of clauses in a sentence according to the subject they are treating and the effect they are trying to have on readers, so can writers vary sentences along the loose-periodic continuum to achieve similar goals.

Sentences vary along the loose-periodic continuum according to how they incorporate extra details in relation to basic sentence elements. As you know, the basic elements of every sentence in English are subjects, verbs, and complements. Here is a sentence with just two basic elements:

> Abraham Lincoln wept.

A loose sentence is a basic sentence with details added *immediately at the end* of the basic sentence elements:

> Abraham Lincoln wept, fearing that the Union would not survive if the southern states seceded.

A periodic sentence is a sentence in which additional details are placed in one of two positions, either *before* the basic sentence elements or *in the middle of them.* Here is a periodic sentence that results from putting additional details before the basic sentence elements:

> Alone in his study, lost in somber thoughts about his beloved country, dejected but not broken in spirit, Abraham Lincoln wept.

And here is a periodic sentence that results from placing additional material in the middle of the basic sentence elements:

> Abraham Lincoln, alone in his study, lost in somber thoughts about his beloved country, dejected but not broken in spirit, wept.

Understanding the concepts of loose and periodic, you can achieve sentence variety by writing sentences that move along a loose-periodic continuum. The next sentence tends more toward loose than periodic:

> Abraham Lincoln considered the Union an inviolable, almost eternally inspired, concept.

And the next one tends more toward periodic than loose:

> Abraham Lincoln, a self-taught philosopher, a political scientist even before there was such a field, considered the Union an inviolable, almost eternally inspired, concept.

You can hear the differences in these sentences—in what is emphasized, as well as in how quickly a reader reads them. Writers use these types of sentences to effect changes in meaning. Readers use them to understand meaning more clearly. Since, as we just mentioned, the most emphatic position in a sentence is often at or near the end, and since the second most emphatic location is the beginning, recognizing and creating loose and periodic sentences enable the reader and the writer to make wise decisions about varying sentence structure for emphasis. Even more importantly, the structure of a sentence affects the pacing of a text. A loose sentence moves quickly, and a succession of loose sentences can make a piece of prose fairly gallop along. A periodic sentence works with delay—it postpones completing the sentence until after it has provided the details. In passages where a writer wants to sound crisp, businesslike, and efficient, the loose sentence will serve the writer well. In passages where a writer wants to sound balanced, deliberate, and thoughtful, a periodic sentence will be a useful tool.

Good writers make informed decisions about sentence structure. They know their sentences not only carry meaning but also affect readers, causing them, often subconsciously, to evaluate the **ethos** of the writer and empathize with the writer's position. Sentence structure says much about the writer and his or her purpose, credibility, and goals.

Activities

1. Do you think the following sentence from Booker T. Washington's *Up from Slavery* is loose or periodic?

   > In order to defend and protect the women and children who were left on the plantation when the white males went to war, the slaves would lay down their lives.

   Rewrite the sentence in a couple of ways, experimenting with making it more loose and more periodic. In a small group, discuss how changes affect tone, purpose, and the ethos of the speaker.

2. Change the first sentence of an essay you are working on to make it more periodic or more loose. What difference does the change make in your piece or in your voice?

Parallel Structure

One particular feature of style that good writers know how to use and careful readers frequently notice is **parallelism,** or parallel structure. The basic principle of parallel structure is quite simple: When a passage, a paragraph, or a sentence contains two or more ideas that are fulfilling a similar function, a writer who wants to sound measured, deliberate, and balanced will express those ideas in the same grammatical form—words balance words, phrases balance phrases, clauses balance clauses, and sentences balance sentences.

One way to learn about parallel structure is to recognize passages or sentences that violate it. Consider, for example, the following sentence from a student's paper about a short story by Larry Kramer:

> In these moments, Rivka discovers the bitter truth about her husband's hidden life, her son's death, and that Herman was not sending her the letters all along.

This sentence, as you can see, contains three elements, all serving the same function—they are all the things that Rivka "discovers the bitter truth about." The sentence doesn't work stylistically, though, because not all three elements are in the same grammatical form. The first two are noun phrases—a noun preceded by modifiers—while the third is a clause, a group of words with a subject and verb. There are two ways to revise the sentence to achieve parallel structure, both of which make the writer sound more careful, deliberate, and controlled:

> In these moments, Rivka discovers the bitter truth about her husband's hidden life, her son's death, and Herman's deceit about the letters. [a revision making all three elements noun phrases]
>   In these moments, Rivka discovers the bitter truth about how her husband had lived, her son had died, and Herman had deceived her about the letters. [a revision making all three elements clauses]
>   In these moments, Rivka discovers the bitter truth that her husband had led a hidden life, her son had died, and Herman had not sent her the letters all along. [an alternative revision with three clauses]

Here's another example of a breakdown in parallel structure, this one from a published magazine article:

> What happens to a leading writer after he gets a MacArthur genius grant, a Getty fellowship, and his new book hits number one on the nonfiction bestseller list?

Notice the three elements serving the same function in this sentence—three things that happen to this "leading writer." The sentence is a stylistic clunker, though—the writer sounds less deliberate and balanced than she might—because the three elements are not in the same grammatical form. Look at how the sentence might be revised:

> What happens to a leading writer after he gets a MacArthur genius grant, wins a Getty fellowship, and has a book in the number-one position on the nonfiction bestseller list? [three elements as verbs followed by direct objects and modifiers]
>   What happens to a leading writer after he gets a MacArthur genius grant, a Getty fellowship, and a number-one ranking on the nonfiction bestseller list? [three elements as noun phrases serving as objects of *gets*]

With practice, you'll learn to notice parallel structure in sentences you read, to change nonparallel elements as you read, and to create parallel structures in your own compositions. (Notice the parallel structure in that sentence? Three things fulfilling the same function, all signaled by the infinitive *to*). An even greater challenge than working with parallel structure at the sentence level, however, is to analyze it in longer passages you might read and to create such a passage in your own writing. Abraham Lincoln was a master at the parallel construction. His most famous work, the brief but eloquent Gettysburg Address, ends with a paragraph that is a tour-de-force of parallel structure.

> But in a larger sense, we cannot dedicate, we cannot consecrate, we cannot hallow this ground. The brave men, living and dead who struggled here, have consecrated it far above our poor power to add or detract. The world will little note nor long

remember what we say here, but it can never forget what they did here. It is for us the living rather to be dedicated here to the unfinished work, which they who fought here have thus far so nobly advanced. It is rather for us to be here dedicated to the great task remaining before us—that from these honored dead we take increased devotion to that cause for which they gave the last full measure of devotion—that we here highly resolve that these dead shall not have died in vain, that this nation under God shall have a new birth of freedom, and that government of the people, by the people, for the people shall not perish from the earth.

Notice the sense of measured balance in this paragraph created by the repeated parallel structures. In the first sentence, Lincoln creates a strong triplet of clauses, all with the same direct object:

we cannot dedicate, we cannot consecrate, we cannot hallow this ground

In the third sentence, he balances two verbs, each modified by an adverb:

The world will little note nor long remember

The final sentence brings the speech to a powerful conclusion with two sets of parallel structures: a set of three clauses beginning with *that*

that we here highly resolve, that this nation under God shall have, and that the government of the people

plus three of the most famous prepositional phrases in the English language

government of the people, by the people, and for the people

Activities

1. Consider the following passage by Patricia Williams, a prominent lawyer and legal theorist. In a small group, point out Williams's use of parallel structure, and discuss how it appeals to readers.

   Money buys self-esteem. If you're poor, you can't be happy because you're the object of revulsion and ridicule; if you're poor, you can't accept it as fate because poverty is your fault; and if you're poor, you have to resent the upper classes because competition—or economic revenge—is the name of the game, the only way out.

2. Using parallel construction, write the first sentence for one of these stereotypical first-day-of-class assignments:

   My Favorite Hobbies
   Summer Vacation
   When I'm Fifty

Words

When skillful writers make decisions about style and when perceptive readers analyze the style of a document they read, they pay careful attention to diction, or the choice of words. **Diction** strikes some people as an odd term to refer to word choice—to many people, *diction* means "pronunciation." The word *diction* comes from Latin *dictio,* which means "style of speech." In ancient Greece and Rome, when rhetoricians were more concerned with speaking than writing, *dictio* meant "choice of words," and *pronunciatio* referred to the actual speaking of them. When this book uses *diction,* it reflects the classical meaning.

As with sentences, a study of diction depends on situation and genre. In other words, when you are writing a paper and you wonder about using a certain word in a sentence, you need to ask yourself first of all, "What is my purpose, who is my audience, and what kind of text am I writing?" Then ask, "Is it *appropriate* to use the word?" A word that might work perfectly well in one situation and in one type of writing could be completely out of place in another situation and genre.

To make these considerations more real, think about three different types of compositions you might be called upon to produce about the same subject. We'll carry this hypothetical set of writing tasks through the chapter to give some illustrations of the terms we bring up. Imagine you are writing about recreational sports at your school—not organized or competitive sports but activities such as intramural sports teams, recreation nights for the community, and clubs. Think about the kind of document you'd produce in three different settings, or contexts.

- In a public-health class where research is important, you'd produce a researched, documented position paper about the benefits of recreational sports.
- For a Web site sponsored by a real-estate company, you'd write informative pages about the types of recreational sports the schools offer to students and to citizens who live in the community.
- In a letter to a friend, you'd write about your own participation in recreational sports.

Imagine that in each case you'll have a section in the document to explain the advantages of participating in recreational sports—improved physical health, improved mental health, improved coordination, and social benefits. In each piece, you'd vary your word choice to describe those advantages.

Activity

Write the first sentence of your imaginary piece on recreational sports in each of the three settings.

General Versus Specific Words

The famous twentieth-century language expert S. I. Hayakawa in his book *Language in Thought and Action* described a phenomenon he called "the ladder of abstraction." At the top of the ladder were general, often quite abstract terms, like *transportation* and *justice;* near the middle rungs were slightly more specific terms, like *automobiles* and *juvenile court;* and near the bottom of the ladder were specific, concrete terms like *my 2001 green Subaru Forester* and *the offender's five-year probation sentence for shoplifting.* A good writer, Hayakawa claimed, is able to move up and down the ladder of abstraction like a monkey in a tree.

Notice how you could use the ladder of abstraction to vary the key terms in your explanation of the benefits of participating in recreational sports. Just considering one of the four benefits at the abstract, general level, you could refer to *physical health benefits.* Slightly more specifically, you could refer to the same thing as *cardiovascular health benefits.* Slightly more specifically, you could write about *benefits to the heart.* Near the bottom of the ladder of abstraction, you could concentrate on *the benefits to the small blood vessels around your heart.* But why, you might wonder, would any writer want to vary his or her diction in this way? The answer lies in the situation and the genre. A community of scholars in public health might look in a research paper, like the hypothetical one you're writing, for information about *cardiovascular health benefits.* Readers of a Web site about schools might simply want to see that your school's recreational sports program emphasizes general *physical health benefits.* Your distant friend, to whom you have written an e-mail about participating in your school's intramural sports program, might be most interested to know that a strenuous game of volleyball can strengthen and create *small blood vessels around your heart.* You vary the generality or specificity of your diction in order to address your readers in terms most useful to them.

Formal Versus Informal Words

Varying your diction on this dimension is like going to a dance. For an informal occasion at someone's house or a local club, the dress is casual—jeans, T-shirts, and so on. But for a formal dance like a prom, the dress is formal—tuxedos and gowns. Your writing situations can be seen as occasions that require an understanding of the level of formality, and your diction ought to suit the occasion.

What are some of the ways in which diction varies in formality? Some of the ways to make your diction more formal will be considered in the following sections, which take up Latinate or Anglo-Saxon words and slang or colloquialisms. For now, let's consider just two areas that raise formal-versus-informal concerns: contractions and pronoun reference.

A research paper for an academic class, such as the hypothetical one you're writing for your public health class, represents a formal writing occasion, and in such a paper, you should probably prefer *have not* to *haven't, would have* to *would've,* and *is not* to *isn't.* Your contribution to the Web site about the recreational sports program at your school is a slightly less formal writing occasion than the research paper; nonetheless, you might prefer the full words instead of the contractions. The e-mail to your friend, however, would be informal, so contractions would be more appropriate. (Notice that we, the two authors, consider this book to be somewhere in the middle of this formal-to-informal continuum, so we feel free to use contractions.)

Is it appropriate to use first-person references (*I, me, my, mine, we, us, our, ours*) in a paper? Like most other stylistic decisions, situation and genre determine appropriateness. Most teachers and editors prefer that writers do not write in the first person in formal writing situations such as the one calling for the research paper. The Web site might effectively use first-person pronouns if you were describing your personal involvement in the recreational activities. And, of course, a friend would worry if you didn't use first person when you e-mailed.

The question of pronoun use in formal and informal papers raises two additional issues. The first is the use of the impersonal *we* in formal papers. Consider three sentences that might go into your hypothetical research paper:

> I develop multiple intelligences by participating in recreational sports.
> We develop multiple intelligences by participating in recreational sports.
> Participating in recreational sports helps develop multiple intelligences.

The first would probably not be appropriate since the aim of research is to investigate the subject rather than the writer. The second sentence also seems inappropriate since the *we* is unspecified. The impersonal *we* is used most frequently in newspaper editorials or in documents where the writer can actually be sure he or she is writing on behalf of a collective body—such as the editorial board of the newspaper, the governing board of the corporation, or the leaders of the political party. Although there are exceptions—in some science research, for example—you're probably on safest ground using the third sentence in formal research essays, the one with no pronoun reference at all.

The second issue involving pronoun reference is the grammatical concern of pronoun-antecedent agreement. In formal grammar, a pronoun is supposed to agree in number and gender with the word it refers to, its antecedent, and the phrase *a person* is a singular construction. If you were to write

> A person learns to take advantage of a different part of their intelligence than they normally use.

your pronoun and antecedent won't agree. How could you write the same sentence and stay within the boundaries of the rule? You have several options. One is to use singular pronouns:

> A person learns to take advantage of a different part of his intelligence than he normally uses.

OR

> A person learns to take advantage of a different part of her intelligence than she normally uses.

If you choose to follow this option, you should make an effort to *alternate* the use of the singular pronouns, sometimes using the masculine and sometimes the feminine.

A second option is to use *he or she,* or *him or her.* Alternatively, you may use a hyphenated or slashed phrase that includes both the masculine and the feminine in your reference:

> A person learns to take advantage of a different part of his/her intelligence than he/she normally uses.

This option takes care of pronoun-antecedent agreement and includes both the masculine and feminine reference but is stylistically awkward and reads poorly. A third option pluralizes the antecedent, allowing you to make your pronoun and antecedent agree:

> People learn to take advantage of a different part of their intelligence than they normally use.

Latinate Versus Anglo-Saxon Words

Historically, English is something of a mongrel language. The ancestor of the English we speak and write today was called Old English, which was a Germanic language. The Old English spoken in the British Isles from around the fourth century to the eleventh century C.E. has been labeled Anglo-Saxon English because the two tribes of people who spoke it were the Angles and the Saxons. But around 1100 C.E., the language began to change. In 1066 C.E., England was invaded—and the English king overthrown—by a French king, William of Normandy. The Norman Invasion opened the door to a substantial infusion into English of words and phrases from the languages spoken in western Europe, notably France, Spain, and Italy. French, Spanish, and Italian are historically **Romance languages,** so called because of their common roots in Latin, the language spoken in ancient Rome. After the Norman Invasion, and throughout the Renaissance, English came to acquire more and more words and phrases that had their origins in Latin. And because the people who helped bring this Latinate influence into the language tended to be the powerful nobility, the use of what is called **Latinate diction** has come to be associated with writing in more formal situations, while the use of what is called **Anglo-Saxon diction** has come to be linked with writing in more informal situations.

In general, you can recognize Latinate words by their multisyllabic construction in contrast to monosyllabic Anglo-Saxon words. A Latinate word usually consists of a root, derived from Latin, plus a prefix that qualifies the meaning of the root, a suffix that designates what part of speech the word is, or both. Consider, for example, the word *magnanimous*. The root is *anim*, which means "soul" or "spirit." The prefix is *magn*, which means "large." The suffix is *ous*, which indicates that the word is an adjective. Thus, *magnanimous* is an English word, with Latinate word parts, meaning "kind, noble, or honorable." Notice that the brief Anglo-Saxon word *kind* is simpler and seems more direct, and in many writing situations, you might use *kind* instead of *magnanimous*. In others, you'd choose the longer word for its appropriateness to the situation and genre or for the subtle difference in meaning between the two words.

How might the Latinate versus Anglo-Saxon distinction affect your writing of your three pieces about recreational sports? You could refer to the activity as *participating* (a Latinate word) in recreational sports or *playing* (an Anglo-Saxon word) recreational sports. You could claim that "participating in recreational sports employs multiple intelligences" (several Latinate words), or you could say that "playing recreational sports uses different parts of your mind" (several Anglo-Saxon words). You could assert that "participating in recreational sports facilitates social interaction" (several Latinate words), or you could write that "playing recreational sports helps you make friends" (several Anglo-Saxon words). The Latinate constructions seem more formal and might be more appropriate in the research paper than on the Web site or in the e-mail to your friend.

Activity

Consider several pairs of terms that illustrate both Latinate diction and Anglo-Saxon diction in English:

- *Facilitate* **(Latinate) versus** *help* **(Anglo-Saxon):** both words mean "to make easier."
- *Manufacture* **(Latinate) versus** *make* **(Anglo-Saxon):** the roots of *manufacture* suggest that it means "to make by hand," but over the centuries, it has come simply to mean "to make."
- *Interrogate* **(Latinate) versus** *ask* **(Anglo-Saxon):** *interrogate* derives from both the Latin for "to ask," *rogare*, and the prefix *inter*, meaning "between or among."
- *Maximize* and *minimize* (Latinate) versus *grow* and *shrink* (Anglo-Saxon).

In a small group, talk in specific terms about what kinds of writing situations would call for the more Latinate diction and what kinds of writing situations would call for the more Anglo-Saxon diction. Explain the difference in meaning and effect between the two words in each pair.

Common Terms Versus Slang or Jargon

Slang and jargon generally get a bad rap. Just look at how a popular online reference source, *Merriam-Webster's Collegiate Dictionary*, defines these two terms. **Slang** is either "language peculiar to a particular group" or "an informal, nonstandard vocabulary composed typically of coinages, arbitrarily changed words, and extravagant, forced, or facetious figures of speech." If you were to encounter the following sentence in a novel, you would probably recognize it as slang from the 1920s, known in America as the Jazz Age:

> I'd say let's ankle to the joint, but I got a gimp. Other than that, everything's jake.

What the character is saying is,

> I'd say let's walk to the restaurant, but I'm limping. Other than that, everything's fine.

Jargon is "confused, unintelligible language"; "a strange, outlandish, or barbarous language or **dialect**"; "a hybrid language or dialect simplified in vocabulary and grammar and used for communication between peoples of different speech"; "the technical terminology or characteristic idiom of a special activity or group"; or "obscure and often pretentious language marked by circumlocutions and long words." If you were to use the terms *drop-down menu* and *DKDC*, you would be using jargon common to online writing among Internet aficionados. A more common way to refer to these terms would be "a screen menu that drops down from a term when you point the cursor toward the term" and "don't know don't care."

Should you use slang or jargon in any of the hypothetical papers you are writing about recreational sports? A sentence such as the following would be out of place in the researched paper or the informative Web site:

> While some folks think playing volleyball is way old skool, others know it's a way to meet some phat friends and escape the rents for a couple hours.

That sentence might work in the e-mail to the friend, assuming the friend understands the slang terms. A sentence like this might work in your research paper:

> Some critics of intramural recreation programs find fault with their social hegemonic nature.

while readers of the Web site or your friend might be confused or put off by the social-science jargon.

Both slang and jargon seem like dangerous territory for a writer because both employ language that might obscure a writer's message rather than clarify and simplify it. To a certain extent, that is true, and savvy writers ought to be aware of the simpler, more direct, more common words they could use. But, as with all questions involving style, a writer's decision about whether to use slang or jargon depends on the situation in which he or she is writing. As always, the question is this: "Given this subject matter, this purpose, this audience, and this type of writing, would slang or jargon be *appropriate?*" Sometimes the answer is yes. The use of slang or jargon can signal to your readers that you are a member of their group, that you are in solidarity with them, and that you have done your homework about a particularly complicated topic that is important to the community.

Denotation Versus Connotation

Intuitively, we all know that words can be loaded. A careful reader always notes how a text capitalizes on the multiple meanings of words, and a careful writer chooses and arranges words so that the reader catches subtle, suggested meanings.

Consider these two simple sentences:

Wilbert Newton is a perfect example of a statesman.
Wilbert Newton is a perfect example of a politician.

This Newton fellow would probably be pleased if someone said the first sentence about him. *Statesman* suggests responsibility, intelligence, and high-mindedness. But he might be unhappy if someone said the second sentence about him, since *politician* often these days suggests self-serving or unprincipled behavior. The differences in meaning in these two sentences illustrate what scholars of language refer to as **denotation** and **connotation.** Denotation refers to a literal meaning of a word, while connotation refers to an association, emotional or otherwise, that the word evokes. Both sentences just presented use words that might have the same denotative meaning—elected official—but carry quite different connotations.

Figures of Rhetoric: Schemes and Tropes

One of the most time-honored methods of elaborating one's style is to employ **figures of rhetoric** in a piece of writing. A critical reader will learn to recognize when a writer is using one or more of the figures, just as a good writer will learn how to incorporate them effectively in a composition.

People have been teaching and learning about the figures since ancient Greece and Rome, when rhetoric began to be studied as an organized subject. In general, the classical rhetoricians divided the figures into two broad categories: schemes and tropes.

- A **scheme** is any artful variation from the typical arrangement of words in a sentence.
- A **trope** is any artful variation from the typical or expected way a word or idea is expressed.

In ancient Rome, and later in the European Middle Ages and Renaissance, scholars developed substantial lists of figures, categorizing them under these two general labels, and schoolchildren had to learn the definitions and find examples of the figures in literary works and public discourse. It would not have been unusual, for example, for a grammar school student in Renaissance England to be given a list of 300 or so names of schemes and tropes and to be required to memorize the definitions and produce an example of any one of them on demand. Students undertook this task not simply to learn how to vary their words, phrases, and sentences. They did so because their teachers believed that a different way of *saying* something about the world was also a different way of *seeing* something about the world. In other words, they taught that using figurative language to express ideas helped to clarify and sharpen a person's thinking—not a bad lesson for students even today.

You don't have to memorize 300 definitions to use figures. (You can consult any number of excellent handbooks and Internet sites. One particularly helpful resource is Professor Gideon Burton's Web site at Brigham Young University called *Silva Rhetoricae*, literally "the forest of rhetoric" at http://humanities.byu.edu/rhetoric/silva.htm.) But you can learn to recognize schemes and tropes by their functions and understand their effect on readers.

Schemes Involving Balance

The most common scheme involving balance is parallelism, which uses the same grammatical structure for similar items (see pages 70–72). Readers understand the equivalency of items in parallel construction and exercise the logical, systematic thinking abilities. In your sports paper, you might write parallel sentences like the following:

- **Parallelism of words:** Exercise physiologists argue that body-pump aerobics sessions benefit a person's heart and lungs, muscles and nerves, and joints and cartilage.
- **Parallelism of phrases:** Exercise physiologists argue that body-pump aerobics sessions help a person breathe more effectively, move with less discomfort, and avoid injury.
- **Parallelism of clauses:** Exercise physiologists argue that body-pump aerobics is the most efficient exercise class, that body-pump participants show greater gains in stamina than participants in comparable exercise programs, and that body-pump aerobics is less expensive in terms of equipment and training needed to lead or take classes.

Coincidentally, each of these three parallel schemes is also called a **zeugma,** a figure in which more than one item in a sentence is governed by a single word, usually a verb. Each of the three examples of parallelism involves a single verb, *argue,* that introduces a list of three words, phrases, or clauses.

A related scheme involving balance is **antithesis,** in which parallelism is used to juxtapose words, phrases, or clauses that contrast. With an antithesis, a writer tries to point out to the reader differences between two juxtaposed ideas rather than similarities. Here are three antitheses (note how to spell the plural) that might be appropriate in your sports research paper:

- **Antithesis of words:** When distance runners reach the state they call the zone, they find themselves mentally *engaged* yet *detached.*
- **Antithesis of phrases:** When distance runners reach the state they call the zone, they find themselves mentally *engaged with their physical surroundings* yet *detached from moment-to-moment concerns about their conditioning.*
- **Antithesis of clauses:** When distance runners reach the state they call the zone, they find *that they are empirically engaged with their physical surroundings,* yet *they are also completely detached from moment-to-moment concerns about their conditioning.*

A famous example of antithesis in clauses is "To err is human; to forgive, divine."

Another scheme that looks a great deal like antithesis is an **antimetabole** (anti-muh-**TI**-boh-lee), in which words are repeated in different grammatical forms. Well-known examples of antimetabole are "When the going gets tough, the tough get going" (adjective becomes noun; noun becomes verb); "You can take the kid out of the country, but you can't take the country out of the kid"; and the famous line from President John F. Kennedy's inaugural address; "Ask not what your country can do for you—ask what you can do for your country."

Schemes Involving Interruption

Sometimes, a writer needs to interrupt the flow of a passage in order to provide necessary, on-the-spot information or ideas to readers. Two schemes are especially useful for this purpose. The first goes by the name of **parenthesis** (the same word as the singular of parentheses, the punctuation marks). Here is a parenthesis embedded in a sentence from your hypothetical letter to your friend:

> Sports night at the school always brings out the would-be jocks—who would expect any different?—ready to show that they're potentially as good as the varsity players.

Notice that this parenthesis is set off by dashes, the punctuation marks most commonly used to set off an interruptive word, phrase, or clause. When you use dashes to set off an interruption, be sure to include them at the beginning and the end of the interruption. A parenthesis, however, can also be set off from the remainder of the sentences with parentheses:

> Sports night at the school always brings out the would-be jocks (who would expect any different?) ready to show that they're potentially as good as the varsity players.

Notice that a parenthesis in the form of a question, as in the example above, needs to be punctuated with a question mark. The same would hold true for a exclamatory word, phrase, or clause

> When sports night is canceled—oh, sorrowful day!—all the would-be jocks get a case of show-off withdrawal.

but not for a simple declarative sentence:

> Sports night supervisors have to stop people from trying to slam dunk—this is the ultimate showboat move—for fear that one of the would-be jocks might hurt himself.

A second scheme useful for setting off additional material is an **appositive.** An appositive is a construction in which two coordinating elements are set side by side, and the second explains or modifies the first:

> Joe Weider, *a pioneer in personal weight training,* would marvel at the facilities open to today's student athletes.

Schemes Involving Omission

A writer occasionally needs to omit material from a sentence so that its rhythm is heightened and often accelerated and so that the readers will pay close attention to the potentially dramatic effect of the prose. Two schemes useful for this purpose are ellipsis and asyndeton (uh-**SIN**-duh-ton). An **ellipsis** is any omission of words, the meaning of which is provided by the overall context of the passage:

> In a hockey power play, if you pass the puck to the wing, and he to you, then you can close in on the goal.

The phrase *and he to you* omits the words *passes it,* but a reader can clearly infer the meaning. An **asyndeton** is an omission of conjunctions between related clauses:

> I skated, I shot, I scored, I cheered—what a glorious moment of sport!

Schemes Involving Repetition

Beginning writers are often warned not to be repetitive. That's good advice, as far as it goes; but it actually should be "Don't be repetitive, but use repetition." Several schemes involving repeating sounds or words can actually lead the reader to pay closer attention to the prose and to see the writer as a purposeful, forceful, even artistic writer. Some of these schemes will be familiar to you from studying literature.

- **Alliteration:** repetition of consonant sounds at the beginning or in the middle of two or more adjacent words:

    Intramural hockey is a strenuous, stimulating, satisfying sport.

- **Assonance:** repetition of vowel sounds in the stressed syllables of two or more adjacent words:

    A workout partner is finally a kind, reliable, right-minded helper.

- **Anaphora:** (uh-**NA**-fuh-ruh): repetition of the same group of words at the beginning of successive clauses:

    Exercise builds stamina in young children; exercise builds stamina in teenagers and young adults; exercise builds stamina in older adults and senior citizens.

- **Epistrophe:** (e-**PIS**-truh-fee): repetition of the same group of words at the end of successive clauses:

    To become a top-notch player, I thought like an athlete, I trained like an athlete, I ate like an athlete.

- **Anadiplosis:** (a-nuh-duh-**PLOH**-suhs): repetition of the last word of one clause at the beginning of the following clause:

    Mental preparation leads to training; training builds muscle tone and coordination; muscle tone and coordination, combined with focused thinking, produce athletic excellence.

- **Climax:** repetition of words, phrases, or clauses in order of increasing number or importance:

    Excellent athletes need to be respectful of themselves, their teammates, their schools, and their communities.

Anadiplosis and climax are closely enough related that some teachers of the figures refer to the two schemes together as **climbing the ladder.**

Activity

Reread carefully a paper you are working on. Identify a passage where you can consciously use one or more of the schemes that affect balance, and add them.

Tropes Involving Comparisons

The most important trope in this category, the one upon which all the others in this group are based, is metaphor, an implied comparison between two things that, on the surface, seem dissimilar but that, upon further examination, share common characteristics:

    Many an athletic contest is lost when the player's mind is an idling engine.

Clearly, an athlete's mind and an automobile engine are dissimilar. Yet the metaphor here suggests that, to be successful, an athlete must put his or her mind to purposeful work, just as a driver puts an automobile engine in gear to drive the car. A **simile** resembles a metaphor except that with a simile, the comparison between the two things is made explicit with the use of the word *like* or *as*, rather than remaining implicit, as it does in a metaphor:

> An athlete's mind must be like a well-tuned engine, in gear and responding to the twists and curves of the contest.

Notice that this sentence, which begins with a simile, ends with an **implied metaphor**—the athletic contest is compared to a twisting, curving road.

Other tropes involving comparison include the following:

- **Synecdoche** (suh-**NEK**-duh-kee): A part of something is used to refer to the whole.

  > We decided we could rearrange the gym equipment if everyone would lend a hand.

  (Obviously, everyone needed to use hands, arms, legs, shoulders, and so on, but *hand* stands for them all.)
- **Metonymy** (muh-**TAH**-nuh-mee): An entity is referred to by one of its attributes.

  > The central office announced today new regulations for sports night.

  (The central office can't speak, of course, but the noun is an attribute of the person or an association with the person who works in the central office.)
- **Personification:** Inanimate objects are given human characteristics.

  > After almost three periods of searching, the puck finally found the goal.

- **Periphrasis** (puh-**RI**-frah-suhs): A descriptive word or phrase is used to refer to a proper name.

  > The New York Rangers and the New York Islanders vie to be the best hockey team in the Big Apple.

Tropes Involving Word Play

Some writers like to entertain (and enlighten) their readers simply by playing with the sounds and meanings of words. The most common trope for doing so is the **pun,** a word that suggests two of its meanings or the meaning of a homonym. Puns have a bad reputation—and it's often well deserved. But sometimes a good pun can really attract a reader's attention:

> The tipped-but-caught third strike, ending a bases-loaded rally, was a foul most foul.

Two additional word-play tropes are:

- **Anthimeria** (an-thuh-**MEER**-ee-uh): One part of speech, usually a verb, substitutes for another, usually a noun.

  > When the Little Leaguers lost the championship, they needed just to have a good cry before they could feel okay about their season.

- **Onomatopoeia:** Sounds of the words used are related to their meaning.

  > The puck whizzed and zipped over the ice, then clattered into the goal.

Tropes Involving Overstatement or Understatement

A writer, ironically, can help readers see an idea or point clearly by overstating it or understating it. The trope of **overstatement** is called **hyperbole** (hye-**PUHR**-boh-lee):

> He couldn't make that shot again if he tried a million times

while the trope for **understatement** is called **litotes** (**LYE**-tuh-tees):

> Shutting out the opponents for three straight games is no small feat for a goaltender.

Tropes Involving the Management of Meaning

Some tropes can be seen as techniques that simply allow a writer to play with the meaning and development of ideas in strategic ways.

- **Irony:** Words are meant to convey the opposite of their literal meaning.

  > Their center is over seven feet tall—where do they come up with these little pip-squeaks?
  > When irony has a particularly biting or bitter tone, it is called **sarcasm.**

- **Oxymoron:** Words that have apparently contradictory meanings are placed near each other.

  > When you have to face your best friend in competition, whoever wins feels an aching pleasure.

- **Rhetorical question:** A question is designed not to secure an answer but to move the development of an idea forward and suggest a point.

  > Hasn't the state of intercollegiate athletics reached the point where the line between professionalism and amateurism is blurred?

Activity

Turn again to a paper you are currently working on. Find a section into which you can incorporate one or more of the tropes just described. Do so, and then discuss in a small group whether your rewritten version is appropriate for the audience and purpose of your paper.

Delivery

The canon of delivery, like memory, assumed its place in the rhetoric curriculum because ancient Greece and Rome were primarily oral cultures. Speakers who wanted to excel in politics and public affairs needed to learn how to use their voices effectively, how to enunciate clearly, and how to use their bodies to gesture appropriately while they were giving a speech. One of the most famous stories in the lore of rhetoric, indeed, involves Demosthenes, a celebrated orator in fourth-century B.C.E. Athens. As a youth, Demosthenes had a speech impediment, so to perfect his craft, he practiced enunciation with his mouth full of pebbles, he recited speeches while he was running, and he declaimed at the seashore, strengthening his voice by speaking over the roar of the waves. When asked which was the most important of the five canons, Demosthenes is reputed to have answered, "Delivery, delivery, and delivery."

In our culture, where written documents tend to do more knowledge work than speeches, delivery has taken on new meanings. Delivery now refers to how the written text is, well, delivered. Among the many questions a contemporary student can ask now in analyzing delivery, or in planning his or her own, are these:

- Does the writer choose an electronic or print format?
- If the former, does the writer choose to include any hypertextual links? How effective are they?
- Does the writer use any photographs or other kinds of images to accompany the written text?
- Does the writer choose to put a cover of any kind on a printed text?
- How does the writer use such features as font sizes and styles, bullets or numbered lists, and white space?

Delivery may also include stylistic choices that let readers hear some words more loudly than others—setting off words in a paragraph, for example, with hyphens or ellipsis marks, or capitalizing words or making all lowercase. "My name is ELOISE. I live at the PLAZA," says the main character in the delightful children's books. Erik Larson begins his history of the Columbian World's Fair Exposition in Chicago, *The Devil in the White City* (2003), in this all-cap way: "HOW EASY IT WAS TO DISAPPEAR." Dorothy Allison's memoir of poverty-stricken southern childhood includes a refrain that appears in every section of the book and in italics: *"Two or three things I know for sure, and one of them is. . . ."* These decisions affect the way readers hear the words and the message. The delivery alters the meaning. Re-creating dialect in spelling or word choice is another decision that affects delivery. Delivery has to do with how a text looks, but it also has to do with how it's heard. Classical rhetoricians emphasized delivery by using a set of techniques called **declaiming**. In declamation, the speaker heightens the message by carefully emphasizing pitch, volume, and pause while speaking and by using gestures and movements that accompany and highlight elements of the spoken text. The formality of preparing a speech, then standing and delivering it, is good practice for all rhetors. Delivery has changed in the twenty-first century, but it remains a vital component in making a written or spoken text most effective. All of these features, and others that involve the delivery of the text, affect how clearly the writer conveys the central ideas of a piece and what kind of credible, trustworthy person the readers perceive the writer to be.

Activity

Write the paragraph above or another one of your choice in slang or dialect, using punctuation, typeface, paragraphing, or other format changes to highlight how the paragraph sounds or how it would be spoken.

Rhetorical Analysis

Now that you understand a great deal about how the three rhetorical appeals—logos, ethos, and pathos—work and about how writers can tap into the strategies of invention, arrangement, style, memory, and delivery to create texts that appeal to reason, credibility, and emotion, how can you use your knowledge? Certainly, you can think about the connection of context, appeals, and canons when you write your own papers. You can also use your new knowledge to guide a rhetorical analysis of any text you might be asked to examine.

The following text is an editorial from the *Washington Post* of May 12, 2007. Read the editorial carefully, and then study the rhetorical analysis that comes after it.

TESTING, TESTING

Making the U.S. citizenship test more "meaningful"

What is or should be required to become an American?

According to U.S. law, the criteria include basic knowledge of English and U.S. civics. What "basic knowledge" means, however, varies from region to region. Citizenship applicants must answer 10 of the 96 civics questions produced by the U.S. Citizenship and Immigration Services. But which 10 questions, whether the hardest 10 or the easiest 10, and whether they are written or oral, is determined by the office or the person administering the test. As a result, cities can have different tests and different pass rates.

Now, concluding a decade-long project to standardize the naturalization process, Citizenship and Immigration Services is trying out a new test in 10 cities. Agency spokeswoman Chris Rhatigan says the pilot test questions are selected randomly by computer, with a balance of hard and easy questions and a consistent mix of questions from different topics such as history and geography. Citizenship and Immigration Services has also infused the vocabulary lists for the English portion of the test with more civics-related terms such as "first lady."

The more controversial change to the test is the refocusing of the civics questions on American "concepts" rather than tight facts. The 142 pilot questions, of which about 100 will be kept, are meant to make the naturalization test "more meaningful," the agency says. Some pro-immigrant groups fear that "more meaningful" may be code for "harder." Many of the pilot questions are most abstract, such as asking what the rule of law means or what Ben Franklin was famous for. These open-ended questions seem to undercut the standardization goal since they are inherently more subjective. Citizenship and Immigration Services has released a list of the questions and correct answers, but they do not include every possible answer.

Other pilot questions seem beyond the scope of what American citizens, native-born or immigrant, are expected to know. We'd like to think everyone can name the authors of the Federalist Papers (Madison, Hamilton, and Jay, writing under the name "Publius") or identify the alliance of North American and European countries created during the Cold War (NATO), but should you be barred from citizenship if you can't? Given that naturalization applicants have already been legal permanent residents for years and have passed FBI background checks, there's no need to make them jump through hoops that most current citizens couldn't wriggle through without consulting Wikipedia. We hope that once the study is completed in a few weeks, officials will craft a test that maintains the current national pass rate of 84 percent, as they have said they will.

A SAMPLE RHETORICAL ANALYSIS OF "TESTING, TESTING"

One can begin to understand the meaning and purpose of "Testing, Testing" by casting its main point—its logos, or appeal to reasoning—as an **enthymeme.** The editorial writer (who refers to himself or herself as *we* and represents the *Washington Post* as a whole) crafts meaning by reasoning as follows:

> It is the responsibility of the U.S. Citizenship and Immigration Services to test, fairly and objectively, those people who want to become U.S. citizens, asking them the kinds of questions that current U.S. citizens should be able to answer.
>
> The proposed new citizenship test may contain questions that are subjective or beyond the scope of what most U.S. citizens actually do know.
>
> Therefore, the proposed new test may be unfair, and prospective new citizens may not be able to pass at the rate applicants for citizenship currently do. The purpose of the editorial, therefore, is to raise a flag of caution about the proposed new citizenship test and to serve notice to the U.S. Citizenship and Immigration Services bureau that the *Washington Post* is watching its every move.

As with most enthymemes, not all three sentences in the above paraphrase of the argument are actually stated directly in the editorial. The middle sentence (which would be the **minor premise** if this were a **syllogism**) is conveyed in a straightforward manner in the first sentence of the final paragraph. The other two sentences must come from the readers' reasoning. The first sentence (which would be the **major premise** if this were a syllogism) is an assumption that the editorialist presumes readers readily agree with. The third sentence (which would be the **conclusion** if this were a syllogism) derives from implication: If a fair test contains objective items and items that test-takers can be expected to know, and if the proposed new test contains subjective items and items that test-takers cannot be expected to know, then the proposed new test is unfair.

While this enthymeme sits at the center of the editorialist's invention, it's also safe to assume that the writer could have employed three additional invention strategies when developing material for this piece. First, observe that even though this is not a straight news story, the basic journalist's questions—who? what? when? where? why? and how?—are taken up in the editorial. Second, notice that the editorial exploits one of the **ratios**—*agency-act*—from Kenneth Burke's **dramatistic pentad** to generate material. The editorialist focuses on gaining citizenship as the **act** in the **casuistry** and the proposed new test as the **agency** for achieving this act. In most situations, one would think that the agency should be fitting and congruent with the act—that the means of gaining citizenship actually fits with the concept of citizenship itself. The editorialist is suggesting that this congruency might not be the case—that the agency (the proposed new test) is not appropriate for the act (gaining citizenship). Third, notice that the editorialist makes use of two of the **common topics** of invention: definition and testimony. The second paragraph focuses on defining the criteria for becoming a citizen, while the third paragraph contains testimony from an official of U.S. Citizenship and Immigration Services.

The arrangement follows a very typical pattern for a newspaper editorial. It begins with a very brief introduction of the issue at hand, addresses the issue with descriptive, factual, and evaluative evidence, and then closes with a call for action, case in the first-person plural *we* of the newspaper.

It is in the stylistic choices the editorialist makes that we most clearly see the piece's vigilante purpose—to question the fairness of the proposed test and to assert the newspaper's watchdog function vis-à-vis Citizenship and Immigration. The first paragraph consists of a single sentence, a **rhetorical question** shaped in such a way that the reader knows that the editorial is going to interrogate and scrutinize the proposed new citizenship test, not support it. The second paragraph is dominated by a long, periodic sentence that begins with an adversative conjunction, "But," and moves the important information, the past tradition of local control and test administration, to the end of the sentence, where readers will remember it. This long periodic sentence leads directly to the problem that Citizenship and Immigration is trying to address with the proposed new test: "cities can have different tests and different pass rates." So maybe, the reader is saying, we *need* a new, more standardized test for citizenship. The editorialist would probably agree.

The third paragraph describes the noncontroversial aspects of the new test in an exceedingly plain style. The sentences are all about the same length and are mostly simple, declarative, active-voice sentences. No problem in this paragraph, the editorialist seems to be implying.

The fourth paragraph, however, capitalizes on the stylistic concept of connotation to convey the writer's meaning and purpose. By putting *concepts* in quotation marks and tacitly contrasting that term with *tight facts*, the editorialist is suggesting that the former are inherently more subjective than the latter. Further along, the writer openly acknowledges that for some *pro-immigrant groups,* Citizenship and Immigration's adjective *more meaningful* actually openly connotes *harder*. And, certainly, when anyone refers to an examination question as *more abstract*, as the editorialist does, the connotation is that the question at least borders on being too sophisticated.

Having established stylistically in the fourth paragraph the **claim** that the proposed new test may be subjective, the editorialist deploys a range of stylistic moves in the final paragraph to establish the point that most current U.S. citizens couldn't answer many of the questions on the proposed new test, thereby rendering it unfair. The second sentence in the final paragraph contains another rhetorical question, this one designed to highlight the arcane and arbitrary nature of some of the new questions. Further, the writer uses a common **metaphor** and simple diction to evoke a vivid visual **image** when characterizing the proposed new test as making people "jump through hoops that most current citizens couldn't wriggle through. . . ."

Finally, notice that the editorial both begins and ends by invoking items from our cultural memory that support the piece's meaning and purpose. The title "Testing, Testing" is familiar to anyone who has ever sat in an auditorium and listened to someone trying out the sound system. The title is exactly what its words suggest: empty, meaningless language, mere noise. Is the editorialist suggesting that the proposed new citizenship test, like most bureaucratic products, is nothing but a lot of empty noise itself? *Wikipedia*, mentioned at the end of the editorial, is an Internet reference site that, while useful in some measure, is also notorious for being a repository of abundantly esoteric knowledge that relatively few people know, or perhaps care, about. Is the editorialist suggesting that the questions on the proposed new test are like those one finds in Wikipedia, rather than ones that every American citizen ought to be able to answer? I would answer "yes" to both of the questions I've raised in this paragraph.

Interchapter

Overview of the Major Points in Chapter 3

- The canon of arrangement offers techniques that writers can use to give appropriate and effective order and structure to texts.
- The canon of style represents an extensive array of strategies that writers can use to craft their sentences, phrases, and words in ways that are appropriate and effective in the particular writing situation.
- The canon of delivery today helps writers decide how to format their compositions, either in print or electronically, in a way that is most effective for readers.

Activities and Discussion Questions for Chapter 3   Use these questions and comments as guides for your own discussion and writing about these works.

Henry David Thoreau, "An Essay on Civil Disobedience" (published 1849)

The text appears on pages 221–237. In a discussion with a group of your classmates, or in a well-developed essay, address one or both of the following questions.

1. Using the six numbered questions on pages 60–61, divide "Civil Disobedience" into functional sections. Then, using the bulleted questions on pages 61–63, analyze the effectiveness of arrangement in *one* of the functional sections.

2. Select one specific paragraph that you believe represents the most interesting, most vivid passage in "Civil Disobedience." Describe as much about the style of that passage as you can. For every stylistic feature you notice, explain what you see as its effect on the appeal of "Civil Disobedience" to the development of the central idea, to the credibility of Thoreau, or to the emotional power of the piece.

Eavan Boland, "It's a Woman's World" (published 1982)

The text appears on pages 237–239. In a discussion with a group of your classmates or in an essay, address one or more of the following questions:

1. Does the poem move from general to specific or specific to general, or are specific references and general claims mixed? What is the effect of the arrangement of general claims and specific details in the poem?
2. Paying careful attention to schemes of repetition and balance, analyze what you see as the major stylistic effects of "It's a Woman's World."
3. Describe and analyze the delivery of the poem on the page. How do the line lengths and the stanza divisions influence the effectiveness of the poem?

Alice Walker, "Everyday Use" (published 1973)

The text appears on pages 239–246. In a discussion with a group of your classmates, or in a well-organized essay, address one or more of the following questions:

1. How does Walker use time as an ordering device in "Everyday Use"? Consider the events mentioned, even in passing, in the story, and arrange them in an exact chronological order. Then contrast the chronological order with the order Walker uses, and explain the effect of Walker's choice of arrangement.
2. Look carefully at the section of "Everyday Use" where Dee/Wangero shows up at the house with Asalamalakim. Describe how the order of details contributes to the effectiveness of this arrival scene.
3. Describe and analyze the way Walker uses diction to create the character of the narrator of the story, the mother.

Rhetoric and the Writer

4

"Let's say you want to write an award-winning short story—you just push this key, here . . . "

Working your way through the first three chapters of this book, you have assembled a considerable storehouse of new ideas and strategies to use as a reader, writer, speaker, and thinker. You know now that **rhetoric** is a set of strategies you employ every day as you use language in your roles as a student, a family member, and a participant in your community, nation, and world. What's more, you have acquired at least a beginning sense of how those strategies work to accomplish a **purpose**. And you know now that these strategies can be classified under the five **canons** of rhetoric: **invention, arrangement, style, memory,** and **delivery**.

As you consider all this information, you may be wondering how you might use all these definitions, strategies, and techniques. How can you make your understandings about rhetoric work for you? The aim of this chapter is to help you understand how to make rhetorical choices—choices involving invention, arrangement, style, memory, and delivery—in a writing process that is guided by your developing purpose, or intentions, as a writer. In this chapter, we will show real writers at work—writers much like you—and show how these writers understand the **rhetorical situation** they have at hand, make the situation their own by discovering their own **intentions** within it, and respond to the situation and their own purposes effectively. We offer real stories of writers making choices about the processes they engage in, the material they decide to incorporate, the organizational strategies they employ, and the language they use.

Before moving to these writers' stories—and to give us some common language to use in examining them—we need to review some terms and concepts that you have probably studied before, definitions of the **writing process** and its components. But we hope your new perspective on rhetoric can help you examine the writing process in a considerably different light. The writing process, as we will explain below, is most usefully seen not as a set of isolated moments but instead as a collection of strategic moves designed to help a writer achieve a purpose for an **audience**. In other words, the writing process is ultimately a rhetorical process.

Writing as Process: Making the Right Moves for Context

Every good writer knows that writing involves a series of processes. It would be nice if you could simply sit down at the word processor or with a pad and pencil and, voilà, the words magically appeared on the screen or the page. It doesn't work that way. Instead, writers must generate good writing: build it, cook it, incubate it, massage it, live with it, whatever-growth-metaphor-you-choose with it.

When teachers and students talk about generating good writing over time, they frequently name their activity "following the writing process." But even though it's usually referred to in the singular, *the* writing process is actually *several* processes; different people use different labels to describe them.

Since what gets called the writing process can be described in many ways, bear in mind that seeing writing as a process means understanding that what all writers do, repeatedly and simultaneously, is invent and revise. Think back over something you have written that you were proud of, and try to remember what it felt like when you were deep into the process. It's probably hard to remember a moment in your work on this piece when you were not thinking up new material—ideas, specific sentences, phrases, and words—and, at the same time, evaluating its quality and making appropriate changes. You were almost simultaneously inventing and revising. While acknowledging that the heart of writing as process is this continual interplay of inventing and revising, we nevertheless provide a seven-term overview of writing processes—not only to do justice to the complexity of writing but also to suggest how this inventing-revising interaction works. If writing processes did not occur so interactively, we might say that the first three of the points in the process could be subsumed under inventing, while the last three could be considered as **revising**, with the middle process, **drafting**, considered under both labels.

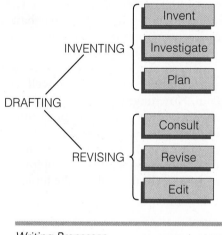

Writing Processes

But we can't make this claim because the processes are fluid. Good writers allow themselves to move among the processes as the need arises.

Writing as a Rhetorical Process

In a substantial writing project—one that requires research, rethinking, taking on more than one perspective, experimentation, and so on—good writers almost always engage in these acts within their writing process, knowing that the rhetorical context will help them decide how to proceed through each **act** and how much time and energy to devote to each one—to inventing, investigating, planning, drafting, consulting, revising, and editing.

Inventing

Inventing is the general term for the activities that writers undertake to extract information from the "database" of their memories or experiences and to evaluate and reflect on what they've uncovered for its usefulness in the writing task at hand. As you recall, invention is the first of the five canons of classical rhetoric. You've practiced invention activities in Chapter 2.

Investigating

Investigating is the general name for the activities people undertake to discover information and generate a fund of knowledge about which they will write. Not everyone includes investigating in the *writing* process; some teachers consider it instead a process that precedes the actual writing. There are good reasons, however, for including it. The rhetorical situation, as outlined in Chapter 1, including the kind, or **genre,** of writing a writer aims to produce, influences the nature of a writer's investigation.

Consider this rhetorical situation, for example: You have to write a paper for a psychology class analyzing how preschool children behave after their parents drop them off at a day-care center. Your audience consists of the other students in your class and your teacher, but your teacher has urged you to write a paper that would speak to the intellectual and professional interests of child psychologists and that would particularize your study, as well as prevent you from making too general a claim. How might you investigate this topic? You might read books and articles about children's behaviors or consult your parents about your own behavior in day care. An effective investigation might well begin with actual observation in a day-care facility. Especially if your psychology class has studied experimentation and observation, this kind of investigation will be appropriate as a beginning for your thinking about the topic.

Activity

Read several essays on the opinion page of a major daily newspaper. In a small group, discuss these editorial pieces, and then, with your group, write just the beginning of two essays analyzing the editorials. Assume one essay is for an English class and one for a political science or U.S. government class. What do you need to investigate to write each of these pieces?

Planning

Planning occurs when a writer determines (1) who the audience for the writing might be and (2) what purpose or purposes the paper can accomplish, given its contexts and constraints, and then decides how to state and reflect on ideas most effectively.

Planning might better be labeled **brainstorming.** When writers plan, they must be keenly aware of the occasion for writing, the subject, the purpose, the audience, as well as the genre and the length considerations.

Consider this rhetorical situation: You have been assigned to write a paper for your U.S. government class about some issue relating to government and education. Your preliminary planning or brainstorming looks, or perhaps *sounds,* something like this:

> Writing a paper that my U.S. government teacher will read. I want to convince her that the federal government hasn't really considered the drawbacks of too much standardized testing. But my teacher is just one person of a larger group interested in the politics of education, so I might consider other possible readers too. With this audience and purpose, how should I begin? With an **anecdote** about how many days every school year are given over to standardized testing? Then I can talk about the brain-numbing effect those days have. I could tell a story here—or maybe that's not going to be good evidence. It is supposed to be formal. I'll ask the teacher. Then I can try to show how legislators think only about the bottom line of standardized testing and don't consider how it actually affects education day to day. I want to make clear what students, parents, and interested citizens can do to change the testing environment in schools. But I know I'll need to suggest my main ideas up front. What sections should I have?

Planning is an incredibly active process. It's not just imagining an audience and achieving a purpose; it's understanding and working with the *interaction* of audience and purpose; it's capitalizing on the *synergy* that this subject-audience-purpose dynamic creates; it's thinking aloud, sometimes to yourself and sometimes to a writing partner or group, about the possible directions a paper might take to be persuasive with an audience.

Activity

Imagine that you were asked to write a piece for the op-ed page of your local newspaper describing the *best* thing that happens at your school to improve students' educational opportunities. With a partner or in a small group, plan this piece, considering all ideas about what *is* best. Think about your audience (your local community), and consider why you're writing to this audience (and why the newspaper might have asked you to write). Your plan might be reflective notes, as in the previous example, or a list or an outline.

Drafting

Drafting is the process by which writers simply get something written on paper or in a computer file so that they can develop their ideas and begin moving toward an end, a start-to-finish product. Good writers realize that no piece of writing emerges immediately in finished form. They see a draft as raw material for what will become the final product, and they know this raw material will need expanding, reducing, rearranging, and rethinking. When they draft, many successful writers tell themselves (perhaps subconsciously, but forcefully), "For the time being, stop investigating, stop planning, and stop inventing. Don't worry about perfection. Just write."

How a writer produces a draft is influenced by how familiar he or she is with the rhetorical situation. Writers in English classes who regularly write one-page response papers, in which they reflect informally on the texts they read, and use these papers to begin class discussion, might write a draft that appears in nearly final form. Their familiarity with the rhetorical situation—the fact that the paper won't be graded, that it's quick, and that they can use it to speak from—helps the draft develop. But writers in that same English class who are asked for the first time to write up research on a recurring theme in literature over several historical periods and to assume an audience of literary scholars can expect less ease in the drafting of their papers.

Activity

With a partner or in a writing group, discuss a paper you have written in the past that you found easy to draft and one that you found difficult and time consuming to draft. How can you account for the difference?

Consulting

Sometimes referred to as **peer review, consulting** is the activity of seeking the help of a "fresh" reader and asking him or her to tell you what is good about a draft, what is questionable, and what definitely needs change and improvement. There's an old saying that circulates in the hills of Appalachia, where both of the authors of this book grew up: "There's no child so homely that its mother doesn't love it." There's an analogy to writing here. When you write something, especially something you have worked very hard at drafting, you justifiably feel proud of it. It's part of you—your ideas taking shape as words on the page. But for important pieces of work, it's vital to get someone else to read your work and be frank and honest in appraising it.

Notice that working with a consultant does not mean finding someone to proofread, edit, or correct your writing. It means finding someone to read your work once you have produced a comprehensible draft, not a final product. Consulting readers of your drafts can be representatives, either actual participants or role-playing stand-ins, of the rhetorical context at hand; that is, they can say, "As a reader, here's my honest reaction to the way you have developed your idea to achieve the purpose you have in mind for your audience." Consulting readers can give you their opinions about the good, the bad, and the questionable in your draft. In the task we mentioned earlier, to write up research on literary themes over time, consulting readers with greater experience and expertise in genre, methods, and evidence—teachers, avid readers of literature, and/or students who are writing about similar research—can be invaluable.

Working with a consulting reader often requires that you take a big gulp, swallow your pride momentarily, and put your ego aside. You may hear responses to your draft that you had not expected and do not necessarily enjoy. On the other hand, you will probably discover things about your draft that you never expected to find out. It will be up to you whether to actually do anything in response to your consulting readers' comments. But getting someone to consult with you about a draft affords you an objective person's (or persons') views of how your work is shaping up.

Revising

When writers return to their drafts, reread and rethink them, and then decide what to change in order to improve them, they are revising. Revising is a process that activates other processes. For example, when you revise, you may engage in planning: "How can I approach my audience better to make my purpose clearer?" When you revise, you may return to investigating: "Do I need to read more to be convincing? Is there a place I should visit and observe?" When you revise, you may engage in more invention strategies: "I know I need more examples. Let me think of stories I've heard." When you revise, you almost always realize that the draft isn't quite finished. And you often realize that it has not "settled" into its rhetorical situation yet—it's not doing all it can do to achieve its purpose with the audience at hand. So you revise—literally, "resee" and then rethink—the composition as a whole, as well as its sections.

Activity

With a partner or in a small group, revise a short piece you've written recently in class. Follow these steps: (1) write a note about what you'd like to add or change, (2) read the piece aloud, (3) ask the group to suggest changes and discuss reactions, and (4) make a note about their responses.

Editing

This is your final interaction with your composition before you submit it to the audience—publisher, peers, teachers—for response and evaluation. **Editing** occurs when writers read over their texts slowly, looking for lapses in usage, in sense or coherence, and in spelling or punctuation. As with the other processes, the rhetorical situation strongly influences how a writer edits. If you know your audience holds standards of excellence in spelling, grammar, mechanics, and punctuation, and you want your paper to make a strong statement to this audience, it has to meet those standards. If an audience expects a draft of a work in progress, you will edit less strenuously.

Activity

Take a careful look at a paper you have recently written for a class, and select two paragraphs from the middle of this paper. Read one of these paragraphs aloud. Then read the other aloud, but backward, starting with the last word and moving to the first one. Edit both paragraphs. What do you notice about the different levels of attention you pay to individual words and punctuation marks in the two reading experiences? Does reading backward help you edit?

Real Writers at Work:
Cases for Studying Writing and Rhetoric

Rhetoric is not some disembodied academic pursuit. Rhetoric involves real readers, writers, speakers, and listeners in real situations. In the rest of this chapter, therefore, we present four cases: stories about real writers like you who are working hard to become the kinds of rhetorically effective, perceptive writers and readers who succeed in school and beyond. Each case begins with a series of focusing questions, then follows a **narrative** of the writer at work. Within the narratives are activities that you can do alone or in a small group. Working through each of these cases, and then taking on a case of your own, you will put into play what you have learned about understanding rhetorical purpose, operating within **context**, employing the **appeals**, using the canons, and seeing the writing process as a rhetorical one.

Erica: Slow Starter

As you study Erica's case, keep the following questions in mind. Discuss them with your group when you can.

1. What does Erica need to do to clarify the rhetorical purpose?
2. What does Erica need to do to understand her audience more thoroughly?
3. What does Erica need to do to invent material for her new composition?
4. How might Erica go about planning her new composition?
5. How might Erica get started drafting her composition and keep the drafting process going?

"I don't know where to start," Erica tells her teacher as she's explaining her problem in writing a paper. "I know what I want to say, sort of, but I don't know how to say it."

The student's frustration is probably familiar to you. We all have moments, usually at the beginning of writing something, when we just can't think how or where to start. It's hard to put fingers to the keyboard or pen to paper when we can't figure out what should go first or why. Sometimes, that feeling is enough to make a writer put away the pen or get up from the computer and delay the start of the process for as long as possible. When words do begin to come, it's because they're being forced out under the pressure of a nonnegotiable and usually very immediate deadline.

Erica's assignment is to analyze one essay from a collection of articles on identity and cultural diversity. She has picked a good essay, but a difficult one, on stereotyping. She has shown herself in earlier assignments to be a careful and adept writer, and the first question her teacher has for her is why the paper she had completed the week before—a paper about her first name—hadn't presented her with problems. "Well, it was about me," she smiles. "I got to talk about my name and where it came from. I knew about that stuff."

"But how did you know how to begin?" the teacher asks.

"It's the funniest thing about the name. Where it came from."

This was the first line of her piece: "I am named for a cow." It was a funny and poignant essay about her mother's friendship with a German neighbor who kept a cow in her backyard. Erica had known how to begin because, as she said, she knew about herself and her story. But it was also because she felt confident about the way it should be told, perhaps because she had told the story often before. She felt sure of her audience too, students in her class who she knew would like the opening, its quickness, its unexpectedness. She was right. When she read it aloud to her classmates, they all laughed, and, after she finished reading, they commented on how effectively she had written.

One other factor seems important to explain why Erica had little problem in beginning her essay on her name. The class had already been talking about the issue that Erica would explore: the importance of names and of naming something. They had read the beginning section of Sandra Cisneros's *House on Mango Street*, which begins, "My name is Esperanza."

MY NAME

In English my name means hope. In Spanish it means too many letters. It means sadness, it means waiting. It is like the number nine. A muddy color. It is the Mexican records my father plays on Sunday mornings when he is shaving, songs like sobbing.

It was my great-grandmother's name and now it is mine. She was a horse woman too, born like me in the Chinese year of the horse—which is supposed to be bad luck if you're born female—but I think this is a Chinese lie because the Chinese, like the Mexicans, don't like their women strong.

My great-grandmother. I would've liked to have known her, a wild horse of a woman, so wild she wouldn't marry. Until my great-grandfather threw a sack over her head and carried her off. Just like that, as if she were a fancy chandelier. That's the way he did it.

And the story goes she never forgave him. She looked out the window her whole life, the way so many women sit their sadness on an elbow. I wonder if she made the best with what she got or was she sorry because she couldn't be all the things she wanted to be. Esperanza. I have inherited her name, but I don't want to inherit her place by the window.

At school they say my name funny as if the syllables were made out of tin and hurt the roof of your mouth. But in Spanish my name is made out of a softer something, like silver, not quite as thick as sister's name—Magdalena—which is uglier than mine. Magdalena who at least can come home and become Nenny. But I am always Esperanza.

> I would like to baptize myself under a new name, a name more like the real me, the one nobody sees. Esperanza as Lisandra or Martiza or Zeze the X. Yes. Something like Zeze the X will do.

Cisneros's narrator translates her name, talks about its derivation and its connection to her family's past, and considers her feelings about it and her grandmother, the person she is named for. You might hear the echo of Cisneros's opening in Erica's "I am named for a cow." Its simplicity, its brevity, its no-nonsense tone strike a note similar to Cisneros's sentence. Erica had known how to begin in part because she had already heard a beginning that sounded like something she might try herself. And it worked.

So Erica's success in inventing, planning, and drafting her name paper came about because (1) she knew her subject well, (2) she knew how her audience might respond to the subject, (3) she had experience and examples that she could use to develop her writing, and (4) she understood why she was writing. All these elements made Erica feel sure of herself as she completed a draft. She revised extensively after working with her small group, who talked with her about how to make her intention—to tell a funny story and to honor her mother and her friend—most effective for them.

But what about the problem with the second assignment? With this task, Erica seems to have none of the understandings that had allowed her to gather ideas and begin so easily when she wrote about her name. She fears her subject (she asks herself silently, "Do I really understand the point of this essay?"). She ignores her audience (she asks herself, "If I don't understand it, how do I expect anybody else to?"). She doesn't trust any of her own experiences and doesn't think of any examples that might help her (she frets to herself, "I don't know how I'm supposed to sound"). And, most of all, she doesn't understand why she is writing.

The topic she is supposed to be writing about is one similar to many school assignments. It asks for an analysis of a text and requires careful reading of the text, cogent assessment of details in the text, and well-supported conclusions about it. Erica is focusing much more on the possibility of being wrong about what she says and the way she says it than she did in her first essay, and her worry has begun to prevent her from writing at all.

In brief, Erica isn't clear about her *intention* (other than her intention to complete the assignment). She is stymied. So what does Erica need to do?

Activity

Think carefully about two papers you have written in the past, one for which you felt a strong sense of intention and another for which this sense was largely absent. In your group, discuss how the processes of drafting and revising seemed different to you for each of these papers. Or write about an assignment that gave you the kind of trouble Erica faces. What was the assignment? How did you resolve the problem? Share your response with your small group.

Erica's Intention and Invention

Recently, high school students in an advanced-placement English class discussed what they found most difficult about the process of writing. Five or six explained that the thesis presented the most difficulties for them; several mentioned form; and two more talked about gathering enough details. Only one said, "Getting started! That's the hardest thing for me." But when she spoke, almost all of the students nodded their heads. "Oh, yes. It's just jumping in. I put it off for as long as I can." Or "I start over and over again trying to get it right." What the students found as they talked was that the beginning of the process, particularly invention and drafting, presented the most challenges and frustrations for them. "Sometimes I wait so long that I don't have time to revise. I just turn it in and hope for the best," one admitted.

To begin inventing—considering ideas and scenarios, gathering material, and thinking through possibilities—a writer has to believe there's a reason to write. The writer has to believe in an *intention* for the text. After all, people write best when there's a reason to do so. But the reason must not be simply *extrinsic*—something outside, like a teacher or an assignment or a grade—that compels the writer. Rather, the reason should be at least in part *intrinsic*—something within the topic or the argument that compels the writer.

But here's the problem: A writer may not feel a sense of intention when starting work on the composition. Intention often emerges *while* the writer is in the process of writing. In other words, a writer's intention will, and should, change as he or she finds material or considers alternatives or uses a particular story or metaphor to explain a point.

How might Erica gather intention and thus improve her ability to invent ideas on the topic she is exploring? First, she might consider what she knows already. Interestingly enough, her name paper can give her background information and experience for examining the article on stereotyping and cultural diversity that she is trying to analyze. Stereotyping is a kind of naming. And knowing the importance of her own name to her can help Erica think through the issues about being called a name that doesn't fit or that hurts or that carries lots of negative associations. Finding out that she brings something to the assignment improves her confidence immediately and makes her able to look at the text more closely, discovering the details that begin to support her feeling about the power of naming. As her intention becomes clearer, her ability to talk with others about what she's thinking develops, and she brings to her group the following, a potential beginning paragraph:

> Words, especially names, make a difference. What a person is called gives her an identity, a kind of place. In Sandra Cisneros's story, the main character dislikes what she's called because she doesn't want the identity that goes with it. Her grandmother lived a sad life, and Esperanza fears that her grandmother's identity, as well as her name, might be passed down to her. In the article "The Function of Stereotypes," the author shows how defining people with stereotypes misrepresents them and gives them an identity that is so hard to escape.

Erica has found a way into her text analysis by linking her task in this assignment to issues she's already thought about, to experiences she already knows. She is beginning to discover her intention and beginning the process of analyzing the argument in the article. She changes some of that first paragraph later, after she's written more, but she retains the connections to the Cisneros story in her later version. She's been able to hear her own **voice** more clearly because she feels more assurance about her position on the article, so she can find the details in the article that support her own emerging **argument**.

Activity

Write your whole name, or a nickname, and then jot down some ideas about it. Are you named for someone? Do you like your name? Is there a funny story associated with your name, how it's pronounced, or how it's spelled? Are there things you don't know about your name—why your parents gave it to you or what the word means? Write those questions too. Write quickly without stopping much to consider how you sound or where you're headed. The idea is to get your initial thoughts on the page or screen where you can see them.

Apply Erica's Solution

You've begun to search for **rhetorical intention** now, with your notes and questions. You already know a lot, but you may find that there are things you still need to know before you might write a whole essay about your name. You might need to investigate a little, talking to a family member or looking up the derivation of the name. You might need to plan where you will tell a story about being named or how you'll argue that your name fits you or doesn't.

Your notes and comments may seem chaotic as you look back at them. How might they fit together? What's your point in writing them? But chaos is not necessarily bad. In fact, for a writer it's a necessary step in the process. Generating ideas and considering possibilities are both chaotic. At first, there seem to be too many choices. One reason that writers fear beginning a writing task is their apprehension about the chaos of ideas that inevitably comes with invention. But, as the writing teacher and theorist Ann Berthoff says, "Chaos begins the forming." The questions and comments you've jotted down, the memories you've stirred with the words you've written, and the ideas you've begun to consider are not simply chaotic; they are generative. They help you begin the process of formulating ideas into a plan, an approach, and a direction.

That direction gets set as writers understand more about rhetorical situations—the interaction of the subject with the audience and the purpose. If you are writing your piece for your family, you'll no doubt begin differently than if you're writing for the school newspaper. If you're writing about your name because your teacher has given you the assignment, you'll approach it somewhat differently than if you came up with your own idea for a discussion of names. If you want to make an argument that people should be more careful about what they call others, you might add details that wouldn't appear if you were writing to explain how names get changed. Your readers, your purpose, and your **context** will affect your **persona**, the type of person you present yourself to be to your readers. All the elements of the **Aristotelian triangle**, as we explained in Chapter 1, will direct the way you come up with ideas and details as you write.

Recall that in Chapter 2, we set out a wide range of systematic invention strategies, techniques you can use to analyze how a writer comes up with ideas for a composition and to plan how to generate ideas for your own papers. Erica's story provides the raw material for using these techniques. It illustrates the individual sources writers can tap into to discover the material for their work. As Erica's story suggests, writers generate ideas from all kinds of sources. They invent by using what's available to them, both from their own backgrounds and from what they're able to investigate. Remember Aristotle's definition: Rhetoricians observe the *available means* in order to effect their purpose, in order to persuade their readers. As you examine the following "available means," think about how Erica (or you) could use each of these sources to invent material through the journalist's questions, Burke's **pentad**, the **topics**, or the **enthymeme**.

- **Experience.** The writer's life in a family, in a school, or in the community can be useful both to understand situations he or she reads about and to employ as an illustration or as a narrative to provoke or connect with readers. Cisneros's character Esperanza speaks of her past and present to explain the power of names. Erica uses the story of her mother's friendship with a neighbor to make a connection with her readers. Some subjects lend themselves more easily than others to the overt use of past experience in an essay. But experience is always important as people read and write. If you've read a John Updike novel in the past, you'll carry attitudes about his style that will affect the way you read any other Updike story. If you are assigned to write about the grocery boy narrator in Updike's short story "A&P," you'll connect what you know about being a grocery bagger in your local market to the character even if you never write about your own experience in your final text.

- **Observation.** All good writers are good observers. They watch the world around them as well as participate in it. They learn about what motivates people, what scares them, what entertains them—because they take note of the world around them. They use their understandings as they write to make connections with their readers. In other words, they pay attention to what they see and hear. Aristotle spoke of how to appeal to various kinds of audiences—old men, soldiers, young people, politicians—giving advice about approaches to subjects that would work best with each group. He had obviously observed the reactions and understood the motivations of these men.

- **Research.** Both observation and past experience represent kinds of research. But research also means the writer's investigation of sources outside the self and outside direct observation. Library and online research in a variety of sources—newspapers, journals, books, and documents—helps writers gather information that contributes to the strength of their arguments or the development of their explanations. Talking to experts—people who are knowledgeable about a particular issue or event—is a different kind of research. Becoming a recorder and observer in a scene, doing what's called *ethnographic* research, is yet another method of accomplishing research.

- **Sharing.** Talking about issues, ideas, and emerging opinions with others is useful for all writers. Listening to objections to an opinion prepares writers to counter those objections when they write or helps them qualify or complicate their positions. When writers articulate what they're thinking about a subject or about a text they have read, they are generating ideas about that subject or text. And, as a small group or a conversation partner asks questions or gives an alternate opinion, writers rethink and reform their own thinking.

- **Reading.** Reading, of course, is a kind of experience and a kind of research. We separate it here to highlight the importance of reading widely from popular magazines and Internet Web sites, from letters and journals, and from textbooks. Reading for pleasure as well as for information gives a writer a rich mine from which to draw ideas and explore new directions. And reading allows writers to sharpen their own ears, to hear voices and styles that can strengthen their own.

Activity

Think about something you've written recently, and consider how you've made use of the possibilities just described—experience, observations, research, sharing, and reading—for inventing ideas. With a partner or in your group, discuss whether there are possibilities you might have explored but didn't.

Chan: Confused About Context

As you study Chan's case, keep the following questions in mind. Discuss them with your group when you can.

1. How does the context affect the way Chan engages in invention strategies?
2. How does the context affect the way Chan investigates a subject in order to write about it?
3. How does the context affect the way Chan goes about planning a composition?

Our second case is about Chan, and his story leads us to think about how the context of a writing project affects the ways a writer goes about completing it. In much of the writing you do in school, the assignment provided by the teacher is the informative clue about the context. In some ways, Chan's story is the mirror image of Erica's. Erica felt a sense of intention with a topic of her own choosing and had difficulty with one assigned to her. Chan, on the other hand, finds it difficult to come up with a sense of intention when the teacher does not assign a specific task or subject.

Chan is a transfer student, moving to a new school at the semester break, and he is fairly confident that he will be able to continue doing well in his new writing course. In the course he took at his previous school, he had usually done well on the assignments, which required students to read short stories, identify important themes or issues in them, and then write three- to five-page compositions demonstrating how the identified themes and issues might be relevant in contemporary life. Chan had interesting insights on this literature-life connection, and his teacher both praised him for his incisive readings and helped him learn more about how to write about them clearly.

But the first assignment that Chan faces in his new writing class throws him for a loop. Here is the assignment:

WRITING PIECE #1

Make your argument. State your claim. Have your say.

One of the biggest, most popular areas of nonfiction writing is the personal opinion piece. Take a look on the last page of *Time* magazine at the "My Turn" essay. Look at the editorial writers' pieces on the last inside pages of the front section of the *News and Record.* (I'm including one of these for you to examine.) Look at collections of columns from writers like Dave Barry, Ellen Goodman, Katha Pollitt, William Raspberry, and Molly Ivins. Think of writers in past decades or centuries who wrote commentary that expressed personal opinion on some matter of the day; writers from Jonathan Swift to Mary Wollstonecraft to Oscar Wilde all wrote opinion essays, or what you might call argument.

Your task is to discover your own argument and have your say. What do you want to have a say about? Something funny like why Harris Teeter has stopped carrying Golden Fleece pot cleaners? (I bet you don't know what that is!) Something serious like why states are executing innocent men? You can comment on an event, a cultural phenomenon (why were we glued to the TV to watch the Survivors eat grubs?), a societal problem, or a coming change in local or national life. Once you have your idea, you'll begin to discover form and tone. The writers above vary wildly in terms of style and format. Some use humor; others use anger, irony, or compassion to get across their views and to persuade others to agree with their point. Think about how you will best convey your idea and make an appeal to your reader. Notice that most personal opinion pieces are relatively short; you should consider length as you write. Your piece should probably be not less than two pages and not more than five.

Have fun. Have a point. Have a title.

Chan feels quite uncomfortable when he starts to work on this assignment. Why is it so long? What is he supposed to make of the distinctive teacher voice that he hears in the assignment? What idea should he choose when the topic is not even indicated? What kind of voice and **tone** would be appropriate? What form should the paper take? Chan needs to imagine his task differently from the writing-about-literature assignments he was comfortable with writing at his previous school, and, frankly, he isn't prepared to do so. Working through this difficulty, Chan discovers the responsibility that attends writing: that good writers not only complete the assignment but also make it their own.

Take another look at the assignment, and notice which elements of the rhetorical situation Chan might connect with.

- First of all, the context that surrounds this writing task assumes an ongoing class discussion. Are there things you don't understand when you read the assignment? (Why the mention of Golden Fleece pot cleaners?) It's in the context of that discussion that the assignment occurs, so it will help Chan, as he starts to work, to re-create mentally the classroom conversation. The voice of the teacher, the one who has initiated the assignment, is low-key conversational, and humorous; the teacher deliberately chose that voice to make writers feel relaxed rather than pressured.

- Second, the assignment makes it clear that students should read published personal opinion pieces from a variety of sources that will give them some ideas—about form, voice, and details—and that writers should feel encouraged to use their reading as guides to genre considerations or to subject matter as they begin their own pieces.

- Third, the assignment indicates a presumed audience as well: not only the teacher who will read students' writing but also regular readers of columns like "My Turn," so it might benefit Chan to examine a column like this to see how the column addresses its audience.

- Finally, the persona the writer develops in the piece is implied when the assignment suggests that the writer should have a real stake in the writing, should explore an issue that means something personally and that the writer wants to share an opinion about.

What's missing from this context is the subject, and that's what perplexes Chan the most. In this assignment, students have to find their own subjects, the issues and ideas that they have experienced and want to investigate on their own.

Activity

In your group, brainstorm for ten minutes on this assignment: "You must teach a class session about some literary technique." Then, again in your group, brainstorm for ten minutes on this assignment: "You must teach a class about the definitions of *hero* and *villain* in literary works." After you have finished brainstorming, talk in your group about the differences in the two planning experiences.

Chan, Context, and Notes

Chan feels considerably more at home with the next assignment, when the class begins reading a novel and is asked to write about it. Many students share Chan's comfort with this kind of assignment because they are more familiar with one in which the subject matter and rhetorical requirements are fully described. Here is the next assignment that Chan gets:

ESSAY ON *THE SCARLET LETTER*

Write a two- to three-page description of the real villain in *The Scarlet Letter.* Remember that you'll have to decide for yourself who the real villain is and prove it in the way you support your idea with details and examples from the text. Be careful not to simply summarize the plot. Making use of quotes from the novel will add to the specificity of your examples and your argument.

Notice that this assignment indicates much of the rhetorical situation for Chan to use as he begins to invent ideas for the paper. Length is specified, suggesting that Chan needs to understand something about the depth he should go into in his description of the villain. If the paper were to be longer, he might add short descriptions of the other characters or include criticism from some outside source that would add to his claim, but the brevity called for in the assignment tells Chan that he needs to get to the point quickly and clearly.

The form that the paper should take is also indicated by the request to add details and examples and by the direct suggestion that quotations will make papers more effective. We don't know much about the actual classroom context for the assignment, but it's fair to say that the teacher expects Chan and the other students to know something already about how to use details to support a position. And they have obviously already read the novel, so they can use their reading experience to help them make a decision about the villain. One other thing: the assignment implies that the identity of the villain is open to question, that it's a matter for debate. Chan won't be judged to be incorrect if he chooses a character who may not be the most obvious evil character in the novel.

In deciding upon the character to describe, Chan needs to find his own angle on the assignment. Clearly, the fact that he has been reading *The Scarlet Letter* in order to write a paper about it has affected the way he reads—a person reads fiction with a different eye if he or she is reading for pleasure rather than performance. Chan's invention strategies for the paper will depend on what he has been thinking as he's been reading about the characters and their actions. He might use the journalist's questions (pages 36–38) or Burke's pentad (pages 39–42) to generate insights about characters and motives. He might consider one of the classical topics of relationship, comparison and contrast (pages 48–49), as a perspective for considering varying motives and actions. His strategies will depend on what's been discussed in class and in small-group discussions about morality and revenge and hypocrisy, all issues for the characters in the novel. Since the teacher has indicated an audience of classmates and interested readers, Chan's planning strategies—considerations of who will be reading his work and how he needs to support his points—will be affected by class discussions as well.

As he reads the assignment, Chan already knows the character he'll choose based on his reading and discussion, and his aim for the essay will center on how to be most convincing about his choice.

Here are sample notes that Chan makes as he starts working on the assignment.

> Hester: obvious guilt with the A on her dress. More than that?
> Chillingworth: her husband and angry about what she's done. Mean and gets uglier throughout the book. The way somebody looks is sometimes a key to how they are inside (check).
> Dimmesdale: well, he's just a coward. Makes me mad that he lets Hester carry it all.

These notes show Chan figuring out which of the characters he finds most guilty or evil. He hasn't quite decided, perhaps, but you can tell from his notes that he leans toward Dimmesdale, the one who "makes me mad."

Chan's method here is worth emulating. Writing notes to yourself at the very beginning of a writing task is a good way to begin the invention process without much pressure. If they're just notes, you're not held accountable for them, and they won't be the first sentence of your final essay. This kind of thinking on paper or computer helps you formulate ideas quickly and allows you to continue writing and thinking rather than procrastinating because you feel too much pressure to perform.

Once Chan establishes his opinion, he can begin the data gathering that will constitute his evidence. Lines from the book, events and their consequences, and other situations from Chan's own experience or other reading all might help with the argument he intends to make. Notice that even in the early notes, above, Chan has shown why he leans toward Dimmesdale as the villain. "He's just a coward." That reaction might help Chan as he looks for evidence in the text (Where does Dimmesdale show his cowardice? What happens because of it? How does his cowardice affect others?) and sustains a developing argument about Dimmesdale's character.

One invention technique Chan's teacher suggests that he begin to use is keeping a journal. Following up on this suggestion helps Chan discover the seeds of lots of good ideas for his assignment on the villainous character and later on, for that matter, for essays on any number of topics.

A **reading journal**, a log that the reader uses to trace and monitor developing ideas and reactions to the reading, is a fine way to stimulate invention. Readers write about the characters in a book ("Interesting that Hawthorne compares Hester to a Madonna"), their own connections to the themes or context ("I went to Boston once, and it still feels like a Puritan place"), what they like or dislike, what they don't understand, and what they predict. The reading journal becomes a record of ideas developing and a source of pleasure as readers give voice to their reactions in ways they sometimes aren't able to in classroom discussion.

The best thing about journals kept by writers in a classroom or on their own is that in the journal the writer feels free of many of the rhetorical constraints that are present in assignments like the two given above. The audience may be a teacher or a reading partner, but that audience is not evaluating or judging the journal; instead, the journal is operating as a kind of sounding board for ideas. The subject is the book at hand, but, within that constraint, readers choose any topic that occurs to them to comment and reflect on. The persona of the writer in the reader's journal is determined by the writer's own mood and inclination, not by the demands of correctness or of overt persuasion. The language of this kind of journal is exploratory, with an aim of discovery and explanation to the self rather than to an outside *other*; it is concerned with speculating on possibilities rather than with right or wrong responses. Here is a portion of Chan's journal that he wrote while working on the *Scarlet Letter* assignment:

> I've got to say I just don't get it when Hester refuses to tell everybody who the father of her baby is. If she would just tell, then everybody would have to face up to things, including the fact that people we want to think are so great—pillars of the community, ministers—are just like the rest of us. I wish she'd be braver. Why do people always think it's so brave not to tell on somebody? Sometimes that's the bravest thing.

Apply Chan's Solution

The freedom of thought offered by the journal often results in fluent, interesting, and perceptive writing. Writers who feel free to voice opinions and questions, who aren't burdened by demands for particular forms or length requirements, demonstrate confidence and skill, as well as creativity. And writing in a journal can transfer to other, more formal writing tasks. It's a habit all writers should get into, taking time to write ideas and questions in a journal.

Aristotle believed speakers could understand audiences well because speakers themselves were also audiences. In other words, the more speakers knew themselves, the more they inevitably knew about their listeners. Socrates's famous injunction, "Know thyself," becomes a command to writers who want to reach readers. Writing in a journal, about books or events or plans, is one of the most effective ways for writers to know themselves—and thus, as Aristotle tells us, to begin to know those we're trying to reach.

Activity

Keep a journal of your own for two weeks, writing three times a week. Write about what's going on in the news, what you feel about the work you're doing in class, and what you like or don't understand about the texts you're reading in school. When you're given an assignment, write a journal entry that speculates how you might go about it, what you think you'll need to do to accomplish it, and what you're worried about.

Tasha, Lewis, and Susan: A Group at Work on Writing

As you consider the case of Tasha, Lewis, and Susan, keep the following questions in mind. Discuss them with your group when you can.

1. Since thinking about who your readers are, what they know about your subject, and how you need to interact with them is such a vital part of planning, how does working in a writing group help you plan your writing?

2. How can you use the insights of the other members of a writing group to help you invent effective material for your writing?

As Aristotle taught his students, and as we've shown throughout this book, writers always invent, draft, and revise more effectively if they think carefully about their audience. Our next three writers—Tasha, Lewis, and Susan—show us not only how sharing ideas in a group discussion can help you know your audience better but also how such conversations help you generate more useful material for your compositions. These three writers are working collaboratively on a book review, and their teacher has told them that they should write to an audience of people like themselves—curious, educated students.

What exactly does thinking about an audience do for you as a writer? If you know who's listening or reading, you'll have a better idea of examples that will be effective, stories that will strike familiar notes, and evidence that will be compelling. You know something about how long you should go on because you can infer the tolerance level of your audience; you know something about what you should repeat or omit because you sense their level of experience or understanding.

An audience is much broader than simply who's in an auditorium listening to your speech or who's likely to read your essay in the school newspaper. An audience also has a part to play in helping give writers ideas and helping writers test those ideas. The small group is one place to find such an audience. The talk that students engage in when they're in a group fosters the development of ideas, as students learn both to articulate and to adjust as they speak and listen.

Here's a brief exchange from Tasha, Lewis, and Susan's preliminary discussions of collaboratively writing a review of the book they have just finished reading:

TASHA: I don't think we need to tell too much about her, do you?

LEWIS: You mean the writer? 'Cause I think she's really important to the whole thing. I mean, did you read that part where she talks about being a Quaker?

TASHA: Where was that?

SUSAN: In the intro; it wasn't even in the first chapter. And she never mentions it.

LEWIS: But now you can see why she's so worried about peace.

TASHA: Yeah, I thought, "Why is she talking about wars when it's education we're supposed to be reading about?" But, yeah, I see why we should put that into the report.

SUSAN: I think we should start with it, don't you?

This fragment of a conversation shows how one person's ideas and experience might alter the thinking of somebody else. Tasha begins by saying to her group that the author's life isn't important to the review. She's ready to move on to what she thinks is important: the book's ideas about education, which Tasha alludes to when she says, "It's education we're supposed to be reading about." Lewis has read the introduction, where the writer speaks of her Quaker background and its effect on her teaching; his knowledge changes the way the group sees its task. Tasha uses Lewis's information to reframe her thinking about the report the group is writing, and Susan begins to see the form the report will take, opening with the biographical piece of information that Tasha began the conversation by rejecting.

When a group produces a collaborative product—a report, a presentation, a review—each group member has a *writerly* investment in gathering ideas, presenting evidence, and deciding on organization. Everybody in the group has an idea about these matters because everybody engaged in a collaborative project is a writer of the project. That's one of the difficulties of writing with a partner or with a group, and also one of the benefits. Writers learn how to articulate ideas and decide on opening sentences, supporting details, and effective sentence constructions as they listen to others' writing decisions, and they learn how to negotiate, challenge, and alter ideas in that social context. In other words, their own writing is strengthened by their connection with others' writing.

The advantages of talk about writing in a group are particularly evident when writers are inventing ideas for writing. As in the conversation above, writers invent both what they will talk about and how by listening to each other and offering ideas. A writer can generate questions to discuss in a group by using the strategies of invention explained in Chapter 2: the journalist's questions (pages 36–39), the pentad (pages 39–42), the topics (pages 46–51), and the enthymeme (pages 42–46).

- **Hearing other perspectives.**   Let's say that in the conversation above, one of the group members was a member of the Quaker faith. His perspective and experience would add both information and ideas to the discussion and might, in addition, change a group member's belief or opinion or strengthen it. Group talk about writing increases a writer's storehouse of information, and the interaction of several readers and writers creates new knowledge that every group member potentially can make use of.

- **Articulating thoughts.**   When writers talk to others about plans or ideas for a piece of writing, they learn what they think about those plans and ideas because they have had to frame what might be unconscious or undeveloped thoughts into language that someone else can understand.

The group asks questions such as "Why do you want to begin with a definition?" or "What will you say next?" In the act of responding, writers discover why they're making particular decisions and proceeding in certain directions. Writers become more conscious, in other words, of how they're generating ideas when they must account for those ideas within the group. The role of talk in helping writers make ideas conscious is similar to the way in which the journal can work by helping writers "see" what they think.

- **Understanding what works and what doesn't.**   Effective group members let writers know when the decisions they're making seem appropriate and useful. They reinforce writers' ideas by adding information, suggesting details, questioning, and affirming. They also suggest changes or additions to a plan, or they question when they don't understand writers' intentions. In this way, writers become aware of how their own writing plans and decisions need to alter to accommodate a reader's needs. In later stages of drafting and revising, writers learn from talk in the group about how well **evidence** and **logic** work in their papers, how suitable their **diction** is, how clearly they move from point to point, and how effectively their voice carries.

Activity

Using the first chapter of Sandra Cisneros's *House on Mango Street* or any other piece you and your class have read recently, find one problem or issue that you think is important to discuss. It might be something about family from the Cisneros story, for example. Use one or more of the invention strategies from Chapter 2 to generate some ideas about the issue. Then write a paragraph that speculates about the issue. Try out your ideas in a discussion with your group. After the group discussion, rewrite the paragraph so that it incorporates in some way the perceptions, questions, or additions provided by someone in your group.

Nell: The Rhetorical Reviser

As you read Nell's case, consider the following questions and discuss them in your group when you can.

1. In general, what considerations seem most important to you when you're revising a piece of writing?
2. How is a writer's need to revise a piece of writing related to the need to do additional inventing, planning, or drafting?

So far in this chapter, we've been studying invention and revision, and looking at writers working alone or in groups, gathering ideas, and creating scenarios to make their ideas emerge. Now let's examine a writer who devotes a lot of attention to focusing her ideas, omitting what she sees as extraneous material, and changing her ideas. As you read about Nell's revision process, remember the point we made at the outset of this chapter: writers invent all the time during the process of writing, and they revise all the time too. That's why writing is called **recursive:** because it moves back and forth rather than in a straight line from beginning to end.

Nell is planning an editorial for the school newspaper about racial issues in her community, and she comes to talk to her instructor about her ideas: "I thought it would be useful to talk about the progress that's being made in our school on the issue of race. We hear so many bad things, and it's good sometimes to hear about the positive ones." She pauses. "So I thought I'd talk about what the student body did for Martin Luther King Day last year, when we had that special assembly." Her teacher nods. She continues: "But maybe I should start with all the problems we've had here in the past. I don't want to sound like I don't know how prejudiced we've been."

Nell thinks out loud as she's talking to her teacher. As she's inventing possibilities, she's also revising out loud. She sets her **aim**—to demonstrate that progress has been made in racial issues at her school. She offers evidence—Martin Luther King Day assemblies—and she considers the audience, who she feels have heard "so many bad things" that they might need to hear something positive. But you can see that she's also revising her initial idea as she decides that she must acknowledge racial problems. She's considering her audience here as well; she doesn't want her readers to think that she isn't aware of problems or is trying to ignore past racial difficulties. All this invention and revision occur in the space of a minute or so of talk!

Although revision occurs during the entire writing process, it's when writers have put words and paragraphs down on paper that they most consciously consider purpose, audience, and voice. Once ideas have been shaped onto the page, a writer begins to decide more directly how those ideas work together, how the voice sounds in presenting them, and how readers might react to them. Writers begin the process of changing and adding and deleting as they invent new ideas, and they consider the effect of their language and organization on communication with readers and on their emerging aim.

The journal and the writer's group are both useful in this part of the writing process, too, when writers are rethinking or reseeing their work. As we've suggested, the journal is a way to speculate and explore, to try out ideas and voices. Writers who get stuck or "blocked" in the middle of writing a paper can use the journal to get unstuck. Writer's block often happens because writers feel sudden or intense pressure: the time is too short, they don't like the previous paragraph, they don't know what comes next, or they don't sound knowledgeable enough. These writers are feeling the rhetorical constraints of voice, subject, aim, or audience too intensely and find it hard to proceed.

Audience is the constraint that most often blocks student writers, since so often their audience is an evaluator who will grade or score their performance, who may or may not talk to them about it, and who seems to have in mind already what constitutes an acceptable writing performance. The journal, taken up in the middle of a writing assignment, can free writers once again to explore ideas even if they choose not to write about the issue at hand in their journal entry.

Next time you feel blocked in your own writing, write in your journal about your problems with the assignment. "I think I know where I'm going, but I don't seem to be able to get there. It's like I'm on a highway with no exit," one student wrote to his teacher about his trouble in completing a draft. Writing through his anxiety helped him continue. Or write about something totally unrelated to your draft: observe somebody in the hall, write a character sketch, or write about a funny moment in class. Any experience or speculation that you write about with some attention will work to build your confidence. And confidence is what writers who feel blocked need.

Activity

As quickly as you can, write a first draft of what you think would be a good first paragraph for the composition Nell is working on. Then, in your group, compare your first drafts, and talk about what you would do to revise them if you continued working on this assignment.

You Pull It All Together

As you work on this final case, consider the following questions, and discuss them in your group when you can.

1. How do you connect your own experiences to the texts you read when you're planning a composition?
2. How do you develop your own persona when you're also paying attention to the voices and positions from the texts you're reading?
3. How do you persuade an audience when you're writing about a controversial issue or one that provokes strong feelings?

Let's conclude this chapter with a flourish—with a project that asks you to practice some of the major considerations you take into account with a substantial writing project. Your writing processes here will include invention, drafting, and revising.

Following are two articles taken from the Greensboro, North Carolina, *News and Record*. The newspaper publishes articles on racial issues every Sunday during February in its "Ideas" section as part of its recognition of Black History Month. The first, written by the white director of a branch library in town, comments on the need for a civil rights museum in the city and uses his own family history to help argue his point. The second is a reprint of a speech given by an African American professor speaking at a celebration of Martin Luther King Day at Bennett College in Greensboro. Read the two articles, and pay attention to the persona of the writers, the way they use evidence, and how they appeal to their audiences.

WHY WHITE PEOPLE NEED A CIVIL RIGHTS MUSEUM IN GREENSBORO

I always had taken comfort in the fact that I was from a family too poor to own slaves. As far as I knew, our ancestors were all dirt-poor farmers, sharecroppers and mill workers. I felt sure that no one with a DNA link to me was guilty of the sin of slavery. In fact, my grandfather had told us that one of our South Carolina ancestors had been openly opposed to slavery and had taught slaves to read, even though it was illegal to do so. Needless to say, I liked that story and I wanted to go to my grave thinking that my ancestry was a combination of poor sharecroppers and good abolitionist stock.

But my brother is a scientist and he answered my question with the facts: One branch of our family did have enough money to own a small number of slaves.

In Dr. King's most famous speech, he cried out for a day of equality and harmony between the "sons of former slaves and sons of former slave owners." Before that day, I hadn't felt that I was kin to either of these groups, but suddenly I felt as if my DNA had rearranged itself and linked me, against my will, to the plantation owners of the Mississippi Delta. My working class heritage, of which I am proud, was now tainted by a bloodline connection to slave owners. I sat there, a few miles away from the levees and the plantations, feeling that I had gone deeper into the South and deeper into my own heritage than I had really wanted to go.

. . .

History is like family ancestry: We can't selectively decide whom we want to be related to, and we shouldn't selectively decide which parts of history we want to remember. History, like our DNA, continues to shape the present in ways we cannot recognize. . . . We will not be able to understand current issues such as racial profiling, achievement gaps, racial mistrust and school redistricting until we understand the full implication of what transpired between blacks and whites when the river rose over the levees in Greenville and when the demonstrators in Greensboro were abused.

IS RACISM STILL ALIVE? OR HAVE WE OVERCOME?

Racism is our shibboleth. It is the sign and symbol by which we are known and remembered around the world, for this civilization cursed itself long before it became a nation. The white men and women who founded it with such high purpose let that purpose be demeaned by the enslavement of those black men and women called to maintain and develop what they founded.

. . .

We turn again to the memory of Martin Luther King, whose life was itself the clearest expression of what America claimed to be but never was. We look again at the America he knew and the America he dreamed about, and because we share his dreams we wish that somehow he could be here now, alas! not to see those dreams fulfilled, for that is a long way off, but to bring us together again and to revive us in the continuing struggle toward the realization of what he dreamed about.

Activity

In a sentence or two, describe the argument that each of these writers is making about race. Now consider how each man is making his argument. What evidence do they offer? What support do they give for their positions? Are those positions more alike or different? What do these pieces assume about readers?

Using What You Read

If you were writing your own piece for the newspaper about race or giving a speech about it to your school, you would no doubt revise what the writers above have said to make use of your own context, to fit your own ideas and experience. And that's the essence of all revision: to rethink what you've read and heard—including what you've read and heard in your own draft—to get closer to what you're discovering to be the purpose of the writing. So, having read these two pieces, try the following activity.

Activity

Write a beginning discussion of race as you see it, from your own personal experience, your understanding of culture and history, and books you've read. Use the ideas presented by one or both of the writers above for your own emerging argument or speculation about race. You'll be revising your ideas based on the need to include one or both of these examples; you'll be revising the examples as you fit them into your own context. Once you have a short draft, read your work aloud to your group. See if they feel you've been fair to the writers as you've included them in your argument. See if you can describe your speaker's voice and your aim to them. Does your group agree with you? Your group will help you revise, too, to help you get closer to what you want to achieve, especially in having someone else understand what you're trying to say.

Revising Your First Effort

When you revise, you test your own truth as a writer. How do you conduct this test for truth? You look back to find out how you sound and to find when you hear your own voice speaking. It sounds different than it does when you first compose because now you're hearing the words on the page as a *reader* as well as a writer.

Suppose you began your draft this way: "Race is still a problem, but progress has been achieved." You might read back and cross out that sentence. "Race is still a problem, but we've made progress." What made you decide to change the first sentence? You can hear the difference in the two. The first sentence sounds more formal, distant. And why is that? The word *achieved* carries more precise definition somehow than *made* and so feels explanatory. And the passive construction *has been achieved* puts you, the writer, out of the message, making your voice sound far away from the subject and from your readers. In some cases, of course, you want to achieve that distance. You've written essays or reports in which you wanted to highlight findings rather than your part in discovering those findings. And taking the "person" out of the writing is one way to do that.

But suppose you make the change above. Why do you revise the sentence? Apparently, you've decided you don't want to be far removed from the subject; you want somehow to be involved in it. And you want your reader to be involved too. You use the word *we* to signal that you see yourself, and your readers, as part of something, such as a community or a culture. Revising with a notion of voice or persona, with a sense of readers, and with an idea of subject, you are making changes rhetorically. You're using the elements of Aristotle's triangle to achieve your purpose more effectively.

Whether you're conscious of it or not, you are thinking rhetorically as you make the change from the more to the less formal sentence. When you revise, you read back and make changes in part to "get it right with the self," as British language theorist James Britton said. You listen to yourself, ask questions of yourself, and try changes in words, punctuation, and paragraphing to see if the writing seems to "work" better, or "sound right." Sometimes when you revise, you're trying to make sure your text is correct or you're adding sentences to make it longer, but these are concerns with audience, not with your own ideas about the text you've written.

As you're getting your piece to sound right to you, you're also thinking about other rhetorical concerns that will make it sound right to others. Becoming conscious of these, you can become an even more effective reviser of your own work.

Revising for Persona

The writer's personality on the page, his or her voice, can be the most powerful tool a writer possesses. The best way to revise for voice, or persona, is to listen to that voice and test its sound. Like tuning a guitar, you'll get in the habit of hearing the note that's a little too high or too loud, and you'll adjust your word, sentence, or punctuation to make the chord harmonious.

You sometimes find your persona in the acts of writing and revising. You realize in the process of formulating your ideas and planning your approach that you sound informed or passionate or objective or distant. And developing your persona as you revise helps you to come up with new ideas, new illustrations, and new word choices.

But often your persona is implicitly given to you in an assignment. When you write your college admissions essay and the directions are to tell of an experience that has shaped you as a student, you understand that you need to write as a teenager, as a student, and, because it's an essay that will help get you admitted to a university, as someone who cares about education and learning. You want to show that you understand the conventions of academic and formal writing, so you avoid clichés, slang, and digressions. You check to make sure that you've spelled words correctly, that you haven't made punctuation errors. And you want to sound interested and appealing; you're asking readers to see you as a good candidate, a good student, and a reflective thinker. Understanding the persona your words create can make you a persuasive writer.

Activity

Here's a quick exercise: Make the voice in this sentence sound more angry.

"The mass of men live lives of quiet desperation."

Now make the voice sound more informal.

Do you see how quickly you can change the feeling an audience might form about the writer and the subject by changing the words that give them a sense of the writer's persona?

Revising for Audience

The people your writing interacts with constantly influence your thinking. For much of the writing you accomplish in school, you know your audience well. It's a teacher, who has indicated to you in comments and evaluations of your work what he or she expects or hopes for from the writing. Think about what you know of your teacher's expectations: clarity, development of ideas, knowledge of subject, use of detail. There are probably lots of others. And for different courses, the teacher as audience has some varying expectations. In writing for a biology class, your audience wants to be able to repeat experiments and so expects no omissions of procedure. In asking you to write a paraphrase for a history class, your teacher expects no digressions or personal asides; he or she wants you to demonstrate your understanding of the texts. In some classes, originality is prized; in others, brevity. As a student, you learn, sometimes almost unconsciously, about audience through a teacher's conversation and responses.

When you write other pieces for which the teacher is not the main audience—the school newspaper, a journal, a group presentation—you take into account expectations too, even though sometimes you're not as sure about those expectations as you might be with teachers, since you don't get the same kind of direct feedback from newspaper readers or your fellow students. And when you write for distant audiences, as in the college admissions essay or an Advanced Placement exam, you infer from the directions and from reading similar pieces what the audience members believe, need, or expect from you. In these cases, the Socratic maxim "Know thyself" can help you. You know what makes you interested or bored, convinced or doubtful, and you can use this knowledge as you revise your writing.

Revising Subject

The content, point, or subject matter of a piece of writing is a complex concern for a writer. Writers often believe that the main point in the rhetorical triangle is the subject point. "I just read about whatever topic they assigned and found out as much as I could about it. Then just wrote it up," one writer explained as she was describing her writing process in a composition class. For many assignments, knowing the subject does seem to be the most important thing. Writers need proof, they need evidence, and they need detail to be convincing.

Revising with subject in mind, a writer may go back to the library or to the Internet to find additional support for descriptions of the rain forest climate along the Amazon or for an explanation of chaos theory or for an argument about the value of the space program or for a claim that Huck Finn is not naïve. The **thesis** about the subject can also be developed by talking to others and by jotting down ideas as they suggest themselves in reading the beginning of a draft. The more you think and talk about a subject, the more you know of it.

Revising Evidence

You need proof that helps persuade a reader, and evidence comes in many forms. Writers decide how much evidence and what kinds of evidence to use based on their growing understanding of the subject, of voice, and of the audience. They revise that evidence to make their writing increasingly convincing.

- **Narrative.**   Stories, **anecdotes**, and **examples** all serve as evidence and as ways to develop subjects. Look back at your essay on race. Did you use a story? If so, why? The first article on race (page 117) uses narrative to explain the subject—the need for a civil rights museum—and to frame the argument. The advantage of narrative is clear: readers get to know the writer and understand his or her persona through a story, even when it's not a story about the writer. And readers like stories because they're usually easily understood and easily connected to the readers' own experiences. Of course, narrative is more appropriate for some writing tasks than for others. A narrative can be merely a distraction if you're writing to explore the rhetorical techniques in Frederick Douglass's prose. It might be clearly inappropriate in a reflection on an experiment. You might edit a story out of a final draft for these reasons. Or you might insert one as you revise.

- **Logic.**   Writers use the logic of ideas—how one idea necessarily follows another, how one **claim** justifies another—constantly in their writing. As we explained in Chapter 2, Aristotle used two terms to define this logical manipulation of ideas, the **syllogism** and the **enthymeme.** The syllogism suggests two premises, neither of which is arguable, and then draws the inescapable conclusion.

    Van is a politician.

    Politicians all have suspect motives.

    Van's motives are suspect.

Logical reasoning using either the syllogism or the enthymeme (syllogistic reasoning with one premise assumed rather than stated, as in "Van is a politician, and I'm suspicious") is often highly persuasive, and academic writing uses this kind of reasoning all the time. You should be ready to revise with an idea of logical order in mind. What are your unstated premises? Are they probable or useful? Do readers understand the progression of your ideas so that they follow your line of thinking and might be inclined to agree?

- **Data.** Probably the kind of evidence you're most familiar with and use most consciously is data—research that supports the conclusions you're drawing. You locate this research in the books and articles you read on your subject, in reports and findings from researchers, and in newspaper articles, interviews, and case studies. Data help make your case, providing support outside your own experience or logic, that the position you take has merit. In your essay on race, your data may come from cultural criticism, biographies of civil rights figures, primary documents from the 1960s, or interviews and other sources. As you revise your work, you examine your data, testing to make sure that you have enough, that you've dealt with the data fairly, and that you haven't hidden data that present an opposite position.

How, and if, any kind of data gets used depends on all the rhetorical factors we've been discussing, but most especially on the context for your writing. The rhetorical situation—what purpose you're trying to accomplish, who your readers are, and what kind of assignment you have—determines the data you'll use as evidence. Knowing and acting on that rhetorical situation is perhaps the single most important element in learning to revise and invent throughout your writing process.

Interchapter

4

Overviews of the Major Points in Chapter 4

- Writers develop substantial pieces of writing by following a complex, recursive process. All aspects of the writing process are influenced by the rhetorical situation in which the writer is working.

- As writers work through a process on a piece of writing, they develop a sense of intention, a belief that what they are writing is important to them, and a sense that they have a reason to write beyond fulfilling an assignment.

- The central acts of writing are invention and revision, both of which operate continually throughout a writer's process.

- Writers become more fluent and effective by tapping into many sources to discover material for their writing, by keeping journals, and by discussing their emerging work regularly with classmates and/or a writing group.

Activities and Discussion Questions for Chapter 4   Use these questions and comments to guide your own discussion and to guide your writing about these literary works.

Henry David Thoreau, "An Essay on Civil Disobedience" (published 1849)

The text appears on pages 221–237. Suppose that you decide to write on some aspect of a citizen's duty to either respect his or her government or resist it. Describe what such a composition would be—an essay, a letter, a Web site, an editorial, a speech? How would you develop a sense of intention? How would you go about writing it?

Eavan Boland, "It's a Woman's World" (published 1982)

The text appears on pages 238–239. You decide to write on some aspect of a woman's rights and roles in our society. Describe the form such a piece of writing might take—a **dialogue**, a researched essay, a journal entry, a poem. How would you develop a sense of intention? How would you proceed as you begin to write?

Alice Walker, "Everyday Use" (published 1973)

The text appears on pages 240–246. You decide to write on some aspect of either ethnic identity or family relationships. Describe the form your piece of writing might take—a story, an interview, a feature story for a newspaper, a history. How would you develop a sense of intention? How would you proceed as you begin to write?

Rhetoric and the Reader

5

" 'And'—what do you know?—'they all lived happily ever after.' "

One must be an inventor to read well.

Ralph Waldo Emerson, "The American Scholar"

Just as writers envision and realize an **intention** with the texts they write, readers predict and create intentions with the texts they read. Readers go through processes similar to the ones writers engage in and that we've investigated in previous chapters: they use strategies to foster **invention** of ideas (notice Emerson's line, above, about the necessity of invention for readers); they make predictions about **aims** and **effects**; they revise ideas based on what they are learning about the text's **genre** and **style**; they come to understandings about the meaning and significance of what they've read.

Readers are, above all, actively involved in what they read; if they can't be active, they can't read very well. At that point, they stop listening to the text and just look at words. Aristotle knew that the **audience** who listened to a speech brought with them particular beliefs and experiences that shaped what they'd hear. It was up to the **speaker** to use those beliefs and experiences to help the audience understand or appreciate the message—or even to change their minds—as they listened to the speech. Today, speakers and writers expect their listeners and readers to do the same: bring beliefs and experiences to bear on texts they hear and read and, in so doing, make meaning.

Predicting What's Next

Once upon a time . . . What's the next word? Most readers have no trouble predicting that the word that follows that phrase is *there*. How do readers know that word? It doesn't follow the ordinary English sentence pattern to put the word "there" next. If it were an ordinary English sentence, it would read something like "Once upon a time a wicked witch lived. . . . " But somehow that doesn't sound right—because readers know that *Once upon a time* begins a fairy tale, and fairy tales *always* have *there* after *Once upon a time:* "Once upon a time, *there* lived a wicked, frightening, hideous old witch. She lived in a cave all alone, so wicked and so frightening that even the bats hid from her in the farthest corners of the rock." What will happen next? You might not know the exact words (and there aren't any, since we're making this fairy tale up), but you could predict that sometime soon there'll be a sentence that will read something like *And then one day. . . .* In fairy tales, there's always a turn like that; somebody or something new comes into the forest and changes fairy tale life. Finish the sentence for yourself. Then ask your friends how they finished it. There will probably be some similarities because many of you will have the same expectations for the tale. Will there be a princess? A prince? A magic spell?

Readers predict like this all the time. In fact, in order to read, they *must* predict. How do they make predictions? They read in units, or "chunks" of meaning, not word by word. Readers are always reading for meaning, reading fast and moving ahead to find the next bit of meaning they can hold onto. In fact, if you were to get very close to someone reading intently, you could see that the eye moving across the page doesn't move in just one direction. It moves back and forth very quickly, reading ahead and then looking back to retrieve necessary bits of information not attended to at first.

The process is fast, this going back and forth, and unconscious for the most part. Lots of readers believe they read every word, for example. Or they believe they're much slower readers than they actually are. Readers become conscious of how they predict and revise predictions, make choices and remake them, only when they encounter a text that's too difficult for them, one where they must reread often, go back continually to check what they might have missed. If you've ever read a text too difficult for you because you didn't have enough information or experience to bring to the text or because the language was too difficult or specialized, and you've had to read word by word, you know how you lose interest fast. You can't read fast enough to predict, so you can't enjoy or understand what you're reading.

Readers make their predictions about what they read based on all kinds of factors. They predict based on what they know about the kind of text—the genre—they're reading, as you did with the fairy tale. They predict based on their own experience with the subject of the text, the sound of the writer's voice, and their knowledge of grammar and sentence structure. *Everything* that readers know helps them to read a text and predict accurately. As readers read, they gather more and more data about the narrator, the genre, the **tone**, and the sentence structure, and understand more and more clearly which of their own experiences are most helpful to their reading. As a result, readers get better at predicting the further into a text they read.

Activity

Here's a test to illustrate how much, and how well, you predict when you read. It's called a **cloze test,** and it's based on the idea that readers read in chunks, rather than in words. The educational theorist George Herbert Mead determined that for most readers, a chunk includes seven or so words, so the cloze test leaves about every seventh word blank and asks the reader to figure out what word makes sense in the blank.

> They lived in a hamlet swept _____ by winds from the land and _____ from the sea.

The first sentence of this paragraph reads, "They lived in a hamlet swept *alternately* by winds from the land and *winds* from the sea."

If you had been reading along and had noted the word *alternately*, you would have likely predicted *winds* as the word for the second blank. If you had skipped over *alternately*, you'd have likely predicted another word like *waves*, perhaps, for the second blank. *Waves* would be a good choice, in fact, because of the alliterative balance with the *w* sound in *winds*.

Try the rest of the paragraph. In your mind, fill in the blanks as you read. Suggest only one word for each blank.

A steep road _____ along by cliffs and wastelands, leading, it _____ , to nothing human. And that was _____ it was called the deserted _____ , L'Abandonée. At certain times everyone there _____ be filled with dread, like travelers in a strange land. Still young _____ strong, always dressed in a worker's _____ , Minerva had a glossy, light mahogany _____ and black eyes brimming over with _____ . She had an unshakable faith in _____ . When things went wrong she would _____ that nothing, no one, would ever _____ out the soul God had chosen _____ for her and put in her _____ . All the year round she fertilized _____ , picked coffee, hoed the banana groves, _____ weeded the rows of sweet potatoes. _____ her daughter Toussine was no more _____ to dreaming than she.

After you make guesses for as many blanks as you can (there may be blanks you can't figure out easily, so skip them), move into your small group, and try to come up with a word for every blank. You'll need to decide together about which word fits best in each blank. Think about how you make decisions about which word to choose.

In this activity, the paragraph in the cloze test is from the first chapter of the novel *The Bridge of Beyond* by Caribbean writer Simone Schwarz-Bart. As you go over the actual words from the novel (the missing words appear at the end of this chapter), you will probably discover that your guesses get more accurate the further into the paragraph you read. Why? You are building up information and making decisions about what kind of **character** Minerva might be, about where the story takes place, about what kinds of events might happen. You'll notice that some words—conjunctions, prepositions—are easy to figure out. Other words, adjectives especially, are more difficult to think of. But your understanding of **narrative,** of the forms stories take, might make you able to predict fairly smoothly. Many words you selected will be synonyms for the actual words in the text, showing how well you understand the conventions of sentences and of the genre of the story.

Activity

Cloze tests based on nonfiction present more challenges sometimes, since nonfiction often uses more specialized vocabulary and is less dependent on a familiar story line. Try this piece of nonfiction. As before, guess which words belong in the blanks, and then confer with your group to see if you can agree on most of the words.

Chaos breaks across the lines that _____ scientific disciplines. Because it is a _____ of the global nature of systems, _____ has brought together thinkers from fields _____ had been widely separated. "Fifteen years _____ , science was heading for a _____ of increasing specialization," a Navy official _____ charge of scientific financing remarked to _____ audience of mathematicians, biologists, physicists, and _____ doctors. "Dramatically, that specialization has reversed _____ of chaos." Chaos poses problems that _____ accepted ways of working in science. _____ makes strong claims about the universal _____ of complexity. The first chaos theorists, _____ scientists who set the discipline in _____, shared certain sensibilities. They had an _____ for pattern, especially pattern that _____ on different scales at the same time. They had a taste for randomness and complexity, for jagged edges and sudden _____. _____ in chaos—and they sometimes call _____ believers, or converts, or evangelists— _____ about determinism and free will, _____ evolution, about the nature of conscious _____.

In this paragraph, from the beginning chapter of James Gleick's book *Chaos*, the discussion centers on how theory in physics has begun to redefine areas of thought and to forge links across disciplinary boundaries. Although it's about physics, this book is written for nonspecialists, as perhaps you can tell even in this little sample; the word choice is not overly specialized, and there are beginning definitions and a kind of story that weaves the information together. Still, it may be harder for you to make decisions about how to fill in the blanks best. See which words seem to be easiest for you and your group to agree upon. Look at the end of the chapter (page 147) to find the missing words in this cloze test.

Understanding How Readers Predict

In these two activities, part of your decision as you predicted and changed your predictions based on rereading and on your group's discussion came about as you began to understand more about the rhetoric of the paragraphs you read. As you read, you made inferences about the speaker's or narrator's **persona,** about the subject, and about what you as a reader are expected to know or to want to learn. In the opening from *The Bridge of Beyond*, for example, the narrator chooses words that begin to tell the reader about important elements in the character of Minerva. She's strong, has an unshakable faith in *herself*, and works hard, dressed as always in a worker's *overall*. She is kind and beautiful, the emblem of the fairy tale heroine. In fact, *The Bridge of Beyond* is a kind of fairy tale, a myth with magic and danger and a happily-ever-after ending. You no doubt can find places in the paragraph that suggest the faraway character of the novel or its mythical qualities. Think of the name of the village, for example.

In the paragraph from *Chaos*, the writer adopts an almost jovial tone (can you pick out words that indicate that tone?), although he's talking about difficult scientific issues. He uses a narrative—beginning with *fifteen years ago*—to help the reader. And he humanizes the scientists who first made the discoveries that were to lead to the development of chaos theory: "They had an *eye* for pattern," he tells us. Consider how different the tone might be if he had chosen instead to say, "The first chaos theorists were interested in pattern." You wouldn't be as interested. You might speculate about why the speaker creates this tone and uses narrative at the opening of this book on a new theory in physics.

A writer's choice of words reflects the depiction of character and the writer's intention, and you get better at predicting qualities of character and writer's intentions as you read further. Of course, you bring your own knowledge and beliefs to what you read as well. How you value your own experiences as a reader and writer, what you know about the kind of text you're beginning, how you feel about the subject—all of these will be factors in determining how you read the writer's intentions. The process of making meaning is interactive: Readers and writers work together to create meaning in texts.

Rosenblatt and Interaction: Two Kinds of Reading

Reading theorist Louise Rosenblatt explains the interaction between the reader and the writer's text this way.

Rosenblatt shows that it's in the combination between readers (and all they bring with them) and texts (and all they offer) that what she calls the **poem** happens. When Rosenblatt uses the term *poem,* she is not referring to a specific type of text, one that may have line divisions, meter, or rhyme scheme. *Poem* is the term Rosenblatt uses for interpretation, for meaning making, and this process happens only in interaction between readers and texts. If readers can't, or won't, bring their own experiences and ideas to their reading of a text, then interpretation, or meaning, is lost. Readers might understand words on the page but little about their importance or their context. As Rosenblatt's scheme suggests, reading must in some sense always be made personal for it to be made meaningful.

Rosenblatt also discusses *kinds* of readers or reading behaviors. As readers, we read with varying intentions—aims or purposes. Texts remain the same, but readers vary, and their reasons for reading those texts vary. Rosenblatt defines two kinds of reading that you'll be familiar with from your own experience.

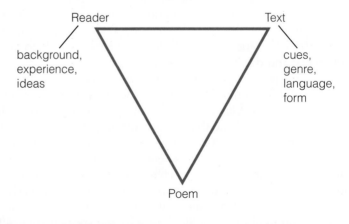

Rosenblatt's Tringle

Efferent reading is the kind of reading you do when you're looking for information, for the facts or ideas that readers can *do* something with. The word *efferent* comes from the Latin word *efferre,* which means "to carry away." Readers reading efferently hope to carry away from the text something they will put to use. Readers usually read textbooks efferently; they read recipes, manuals, handbooks, directions, musical scores, and lots of other texts for what those texts will allow them to do. Did you read the opening from *Chaos* efferently once you had all the words?

Aesthetic reading is reading for experience, for the chance to enter the world that the text presents, to become immersed in the words, ideas, images, and story within the text. Readers reading aesthetically are not so much interested in carrying away information for particular uses of their own as they are in carrying themselves into the text. Readers often read fiction and poetry aesthetically; they read drama, letters, and their own journals for how those texts let them feel, or to experience what's in the text. Look again at the opening to *The Bridge of Beyond.* Did you pay attention to its language? Did you try to imagine what the character looked like and who she was? If so, you responded aesthetically to the novel's opening.

But it's certainly possible to read a novel efferently or a science book aesthetically. If you are searching for metaphors in Schwarz-Bart's book (or filling in blanks), you're reading the novel efferently. When you read a novel looking only for what you can carry away with you to use in an essay or to answer a question on an exam, you miss the aesthetic response. Readers who listen for Gleick's subtle humor or who imagine the chaos scientists as detectives read aesthetically, just as readers do who hear subtle chord changes when they read sheet music or who examine a quadratic equation for its beauty of balance. Even a textbook could be read aesthetically for its design or its **voice.**

Activity

Imagine that you were instructed to begin reading a text that someone had told you was written by a paleontologist about a perspective on evolutionary history as it has been located in a group of ancient fossils. Before beginning this reading, discuss with your group members your expectations about tone, word choice, and level of interest and engagement. Talk openly about how these expectations would affect your reading.

Now, read a segment of that book:

FROM CHAPTER 1 OF *WONDERFUL LIFE*
A Prologue in Pictures
by Stephen Jay Gould

> And I will lay sinews upon you, and will bring up flesh upon you, and cover you with skin, and put breath in you, and ye shall live.
>
> —*Ezekiel 37:6*

Not since the Lord himself showed his stuff to Ezekiel in the valley of dry bones had anyone shown such grace and skill in the reconstruction of animals from disarticulated skeletons. Charles R. Knight, the most celebrated of artists in the reanimation of fossils, painted all the canonical figures of dinosaurs that fire our fear and imagination to this day. In February 1942, Knight designed a chronological series of panoramas, depicting the history of life from the advent of multicellular animals to the triumph of *Homo sapiens*, for the *National Geographic*. (This is the one issue that's always saved and therefore always missing when you see a "complete" run of the magazine on sale for two bits an issue on the back shelves of the general store in Bucolia, Maine.) He based his first painting in the series—shown on the jacket of this book—on the animals of the Burgess Shale.

Without hesitation or ambiguity, and fully mindful of such paleontological wonders as large dinosaurs and African ape-men, I state that the invertebrates of the Burgess Shale, found high in the Canadian Rockies in Yoho National Park, on the eastern border of British Columbia, are the world's most important animal fossils. Modern multicellular animals make their first uncontested appearance in the fossil record some 570 million years ago—and with a bang, not a protracted crescendo. This "Cambrian explosion" marks the advent (at least into direct evidence) of virtually all major groups of modern animals—and all within the minuscule span, geologically speaking, of a few million years. The Burgess Shale represents a period just after this explosion, a time when the full range of its products inhabited our seas. These Canadian fossils are precious because they preserve in exquisite detail, down to the last filament of a trilobite's gill, or the components of a last meal in a worm's gut, the soft anatomy of organisms. Our fossil record is almost exclusively the story of hard parts. But most animals have none, and those that do often reveal very little about their anatomies in their outer coverings (what could you infer about a clam from its shell alone?). Hence, the rare soft-bodied faunas of the fossil record are precious windows into the true range and diversity of ancient life. The Burgess Shale is our only extensive, well-documented window upon that most crucial event in the history of animal life, the first flowering of the Cambrian explosion.

The story of the Burgess Shale is also fascinating in human terms. The fauna was discovered in 1909 by America's greatest paleontologist and scientific administrator, Charles Doolittle Walcott, secretary (their name for boss) of the Smithsonian Institution. Walcott proceeded to misinterpret these fossils in a comprehensive and thoroughly consistent manner arising directly from his conventional view of life: In short, he shoehorned every last Burgess animal into a modern group, viewing the fauna collectively as a set of primitive or ancestral versions of later, improved forms. Walcott's work was not consistently challenged for more than fifty years. In 1971, Professor Harry Whittington of Cambridge University published the first monograph in a comprehensive reexamination that began with Walcott's assumptions and ended with a radical interpretation not only for the Burgess Shale, but (by implication) for the entire history of life, including our own evolution.

Once you have finished the reading, discuss with your group members how the voice and **stance** of the author (the late Stephen Jay Gould) influenced your reading. Did the voice and stance lead you to alter your expectations as you began reading? You might hear the word *paleontologist* and expect a text dry and difficult to read—specialized and data-driven. But Gould's enthusiasm and energy might have encouraged you to read with more pleasure and interest than you expected. The Burgess Shale discovery changes the whole history of life. Gould's stance provokes readers' efferent and aethestic responses. We need to read on.

Rosenblatt, Reading, and Rhetoric

Rosenblatt's primary goal in identifying efferent and aesthetic readings is to help readers respond appropriately to the texts they read. If you attend a poetry reading, the experience of the "reading"—that is, listening to the poet read—is meant to be aesthetic, designed to have you experience emotions and ideas through the interesting turns of its language. On the other hand, if you're in a computer lab listening to a speaker describing how to create a Web page, you're meant to "read" the talk efferently, by taking notes or following instructions on your own machine. Should you consider only the way the speaker phrases sentences or repeats a metaphor, you might miss the overall point and fail to learn much about Web pages. To understand your efferent and aesthetic possibilities as a reader is to begin the process of reading well. Rosenblatt's discussion also shows readers just how powerful they are in the act of reading, and how much their own disposition affects how they'll read and understand the texts they encounter.

You probably can see the rhetorical implications of Rosenblatt's work. The writer producing the text has to know how to create possibilities for readers to engage with the words on the page, to bring what they know to bear on what they read. The writer uses those "cues" to help guide readers' responses and to attempt to persuade readers to the position the writer wants them to adopt. Sometimes that persuasion is as simple as "You're really going to like this piece, I promise, so keep reading." Fiction often has that as a persuasive message. James Gleick's *Chaos* might be saying something like, "You may think this is tough stuff, but chaos theory is all around you, and you ought to read this because it is so exciting." Both messages say, "Keep reading." Gleick is also persuading his readers that chaos theory makes sense and offers new areas of study and cooperation to science and philosophy. Simone Schwarz-Bart may be persuading her readers of the value of oral culture, of dialect, and of the beauty of the island myths. Both writers use words and the forms they choose to make connections with readers strong enough to convey their persuasive intentions.

As a reader, then, you analyze and respond to the intention of the author and to the text itself. You pick up on the writer's cues—the indications given about aim through words and punctuation and sentence structure, as well as through the tropes and figures you worked with in Chapter 3. You understand the role you're being asked to play as the reader, and you decide whether your primary response is to enter the text or to take something from it, to become an aesthetic or an efferent reader. In doing this kind of response and analysis, you predict. As you predict your role as a reader, you decide whether and how you'll play it. As you predict the writer's intention, you decide whether you believe it or agree with it. When you respond in this way, you are engaging in the process of rhetorical analysis, of looking at the elements of rhetoric and how they combine to produce their effects on you as a reader.

Rhetorical Analysis of Chaos

To illustrate how the principles of rhetoric work in a text—that is, to show how a rhetorical analysis might be accomplished—we'll examine the rhetoric in the excerpt from *Chaos*. It's important to remember that what we'll analyze is just a small fragment, but even a paragraph or two can reveal much about intention and effect. Here is the beginning of a rhetorical analysis of Gleick's book.

> James Gleick wants to introduce readers to chaos theory and establish that it has beneficial possibilities for science. He makes his argument by creating a writer's voice that's both readable and knowledgeable. And he invites readers to share the chaos theorists' belief that looking everywhere for knowledge rather than in just one specialized area leads to new and better knowledge.

Notice that this first paragraph of the rhetorical analysis touches on all the points in Aristotle's triangle. It mentions purpose—"the beneficial possibilities" of chaos theory. It describes Gleick's persona—"readable and knowledgeable." It acknowledges audience—"invites readers to share" in understanding the chaos theorists' position. The **subject,** chaos theory, is mentioned in the first sentence.

What should happen next? As the writer analyzing Gleick, you might want to illustrate your **claims** about the rhetoric of the piece by demonstrating, through examples from the paragraph, how they work.

> Gleick begins with a definition of chaos as a science of "the global nature of systems." He quickly moves to claim that the connection of areas of science that have been traditionally separated has been the result of chaos theory and that it's a useful benefit for science. Quoting a Navy official who speaks approvingly of chaos having begun to reverse the dangers of "increasing specialization" in science, Gleick demonstrates his own position: that posing new problems in science might lead to new breakthroughs in scientific knowledge.
>
> Throughout the paragraph, Gleick's voice is conversational, even easygoing. "They had an eye for pattern," he says, speaking of the first chaos researchers. "They had a taste for randomness." The personal qualities of the scientists themselves makes even readers who might be leery of reading such a scientific book relax. Gleick clearly wants to introduce readers to a theory he believes has possibilities for changing the way we all think.

The reader analyzing Gleick could, and should, go on to speak of other rhetorical moves in the text—for example, the statements of definition, the non-specialized language, and Gleick's mostly unstated belief in the importance of new ways of thinking that gets inserted into the paragraph in several places. But the three beginning paragraphs are enough for you to see how you might proceed to analyze a piece rhetorically, looking at its elements and making claims about its intent. A reader who analyzes a piece of writing rhetorically could also at some point talk about its effect—how a reader might or does react to the piece. Of course, whether you choose to emphasize effect or not, a rhetorical analysis always assumes that the reader's response is key and always explains that response, since the reader is a point on the **rhetorical triangle.**

Matching Experience and Intention

Writers consciously and unconsciously use readers' experiences and beliefs to guide their own decisions in the texts they write. The formats they employ, the narrators they choose, the level of language they use, and the evidence they provide are all in great measure based on the predictions they make about how their audiences will read their work. And they are able to make these predictions because they are readers themselves.

"Form is the appeal," philosopher Kenneth Burke says, and form—length, paragraph breaks, dialogue, chapter headings, and so on—guides readers in their expectations and predictions. We pick up a novel. Before we read the title or author, we already begin to make predictions and develop expectations. The book will have characters, conflicts, messages. It will have chapters. If the novel is long, we wonder about its complexity and its scope. We consider how much time might elapse from first to last chapter, and how much time we'll devote to reading it. If we pick up a short story instead, we'll expect less time to elapse, perhaps; we won't expect chapters.

Burke uses a scene from *Hamlet* to talk about the importance of readers' sense of form. In the scene, Hamlet speaks about the ghost of his father appearing to him. The scene is set up to make the audience anticipate the ghost. When, instead, the soldiers at watch begin a playful conversation, readers are momentarily frustrated and then lulled into their conversation, for the moment forgetting the ghost. When he does appear, the moment is all the more striking for its delay, and Burke shows how the audience finds pleasure in having their expectations for form heightened by the delay before they're gratified.

Whatever readers read, they use what they know about forms to make interpretive decisions about the text and to guide themselves in making meaning. Readers are asked to fill in a lot of information from their experience and ideas. The first chapter of *David Copperfield* by Charles Dickens begins with the chapter title "I Am Born." We immediately assume that the title of the book refers to the "I" in the chapter heading. This is to be the story of David Copperfield, then, and it will begin at the beginning, with his birth. We might already have questions about why Dickens should begin there. Is the birth particularly significant? Will the novel spend a lot of time with Copperfield as an infant or young child? And how old is David when he's writing?

The first chapter ends with infant David lying in his basket, his mother in her bed, and his aunt leaving the scene, disappointed that he is born a boy. The second chapter begins this way:

> The first objects that assume a distinct presence before me, as I look far back into the
> blank of my infancy, are my mother—with her pretty hair and youthful shape—and

Peggotty, with no shape at all, and eyes so dark that they seemed to darken their whole neighborhood in her face, and cheeks and arms so hard and red that I wondered the birds didn't peck at her in preference to apples.

When a chapter ends and another begins, readers provide the transition. Notice that as a reader, you had to move forward in time from the baby in the basket to the narrator as an older person remembering his mother and his nurse. You filled in the gap between the chapters with your understanding that the novel would flash back and forth in time.

These gaps in the text are the places where readers are most active in using their expectations to make decisions about the meaning of the text and the writer's intention. In fact, writers often make gaps part of their rhetorical strategy to keep readers active and engaged as they read. The space between one character's speech and another's is a gap that readers are invited to fill in with ideas about expression, gesture, or movement. Sometimes gestures are written in without speech. "After he finished his tirade, she quietly refilled her cup." Readers fill in the gap with speculations about what "she" might be thinking and not saying. When a writer begins a new chapter with a line like "The next year was a blur" or ends a chapter with that line, readers move through time quickly, filling in the gap of time with their own speculations and settling quickly into the next moment. Readers are able to add information, create dialogue, and understand what happens between one moment and the next because of their experiences in the world outside the text and because, as they read, they become increasingly part of the world inside the text. By a few chapters into *The Scarlet Letter*, readers can predict how Hester will respond to a question from the townspeople because they've heard her respond before and have seen her in similar situations in earlier sections of the novel.

In nonfiction reading and writing, gaps occur as writers invite readers to fill in parts of **arguments** or explanations. Readers predict the kinds of evidence that might be offered, the type of opinion the writer might develop, and the organizational strategy the writer might follow. If the writer makes an argument or takes a position, readers will expect to fill in the **premises** that the writer leaves out.

Here is the opening from Toni Morrison's Nobel Prize speech, delivered to the members of the Swedish Academy in 1993. (The body of the speech appears on pages 258–264.) As you read, consider where you are invited to fill in gaps in the text.

Members of the Swedish Academy, Ladies and Gentlemen:

Narrative has never been merely entertainment for me. It is, I believe, one of the principal ways in which we absorb knowledge. I hope you will understand, then, why I begin these remarks with the opening phrase of what must be the oldest sentence in the world, and the earliest one we remember from childhood: "Once upon a time. . . ."

"Once upon a time there was an old woman. Blind but wise." Or was it an old man? A guru, perhaps. Or a *griot* soothing restless children. I have heard this story, or one exactly like it, in the lore of several cultures.

"Once upon a time there was an old woman. Blind. Wise."

In the version I know the woman is the daughter of slaves, black, American, and lives alone in a small house outside of town. Her reputation for wisdom is without peer and without question. Among her people she is both the law and its transgression. The honor she is paid and the awe in which she is held reach beyond her neighborhood to places far away; to the city where the intelligence of rural prophets is the source of much amusement.

You, the reader reading the speech, begin with the idea of the text *as* a speech, so the first gap you must fill in has to do with context, or **setting**. Toni Morrison is standing before an audience of Nobel Prize judges and officials and invited guests. She is there to receive literature's highest honor. Once she begins to speak, readers fill in other gaps about her intention for that audience, about her own persona as writer and speaker, about what they know about fairy tales and old women. They might puzzle over the word *griot*, filling in the possible gap of definition by connecting it to the wise village elder that Morrison describes. They consider associations between wisdom and age, between power and race and gender. They predict that soon in the speech will come the line "And then one day. . . ."
And it does.

One day the woman is visited by some young people who seem to be bent on disproving her clairvoyance and showing her up for the fraud they believe she is.

Readers understand that the fairy tale Morrison offers will serve as an example of an argument she will make in the speech, and they already predict that the argument will have something to do with the power of narrative.

Be it grand or slender, burrowing, blasting, or refusing to sanctify; whether it laughs out loud or is a cry without an alphabet, the choice word or the chosen silence, unmolested language surges toward knowledge, not its destruction. But who does not know of literature banned because it is interrogative; discredited because it is critical; erased because alternate? And how many are outraged by the thought of a self-ravaged tongue?
   Word-work is sublime, she thinks, because it is generative; it makes meaning that secures our difference, our human difference—the way in which we are like no other life.
   We die. That may be the meaning of life. But we *do* language. That may be the measure of our lives.

Notice that the questions are ways of asking readers to fill in gaps, as they invite readers to reflect on censorship and freedom in writing as well as on the power of language.
   In conversation, too, speakers and listeners use gaps all the time. "I'm a Quaker," a college student might say to explain a decision to take part in a peace demonstration. Listeners would easily fill in the missing part of the explanation—that part of the Quaker religion is its belief in pacifism. Therefore, identifying himself as a Quaker is enough information for the speaker to give about his reasons for his action. These reading/listening gaps are a kind of **enthymeme**, just as we explained in Chapter 2. The logic of syllogistic reasoning moves in a cause-effect pattern. *If* one premise is so, *and* a second premise is also true, *then* a conclusion about the second premise can be made.

The enthymeme "John is a Quaker; *therefore,* John is a pacifist" omits the premise that all Quakers are pacifists. Like literary moments where the reader fills in missing information, the enthymeme is structured as a gap in the text, and it forces readers to become active meaning makers as they read. The use of syllogistic reasoning and of gaps in texts not only fosters logical meaning making and the logical persona of the writer but also assures that readers become part of the transaction in making sense of the texts they read.

Much of the time, premises omitted by speakers and writers are obvious ones, as in the Quaker example above. But writers can also assume agreement by ignoring a premise that all readers might not believe or understand or by jumping to a **conclusion** without stating the premises for it. Readers might be led to a conclusion and accept it without understanding all the premises the conclusion is based upon. A writer who says, "We should give to charity. We're Americans," omits a premise that might be stated as "Americans are generous and always help those less fortunate." Perhaps not everyone would agree if the major premise were stated, and that is one reason why it's important to recognize how writers use gaps and enthymemes to structure their ideas. Recognizing the underlying reasons for a claim, readers fill in gaps that make them analyze arguments effectively and make them active cocreators of what they read.

Activity

Read this segment of an essay by Amy Tan on her mother's heavily Chinese-inflected English dialect and language differences in general. With your group, create an enthymeme that expresses what you believe Tan's position to be. Remember that there should be a premise and a conclusion stated and one premise left implicit so that the reader fills it in.

> Lately, I've been giving more thought to the kind of English my mother speaks. Like others, I have described it to people as "broken" or "fractured" English. But I wince when I say that. It has always bothered me that I can think of no way to describe it other than "broken," as if it were damaged and needed to be fixed, as if it lacked a certain wholeness and soundness. I've heard other terms used, "limited English," for example. But they seem just as bad, as if everything is limited, including people's perception of the limited English speaker.
>
> I know this for a fact, because when I was growing up, my mother's "limited" English limited *my* perception of her. I was ashamed of her English. I believed that her English reflected the quality of what she had to say. That is, because she expressed them imperfectly her thoughts were imperfect. And I had plenty of empirical evidence to support me: the fact that people in department stores, at banks, at restaurants did not take her seriously, did not give her good service, pretended not to understand her, or even acted as if they did not hear her.

You will find more than one line of reasoning in these two paragraphs, more than one set of premises and conclusions. See what you come up with as your group shares its findings with other groups in the class.

Activity

Tan gives some background and experience to begin to develop an argument about language and thought, and as a reader you likely can sense the direction she will head in the essay. Now read the opening to another essay, this one by William Zinsser. The essay begins in a more deductive way, with a group of letters from students.

COLLEGE PRESSURES

Dear Carlos: I desperately need a dean's excuse for my chem midterm which will begin in about 1 hour. All I can say is that I totally blew it this week. I've fallen incredibly, inconceivably behind.

Carlos: Help! I'm anxious to hear from you. I'll be in my room and won't leave it until I hear from you. Tomorrow is the last day for . . .

Carlos: I left town because I started bugging out again. I stayed up all night to finish a take-home make-up exam & am typing it to hand in on the 10th. It was due on the 5th. P.S. I'm going to the dentist. Pain is pretty bad.

Carlos: Probably by Friday I'll be able to get back to my studies. Right now I'm going to take a long walk. This whole thing has taken a lot out of me.

Carlos: I'm really up the proverbial creek. The problem is that I really *bombed* the history final. Since I need that course for my major I . . .

Carlos: Here follows a tale of woe. I went home this weekend, had to help Mom, and caught a fever so didn't have much time to study. My professor . . .

Carlos: Aargh! Trouble. Nothing original but everything's piling up at once. To be brief, my job interview . . .

Hey Carlos, good news! I've got mononucleosis.

In your group, consider these questions:

- What do you deduce the aim of Zinsser's essay might be?
- What's the rhetorical effect of beginning with the group of notes from students to their counselor?
- What line of syllogistic reasoning might follow from what you assume the aim of Zinsser's piece to be?

Rhetorical Analysis: You Try It

Now that you have read brief rhetorical analyses of the opening to *Chaos* and of a portion of Toni Morrison's Nobel Prize speech, you have some idea of the kinds of approaches you might use as you analyze a piece rhetorically and examine the underlying patterns of argument and the gaps you're invited to fill in. The next step is for you to try a short rhetorical analysis of your own with the opening paragraph of Toni Morrison's novel *Sula*.

First, a little background on Morrison and her work is helpful to set the rhetorical context for your analysis. As you might have concluded from reading the excerpt from her Nobel Prize speech, Morrison is overtly a rhetorician, often speaking directly of her aim and her intended effect on readers with the language she chooses and the perspective on events she takes. She doesn't diminish her craft or her desire to affect an audience, her need to communicate a point or an argument most powerfully and effectively. In an interview on PBS several years ago, Morrison talked about her novel *Beloved,* which had just won the Pulitzer Prize for fiction. Asked her reason for writing about the horrific events the novel describes, the murder of a child by its mother to prevent the child from being taken into slavery, Morrison said, "I wanted to bring to slavery a personal face." She stated clearly her *rhetorical* intent, her desire to have readers understand in a human and narrative way what slavery had meant to the millions who suffered under it.

This clarity about her own aim with regard to her subject matter and her audience is evident in all her work. Several years ago, in a talk at the University of North Carolina, where she explored her writing process, Morrison discussed how she deliberately chose the plants *nightshade* and *blackberry* in the opening line to her novel *Sula.* She understood both the effect she wanted and the likely connections her readers would make to the words, their sound, and their meaning.

Sula is a novel about African American families living in a small segregated hilltop neighborhood in southern Ohio called, ironically, the Bottom. It's a story of pride and self-doubt, of racism and tragedy, of love and forgiveness. The main character is Sula herself, a woman who escapes the Bottom and then returns to unsettle the lives of everybody who lives in the Bottom.

Activity

Here is the opening paragraph of *Sula.* You will write a rhetorical analysis of it. Think about what you've just read about Morrison and her work. Read the excerpt quickly, and then go back and read it again, noting words or phrases that seem especially evocative to you as you read. You want to read *aesthetically* at first, drawing yourself into the world that Morrison presents. When you look back at individual elements in the passage, you'll be searching for information to help you explain your response. That more *efferent* activity will be enriched by reading first to enjoy and speculate.

> In that place, where they tore the nightshade and blackberry patches from their roots to make room for the Medallion City Golf Course, there was once a neighborhood. It stood in the hills above the valley town of Medallion and spread all the way to the river. It is called the suburbs now, but when black people lived there it was called the Bottom. One road, shaded by beeches, oaks, maples and chestnuts, connected it to the valley. The beeches are gone now, and so are the pear trees where children sat and yelled down through the blossoms to the passersby. Generous funds have been allotted to level the stripped and faded buildings that clutter the road from Medallion up to the golf course. They are

going to raze the Time and a Half Pool Hall, where feet in long tan shoes once pointed down from chair rungs. A steel ball will knock to dust Irene's Palace of Cosmetology, where women used to lean their heads back on sink trays and doze while Irene lathered Nu Nile into their hair. Men in khaki work clothes will pry loose the slats of Reba's Grill, where the owner cooked in her hat because she couldn't remember the ingredients without it.

Here are some questions to help your thinking about the passage:

- How do details contribute to the rhetoric?
- What is the tone? How do you decide?
- How does Morrison make the place itself seem significant?
- Where do you detect **irony** in the voice of the speaker or in the situation the speaker describes?

You might begin your rhetorical analysis by working in your group to think through the elements of rhetoric as they appear in the passage. In your group, choose one of the following questions to respond to. Share your responses with the other groups in your class.

- Who's speaking, and how do you characterize the speaker?
- What is the subject?
- Who is the audience? What do they know and need to know?
- What is the writer's aim as it appears so far?

After talking with your group and listening to other groups, write your analysis. Rhetorical analysis begins with readers' recognition of their own experience with a text, the reaction they get from the writer's words, images, and structures. Remember to pay special attention to the language of the passage itself—its word choice, its use of imagery, and the length and variety of its sentences. And use your reactions (and those of your group members) to help you decide what's most significant in the paragraph.

- Read and describe the feeling you get from the passage. As you consider words that describe your feeling, you begin to name the tone of the passage.
- Read back to account for the words you've chosen to describe your feeling. You'll discover that the **diction,** the particular word choices Morrison makes, affects your choice of words. Identify some of Morrison's word choices that connect with the words you've used to describe your reaction.
- Notice phrases or **images** that seem especially vivid. Accounting for these images will allow you to expand your first reactions.

- Examine how Morrison uses sentences, looking at their length and complexity. Her construction of sentences and sentence patterns (or **syntax**) affects your reading. Notice how sentences balance one another, or how **repetition** of sentence patterns contributes to your response to the passage.

You could go on with the passage from *Sula* by talking about another element that is definitely a part of your reading process and related to your ability to fill in gaps: prediction. As a reader, you are always guessing about matters of character, plot, theme, and conflict, as well as sentence and word meanings. The cloze test showed you how prediction works to make sense of the sentences and words in a passage. Readers build up more effective predicting skills the longer they read because they begin to use what has come before to make sense of what's coming next. Readers always travel back and forth in time this way—for example, remembering what David Copperfield said about his nurse Peggotty in the book's Chapter 2 as they read about her engagement and marriage in Chapter 30.

This ability to move forward and backward with the eye and the brain is essential for good reading to take place, for the *poem* to happen, as Rosenblatt would say. Taking what you've said about *Sula* as a starting place and using what you know about Morrison, what might you predict will happen next, or even finally, in the novel? It's interesting how much gets established early on in the reading of any text and how often readers predict accurately even after the first few pages.

Activity

As you begin to read the next book or play you're working on in class, keep a journal of predictions and revisions. Read the first chapter or so, and then make some guesses about character, argument, or outcome. Write again when you begin to revise some of your ideas; at that point, explain what makes you change your mind. Engaging in this running commentary about your reading will allow you to see how active and creative a reader actually is in the process of reading.

Activity

The following excerpt from Leslie Marmon Silko's "Yellow Woman and a Beauty of the Spirit" grapples with differences between "old time" and "modern" ways of looking at people and the world. Silko grew up on the Laguna

Pueblo reservation in New Mexico and spent a great deal of time as a child with her great-grandmother, listening to stories of the old days.

> Grandma A'mooh would tell about the old days, family stories about relatives who had been killed by Apache raiders who stole the sheep our relatives had been herding near Swahnee. Sometimes she read Bible stories that we kids liked because of the illustrations of Jonah in the mouth of a whale and Daniel surrounded by lions. Grandma A'mooh would send me home when she took her nap, but when the sun got low and the afternoon began to cool off, I would be back on the porch swing, waiting for her to come out to water the plants and to haul in firewood for the evening. When Grandma was eighty-five, she still chopped her own kindling. She used to let me carry in the coal bucket for her, but she would not allow me to use the ax. I carried armloads of kindling too, and I learned to be proud of my strength.
>
> I was allowed to listen quietly when Aunt Susie or Aunt Alice came to visit Grandma. When I got old enough to cross the road alone, I went and visited them almost daily. They were vigorous women who valued books and writing. They were usually busy chopping wood or cooking but never hesitated to take time to answer my questions. Best of all they told me the *hummah-hah* stories, about an earlier time when animals and humans shared a common language. In the old days, the Pueblo people had educated their children in this manner; adults took time out to talk to and teach young people. Everyone was a teacher, and every activity had the potential to teach the child.

Make some predictions about this text based on the introduction to Silko and the excerpt itself. What do you expect the argument to be? Why does the writer begin with the description of Pueblo ways of educating? How might she develop her argument?

Building the Reader's Repertoire

Readers use all their experiences to make sense of what they read. They remember their own pasts. They test their own knowledge. They use what they know about the writer. They call upon their own beliefs and opinions. They compare forms and genres they're familiar with to the ones they're reading. Reading theorist Wolfgang Iser calls this wealth of information and experience within the reader the **repertoire.** Other reading researchers call it nonvisual information or, simply, experience. The idea is that readers can call upon what they need in order to interpret and re-create the text as they're reading. It follows, then, that the more readers know—about reading, authors, life, ideas, history—the richer the repertoires they can draw upon. The broader and deeper the repertoire, the more engaging and satisfying the reading experience.

How might readers go about building their repertoire? Of course, much of that building happens in school with the kinds of experiences and information gathering that school provides. But outside school, reading and generally living in the world build information, experience, and ideas that readers use when they read. Becoming conscious of what you learn by reflecting on it in a journal (either written by hand or on the computer) is a good way of consciously building your repertoire. Taking careful stock, at the beginning of reading, of what you know and what you think you need to know is another way. Reading related texts, investigating Internet sources, talking to other people—all are ways of adding to your own fund of experiences that will deepen and enrich your reading experience.

With *David Copperfield,* consider what you know. You know about children and young boys, about what a mother means to a child. That's important in this novel since David's mother dies early in his life. What might you not know? Details of rural England in the nineteenth century? Child labor laws? These elements might be important in the story, and the story itself might reveal the information. But even if the novel doesn't tell a reader everything about rural life in England over a century ago, readers can use what they *already* know to make sense of what they're learning. Readers may not know much about England or the nineteenth century, but they may know a good deal about small towns in this country or about feeling isolated. The point is that even when you don't know everything you need to know to read most efficiently, you know *something* of what you need to know, and knowing something allows you to read more. As you read, you begin to know more and more of what you need to know.

Reading nonfiction or nonnarrative texts, you use similar strategies, building on what you know already to learn more as you read. In Silko's essay, while you might be unfamiliar with the cultural practices of the Pueblo in New Mexico, you know about generational differences and about how children learn and are taught. You know how people use examples to create arguments and to state positions. You use these understandings as you learn about Silko's own experience and you compare them with yours.

Sometimes readers are asked to read texts that they don't have enough of a repertoire to read effectively. That's why it often happens that a book a reader has read in tenth grade and disliked becomes a favorite if the reader reads it again in college. The book hasn't changed; the reader has. The repertoire has broadened.

As a reader, you are both a consumer and a producer; you respond to the texts you read, and you help create them by using your own experience, opinions, and ideas to make sense of the text and to respond to it appropriately. When you open a textbook, you begin with a certain mind-set that predisposes you to read in special ways, and you read with expectations about the author's tone and voice and the textbook's format—expectations that help you read efficiently and meaningfully. Expectations about style, form, and meaning guide you in reading all kinds of work from textbooks to speeches to poetry. Understanding your role as a reader helps complete the rhetorical transaction among writer, reader, and text and lets you communicate with the texts you read, even when you sometimes don't know everything about the subject or the context of what you read as you begin.

Activity

In your group, discuss any times in which you've read a book more than once and found the second reading experience radically different from the first one. Consider how your repertoire affected your changed response to the book. Discuss the same process using a film you've seen more than once.

Activity

Read the following excerpt, the beginning of the essay "One Moment on Top of the Earth" by Naomi Shihab Nye. Then, in your group, discuss what you already know about her subject or the details she presents and what you still need to know to predict and to understand her position. The entire essay is included at the end of this chapter.

ONE MOMENT ON TOP OF THE EARTH
FOR PALESTINE AND FOR ISRAEL

In February she was dying again, so he flew across the sea to be with her. Doctors came to the village. They listened and tapped and shook their heads. She's a hundred and five, they said. What can we do? She's leaving now. This is how some act when they're leaving. She would take no food or drink in her mouth. The family swabbed her dry lips with water night and day, and the time between. Nothing else. And the rooster next-door still marked each morning though everything else was changing. Her son wrote three letters saying, Surely she will die tonight. She is so weak. Sometimes she knows who I am and sometimes she calls me by the name of her dead sister. She dreams of the dead ones and shakes her head. Fahima said, Don't you want to go be with them? And she said, I don't want to have anything to do with them. You go be with them if you like. Be my guest. We don't know what is best. We sit by her side all the time because she cries if we walk away. She feels it, even with her eyes shut. Her sight is gone. Surely she will die tonight.

Reading Your Own Writing

We've talked in earlier chapters about the importance of revision in the writing process and about the way that creating and altering ideas intertwines for writers as they look ahead and read back. One of your most important tasks as a reader is to know how to read your own writing most helpfully and efficiently. As discussions of writing processes suggest, you read your own writing unconsciously in large measure; with every phrase your eye quickly travels back to check on what you have said and how it sounds. Reading back in this way actually allows you to continue to write. Some research shows that writers who are kept from looking back at their writing as they are producing a draft fairly quickly become hesitant or even stymied at how to proceed. They lose the ability to write because they aren't able to read.

This quick and nearly unconscious reading is, as the writer Eudora Welty put it, your "test for the truth" of your idea. You listen to how you sound, to the words you've chosen; you think about the argument you're trying to develop or the details you're describing or the mood you're capturing. And as you read back, you "write" ahead, considering what you might place next and how you'll move from one point to another. This reading activity is one of the primary tools for all writers.

When you read your own work after you have completed a draft, you're looking at how the end product meets the expectations you've assigned to it as you've been reading back during the process. As a reader of your own text, make sure you can answer the following questions:

- What does the first sentence or first paragraph allow readers to predict?

- What does the vocabulary, your use of examples, or the way you make your argument suggest about the repertoire a reader needs in order to interpret your text effectively?

- What tone do you attempt to carry throughout your text? Point to some words that suggest that tone.

- How clearly do you make connections among the points or ideas you've written about?

- As a reader, do you have to fill in lots of gaps in order to keep reading?

- As a writer, have you paid attention to your reader? As a reader, do you feel that attention has been paid to you?

These questions can be useful when you read drafts by your friends and members of your group. One reason why writers often like to get comments from another reader is that they need to validate their own reading of the text, to see if the way they have read their own text matches another reader's experience. Thinking about your role as a reader of your text allows you to make helpful comments and useful suggestions for writers, including yourself, to follow in the revision of essays. What you do as a reader—gather ideas, predict, revise—is in so many ways what you do as a writer, and you can rely on this similarity to guide your reading as well as shape your writing.

Activity

Choose a draft of an essay that you're working on, and consciously make yourself into a reader of your piece by considering what you're learning, feeling, and thinking as you read the draft. Make notes to yourself; read portions aloud; listen for your voice as you read and write. Point out one place where you use prediction, revision, gaps, and background repertoire.

Here are the two selections from the cloze tests (pages 128 and 128–129), this time reprinted with all their words in place.

FROM *THE BRIDGE OF BEYOND*
by Simone Schwarz-Bart

They lived in a hamlet swept *alternately* by winds from the land and *winds* from the sea. A steep road *ran* along by cliffs and wastelands, leading, it *seemed*, to nothing human. And that was *why* it was called the deserted *village*, L'Abandonnée. At certain times everyone there *would* be filled with dread, like travellers *lost* in a strange land. Still young *and* strong, always dressed in a worker's *overall*, Minerva had a glossy, light mahogany *skin* and black eyes brimming over with *kindness*. She had an unshakable faith in *life*. When things went wrong she would *say* that nothing, no one, would ever *wear* out the soul God had chosen *out* for her and put in her *body*. All the year round she fertilized *vanilla*, picked coffee, hoed the banana groves, *and* weeded the rows of sweet potatoes. *And* her daughter Toussine was no more *given* to dreaming than she.

FROM *CHAOS*
by James Gleick

Chaos breaks across the lines that *separate* scientific disciplines. Because it is a *science* of the global nature of systems, *it* has brought together thinkers from fields *that* had been widely separated. "Fifteen years *ago*, science was heading for a *crisis* of increasing specialization," a Navy official *in* charge of scientific financing remarked to *an* audience of mathematicians, biologists, physicists, and *medical* doctors. "Dramatically, that specialization has reversed *because* of chaos." Chaos poses problems that defy accepted ways of working in science. *It* makes strong claims about the universal *behavior* of complexity. The first chaos theorists, *the* scientists who set the discipline in *motion*, shared certain sensibilities. They had an *eye* for pattern, especially pattern that appeared on different scales at the same time. They had a taste for randomness and complexity, for jagged edges and sudden *leaps*. *Believers* in chaos—and they sometimes call themselves believers, or converts, or evangelists—*speculate* about determinism and free will, *about* evolution, about the nature of conscious *intelligence*.

Here is the complete essay, the first paragraph of which appears on page 145.

ONE MOMENT ON TOP OF THE EARTH
by Naomi Shihab Nye

For Palestine and for Israel

In February she was dying again, so he flew across the sea to be with her. Doctors came to the village. They listened and tapped and shook their heads. She's a hundred and five, they said. What can we do? She's leaving now. This is how some act when they're leaving. She would take no food or drink in her mouth. The family swabbed her dry lips with water night and day, and the time between. Nothing else. And the rooster next-door still marked each morning though everything else was changing. Her son wrote three letters saying, Surely she will die tonight. She is so weak. Sometimes she knows who I am and sometimes she calls me by the name of her dead sister. She dreams of the dead ones and shakes her head. Fahima said, Don't you want to go be with them? And she said, I don't want to have anything to do with them. You go be with them if you like. Be my guest. We don't know what is best. We sit by her side all the time because she cries if we walk away. She feels it, even with her eyes shut. Her sight is gone. Surely she will die tonight.

Then someone else who loved her got on an airplane and flew across the sea. When she heard he was landing, she said, Bring me soup. The kind that is broth with nothing in it. They lit the flame. He came and sat behind her on the bed, where she wanted him to sit, so she could lean on him and soak him up. It was cold and they huddled together, everyone in one room, telling any story five times and stretching it. Laughing in places besides ones which had seemed funny before. Laughing more because they were in that time of sadness that is fluid and soft. She who had almost been gone after no eating and drinking for twenty days was even laughing. And then she took the bread that was torn into small triangles, and the pressed oil, and the soft egg. She took the tiny glass of tea between her lips. She took the match and held it, pressing its tiny sulfuric head between her fingers so she could feel the roughness. Something shifted inside her eyes, so the shapes of people's faces came alive again. Who's that? she said about a woman from another village who had entered her room very quietly with someone else. She's lovely, but who is she? I never saw her before. And they were hiding inside themselves a tenderness about someone being so close to gone and then returning.

She wanted her hair to be washed and combed. She wanted no one arguing in her room or the courtyard outside. She wanted a piece of lamb meat grilled with fat dripping crispily out of it. She wanted a blue velvet dress and a black sweater. And they could see how part of being alive was wanting things again. And they sent someone to the store in the next town, which was a difficult thing since you had to pass by many soldiers. And in all these years not one had ever smiled at them yet.

Then the two men from across the sea had to decide what to do next, which was fly away again, as usual. They wished they could take her with them but she, who had not even entered the Holy City for so long though it was less than an hour away, said yes and no so much about going they knew she meant no. After a hundred and five years. You could not blame her. Even though she wasn't walking anymore, this was definitely her floor. This voice calling from the tower of the little village mosque. This rich damp smell of the stones in the walls.

So they left and I came, on the very next day. We were keeping her busy. She said to me, *Marhabtein*—Hello twice—which is what she always says instead of just Hello and our hands locked tightly together. Her back was still covered with sores, so she did not want to lie down. She wanted to eat whatever I had with me. Pralines studded with pecans, and chocolate cake. They said, Don't give her too much of that. If it's sweet, she'll just keep eating. She wanted cola, water and tea. She wanted the juice of an orange. She said to me, So how is everybody? Tell me about all of them. And I was stumbling in the tongue again, but somehow she has always understood me. They were laughing at how badly I stumbled and they were helping me. It was the day which has no seams in it at the end of a long chain of days, the golden charm. They were coming in to welcome me, Abu Ahmad with his black cloak and his cane and his son still in Australia, and my oldest cousin Fowzl the king of smiling, and Ribhia with her flock of children, and the children's children carrying sacks of chips now, it was the first year I ever saw them carrying chips, and my cousin's husband the teller of jokes who was put in prison for nothing like everybody else, and the ones who always came whose names I pretended to know. We were eating and drinking and telling the stories. My grandmother told of a woman who was so delicate you could see the water trickling down her throat as she drank. I had brought her two new headscarves, but of course she only wanted the one that was around my neck. And I wouldn't give it to her. There was energy in teasing. I still smelled like an airplane and we held hands the whole time except when she was picking up crumbs from her blanket or holding something else to eat.

And then it was late and time for sleep. We would sleep in a room together, my grandmother, my aunt Fahima, my cousin Janan of the rosy cheeks, a strange woman, and I. It reminded me of a slumber party. They were putting on their long nightgowns and rewrapping their heads. I asked about the strange woman and they said she came to sleep here every night. Because sometimes in such an upsetting country when you have no man to sleep in the room with you, it feels safer to have an extra woman. She had a bad cold and was sleeping on the bed next to me. I covered my head against her hundred sneezes. I covered my head as my father covered his head when he was a young man and the bombs were blowing up the houses of his friends. I thought about my father and my husband here in this same room just a few days ago and could still feel them warming the corners. I listened to the women's bedtime talking and laughing from far away, as if it were rushing water, the two sleeping on the floor, my grandmother still sitting up in her bed—Lie down, they said to her, and she said, I'm not ready—and then I remembered how at ten o'clock the evening news comes on in English from Jordan and I asked if we could uncover the television set which had stood all day in the corner like a patient animal no one noticed. It stood there on its four thin legs, waiting.

Janan fiddled with dials, voices crisscrossing borders more easily than people cross in this part of the world, and I heard English rolling by like a raft with its rich r's and I jumped on to it. *Today*, the newscaster said, *in the ravaged West Bank . . .* and my ear stopped. I didn't even hear what had happened in this place where I was. Because I was thinking, Today, in this room full of women. In this village on the lip of a beautiful mountain. Today, between blossoming trees and white sheets. The news couldn't see into this room of glowing coals or the ones drinking tea and fluffing pillows who are invisible. And I, who had felt the violence inside myself many times more than once, though I was brought up not to be violent, though no one was ever violent with me in any way, I could not say what it was we all still had to learn, or how we would do it together. But I could tell of a woman who almost died who by summer would be climbing the steep stairs to her roof to look out over the fields once more. Who said one moment on top of the earth is better than a thousand moments under the earth. Who kept on living, again and again. And maybe an old country with many names could be that lucky too, someday, since at least it should have as much hope as invisible women and men.

Interchapter

5

Overview of the Major Points in Chapter 5

- Reading calls for making predictions and revising those predictions.
- Readers carry with them a repertoire of information and experience that helps them read effectively.
- Readers develop hypotheses about what they read and, based on their own repertoires of information, fill in gaps in the text.
- Readers respond to and use rhetorical considerations—of subject, speaker, audience, and purpose—as they read and interpret.
- Readers are like writers.

Activities and Discussion Questions for Chapter 5   Use these questions and comments as guides for your own discussion and writing about these works.

Henry David Thoreau, "On the Duty of Civil Disobedience" (published 1849)

The text appears on pages 222–237. Discuss the following questions with your small group, or write a well-organized essay that you share with your group.

1. How does Thoreau's opening statement, where he describes the best government, help you predict the way in which Thoreau is going to make his arguments? By reading only the first paragraph of his essay, what might a reader predict about other arguments Thoreau might make?

2. What knowledge do you have about Thoreau as a writer or person that influences the way you read this text? What do you know about civil-rights protests in the twentieth century that helps you connect with Thoreau's position?

3. Where in the allusions Thoreau makes do you fill in gaps in the reading? How do you fill them? (Did you find the allusion he makes to his famous piece *Walden?*)

4. How do you respond to Thoreau's argument? Which of his strategies do you find effective? Consider his use of evidence, his persona, and his use of appeals.

5. How does Thoreau use language, especially metaphor, to make his argument clear and strong?

Eavan Boland, "It's a Woman's World" (published 1982)

The text appears on pages 238–239. Use these questions for small-group work or as the basis for an essay on this poem.

1. What associations do you bring with you to the title "It's a Woman's World"?

2. How do you read the tone of the poem? What words signal the tone for you as you read?

3. Rewrite this poem in prose, trying to maintain the same tone. Read your piece to your group, and discuss the effect of the change.

4. How does Boland use history to help make her aim clear? How do you use what you know about history and women to help you connect with her aim?

Alice Walker, "Everyday Use" (published 1973)

The text appears on pages 240–246. Use these questions to help you begin a draft of an essay or to spur discussion with your small group.

1. How do the first words—a dedication—help you predict the events that might take place in the story? How does the dedication help you read the ending?

2. How do you use that dedication to connect with your own experience?

3. What's the rhetorical effect of Walker's use of the second person, "you," in the story?

4. What events or motivations are left out of the plot of the story? How do you fill in those places that the narrator remains silent about?

Readers as Writers, Writers as Readers: Making Connections

6

PEANUTS reprinted by permission of United Feature Syndicate, Inc.

> Ever since I was first read to, then started reading to myself, there has never been a line read that I didn't *hear*. As my eyes followed the sentence, a voice was saying it silently to me. It isn't my mother's voice, or the voice of any person I can identify, certainly not my own. It is human, but inward, and it is inwardly that I listen to it. It is to me the voice of the story or the poem itself. The cadence, whatever it is that asks you to believe, the feeling that resides in the printed word, reaches me through the reader-voice. I have supposed, but never found out, that this is the case with all readers—to read as listeners—and with all writers, to write as listeners. It may be part of the desire to write.
>
> Eudora Welty, *One Writer's Beginnings*

Eudora Welty, who died in 2001 at age 92, wrote *One Writer's Beginnings* in 1982. It is a memoir, a look back at her life as a novelist and short story writer, and it evocatively explores the influences on her writing, especially the importance of her small-town southern upbringing and her storytelling family. Like many memoirs of writers, Welty's book also considers *how* she became a writer. Reading the lines above, you can see Welty emphasizing how the **voice** she heard as a reader and as a writer guided her. For Welty, voice was the element that brought readers and writers together.

In earlier chapters, we discuss voice as we consider how a writer creates a persona on the page and as we describe how a reader comes to understand tone in a written text. In both the lines above and in the following passage from her memoir, Welty suggests something else about voice: how important it is to *hear* when you read and to *listen* when you write.

> The sound of what falls on the page begins the process of testing it for truth, for me. Whether or not I am right to trust so far I don't know. By now I don't know whether I could do either one, reading or writing, without the other.
>
> My own words, when I'm at work on a story, I hear too as they go, in the same voice that I hear when I read in books. When I write and the sound of it comes back to my ears, then I act to make my changes. I have always trusted this voice.

Do Welty's words strike a familiar chord with you? When you read, do you hear what Welty calls the "reader-voice"? When you write, do you listen for that voice to help you decide what word to choose, where to put a comma, how long to make a sentence? In this chapter, we explore how writers improve their skill and confidence by using what they know as readers and how readers expand their critical and interpretive ability by using what they know as writers. In particular, we consider what reading and writing teach us about voice.

Reading and Writing: Different? Similar?

Despite Welty's comment, and our own encouragement to see reading and writing as mutually reinforcing and complementary in this book, it may seem to you that the acts of reading and writing are more different than they are similar. For one thing, while most people identify themselves as readers, far fewer consider themselves writers. Reading seems to be an activity that anyone can do, statistics about the continuing literacy problem in this country notwithstanding. Writing seems to be a more specialized skill. To identify yourself as a reader simply says that you're literate; to say you're a writer is to claim a vocation.

If you were making a list of differences between reading and writing, you might come up with some of these words to describe how the two acts seem different:

Reading	Writing
Receives	Creates
Interprets	Produces
Internalizes	Externalizes
Passive	Active

As we'll see, reading and writing are much more alike than they are different, and once you begin thinking about them together, the separate lists above begin to blend. Reading is as active, as creative, and as productive as writing. And writing is as interpretive, as receptive, and as internalized as reading. Reading and writing are sometimes taught as separate, only tangentially related, activities: a student reads first and then writes to demonstrate that he or she has read, for example, or a student writes so that someone else can read and evaluate the writing. But seeing reading and writing as simultaneous strengthens mightily the skill of interpretation, and the ability to interpret is a rhetorical skill.

Activity

Many people don't remember learning to read. Students will sometimes say that it seems like they always knew how to read, or that one day they just could read, and they don't recall how it happened. They often have vivid memories of learning to write, maybe because writing—taking the big pencil and the wide-lined paper and forming letters—is so much more a physical act than reading.

This activity is designed to help you think about reading and writing connections. Go back to your early childhood or an early time in your schooling—third grade, maybe, or first grade, or even before—and write about a memory of reading or writing. Do you remember something about your first-grade reading group? Having to read aloud? Writing a story that was put on the bulletin board? Being corrected for misspelling? Being read to at night? Pick a memory that stands out for you. Write to evoke the scene—the classroom, the other children around you, yourself. You might speculate about why the scene stands out for you, what it means in terms of how you see yourself now as a reader or writer.

After you write your memory, share it with your group. See if there are similarities in your responses. Describe the voice you hear as you read the memories from each of your group members.

The Literacy Memory

Students who've written about their literacy memories often have a lot to say. They remember being read to—how they knew exactly when to turn the page even before they could read words because they had listened to the story so often. They write about composing poems with great confidence at home and then going to school and being shocked that their teachers didn't find their creations as wonderful as they had thought they were. They write of being afraid to turn in a paper because it would get corrected. They remember being in a slow reading group or a fast one and how they knew without being told whether they were "good" or "bad" readers.

One student writing her literacy memory writes, "I remember being so proud when I could 'read' the sign for McDonald's. I was little, maybe two or three, but I knew that yellow *M*. And I would say McDonald's! My mom would sometimes stop and get me French fries. Maybe that's why I wanted to read. I thought I'd get something."

How does a child *read* before she knows her letters? How does she write before she can spell? People learn to read and write in the same way that they learn to negotiate the world around them; they learn how to understand signs and how to respond to them. They *interpret* words on the page in the same way that they interpret the world and their own experience. And it's this activity of interpretation—understanding and acting on meaning—that links reading and writing and makes them both part of the larger activity of *composing,* or of the imagination.

Children "read" the big *M* on the McDonald's sign and know what it means to them. French fries! It isn't long before the same children read other signs—their own names, the title of a favorite cartoon, the first line of a story. When they go to school, they will learn to read texts as they learned to read *McDonald's,* by understanding what the symbols they see on the page stand for. But in order to read words, they use what they already know about how to read signs—not only the McDonald's sign, but also their mothers' expressions, the cat's meow, and the wind before a rainstorm.

As with reading, children learn to write by using what they already know about how meaningful **symbols** are. Do you remember writing your name when you were very young? Those letters that made up a word stood for *you,* so they were especially meaningful. When writers begin to compose whole sentences and whole stories, they do so with a sense that the words they write carry meaning. Sometimes youngsters *write* scribbles on the page and then "translate" those marks aloud for listeners. The marks carry meaning that the children will willingly explain if readers can't interpret them on their own.

So both reading and writing carry with them the idea of making meaning. And both reading and writing are special instances of making meaning, since we make meaning all the time, from the time we wake up until we dream at night.

Where does **rhetoric** fit into this scheme that brings together reading and writing? Rhetoric, as we've discovered, is about **intention** and **effect**. A writer uses particular words and **images**, **claims** and **evidence**, with an **aim** in mind. A reader has **purposes** for reading, and the way those purposes match the writer's purposes constitutes the effect of the piece. Later, we'll have more to say about how writers and readers link their intentions and decide on effects. For now, it's important to remember that readers and writers are always linked by rhetoric, by their desire to communicate and to interpret ideas.

Activity

Reread your literacy memory piece, and then write a paragraph in which you explain your intention. Identify some of the signals you used to get that intention across. Next, in your group, read one another's literacy memories, and ask group members to write for each other person a short paragraph that explores the voice of the speaker, the attitude toward reading or writing it expresses, the choice of details and images, the use of **figurative language**, or the **argument** it creates. See how your intention statement matches the responses from other members of the group.

The Process of Making Meaning: Readers as Writers

> There is, then, creative reading as well as creative writing.
>
> Ralph Waldo Emerson, *"The American Scholar"*

How does a reader read "creatively"? How important is reading creatively to understanding, interpreting, and analyzing texts well? A significant part of your work as a student is to read skillfully enough to be able to explore texts precisely and analytically. When you take standardized tests for college entrance or write analytical essays for courses in college, you are expected to read closely, with attention to how words and ideas work in the text. Does that view of reading fit with reading creatively?

When readers use a **repertoire** of experiences and ideas and information as they read, they read creatively. And, as we saw in Chapter 5, readers *must* use their repertoire in order to read at all because they're always reading for meaning, expecting it, and lining up what they already know with what they're learning. Readers, then, are creating the text as they respond to it, just as writers create the text as they write it.

When Frank Smith, a prominent reading theorist and teacher, talks about the process of reading, he uses many of the same words that teachers and students use to describe what happens when they write. Using cognitive theory—ideas about how the brain works—Smith shows that the brain processes information in chunks; it can't record everything it sees. Readers don't read every word on a page; if they did, they couldn't read fast enough to make meaning.

You might have listened to struggling young readers pronouncing every word of stories they are reading. They read haltingly, often pointing to each individual word as they say it. If someone stops these readers to ask what the sentence means, they can't answer. They have to work so hard to identify individual words that they can't make sense of the text as a whole, or even of the meaning of the sentence. Think about difficult texts you've encountered as a reader. Have you noticed that you can read a line or a paragraph and not know what you've read after you finish? You're being forced to read too slowly to make meaning. And making meaning is the key to reading.

Because readers can't read every word, because they need to read relatively quickly to get information to the brain, readers *predict*, decide what they *expect* the next word, the next phrase, the next chapter to be about. For young readers, or readers who read texts that are too far beyond their own repertoires, the ability to predict is hampered so much that they can't interpret. They can't read creatively enough to make meaning. Prediction, or creatively deciding on meaning, is crucial to reading, therefore, and the skill of prediction is one that writers use as well.

Activity

1. Complete the word at the end of this sentence:

   The captain ordered the mate to drop the an _____.

2. Make a prediction about the following words:

   Love in the Time of Cholera

Think of the questions you need to answer before you can predict anything about the two groups of words above. Write some of your questions, and then make a prediction about what the sentence in #1 might be about.

You probably predicted easily the end of the word in the sentence above. You were able to predict because of what you know about the words *captain* and *mate*. The **context** of the sentence allowed you to make meaning easily. If you were actually reading the sentence in an essay, you wouldn't even be conscious that you had predicted and would read on without actually seeing the word *anchor*.

In fact, the only way you'd know that you had predicted would be if your prediction turned out to be wrong. Read the rest of the sentence.

   The captain ordered the mate to drop the an _____, and the furry, long-nosed animal scurried across the deck.

Once you complete the sentence, you have to go back to the word you've predicted and revise your guess. You find the word *anteater*, and then you move on; you probably wonder why an anteater is aboard ship, so you make another prediction—that you'll find out more about the anteater in the next sentence.

As readers, we predict, create hypotheses, test them as we read, and revise our guesses. Throughout a story or an essay or a chapter, we continue the process; we acquire more skill and confidence in predicting and **revising** as we build up more and more information from what we've already read.

Now, return to *Love in the Time of Cholera,* the second group of words at the beginning of this activity. What sort of predictions did you make about that group of words? Someone in your group, or you yourself, might have known this phrase already. It's the title of a novel by Gabriel García Márquez, a Colombian author. But even if you didn't know it beforehand, you might have predicted it was a title anyway. It sounds like one. It's not a complete sentence, for one thing, and several words in the phrase begin with a capital letter. Furthermore, the title sounds as if it belongs to a novel rather than a history book; after all, how many history books have *love* in the title? The reason the phrase sounds like a title, the reason you predict that it's a novel, is that you know about stories, about how writers try to engage your interest in them. And if you think about it, you can predict even more. For one thing, you can predict that disease will present complications for the main **characters**, who, you predict, love one another. The **setting** for this story is probably removed from the present day or is a place where cholera epidemics still occur. Once you begin to ask questions of yourself, you discover how much you already know and how much you can predict even before you begin to read.

When you read quickly—for example, on a multiple-choice test that asks you to comprehend bits of text quickly and accurately—your skills of prediction become acute.

Activity

To test the role of prediction on a multiple-choice test, read the following passage and then, in your group, answer the questions that follow it. As you make decisions, talk together about how and why you decide on one answer rather than another.

When I am in a serious humour, I very often walk by myself in Westminster Abbey, where the gloominess of the place, and the use to which it is applied, with the solemnity of the building, and the condition of the people who lie in it, are apt to fill the mind with a kind of melancholy, or rather thoughtfulness, that is not disagreeable. I yesterday passed a whole afternoon in the churchyard, the cloisters, and the church, amusing myself with the tombstones and inscriptions that I met with in those several regions of the dead. Most of them recorded nothing else of the buried person, but that he was born upon one day, and died upon another: the whole history of his life being comprehended in those two circumstances, that are common to all mankind. I could not but look upon these registers of existence, whether of brass or marble, as a kind of satire upon the departed persons; who had left no other memorial of them, but that were born and that they died. They put me in mind of several persons mentioned in the battles of heroic poems, who have sounding names given them, for no other reason but that they may be killed, and are celebrated for nothing but being knocked on the head.

—Joseph Addison, "Westminster Abbey," 1711

1. Which of the following describes the apparent purpose of the entire essay?
   a. To praise the lives of soldiers who have fallen in battle
   b. To describe the intricacies of the architecture found in cemeteries
   c. To explain what one should do when in a bad mood
   d. To ruminate on the contrast between the fullness of life and the terseness of tombstone inscriptions
   e. To provide a tourists' guide to Westminster Abbey

2. The first sentence provides an example to which of the following stylistic features?
   a. A run-on sentence
   b. A periodic sentence
   c. A loose sentence
   d. An ineffective use of the first-person pronoun
   e. A dangling modifier

3. In the fourth sentence, the phrase "registers of existence" refers to
   a. Tombstones
   b. Volumes in the burial vaults of Westminster Abbey
   c. Heroic poems
   d. Victory celebrations
   e. Satirical verses

4. Which of the following best describes the function of the last sentence?
   a. To signal a transition to a new topic in the essay
   b. To move the discussion to a higher level of abstraction
   c. To draw a comparison between the tombstone inscriptions and descriptions in heroic poems
   d. To express bitterness at the transience of life
   e. To recommend heroic poems as models of behavior

In some ways, Question 1 *should* be the hardest—though it probably wasn't. To answer the question, you had only the first paragraph of a longer essay to consult. In other words, you had less information that you needed to predict with complete confidence, although you might have predicted well enough to predict the correct answer, *d*. What words and phrases clue you in that the entire essay is probably a thoughtful rumination?

The other three questions direct you to specific sentences, asking you to recognize stylistic features (Question 2), notice diction (Question 3), and analyze organization (Question 3). Question 2 is most dependent on your prior knowledge, since you have to choose from a list of terms not defined in the text. Students of rhetoric and of sentence structure will recognize *b*, a periodic sentence, as the correct term. (See pages 67–70) for explanations of rhetorically effective choices of sentence structure.) Question 3 depends on your ability to recognize metaphorical language since the correct answer *a*, shows how the phrase "registers of existence" is an implied comparison of the tombstones to birth and death registers. Question 4 asks you to capitalize on the predictions you probably have been making up to that point in the passage. Addison has been reading inscriptions, which strike him as satires. It's only a small step of prediction to move to the correct answer, *c*, and to detect that Addison is now making an explicit connection between the tombstone inscriptions and the descriptions of fallen or injured heroes in famous poems.

More About Prediction and Revision in Reading

The preceding sample of multiple-choice questions illustrates making predictions and revising them. It's a skill that improves with practice, but it essentially mirrors what readers do all the time, in all kinds of reading. They make decisions, formulate ideas, and revise them. The first question in the series, the one for which you had the least information, may have been the easiest to answer in fact because it required the most in terms of prediction and the least in terms of factual knowledge.

Often, a timed set of questions gives you little time to exercise revision, at least directly, and that's why when you answer questions or read for information that you need immediately, you often read the whole piece quickly to get the main idea and to set your predictions most accurately. One question often helps you answer the next with more skill, and so even in a timed reading, you revise as you go along, just as you do when you read more deliberately or when you write.

Here's one more example of reading and prediction, from Beryl Markham's memoir *West with the Night*, about her adventures as a pilot in Africa.

> How is it possible to bring order out of memory? I should like to begin at the beginning, patiently, like a weaver at his loom. I should like to say, "This is the place to start; there can be no other."
>
> But there are a hundred places to start for there are a hundred names—Mwanza, Serengetti, Nungwe, Molo, Nakuru. There are easily a hundred names, and I can begin best by choosing one of them—not because it is first nor of any importance in a wildly adventurous sense, but because here it happens to be, turned uppermost in my logbook. After all, I am no weaver. Weavers create. This is remembrance—revisitation; and names are keys that open corridors no longer fresh in the mind, but nonetheless familiar in the heart.

So the name shall be Nungwe—as good as any other—entered like this in the log, lending reality, if not order, to memory:

DATE—16/6/35

TYPE AIRCRAFT—Avro Avian

MARKINGS—VP—KAN

JOURNEY—Nairobi to Nungwe

TIME—3 hrs. 40 mins.

After that comes, PILOT: Self; and REMARKS—of which there were none. But there might have been.

The writer gives us readers lots of information to make guesses about in her opening. We come up with questions as we read: What is this memoir about? Why are the names so significant? What kind of person is she? What are the remarks left blank in her log? Will the memoir fill them in? Does she die in a plane crash? Our questions help propel us into the reading, help us read for meaning, and allow us to guess and revise those guesses as we read.

We're also thinking, consciously or not, about the writer's rhetoric. How does she engage us in the piece we're about to read? What does she want us to feel or to believe? What is she really writing about—planes or Africa or adventure or something else? We begin to consider, in other words, how Markham attempts to create her effects and how we respond to them.

A few examples from the opening illustrate how readers might take note of Markham's rhetoric. She begins with a **rhetorical question**. You may be familiar with that term (it came up in Chapter 3). It describes a question where no real answer is expected because it's a question either to which the speaker believes there *is* no real answer or to which the answer is implied in the question itself. It's a question designed for effect, to get the reader's attention, to heighten the moment. This question in particular does make readers stop for a minute to consider an answer. How *does* the mind impose order on all the memories it stores? Even though it is a rhetorical question, we sort of expect a response from the writer—maybe because it's the first line of the text—and she gives it to us in a fashion in the next line by telling us first what she can't do. She can't order her memory by beginning at the beginning.

Markham uses the **metaphor** of the weaver to make a comparison between the act of weaving and the act of writing about memories. She'd like to begin like the weaver, she tells us, because then she'd know exactly where and how to start. But, as she points out, remembering is different from weaving. Weaving has order; memory must create it. The weaving metaphor helps readers think about how Markham does decide to begin her story, not by beginning at the beginning, as the weaver must, but by picking up the loose thread of a name, and proceeding from there.

The **format** within the third paragraph—its typeface, sentence structure, paragraphing—is written to look like the actual entry from her pilot's logbook, and its effect is to give a feeling of actuality, of **verisimilitude,** to the memoir.

It feels as though Markham has stopped to consult her log, where she had recorded the bare details of the trip from Nairobi to the name she has picked to begin her story with, Nungwe. She establishes her point about **memory**, which we pick from the wealth of data in our brains more or less randomly, beginning with Nungwe because it's a name "as good as any other." And she ends this section with the one-line paragraph "But there might have been," leading us as readers to anticipate what comes next, the details her log omitted. She draws us in with that line, builds our curiosity and our beginning involvement.

As readers, we've done quite a bit of predicting before we turn the first page of the memoir. We predict adventure and perhaps danger, we predict many names and places of the exotic locales in Africa in the early part of the twentieth century, and we guess about Markham's background and personality. Our predicting leads us to read on. It allows us to begin to make meaning.

Whatever kind of reading you do, whether to complete an exam, acquire information, or be entertained, you write the text you read as you predict and revise in the process of interpretation.

Prediction and Revision in Writing: Writers as Readers

Like reading, writing involves the skills of predicting, working out hypotheses, and revising ideas. You already know a lot about how a piece of writing proceeds in a series of steps or stages. You have an idea or an assignment or maybe just a good opening line—and even that much material can amount to a hypothesis. You predict for yourself what kinds of detail you'll need to include, where you'll add a bit of **dialogue**, when you'll establish your argument.

"Sometimes I just begin," says a first-year college writing student. "I'm not sure where I'm headed, but writing a sentence or two kind of leads me on." When you begin to write, your predictions about where you're headed may not be formulated completely; you may simply have an assignment to write an argument about a topic or to analyze a character. You may have collected information about a topic and have at hand statistics or quotations from published sources but little idea of what you'll do with the data in front of you. If you let yourself begin to write without a definite **thesis statement** or outlined plan, you often will find what composition theorist Peter Elbow calls the "center of gravity," the place where you begin to locate what you want to say and how you'll say it. From that center, you begin to predict what you'll use, where you'll include information, what your voice should sound like on the page. In the final, finished composition, you may end up using very little of what you produce as **freewriting**, but the very process of doing it is productive—it's a great way to start the processes of predicting and revising that are so much a part of successful writing. As productive as freewriting is, however, it can also take time for a center to emerge or for a draft to take shape. Taking quick notes as you read an essay you'll be writing about—copying phrases, asking questions—is another way to begin the vital processes of predicting and revising.

Activity

In the last chapter, you read the opening paragraphs of Toni Morrison's novel *Sula.* Look back at that opening (pages 140–141), and then write a few lines of your own about a place you know of that no longer exists or exists only in your memory. A park where you used to play that's now a mall? A neighborhood that's changed? A store you used to walk to? Call up the place in your memory, and then write as quickly as you can for five or so minutes.

Now look back at what you've written. How does it sound to you? As you answer that question for yourself, as you read the text you've written, begin thinking about what you'd write next. Then write one more line.

The last line you write shows your prediction and revision. It might be a beginning center of gravity for your piece. Writers use what they've already written—and already read—to proceed to the next line or next chunk. Reading aloud helps, and hearing feedback from someone else helps too. Have your group read one another's paragraphs, asking group members to speculate on where they think the writing might go next.

You might choose to continue with this piece after hearing from your group. One thing you might discover in writing about the place that's disappeared is that you have more of an understanding of what Morrison is suggesting in her opening to *Sula* after having written about the issue yourself. You're a better reader because you've written.

More About Prediction and Revision in Writing

In writing and in discussing your writing with others, you exercise both the skills of prediction and revision. Writers typically think of revision in terms of whole texts, but just as with reading, revising writing is ongoing, occurring as soon as you write a word or a line. You make a revision so quickly that it's nearly unconscious. "I don't want to sound too mad," says a writer to herself. "I better not say the word *bitter*." "Go on with that quote," another writer says to himself. "Then you can use the last line to get you to the next point." Writers say things like this all the time to themselves, but they're seldom aware of them because they are almost always below the level of conscious thought. As you write, you can try to slow yourself down enough to hear yourself planning and revising. It's interesting to do, but eventually it will be too slow a process. We predict and revise far too quickly as readers and writers to be conscious all the time of what we're doing.

When you revise whole texts, or whole sections of a paper, you begin to be more conscious of how and why you're making changes. For some writers, this process is the most difficult part of writing. But it begins to seem easier once writers think of themselves as readers. As a reader, you might ask yourself the following: What do I like the best in my piece? What's the best line? Where does the piece come alive? Instead of revising by looking for what's wrong or missing in your draft, look for what's best, what you like. Begin to revise outward from the place you liked when you read it. That place is usually where you, the writer, hear your voice most clearly. Next time you're revising a draft of a paper you're working on, practice revision by beginning as we've suggested, with the sentence or section that feels the most accomplished. You'll be revising using what Welty calls your "reader-voice."

Here are some other suggestions for revising:

- If you have time, let the draft "rest" for a while—a day or a couple of hours—before you look at it again.

- Listen for your voice as you read to yourself a section of your draft. Places where you don't like the voice are usually spots where you've been vague, repetitious, or overly general.

- Get a friend or group member to read a part of your draft to you. Take note of what works and what doesn't as you listen.

Voice and Rhetoric

Writers who hear the reader-voice—in other words, writers who are able to become readers of the texts they write—are paying attention to the rhetoric of their writing. These writers think about how they sound to themselves, how they might sound to others, and how clearly they have communicated their point and their subject. They probably do not consider all these elements at once; in fact, they could stymie themselves if they attempted to think of them all at once; but during the process of writing a piece, all these rhetorical concerns emerge. When writers ask themselves or their writing group questions such as "How do I sound?" and "Does this sentence sound okay?" they are using voice to guide rhetorical choices. And voice is a good guide.

Peter Elbow talks about voice often in his discussions about writers and writing. In teaching writing, he realized that he and his students always liked best the writing that somehow sounded the most real. It had voice. Elbow suggests that writers begin to look for the places—the words, the lines, the paragraphs—where they hear the quality of voice that somehow makes the writing seem real to them. One way to do that is to ask others to tell you where they hear voice most clearly in your work. Another way is to read aloud or to simply listen hard as you read to yourself. "Writing with voice is writing into which someone has breathed," Elbow says.

Some writing, Elbow notes, has no voice: "Writing with no voice is dead, mechanical, faceless. It lacks any sound. Writing with no voice *may* be saying something important, or new; it may be logically organized; it may even be a work of genius. But it is as though the words came through some kind of mixer rather than being uttered by a person." You know this kind of writing; you've read it. Perhaps even written it. One of our students describes her own writing with no voice as "writing just to do the assignment. I don't feel like I own it because I don't care enough except to get it done."

What Elbow doesn't say is that writing with no voice is writing that doesn't pay attention to rhetoric. The reader of a piece of no-voice writing doesn't sense a person behind the words or anybody interesting. The writer hasn't created a relationship with the reader or the subject, or hasn't considered the context of the writing. In some writing, the voice may be fake rather than absent. And having a fake voice—too intimate, too academic, too arch—is the result of not understanding how to use rhetoric to illuminate ideas by creating relationships between reader and writer.

Most of the excerpts in this book have voice, we think, and that's why as readers we appreciate them. Some excerpts use personal examples as well as direct address to readers. Frank DeFord's column in Chapter 1 does those things. Others, like Gleick's *Chaos* excerpt, use no personal examples but establish a relationship of engagement with the subject and with the reader that feels authentic. It feels like writing that's been "breathed into." A piece with voice invites the reader to understand, to participate, to be convinced.

What We Hear When We Read and Write

Writers and readers respond to words, ideas, and arguments in a host of ways that depend on their own contexts—their education, their mood, their personality, their beliefs, their experience. Knowing that words were always tied to meaning for both the speaker and the hearer, Aristotle developed three categories to describe the tools a speaker might use in the process of inventing ideas and making choices. The categories, the three appeals that we introduced in Chapter 1 and explain further in Chapters 2 and 3, apply to the listener as well; they describe the ways that listeners are persuaded to the speaker's **point of view.** Aristotle described them this way:

> There are then these three means of effecting persuasion. The man who is to be in command of them must, it is clear, be able (1) to reason logically, (2) to understand human character and goodness in their various forms, and (3) to understand the emotions—that is, to name them and describe them, to know their causes and the way in which they are excited.

The Logical Appeal: Logos

A speaker can use logical reasoning—**logos**—to appeal to the reasoning function of an **audience.** Speakers who back up their claims with factual evidence and support from sources and who can lead listeners through a logical chain of events toward a conclusion emphasize logos. "Nine out of ten doctors agree," claims an advertisement for a painkiller, and readers are invited to conclude that since the percentage of experts who concur about the value of the product is overwhelming, they should agree on its value as well. Statistics, charts, graphs—all are used often to appeal to readers' sense of objectivity and reason.

Logical reasoning is the simplest way to persuade. A writer states a claim and then supports it, logically or empirically. In a deductive claim, or **deductive reasoning,** the statement comes before the support (even though logically it follows the proof) because the writer wants readers to evaluate the claim as they're reading along. The proof itself may be deductive or the result of **inductive reasoning;** it may begin with general principles and proceed with particulars that follow from those principles, or it may begin with examples (or experiments or cases) and generalize logically from them.

Here's another brief example from James Gleick's book, *Chaos.* (An excerpt from his book appears in Chapter 5.) This example demonstrates how deductive reasoning works in a logical argument.

> In fluid systems and mechanical systems, the nonlinear terms tend to be the features that people want to leave out when they try to get a good, simple understanding. Friction, for example. Without friction, a simple linear equation expresses the amount of energy you need to accelerate a hockey puck. With friction the relationship gets complicated, because the amount of energy changes depending on how fast the puck is already moving. Nonlinearity means that the act of playing the game has a way of changing the rules. You cannot assign a constant importance to friction, because its importance depends on speed. Speed, in turn, depends on friction. That changeability makes nonlinearity hard to calculate, but it also creates rich kinds of that twisted behavior that never occur in linear systems.

Stated as a **syllogism,** the **premises** and **conclusion** of this small paragraph might look something like this:

> The world is complex.
> Nonlinear systems in physics account for complexity.
> Nonlinear systems render a fuller account of the world.

Gleick proves his point with the example of friction and the illustration of friction with the hockey puck. Gleick doesn't state the first premise directly but, instead, assumes the audience already believes it. Gleick does, however, support the first premise with the proof that the friction example offers. The conclusion—that nonlinear systems create a fuller account of the way the world works—is stated directly and reinforces his statement that nonlinear systems in physics account for complexity. When we analyze Gleick's argument as a syllogism, we state the premises explicitly, even though Gleick himself doesn't, and we show how he moves logically from premise to statement to conclusion in order to bring readers to agreement.

The syllogism is an effective form of logical reasoning when the writer can't count on his readers to fill in any missing premises because the ideas are too complex, perhaps, or because a premise might be overlooked. Gleick's specialized subject matter and his desire to keep readers involved in that subject lead him to make his statements directly. Often in syllogisms, the premises are stated rather than implied to provide emphasis. For example, in the famous "Socrates is mortal" syllogism described in Chapter 2, Plato wanted to highlight Socrates's mortality, so he reinforced it by reminding his listeners that Socrates was a man. Writers have to be careful if they state all the premises, however; you've heard people dismiss arguments by saying that the speaker just "stated the obvious." Readers sometimes feel that they are being treated condescendingly if all premises, especially ones that are obvious or universally accepted, are stated.

The **enthymeme**, introduced in Chapter 2, is a kind of syllogism that writers employ continually when they're using logical reasoning, in part to avoid stating the obvious. As writers, we assume certain premises to be common knowledge, such as the fact that Socrates was a man or that *The Scarlet Letter* is a nineteenth-century novel. We use enthymemes as well to be more persuasive than we might be with the syllogism, omitting premises that might be rejected too quickly as obvious if they were stated directly. We invite readers into the argument by allowing them to fill in premises and to reach conclusions through logical progressions of ideas.

In analyzing something you've read, let's say a character in a novel, you use logical appeals when you quote the text and cite scenes from the novel or from secondary sources to support your ideas about the character. For example:

> Hester Prynne only seems to be a victim in *The Scarlet Letter*. In truth, she refuses the role of victim time and again as she acts on her own behalf and on behalf of her child. "Look you to it," she warns Dimmesdale when the town threatens to remove Pearl from her care. She becomes a valued member of her small community by making herself invaluable, at sick beds and in the rooms of the dying as well as in her skill at needlework, so much so that her letter of shame eventually seems to many to stand for "Able" or even "Angel." In his study of the novel, *The Office of the Scarlet Letter,* Sacvan Bercovitch describes Hester in just that way.

You can see in this excerpt the writer's use of logical support—quotations, scenes, and support from a book of literary criticism by Bercovitch—to aid the writer in making a claim about Hester's role in the novel. Readers are convinced by the reasoning behind the claim, reasoning that comes from the writer's careful, close reading of the work. Notice, too, the voice of the piece. The writer doesn't waffle: the reader knows exactly what the writer thinks about Hester's role in the novel and why.

When writers write academic prose, like Gleick's study of nonlinear physics or essays of literary analysis, they typically use logical reasoning. Readers anticipate facts, **data**, **examples**, and **logic** when they read writing meant to inform and convince them. Readers expect the voices of writers using logic to be reasoned as well, not too emotional, and not too intimate. (Of course, much nonfiction writing makes use of all the appeals, just as fiction does.) But other writing—fiction and literary memoir, for example—uses logos as well. Here's an example from Beryl Markham's memoir:

> "We fixed the runway," he said, "as well as we could."
>
> I nodded, looking into a lean-boned, sun-beaten face.
>
> "It's a good job," I assured him—"better than I had hoped for."
>
> "And we rigged up a windsock." He swung his arm in the direction of a slender pole whose base was surrounded by half a dozen flares. At the top of the pole hung a limp cylinder of cheap, white "Americani" cloth looking a bit like an amputated pajama leg.
>
> In such a breeze the cylinder ought to have been fully extended, but instead, and in defiance of the simplest laws of physics, it only dangled in shameless indifference to both the strength of the wind and its direction.
>
> Moving closer, I saw the lower end had been sewn as tightly shut as needle and thread could make it, so that, as an instrument intended to indicate wind tendency, it was rather less efficient than a pair of whole pajamas might have been.
>
> I explained this technical error of design to Ebert and, in the half-light of the oil torches, had the satisfaction of seeing his face relax into what I suspected was his first smile in a long, long time.

Markham explains her own logical reasoning here to demonstrate her competence and expertise. She's a pilot who knows both what a windsock does and how one must be rigged. Logically, the way the amateurs on the ground have put the windsock together won't work. Readers realize it, see its humor, and respond both to her knowledge and the good will of the people trying to help her as she lands her plane in the field.

Activity

Create a syllogism or enthymeme from the paragraph on *The Scarlet Letter.*

The Ethical Appeal: Ethos

When writers create a voice, the **persona** of their piece, they also create a relationship with readers that is based on a kind of trust. Writers ask readers to believe them, to bear with them, to listen to them because, they imply, they're trustworthy and believable, and they have good intentions. They use what Aristotle called the ethical appeal, ethos, by establishing their own accountability in the communicative act of speaking or writing. In any writing, then, ethos finds a place. Readers believe that James Gleick knows what he's talking about as he describes the history of chaos theory; he's established his background and knowledge early in the book, and his careful, reasoned tone and well-documented sources lead readers to accept his authority as a speaker. In the Beryl Markham excerpt just above, readers trust Markham's expertise as well as the goodwill she feels toward the men who've tried to help her.

But writers often highlight the ethical appeal in more direct ways than by creating a credible voice in their writing. If the issue to be discussed is highly contentious, if opinions on the best course of action vary widely, if facts themselves are hard to come by or misleading, writers often use their own sense of ethics and their readers' sense of ethics to persuade. The sentence "Ninety-nine percent of doctors agree" might be logical, but it depends for its effect on the fact that *doctors*, not random population groups or other professional people, agree on the brand of painkiller to use. Readers trust doctors to know about painkillers, and if doctors say a medical product is worthwhile, it's not only logical proof but ethical proof as well. In fact, the medical profession is regarded highly in a general way by many readers. If a doctor speaks, listeners might be more inclined to feel trust than if a person from some less highly regarded profession spoke.

The ethical appeal highlights the character of the speaker. Remember Quintilian's dictum about the "good man speaking well" (page 4). The "good" speaker is good because he or she is ethical, and readers depend on that goodness as they evaluate the argument.

Here's another excerpt from Markham's story that highlights the ethical appeal. She has visited the room of a man dying from blackwater fever, and this is a part of her conversation with him:

> The man on the bed was dying like that. He wanted to talk because it is possible to forget yourself if you talk, but not if you only lie and think.
>
> "Hastings," he said. "You must know Carl Hastings. He was a White Hunter for a while and then he settled down on a coffee plantation west of Ngong. I wonder if he ever married? He used to say he never would, but nobody believed him."
>
> "He did, though," I said. It was a name I had never heard, but it seemed a small enough gesture to lie about a nebulous Carl Hastings—even, if necessary, to give him a wife.
>
> In the four years Bergner had been away, the town of Nairobi had swelled and burst like a ripe seedpod. It was no longer so comfortably small that every inhabitant was a neighbor, or every name that of a friend.
>
> "I thought you knew him," Bergner said; "everybody knows Carl. And when you see him you can tell him he owes me five pounds. It's on a bet we made one Christmas in Mombasa. He bet he'd never get married—not in Africa, anyway. He said you could boast about living in a man's country, but you couldn't expect to find a marriageable woman in it!"
>
> "I'll tell him about it," I said; "he can send it by way of Kisumu."
>
> "That's right, by way of Kisumu."

Here, Markham tells a lie to comfort a dying man she doesn't even know, and readers respond to her kindness. We characterize her as a good person, and our trust in her as a speaker and a person increases as she describes her "small enough" gesture. Writers using the ethical appeal ask a reader to examine their character, to infer from their words the ideals or morals they hold dear. Writers using the ethical appeal make a strong link to their readers, as they suggest that the ideals they believe in are the same ones as, or are similar ones to, those values the readers hold themselves. "I would tell a lie like that," we say to ourselves, "if it could give a dying man a little pleasure or peace in his last moments." We like Markham's character because it responds to something in our own.

The Emotional Appeal: Pathos

The strongest, most direct, and thus most dramatic appeal writers make when they try to persuade their readers is the emotional appeal, or **pathos**. Aristotle calls on speakers to understand the emotions, to name them and describe them, "to know their causes and the way in which they are excited." Knowing about human emotions and understanding how those emotions are created within a person allow a speaker to find the words and the forms that appeal to the emotions the speaker wants to evoke.

We've heard and read many examples of the emotional appeal in our daily lives, in advertisements, in movies and on television, in political speeches, in sermons, and in editorials. Emotions are more immediate and sensory than logic or ethics, so we respond more readily when our emotions are involved. That's why, of course, appeals to the emotions, while dramatic, can also be dangerous. Groups have been incited to perform violent actions under the influence of a speaker who has moved them to anger or desperation. The emotions work quickly, and if speakers want an audience to act, not just think, they often make appeals to the emotions.

Think of advertisements you've seen recently on television or in magazines. One typical advertisement for automobiles shows a car with a backdrop of a beautiful sunset and a beautiful woman leaning on the hood. There's not much logical appeal in such an advertisement; neither the scenery nor the woman accompanies the car when a person buys it. But the emotional connection is clear. "If I drive such a car, might I not be able to go to places like the one shown in the picture? And if I'm the driver, might I not find someone who'd admire my choice enough to travel with me?" Love, lust, pride, excitement, and other emotions can all be provoked in the viewer captivated by the ad.

Here, from Markham's book, is one more example that highlights the emotional appeal. As you read, think of the emotions that the author feels and that she attempts to transmit to her readers.

> I patted Buller and he wagged his lump of a tail to say he understood the need for silence. Buller was my accomplice in everything. He was a past master at stealth and at more other things than any dog I ever owned or knew.
>
> His loyalty to me was undeviating, but I could never think of him as being a sentimental dog, a dog fit for a pretty story of the kind that tears the heartstrings off their pegs; he was too rough, too tough, and too aggressive.
>
> He was cynical toward life, and his black-and-white hide bore, in a cryptology of long, short, and semicircular scars, the history of his fighting career. He fought anything that needed to be fought, and when there was nothing immediately available in this category, he killed cats.

One night a leopard, no doubt the chosen avenger of his species, crept through the open door of my hut and abducted Buller from the foot of my bed. Buller weighed something over sixty-five pounds and most of it was nicely coordinated offensive equipment. The sound and the fury of the first round of that battle sometimes still ring in my ears. But the advantage was with the attacker. Before I could do much more than scramble out of bed, dog and leopard disappeared in the moonless night.

Markham begins this scene with a description of her dog, Buller, and her description is overtly unsentimental. She even notes that Buller himself is not a "sentimental dog" but a ferocious, though loyal, one. The scene that follows, where Buller is pulled from Markham's bed and dragged away by a leopard, is emotionally powerful because readers recognize in the description her love for the dog, her constant companion. Because she writes without exclamation points, in a matter-of-fact style, and with some humor—the leopard she imagines singled out to exact revenge on Buller—our emotional response is even stronger. We feel her terror and then sadness when she realizes Buller has been taken. If readers are animal lovers themselves, their response is even more emotional perhaps than for other readers. Markham uses understatement to heighten our reaction as we are left to imagine for a moment what might have happened to this independent, brave, and beloved animal.

One other example of emotional appeal and emotional response before we leave this section. You no doubt recall your own experience with September 2001, during the days after the attacks on the World Trade Center and the Pentagon. Everyone's emotions during those weeks were intense. You probably remember where you were when you first heard the news and remember as well your first feelings, initially of shock and disbelief, then horror and sadness as all of us began to learn the toll of human life these attacks exacted.

We've talked about how rhetoric operates in all kinds of communication, in images and pictures, in symbols and graphics as well as in words. And images often evoke intense emotional response. The American flag—so evident in those days flying at half-mast on public buildings, stuck in the coat pockets and car windows of millions of citizens, waving in the rubble of what was the World Trade Center, draping coffins of the victims—called up strong emotions: determination, pride, and belief. Lots of other images were used rhetorically in those days to express the writers' or artists' attitude and to connect emotionally with an audience numbed and saddened by the tragedy.

The *New Yorker* cover for the week of September 24, 2001, was one such powerful and emotional rhetorical statement. The cover was completely black, with just the *New Yorker* logo in white lettering at the top. Its blackness suggested tragedy and death, expressed the darkness and fear that many, especially in New York, felt after the planes crashed into the Twin Towers. The cover was so dark that readers might have missed the underlying image, but when they held the magazine at an angle or in strong light and looked at it intently, they realized that the cover was not black but dark gray. Beneath the gray was a darker image, the silhouette of the towers. The image was all the more chilling because viewers discovered it on their own, and the emotions that discovery provokes are extremely powerful.

Readers experience a variety of emotions in response to writers' use of images and other verbal techniques. The variety depends on the readers' personal beliefs, desires, or fears. But writers count on readers to feel at least somewhat similar to the way they feel. That's why Socrates's advice to the thinker to "know thyself" has long been the surest means that writers have for understanding how to appeal to readers and that readers have for understanding how to negotiate and respond to those appeals.

Activity

Look at some recent advertisements to see if you can find examples of emotional appeals. Share them with your group. See if together you can figure out how appeals to logic or to ethics might also be part of the ads you've brought in.

Activity

Recall a stirring speech from a movie you've seen, and analyze it for its emotional appeal. *Braveheart* has such a scene; *Titanic* does, too. Think about the effect of the speech on you as a viewer. Do you respond positively to it? Are you critical of it? (If you find yourself critiquing the scene rather than responding positively to it, something in the words or the ideas behind the words might contradict your own sense of logic or ethics.)

The Appeals Combined

Probably no piece of discourse exhibits only one of the three kinds of appeals, for writers and readers bring a complex set of understandings, experiences, and kinds of knowledge to bear on what they write and read. We've isolated bits of discourse in the pieces above to demonstrate how one appeal might be highlighted for readers and promoted by writers, but it's also true that you may have responded in emotional ways to our example of ethos or ethically to our illustration of pathos. To demonstrate how all the appeals might combine for you as a reader, we've chosen an example of a famous speech, one many of you have read or have heard at least the first few lines of. It's Mark Antony's speech in Shakespeare's play *Julius Caesar*. Antony is speaking at Caesar's funeral, as his friend and follower, and the speech Shakespeare creates for him becomes an elegy to Antony's sovereign and friend.

But it's more than that. Caesar has been assassinated by Brutus and other compatriots who believed that Caesar had become a tyrant and a danger to Rome. The people of Rome have agreed, and they are at first hostile to Antony, whom they see as an **apologist** for Caesar's ambitious, imperious rule. Antony wants to change their minds, but he has to operate subtly and carefully. As you read, notice how Antony uses the rhetorical device of **repetition,** as well as **irony,** to turn the crowd from its belief in Brutus and the rightness of his cause to anger against him.

> ANTONY. Friends, Romans, countrymen, lend me your ears;
> I come to bury Caesar, not to praise him.
> The evil that men do lives after them;
> The good is oft interred with their bones;
> So let it be with Caesar. The noble Brutus
> Hath told you Caesar was ambitious;
> If it were so, it was a grievous fault,
> And grievously hath Caesar answer'd it.
> Here, under leave of Brutus and the rest—
> For Brutus is an honorable man;
> So are they all, all honorable men—
> Come I to speak in Caesar's funeral.
> He was my friend, faithful and just to me;
> But Brutus says he was ambitious;
> And Brutus is an honorable man.
> He hath brought many captives home to Rome,
> Whose ransoms did the general coffers fill:
> Did this in Caesar seem ambitious?
> When that the poor have cried, Caesar hath wept:
> Ambition should be made of sterner stuff:
> Yet Brutus says he was ambitious;
> And Brutus is an honorable man.
> You all did see that on the Lupercal
> I thrice presented him a kingly crown,
> Which he did thrice refuse: was this ambitious?
> Yet Brutus says he was ambitious;
> And, sure, he is an honorable man.
> I speak not to disprove what Brutus spoke,
> But here I am to speak what I do know.
> You all did love him once, not without cause:
> What cause withholds you then, to mourn for him?
> O judgment! Thou art fled to brutish beasts,

And men have lost their reason. Bear with me;

My heart is in the coffin there with Caesar,

And I must pause till it come back to me.

FIRST CITIZEN. Methinks there is much reason in his sayings.

SECOND CITIZEN. If thou consider rightly of the matter, Caesar has had great wrong.

THIRD CITIZEN. Has he, masters? I fear there will be a worse come in his place.

FOURTH CITIZEN. Mark'd ye his words? He would not take the crown;

Therefore' tis certain he was not ambitious.

FIRST CITIZEN. If it be found so, some will dear abide it.

SECOND CITIZEN. Poor soul: his eyes are red as fire with weeping.

THIRD CITIZEN. There's not a nobler man in Rome than Antony.

FOURTH CITIZEN. Now mark him, he begins again to speak.

Act III, scene 2

Antony is successful in changing the minds of Roman citizens about the character both of Caesar and of Brutus and his companions. By the end of his oration, which continues for several more pages, the crowd is inflamed with the desire to find and kill Brutus—"We'll burn the house of Brutus!" "We'll mutiny!"—before the speech a hero and after a traitorous villain. In those remaining lines, Antony stops to gather his emotions, mentions Caesar's will but delays until the end of the speech revealing its contents, asks the listeners to examine Caesar's wounds with him, and finally reads the will, which leaves money to each citizen and bequeaths Caesar's private gardens to the public. "I am no orator, as Brutus is," Antony tells them, but the crowd's reaction and the response of readers and audiences suggest how powerful a speaker Antony is, how much he has understood and used voice.

Mark Antony's manipulation of the audience through rhetorical appeals shows how speakers who understand their listeners can move them to belief and action. Antony understands his audience, perhaps because he understands himself. By the end of the scene, his voice and the voice of the people become one.

Here's one more example of a speech using the appeals in complex and interesting ways. It's from Sojourner Truth's speech to the Women's Rights Convention in Cleveland, Ohio, in 1851. Sojourner Truth, a former slave, was speaking to a group of men and women about the need for women's suffrage. Many men in the audience had jeered at earlier speakers and called out counter-arguments as Sojourner Truth began speaking herself. In some versions of this speech, the recorder of the speech (Truth herself could not read or write) intersperses her own commentary about Truth's actions and gestures as well as crowd reaction in much the same way that Shakespeare writes of the crowd's reaction to Antony's plea. Both Antony and Truth are speaking to a crowd at least partially and initially hostile. As you read, see if you discover other similar patterns in the speeches. (For two other versions of this speech, see pages 278–279.)

AND AIN'T I A WOMAN?

Well children, where there is so much racket there must be somethin' out o'kilter. I think that' twixt the Negroes of the North and the South and the women at the North, all talkin' bout rights, the white men will be in a fix pretty soon. But what's all this here talkin' bout?

That man over there say that women needs to be helped into carriages, and lifted over ditches, and to have the best place everywhere. Nobody ever helps me into carriages, or over mud-puddles, or give me any best place! And ain't I a woman? Look at me! Look at my arm! I have ploughed, and planted, and gathered into barns, and no man could head me! And ain't I a woman? I could work as much and eat as much as a man—when I could get it—and bear the lash as well! And ain't I a woman? I have borne thirteen children, and seen 'em mos' all sold off to slavery, and when I cried out with my mother's grief, none but Jesus heard me! And ain't I a woman?

Then they talk about this thing in the head; what's this they call it? ["Intellect," whispered some one near.] That's it honey. What's that got to do with women's rights or Negro's rights? If my cup won't hold but a pint and yours holds a quart, wouldn't you be mean not to let me have my little measure full?

Then that little man in black there, he says women can't have as much rights as men, cause Christ wasn't a woman! Where did your Christ come from? Where did your Christ come from? From God and a woman! Man had nothin' to do with Him.

If the first woman God ever made was strong enough to turn the world upside down all alone, these women together ought to be able to turn it back and get it right side up again; and now they is asking to do it, they better let 'em. Bliged to you for hearin' me, and now ole Sojourner hasn't got nothin' more to say.

Activity

Examine the excerpt of Mark Antony's speech for the three appeals. Note spots where you find those appeals, and talk together in your group about your reasons for selecting those lines. Notice when in the speech Antony uses which appeals. Consider the responses of the citizens to what they have heard.

Activity

Examine one of your own compositions for the three appeals. Consider your format and organization, your **diction**, and your examples. Analyze your rhetoric. Or trade compositions with a classmate to locate the appeals and their effect on you as a reader.

Reading, Writing, and Synthesis: The Researched Argument

One particular type of writing that you will frequently need to produce in college courses is the researched argument, also called the researched essay and the synthesis essay. In this kind of writing, you state your own position on a question, problem, or issue and develop that position by integrating ideas, information, and perspectives from sources, as well as by providing your own reasoning and explanation. In some courses, the assignment will include the source materials for you to synthesize in your essay. In other courses, you will learn how to find relevant and useful sources. No matter how they are labeled or whether the sources are provided versus searched for, all researched arguments have one thing in common: In them, you, the writer, do more than ~~imply~~ find tidbits of ideas by others and drop them into your paper. You must develop your own argument and integrate material from the sources into it.

Writing the researched argument is the ultimate readers-as-writers/writers-as-readers task. You must read the source materials critically, making meaning by predicting and revising. You must analyze the appeals that the sources make, looking at *logos, ethos,* and *pathos* working in isolation and in combination. You must think carefully about your own position, predicting how readers are going to respond to it. And you must monitor how you modify or expand your initial position as you integrate the source material into it.

Tackling the Researched Argument

How should you tackle the task of writing a researched argument about a question, problem, or issue? Here are six moves you can make. (Notice we hesitate to call them "steps" or "stages"—you might want to do them in the order listed here, but you might need to shift the moves around to suit your needs.)

- First, read the assignment carefully, making notes about exactly what the assignment calls for in terms of purpose, audience, and **genre**. Also preview the sources, and note any initial ideas that they evoke.

- Second, analyze each source, using methods that we have described throughout this book: What claim do you see each source making? What evidence do you see each source offering in support of its claim? What unspoken **assumptions** or beliefs enable you to use the data in the source to support its claim? (Notice that these questions, raised in Chapter 2, lead you to analyze the enthymeme sitting at the center of each source.)

- Third, as you consider the assignment and the sources, generalize about your *potential* stands on the question, problem, or issue: What are two or three possible positions that you *could* take? Which of these positions do you really *want* to take?

- Fourth—and here is where the synthesis really begins—converse (imaginatively) with the author or creator of each source: If you were to argue position A, what would the author or creator of each source say in response to that plan? If you were to argue position B, what would the author or creator say then?

- Fifth, continually modify, shape, and finesse your thinking on the basis of these imaginary conversations, and decide on one position, which will serve as a central contention, a **thesis**, that is as sophisticated and robust as the topic demands.

- Sixth, write an essay in which you argue your position, incorporating the "conversations" you have had with the sources.

Assessing a Researched Argument

What are the characteristics of an exemplary researched argument? Notice first of all that it is not an examination answer, one that simply answers the question as straightforwardly as possible. It is an essay, one in which your argument is central, and the sources support your argument—you control them, not they you. Here are some other important characteristics of the genre:

- It assumes its readers are educated, curious adults who enjoy conversing about challenging issues.

- It assumes its readers have not read the assignment or the sources.

- It begins by providing some context, some background, on the issue at hand.

- It puts forth a central contention, a thesis, that is robust enough to do justice to the topic.

- It often provides an overview of what might be said in support of the thesis before going into detail, and it acknowledges the possibility of opposing views.

- It provides explanation and context for any source material it cites rather than simply dropping the material into the essay.

- It often says implicitly to its readers, "Let's think through this issue together"; therefore, the essay contains effective transitions.

Activity

Consider carefully the following researched argument assignment, presented by Rich Glowacki to his students in Bellevue, Washington. Then examine the sources and the response, starting on pages 186–187, by one of Glowacki's students.

> **DIRECTIONS:**   The following prompt is based on the accompanying sources. This question requires you to integrate a variety of sources into a coherent, well-written argumentative essay. Refer to the sources to support your position; avoid mere paraphrase or summary. Your argument should be central; the sources should support this argument.
>
> **INTRODUCTION:**   As America develops and changes as a nation, the perception of what constitutes progress becomes varied and complex. Progress could simply be measured by technological advances. Is this view of progress valid? Has America progressed? Are there other ways of measuring progress?
>
> **ASSIGNMENT:**   Carefully consider the above introduction, and examine the following sources. Then, in an essay synthesizing at least three of the following sources and also your own observations, take a position that agrees with, disputes, or modifies the claim that America was and is synonymous with progress.

SOURCE A

Ben Franklin

Excerpted from *Autobiography,* "Arriving at Moral Perfection"

It was about this time I conceiv'd the bold and arduous project of arriving at moral perfection. I wish'd to live without committing any fault at any time; I would conquer all that either natural inclination, custom, or company might lead me into. As I knew, or thought I knew, what was right and wrong, I did not see why I might not always do the one and avoid the other. But I soon found I had undertaken a task of more difficulty than I had imagined. While my care was employ'd in guarding against one fault, I was often surprised by another; habit took the advantage of inattention; inclination was sometimes too strong for reason. I concluded, at length, that the mere speculative conviction that it was our interest to be completely virtuous was not sufficient to prevent our slipping; and that the contrary habits must be broken, and good ones acquired and established, before we can have any dependence on a steady, uniform rectitude of conduct. For this purpose I therefore contrived the following method. . . .

I included under thirteen names of virtues all that at that time occurr'd to me as necessary or desirable, and annexed to each a short precept, which fully express'd the extent I gave to its meaning.

These names of virtues, with their precepts, were

1. Temperance. Eat not to dullness; drink not to elevation.
2. Silence. Speak not but what may benefit others or yourself; avoid trifling conversation.
3. Order. Let all your things have their places; let each part of your business have its time.
4. Resolution. Resolve to perform what you ought; perform without fail what you resolve.
5. Frugality. Make no expense but to do good to others or yourself; i.e., waste nothing.
6. Industry. Lose no time; be always employ'd in something useful; cut off all unnecessary actions.
7. Sincerity. Use no hurtful deceit; think innocently and justly, and, if you speak, speak accordingly.
8. Justice. Wrong none by doing injuries or omitting the benefits that are your duty.
9. Moderation. Avoid extremes; forbear resenting injuries so much as you think they deserve.
10. Cleanliness. Tolerate no uncleanliness in body, clothes, or habitation.
11. Tranquility. Be not disturbed at trifles, or at accidents common or unavoidable.
12. Chastity. Rarely use venery but for health or offspring, never to dullness, weakness, or the injury of your own or another's peace or reputation.
13. Humility. Imitate Jesus and Socrates.

SOURCE B

H. D. Thoreau

Excerpted from *Walden,* "Where I Lived, and What I Lived For"

Men think that it is essential that the nation have commerce, and export ice, and talk through a telegraph, and ride thirty miles an hour, without a doubt, whether they do or not; but whether we should live like baboons or like men is a little uncertain. If we do not get out sleepers, and forge rails, and devote days and nights to the work, but go to tinkering upon our lives to improve them, who will build railroads? And if railroads are not built, how shall we get to heaven in season? But if we stay at home and mind our business, who will want railroads? We do not ride on the railroad; it rides upon us. Did you ever think what those sleepers are that underlie the railroad? Each one is a man, an Irishman, or a Yankee man. The rails are laid on them, and they are covered with sand, and the cars run smoothly over them. They are sound sleepers, I assure you. And every few years a new lot is laid down and run over; so that, if some have the pleasure of riding on a rail, others have the misfortune to be ridden upon. And when they run over a man that is walking in his sleep, a supernumerary sleeper in the wrong position, and wake him up, they suddenly stop the cars, and make a hue and cry about it, as if this were an exception. I am glad to know that it takes a gang of men for every five miles to keep the sleepers down and level in their beds as it is, for this is a sign that they may sometime get up again.

SOURCE C

Walt Whitman

"To a Locomotive in Winter"

Thee for my recitative,
Thee in the driving storm even as now, the snow, the winter-day declining,
Thee in thy panoply, thy measur'd dual throbbing and thy beat convulsive,
Thy black cylindric body, golden brass and silvery steel,
Thy ponderous side-bars, parallel and connecting rods, gyrating, shuttling at
    thy sides,
Thy metrical, now swelling pant and roar, now tapering in the distance,
Thy great protruding headlight fix'd in front,
Thy long, pale, floating vapor-pennants, tinged with delicate purple,
The dense and murky clouds out-belching from thy smoke-stack.
Thy knitted frame, thy springs and valves, the tremulous twinkle of thy wheels,
Thy train of cars behind, obedient, merrily following,
Through gale or calm, now swift, now slack, yet steadily careening;
Type of the modern—emblem of motion and power—pulse of the continent,
For once come serve the Muse and merge in verse, even as here I see thee,
With storm and buffeting gusts of wind and falling snow,
By day thy warning ringing bell to sound its notes,
By night thy silent signal lamps to swing.

Fierce-throated beauty!
Roll through my chant with all thy lawless music, thy swinging lamps at night,
Thy madly-whistled laughter, echoing, rumbling like an earthquake, rousing all,
Law of thyself complete, thine old track firmly holding,
(No sweetness debonair of tearful harp or glib piano thine,)
Thy trills and shrieks by rocks and hills return'd,
Launch'd o'er the prairies wide, across the lakes,
To the free skies unpent and glad and strong.

SOURCE D

Lester Ward

Excerpted from "Mind as a Social Factor," 1884

If nature's process is rightly named natural selection, man's process is artificial selection. The survival of the fittest is simply the survival of the strong, which implies, and might as well be called, the destruction of the weak. And if nature progresses through the destruction of the weak, man progresses through the protection of the weak. This is the essential distinction.

SOURCE E

George Bancroft

Excerpted from "The Office of People in Art, Government, and Religion" (an oration delivered before the Adelphi Society of Williamson College, in August of 1835)

The universality of the intellectual and moral powers and the necessity of their development for the progress of the race proclaim the great doctrine of the natural right of every human being to moral and intellectual culture. It is the glory of our fathers to have established in their laws the equal claims of every child to the public care of its morals and its mind. From this principle we may deduce the universal right to leisure; that is, to time not appropriated to material purposes, but reserved for the culture of the moral affections and the mind. It does not tolerate the exclusive enjoyment of leisure by a privileged class, but, defending the rights of labor, would suffer none to sacrifice the higher purposes of existence in unceasing toil for that which is not life. Such is the voice of nature; such the conscious claim of the human mind. The universe opens its pages to every eye; the music of creation rebounds in every ear; the glorious lessons of immortal truth that are written in the sky and on the earth address themselves to every mind, and claim attention from every human being. God has made man upright that he might look before and after; and he calls upon everyone not merely to labor, but to reflect.

SOURCE F

Attributed to Calvin Coolidge, 30th President of the United States (1923–1929)

The man who builds a factory builds a temple. The man who works there worships there, and to each is due not scorn and blame but reverence and praise.

Sources continue on the next page.

SOURCE G

Charles Sheeler's *American Landscape* (1930)

SOURCE H

Excerpted from the *Progressive Party Platform of 1912*

The supreme duty of the Nation is the conservation of human resources through an enlightened measure of social and industrial justice. We pledge ourselves to work unceasingly in State and Nation for:

Effective legislation looking to the prevention of industrial accidents, occupational diseases, overwork, involuntary unemployment, and other injurious effects incident to modern industry;

The fixing of minimum safety and health standards for the various occupations, and the exercise of the public authority of State and Nation including the Federal control over interstate commerce, and the taxing power, to maintain such standards;

The prohibition of child labor;

Minimum wage standards for working women, to provide a "living wage" in all industrial occupations;

The general prohibition of night work for women and the establishment of an eight-hour day for women and young persons;

One day's rest in seven for all wage workers;

Publicity as to wages, hours and conditions of labor; full reports upon industrial accidents and diseases, and the opening to public inspection of all tallies, weights, measures and check systems on labor products;

Standards of compensation for death by industrial accident and injury and trade disease which will transfer the burden of lost earning from the families of working people to the industry, and thus to the community;

The protections of home life against the hazards of sickness, irregular employment and old age through the adoption of a system of social insurance adapted to American use;

The development of creative labor power of America by lifting the last load of illiteracy from American youth and establishing continuation schools for industrial education under public control and encouraging agricultural education and demonstration in rural schools;

The establishment of industrial research laboratories to put the methods and discoveries of science at the service of American producers;

We favor the organization of workers, men and women, as a means of protecting their progress. . . .

SOURCE I

Excerpted from the PBS *American Experience Technology Timeline*

1794 Cotton Gin   Eli Whitney patents his machine to comb and deseed bolls of cotton. His invention makes possible a revolution in the cotton industry and the rise of "King Cotton" as the main cash crop in the South. . . .

1807 Steamboat   Robert Fulton . . . opens American rivers to two-way travel. His steamboat the "Clermont" travels 150 miles upstream between New York and Albany at an average speed of 5 mph.

1814 Plough   Farmers had furrowed the rocky soil of New England with wooden-tipped ploughs. John Jethro Woods of Poplar Ridge, New York, creates a plough with a replaceable cast-iron tip, making farming in America easier.

1842 Ether Anesthesia   Crawford Williamson Long, of Jefferson, Georgia, performs the first operation using an ether-based anesthesia, when he removes a tumor from the neck of Mr. James Yenabla. Long will not reveal his discovery until 1849.

1860 Repeating Rifle   B. Tyler Henry, chief designer for Oliver Fisher Winchester's arms company, adapts a breech-loading rifle invented by Walter B. Hunt and creates a new lever action repeating rifle. First known as the Henry, the rifle will soon be famous as simply the Winchester.

1876 Telephone   Alexander Graham Bell patents his telephone, built with the assistance of young self-trained engineer Thomas A. Watson.

1879 Incandescent Light Bulb   Backed by $30,000 in research funds provided by investors including J. P. Morgan and the Vanderbilts, Thomas Edison perfects an incandescent light bulb.

1884 Thrill Ride   L. N. Thompson, founder of Coney Island's Luna Park, invites the first passengers to board his new thrill ride, the roller coaster. Thompson calls his new attraction the Switchback.

1903 Airplane   At Kitty Hawk, North Carolina, brothers Orville and Wilbur Wright break the powered flight barrier with their gasoline-powered "Flyer I." The first powered, sustained, and controlled airplane flight in history lasts 12 seconds.

1908 Model T   Car maker Henry Ford introduces his Model T automobile. By 1927, when it is discontinued, 15.5 million Model T's will be sold in the U.S. Ford owes much of his success to his improved assembly line process. . . .

1927 Television   Philo Farnsworth demonstrates the first television for potential investors by broadcasting the image of a dollar sign.

1942 Atomic Reaction   A team working under Enrico Fermi at the University of Chicago produces the first controlled, self-sustaining nuclear chain reaction. This experiment and others will result in the development of the atomic bomb.

1958 Explorer I   Three months after the Soviet Union began the Space Age by launching *Sputnik*, the U.S. responds by sending the *Explorer I* satellite into orbit.

1960 Laser   Working at Hughes Research Laboratories, physicist Theodore H. Maiman creates the first laser. The core of his laser consists of a man-made ruby—a material that had been judged unsuitable by other scientists, who rejected crystal cores in favor of various gases.

1972 Video Game   Pong, one of the first mass-produced video games, has become the rage.

1975 Microsoft   Bill Gates and Paul Allen form . . . Microsoft to write computer software. They sell their first software to Ed Roberts at MIT, which has produced the Altair 8800, the first microprocessor-based computer.

1982 Artificial Heart   Dr. Robert Jarvik implants a permanent artificial heart, the Jarvik 7, into Dr. Barney Clark. The heart, powered by an external compressor, keeps Clark alive for 112 days.

1985 Genetic Engineering   The USDA gives the go-ahead for the sale of the first genetically altered organism. The rapidly growing biotech industry will seek numerous patents, including one for a tomato that can be shipped when ripe.

SOURCE J

Taken from <http://www.solidwastedistrict.com/information/uswaste.html>

NATIONAL WASTE TRENDS

How much waste do you produce each day? How about 4.4 lbs? That's the average amount of waste generated, per person, per day in the United States in 2001. In total,

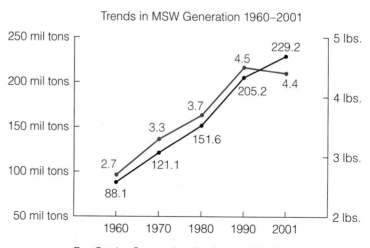

Trends in MSW Generation 1960–2001

we produced some 229 million tons of waste in 2001 alone, of which Indiana contributed some 18 million tons. Sounds like a lot? Well, it is. And like Indiana state numbers, the national numbers have been steadily growing for the past several decades.

As the graph clearly indicates, solid waste generation has nearly tripled in the United States since 1960, increasing from 88.1 million tons to 229.2 million tons. What's the cause of this upward trend? is it just a result of increased population? Not quite. As the blue line indicates, our per capita waste generation has also increased, from 2.7 lbs/person/day to 4.5 lbs/person/day.

SOURCE K

Taken from Bureau of Economic Analysis Web site

<www.bea.gov/newsreleases/national/gdp/gdpnewsrelease>

GROWTH ACCELERATES IN THE SECOND QUARTER

"Advance" Estimate of GDP

Real gross domestic product (GDP) increased 3.4 percent in the second quarter of 2007 after increasing 0.6 percent (revised) in the first, according to estimates released today [July 27, 2007] by the Bureau of Economic Analysis.

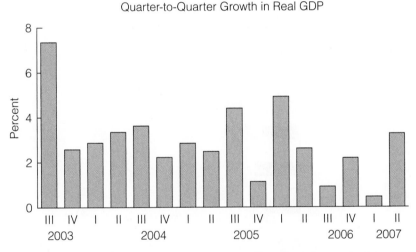

Real GDP growth is measured at seasonally adjusted annual rates.

The acceleration in real GDP growth reflected the following:

- Net exports turned up: exports accelerated, and imports turned down.
- Federal government defense spending and inventory investment turned up.
- Nonresidential fixed investment, mostly structures, accelerated.

SOURCE L

Taken from <http://www.census.gov/population/socdemo/education/phct41/us.pdf>

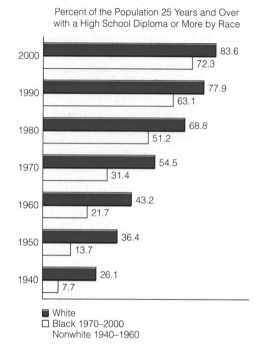

Percent of the Population 25 Years and Over
with a High School Diploma or More by Race

■ White
□ Black 1970–2000
Nonwhite 1940–1960

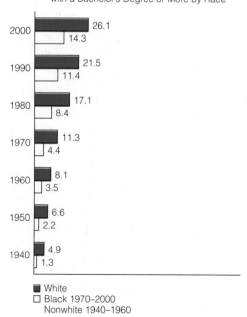

Percent of the Population 25 Years and Over
with a Bachelor's Degree or More by Race

■ White
□ Black 1970–2000
Nonwhite 1940–1960

RESEARCHED ARGUMENT: Here is a researched argument based on the preceding sources. In your group, discuss how you would follow the six moves outlined on pages 177–178 if you were working on this project, and assess the degree to which the student's researched essay fulfills the characteristics of the genre.

THE AMERICAN DREAM: IS IT SIMPLY TECHNOLOGICAL PROGRESS?

America—the American Dream—is often equated with the progress and betterment of the whole world. From America, supposedly, flow justice, technology, and social development to deprived countries and societies worldwide. It is true that America has been a source of technological leaps, especially in the computer age. But has it continued to breed the justice and moral and social progress that the phrase *the American Dream* so romantically conjures up? While America was and is synonymous with technological and industrial advances, it may be fair to say that it has ceased to be synonymous with true social and moral progress, in part because of the emphasis America places on industrial excellence.

If progress is defined in terms of technological and industrial development, America is and was synonymous with progress indeed. As source I indicates, America has been the birthplace of such monumental inventions as the airplane, the steamboat, and the light bulb. It continues to churn out revolutionary technology that has literally transformed our communications networks—a stark example being the microprocessor-based computer and its many applications. Surely, technologically, America is rife with valuable progressive developments. And, as the chart in Source K illustrates, gross domestic product is also on the increase again. Inventions are not the only mark of our progress; so is the economic value of each person. In America, truly, as Calvin Coolidge says, "The man who builds a factory builds a temple. The man who works there worships there, and to each is due not scorn and blame but reverence and praise" (source F).

But is it appropriate—or even desirable—to compare the factory, the symbol of our industrial progress, to a holy place? Has America placed our capitalist economy on such a high pedestal that it has become our God? Charles Sheeler's painting, *American Landscape*, suggests that we have turned the natural landscape into a dry, emotionless industrial plant, chugging out smoke into the once-clean air. As our priorities have focused more and more on our industry, it seems that other kinds of progress have fallen off.

America is certainly no longer, if ever it was, a symbol of moral and social progress. As Thoreau writes, "Did you ever think what those sleepers are that underlie the railroad? Each one is a man. . . ." (source B). We have spent so much time on our technological progress that our moral progress is undermined. What were the Irish and Chinese workers treated like as they slaved over the creation of a railroad, all so that the wealthy could ride faster and in more luxury, or so that more goods could be hauled from one side of the nation to the other? Even today, what do people give up so that they can gain a partnership in their firm—don't they give up family and religious or moral values much too often? More and more technology is pointed at our luxury. But what did the invention of the video game or the repeating rifle, both listed as technological advances in source I, do for our society?

Each made violence cheap and thrilling. Socially, there is a remarkable difference between the marketing millionaires and the family that worries where the next meal will come from. Is this progress?

"All men are created equal," our founding fathers proclaimed. This very nation was built on principles of liberty and justice and a deep-seated moral conviction to follow God. The track of time seems to have worn away at our perception of what true progress is. What is left to be determined is whether we will follow the American Dream that our forefathers had in mind or if we will continue to make industrial progress our all.

Interchapter

6

Overview of the Major Points in Chapter 6

- Both readers and writers listen for the voice of a text in order to interpret the text and to make decisions about what might come next in the text. Listening for the "reader-voice" helps readers and writers test the effectiveness of their texts.

- Words are signs.

- Freewriting helps readers create meanings for texts they read.

- Writers read their own texts as they emerge and use what they've written to guide subsequent writing decisions.

- Active readers co-create the texts they read.

- To complete the transaction between reader and writer, both make use of and respond to rhetorical appeals.

Activities and Discussion Questions for Chapter 6   Use these questions and comments as guides for your own discussion and writing about these works.

Henry David Thoreau, "On the Duty of Civil Disobedience" (published 1849)

The text appears on pages 222–237. In your group, discuss the following questions. You might use some of these questions as the basis for a well-organized essay or journal entry.

1. Identify a section of Thoreau's essay that you find especially dramatic or effective. Read it aloud to your group. How does your voice reading the section change or enrich the meaning of the passage?

2. After rereading the first few paragraphs of the essay, stop to write a response to what you've read, concentrating on the phrases or the positions you hear emerging in Thoreau's argument. How does your piece of writing reinforce or challenge Thoreau's points?

3. Freewrite about Thoreau's essay. Read back over your freewriting, and then write one more sentence. Make that sentence the beginning point for your group's discussion of "Civil Disobedience."

4. How would you define Thoreau's primary appeal to you as a reader? Find examples where Thoreau's use of logic, ethics, or emotion strikes you as effective or where it seems ineffective. Discuss in your group how the appeals work differently for different readers.

5. What are some unstated premises that Thoreau implies in making his argument? Create a syllogism or an enthymeme from one of the points Thoreau makes. Do you agree with the conclusion?

Eavan Boland, "It's a Woman's World" (published 1982)

The text appears on pages 238–239. In your group, discuss the following questions. You might use some of these questions as the basis for a well-organized essay or journal entry.

1. How do you react to the use of *we* and *our*, first-person plural, in the poem? Where does it place you as a reader?

2. Write a short essay that explains how individual word choices in the poem affect your emotions or opinions as your read.

3. How do you feel about the word *outrage* in stanza 11? Write a response that explains Boland's use of the term and your reaction to it.

4. Create an enthymeme to explain Boland's argument in the poem. Discuss these enthymemes in your group as beginning points for an essay on the rhetoric Boland chooses as she writes the poem.

Alice Walker, "Everyday Use" (published 1973)

The text appears on pages 240–246. In your group, discuss the following questions. You might use some of these questions as the basis for a well-organized essay or journal entry.

1. Freewrite briefly about the very general issue of family relationships or sibling relationships. Read at least a few sentences of your response aloud to your group, and discuss how the writing helps you think about the issues of family present in Walker's story.

2. Read aloud a passage where the "I" narrator seems to be an especially strong character and the "you" being addressed seems especially present. What does the reading suggest to you about the relationship between the reader and the speaker?

3. Ask some questions that you don't think this text completely answers. See if you can answer some of those questions with your group or in a journal entry.

4. Consider the ending of the story, looking back to see how the ending is prepared for in earlier sections. If you can come up with a different ending for the story, rewrite the ending, trying to achieve Walker's tone and using Walker's narrator.

Rhetoric in Narrative

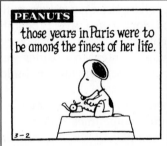

PEANUTS reprinted by permission of United Feature Syndicate, Inc.

> Narrative has never been merely entertainment for me. It is, I believe, one of the principal ways we absorb knowledge.
>
> Toni Morrison, *Nobel Prize lecture*

In her Nobel Prize lecture in 1990, found on pages 259–264, Toni Morrison asked her **audience** to think about the way readers use **narrative** to understand ideas and to gather knowledge about the way a story gets told and about the uses of language to communicate ideas, argue **claims**, and move to action. Morrison is interested in the **rhetoric** of the story—its **aim** and its **effect**. As Morrison says in her speech, "The vitality of language lies in its ability to limn the actual, imagined and possible lives of its speakers, readers, writers."

Morrison emphasizes language as the connecting medium between writer and reader. Not just the subject of the tale but also the art of its telling will determine how readers "absorb knowledge." Morrison underscores the importance of rhetoric as a tool for writers and readers of all kinds of narratives, both fictional and nonfictional. The language of a crafted story, a narrative, is heightened, designed to express, explain, persuade, entertain. Even lyric poetry, though typically without a story line, carries persuasive intent to a reader and uses the same rhetorical tools—**arrangement**, word choice, **persona**—to build its message, make its moves, explore its moment.

In this chapter, we extend our discussion of rhetoric to include other everyday uses. We consider the three **genres** of literature sometimes called *belles lettres*—fiction, poetry, and drama. We've used examples of those genres in other chapters; here we concentrate on the ways in which reading literature through a rhetorical lens changes and deepens readers' responses to the literary work they read in and out of class. We use terms you already know as tools to analyze literary work—*character, setting, plot, theme, narrator, imagery*—to uncover the rhetorical decisions made by writers and readers about intent, method, and effect. Examining literature in this rhetorical way enriches your reading of literature and helps you understand and appreciate what you read and your response to what you read more fully.

> The author cannot choose to use rhetorical heightening. His only choice is of the kind of rhetoric he will use.
>
> Wayne Booth, *The Rhetoric of Fiction*

Wayne Booth's *The Rhetoric of Fiction* was first published in 1961 and quickly became an important resource for critics and teachers interested in how fiction works to achieve its effects on readers. The central premise of the book is that fiction (in a later edition, Booth expanded his ideas to include all narrative, fiction and nonfiction alike) is *inescapably* rhetorical; that is, authors work to achieve effects based on their understanding of the interrelationships among **reader**, **speaker**, and **subject**. As Booth claims in the previous passage, writers *must* use rhetoric. Their only decision is *how* they will use it. As a result, fiction carries persuasive intent just as speeches and letters to the editor do. The message in fiction or drama or poetry may be less direct than the message in other genres; the text may carry many messages rather than just one, or the writer may be persuading the reader only to enter the world of the text. But the communication between reader and writer exists in poetry, fiction, and drama just as in pieces of nonfiction, and understanding how that communication works enriches the experience of reading all kinds of literature.

Rhetoric insists on bringing the reader into the text, on making the reader a part of the transaction as characters speak and act, and as the textual world takes shape. The writer, as well as the narrator, depends on the reader to help complete the transaction to make sense and find resonance in the story—by using what the reader knows about plots and people and life.

One of Booth's insights is how deeply embedded in the story the *author* must be, how much the author orchestrates matters by placing characters in a setting and situation and by reporting the action as it unfolds. Many young writers are familiar with "show, don't tell," a maxim that directs authors to stay behind the scenes, to refuse to manipulate or to refuse to talk directly to the reader about the fact that they are manipulating for effect. In realistic fiction and drama, writers are presumed to be invisible so that audiences might "suspend their disbelief," a phrase the nineteenth-century poet and critic Samuel Taylor Coleridge used to talk about how an audience allow themselves to see the stage as a world. Some authors do attempt invisibility; they let a narrator or a central character "tell" the reader about what might be going on, and they suggest how a reader might be expected to feel. Other writers more overtly make themselves a part of the action by commenting on events and guiding the reader's reactions to those events. In either case, as Booth shows, writers are never really invisible; they use words and create movements among their characters to persuade an audience to believe. When writers show, Booth suggests, they also inescapably tell.

To make his point, Booth uses lots of examples from classic literature like the *Odyssey* to realistic twentieth-century fiction. Booth takes the opening scene from the *Odyssey*, for example, to illustrate how Homer conveys his persuasive intent. At the beginning of the poem in the translation Booth uses, the goddess Athena speaks to Zeus:

> "It is for Odysseus that my heart is wrung—the wise but unlucky Odysseus, who has been parted so long from all his friends and is pining on a lonely island far away in the middle of the seas."

And Zeus replies:

> "How could I ever forget the admirable Odysseus? He is not only the wisest man alive but has been the most generous in his offerings. . . . It is Poseidon . . . who is so implacable towards him."

Readers discover in the opening not just the facts of Odysseus's plight but also how we are supposed to feel about his condition. It's true that readers never learn much about the actual Homer writing the epic, but readers learn quickly how Homer feels about his main character and how he would like us to feel. Homer has Athena use the words *wise* and *unlucky.* He describes Athena's sympathetic reaction by telling readers that her "heart is wrung."

In the rest of this chapter, you'll find examples of writers who intrude themselves deliberately into their stories, writers who hide behind a narrator (sometimes one whom they appear to dislike), and writers who move into the consciousness of many characters or none or one. The way in which writers place themselves in or out of their fictional worlds is itself a rhetorical decision, in part shaped by how writers assume that readers will read and understand the story.

Character

Characters are the actors in a fictional world. They interact in that world in ways that readers recognize or are surprised by based on what readers know of the real world of their own experience. To a great extent, we care about the world of the fictional text because we are engaged by the characters we read about and come to know. We may feel sympathy, dislike, amusement, or horror toward them, but we feel something. Authors present their characters in deliberate ways; they choose language, gesture, action, and appearance that make the clearest, most persuasive description of the character, to help readers respond appropriately and effectively.

If you look back at the bit of dialogue from the *Odyssey,* excerpted earlier, you'll see that Homer has told us almost nothing about the characters who are speaking and much about the character they speak about, Odysseus. To figure out why Homer chose to reveal character in this indirect way, consider that Homer's epic was originally heard rather than read, and the story of the *Odyssey* was a story, like other Greek myths, that the audience of his day already knew well. The early Greeks who first heard the *Odyssey* knew the functions and personalities of all the gods in the myths. They knew Athena as the goddess of war and wisdom, and so recognized the compliment she paid Odysseus when she called him wise. They knew that Zeus, her father, was the supreme god and therefore most powerful in determining the fortunes of men.

Homer, in other words, didn't need to explain the personalities of the two speakers because he could count on his audience using what they knew and believed of the gods to make sense of the gods' dialogue and determine how to feel about the fortunes of Odysseus. Homer places Athena and Zeus at the beginning to show audiences that they should feel sympathy for the hero, just as the gods do. Zeus and Athena are reliable speakers, immortal and wise, and their judgment is meant to be trusted. Homer communicates to his audience—his immediate one in ancient Greece, and his more distant one in the twenty-first century—his own admiration and sympathy for Odysseus through the gods' conversation at the beginning of his poem. We are prepared to admire and like him even before he appears on the scene and speaks.

Activity

Write a small scene (just a few lines or a paragraph) where Odysseus reveals his character through speech or action. You might show Odysseus as wise, brave, unlucky, or embodying any other characteristic that you glean by reading the lines spoken by Athena and Zeus in the earlier dialogue. Then share your paragraph with your group. Notice the variety of approaches group members take as they suggest to their readers how to feel about Odysseus.

Rhetorical Choices for Character

As you wrote your scene for the preceding activity, you gave Odysseus words that demonstrate something about his personality and gave him actions that express something of his character. You made these rhetorical choices deliberately because you counted on your reader's understanding of how those words and actions suggest personal attributes. Knowing how you use rhetoric as a creator of characters will help you to understand the effect of rhetoric on you as a reader of characters.

Here's an example of a character introduced in another way. As you read, listen for the writer's voice underneath the description.

> Thomas Gradgrind, sir. A man of realities. A man of facts and calculations. A man who proceeds upon the principle that two and two are four, and nothing over, and who is not to be talked into allowing for anything over. Thomas Gradgrind, sir—peremptorily Thomas—Thomas Gradgrind. With a rule and a pair of scales, and the multiplication table always in his pocket, sir, ready to weigh and measure any parcel of human nature, and tell you exactly what it comes to. It is a mere question of figures, a case of simple arithmetic. You might hope to get some other nonsensical belief into the head of George Gradgrind, or Augustus Gradgrind, or John Gradgrind, or Joseph Gradgrind (all supposititious, non-existent persons), but into the head of Thomas Gradgrind—no, sir!

This passage comes from Charles Dickens's novel *Hard Times,* which is about education and the working classes, among other things. Dickens's novels often teach lessons—think of the case of Ebenezer Scrooge in *A Christmas Carol*—and Dickens created relationships with his readers that allow them to see readily which of his characters are most sorely in need of a lesson. Scrooge, you remember, needed to learn a lesson about charity, and the three Christmas ghosts taught him. Based on the choices Dickens makes as he describes Gradgrind in *Hard Times,* readers understand quickly that he is not a character to be admired.

Activity

Examine Dickens's description, looking for the signals Dickens gives about Gradgrind's character. Pay special attention to vocabulary and to the **syntax**, or sentence structure, that the writer uses. Share your responses with your group, and you'll see how many examples you've found together.

Flat and Round, Static and Dynamic

Like many writers, Dickens creates vivid characters by identifying them with a few, memorable character traits or physical features. The characters always act *in character*; that is, they never surprise us or confuse us by their complexity or indecision or transformation. Scrooge is transformed, but readers are unsurprised by the change. The entire story, from Scrooge's comment that deaths of the poor would "decrease the surplus population" to the final "God bless us, everyone!" has led us to expect transformation. We know almost from the beginning that Scrooge is a character who can, and will, be rehabilitated. And we're gratified when the transformation happens.

Characters who are less complex, who are readily identifiable by gestures, speech, and actions, are useful for writers as they communicate their ideas to readers. E. M. Forster, literary critic and novelist, called these kinds of characters **flat characters.** It's an unfortunate word in a way because flat characters are not dull, or poorly depicted, as the word itself might suggest. Flat characters simply act as we expect them to and become memorable because they're made identifiable through speech, appearance, or gesture. Mr. Gradgrind is a flat character. His name gives him away, the *grind* suggesting something unrelenting and merciless. Dickens presents another character in *Hard Times,* a school principal, whose name is even clearer: Mr. McChoakumchild. His name tells what he's like and—because Dickens gives him that name and not some other—what Dickens thinks of him.

Characters who are more complex, who change their minds, attitudes, and actions, or who take readers through a process of conflict along with them, are in Forster's terminology **round characters.** Forster defined round characters as ones who "can surprise convincingly." Readers might not expect particular characters to change their minds or move to a new spot or struggle with a decision, but if readers feel that characters' actions make sense, even when they're unexpected, the writer has depicted characters' complexity well.

It's harder to capture a character's roundness in only a paragraph or two because the complexity of the character usually emerges slowly over the course of time and pages in a story, but here's an example of how the round character is employed and depicted by the writer of a contemporary novel.

> At thirty six, bereft, brimming with grief and thwarted love, Quoyle steered away to Newfoundland, the rock that had generated his ancestors, a place he had never been nor thought to go.

A watery place. And Quoyle feared water, could not swim. Again and again the father had broken his clenched grip and thrown him into pools, brooks, lakes and surf. Quoyle knew the flavor of brack and waterweed.

From this youngest son's failure to dogpaddle the father saw other failures multiply like an explosion of virulent cells—failure to speak clearly; failure to sit up straight; failure to get up in the morning; failure in attitude; failure in ambition and ability; indeed, in everything. His own failure.

Quoyle shambled, a head taller than any child around him, was soft. He knew it.

Annie Proulx, The Shipping News

What makes us label Quoyle "round" and not "flat"? For one thing, the physical description doesn't tell us everything about the character, nor does the psychological one. That is, Quoyle doesn't seem to be a character who can be summed up quickly or easily like Mr. Gradgrind can be. Quoyle might be a large, lumbering, awkward, and odd-looking fellow, but he is also painfully conscious of himself. Notice the last line of the passage: "He knew it." Quoyle is sad about his failure and disheartened by his family's reaction to him. He "shambled," a word that suggests head-down embarrassment at his difference. He was "soft," and we're left to imagine if that softness is more than physical, if he is perhaps gentle. We don't know what will become of him; we wonder how he will manage. The careful way that Proulx has described him makes us feel his longing, loneliness, and fear. In sum, we understand that Quoyle is complex, not simple. And we're already prepared, on the first page, to sympathize.

How does Proulx manage to evoke all these reactions in a reader? She places the description as the opening to the novel to let readers know Quoyle's significance; she brings in Quoyle's family background in just a few sentences to suggest the psychological conflicts that haunt Quoyle into adulthood; she selects words that allow for both revulsion and sympathy; she looks unsympathetically at Quoyle's failings, which in a paradoxical way heightens readers' sympathetic reaction. Looking at these techniques, a reader begins to understand Proulx's decisions as rhetorical.

As readers move through the novel, they find Quoyle in a variety of situations, confronting dilemmas, engaging in activities, and considering strategies. Our responses to Quoyle develop and deepen over the course of the novel, and that change in *our* response to Quoyle is another reason that he can be characterized as a round rather than flat character. Readers feel more about him at the end of the story than at the beginning, whereas flat characters usually provoke the same feeling from beginning to end.

Another way to contrast characters is to see them as static or dynamic. The difference between these two types of characters is fairly self-explanatory. **Static characters** don't change or move much; we know everything about them that we need to know from their first introduction. The author uses them in various ways—as foils to other, more complex characters; for humor or ridicule; and/or to establish **tone** or **theme** more decisively in the minds of readers. **Dynamic characters** do change, and they are harder for readers to get a handle on. Often, writers make complex or round characters dynamic and simple or flat characters static, but not always. Mr. Gradgrind is a static character who is also flat, while Scrooge is a flat character who is dynamic. Odysseus is a relatively complex character, with difficult decisions to make and conflicting emotions, but he is also static: his bravery, intelligence, and leadership ability never waver during the course of the story. You might look back at the description of Quoyle to see if you can decide whether he will be static or dynamic and consider why you think so.

Character and the Pentad

A way of considering character and other literary elements rhetorically is to use Kenneth Burke's **pentad**, mentioned in Chapter 3, to explore characters' actions and motives, and to understand the structure of narratives. The pentad includes the **act**, which names what took place in thought or action; the **scene**, the background or situation where the act occurred; the **agent**, or person performing the act; the **agency**, how and with what means the act is performed; and the **purpose**, why the act is done.

The pentad is useful for seeing situations, or plots, in their complexity and for uncovering rhetorical motives in all kinds of narratives and all kinds of acts. It's especially useful in figuring out human motivation and so provides a helpful tool to analyze narratives.

The five points of the pentad operate cooperatively, in **ratios**, as Burke called them. For example, the *scene-act* connection, or ratio, describes how a background—cultural, historical, familial—affects an act, such as a murder, the building of a highway, a marriage, or the passing of a law. The *scene-agent* ratio tells how a background connects to a person; how ideals, personality characteristics, or individual choices are affected by that background; or how the actor uses a background. Let's say two people meet, fall in love despite their families' objections, and commit double suicide. That's the story of *Romeo and Juliet*. The scene-act ratio would examine how family (or society or culture) contributes to the deaths. The scene-agent ratio would describe how society (or family or culture) contributes to the character of Juliet or Romeo. The other elements in the pentad contribute additional perspectives on a situation by exposing additional choices that writers make. Consider, for instance, how agency is important in *Romeo and Juliet*. Because they mislay messages and bungle their attempts to help, both the nurse and the priest become agencies in the deaths of the young lovers.

Say the writer of an analysis of *Romeo and Juliet* begins with the question, "Why did Romeo and Juliet die?" How might the writer use the pentad to help answer the question—that is, explain the act?

- **act-agency:** They died because their plans for escape went awry.

- **act-scene:** Their families' opposition and mutual hatred drove them to commit double suicide.

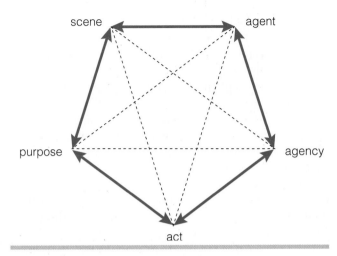

Burke's Pentad

- **act-purpose:**   They wanted to be together so desperately that they chose to die rather than live in a world without one another.

- **act-agent:**   They died when one took poison and the other stabbed herself.

All these explanations are accurate, but some explain more fully the reasons for the deaths than others. A writer might choose to highlight one pair rather than another to guide readers in understanding the motivations that are most appropriate to the writer's own purposes. The way Shakespeare chooses to end the play, as well as his use of the flat characters of the nurse and the priest as agencies for the deaths, might be clues to help readers locate the ratios that most fully explain the tragic outcome of Romeo and Juliet's story.

The pentad is useful for examining all the elements in narrative and their relationship to others. *Setting* is another term for Burke's *scene; theme* can be connected to *purpose; conflict,* to *act.* What Burke's discussion adds is an insistence on seeing each of these elements in combination rather than in isolation so that the complexities of narrative get revealed and the rhetorical possibilities that emerge from highlighting one connection and submerging another get exposed. In the discussion of literary elements that follows, think about how the pentad's combinations might be applied to your reading.

Activity

Choose a novel or a short story your class has read together, and write a brief analysis of one character. Focus on one ratio to explain the actions of that character. You might have each member of your group concentrate on a different ratio, which will add depth and perspective to the text you're analyzing.

Setting

When speakers step to a podium, they use and are affected by the **context** that surrounds them. The auditorium, the stagelights, the time of day and year, the local and national news stories that people have been talking about that day—all contribute to speakers' decisions about how to arrange and deliver the speech. Likewise, events in the world, past and present, can become significant factors in how speakers and writers compose their work and how effective their product is. In fictional narratives, the context, or **setting**, becomes the stage on which characters act out their lives, and writers of fictional narratives must decide how to use this stage to its best rhetorical effect.

As readers and movie audiences, we're quite familiar with the rhetorical effects of setting on the theme, or purpose, of a story, and on the way setting reinforces tone and characters' preoccupations. Stereotypical settings tell us about genre, plot, and theme early on in a narrative. We're prepared to predict that if it's a dark and stormy night, the story must be a mystery and something dangerous, maybe even deadly, is about to happen. You can imagine other stereotypical settings easily by thinking of *genres* of narratives. The fairy tale, the Western, the science fiction story, and the detective thriller often are set in locales that audiences immediately recognize as typical of their genre, and audiences experience the story with that genre in mind. As they present the story, writers make use of an audience's expectations about setting. Sometimes they use audience's expectations to surprise us rather than confirm what we already expect. In some recent films, for example, "It was a dark and stormy night" begins a comedy rather than a horror story.

Stereotypical settings, also called **stock settings,** function as a kind of shorthand method for letting readers know how to engage with the story. More often in the narratives you read and analyze, writers use particular, rather than stock, settings for their plots and characters. But in all kinds of settings, time and place become rhetorical elements in the story, and writers use them to provoke understanding and reaction from the audience and to affect and motivate characters in the story as they respond to what surrounds them.

One way to recognize the rhetorical importance of setting is to notice where writers position descriptions of time and place. The passage from *Sula* you read in Chapter 5 describes the Bottom, the section of a small town in Ohio that is the setting for the novel. Morrison begins the book with the description, "In that place. . . . " Only later do readers get introduced to the characters who live in the Bottom. Morrison makes her setting influence characters' actions—their isolation, their sense of community and belonging—and become part of a message about the continuing effects of slavery and oppression. The name *the Bottom,* placed at the top of the hill, suggests the ironic twist of fate that gives the poor African American population of the town what will become the most prized land. The importance that Morrison places on setting and its relationship to characters (in Burke's terms, the scene-agent ratio) is made clear by her decision to open the novel as she does.

Here's the opening passage of *The Scarlet Letter*. Consider how Nathaniel Hawthorne is using setting as he begins the story:

A throng of bearded men, in sad-coloured garments and gray, steeple-crowned hats, intermixed with women, some wearing hoods, and others bareheaded, was assembled in front of a wooden edifice, the door of which was heavily timbered with oak, and studded with iron spikes.

The founders of a new colony, whatever Utopia of human virtue and happiness might originally project, have invariably recognized it among their earliest practical necessities to allot a portion of the virgin soil as a cemetery, and another portion as the site of a prison. . . . Certain it is, that, some fifteen or twenty years after the settlement of the town, the wooden jail was already marked with weather-stains and other indications of age, which gave a yet darker aspect to its beetle-browed and gloomy front. The rust on the ponderous iron-work of its oaken door looked more antique than anything else in the new world. Like all that pertains to crime, it seemed never to have known a youthful era. Before this ugly edifice, and between it and the wheel-track of the street, was a grass-plot, much overgrown with burdock, pig-weed, apple-peru, and such unsightly vegetation, which evidently found something congenial in the soil that had so early borne the black flower of civilized society, a prison. But, on one side of the portal, and rooted almost at the threshold, was a wild rose-bush, covered, in this month of June, with its delicate gems, which might be imagined to offer their fragrance and fragile beauty to the prisoner as he went in, and to the condemned criminal as he came forth to his doom, in token that the deep heart of Nature could pity and be kind to him.

Notice how the setting gets established first by a quick generalization about the building of a civilization and then a close-in observation of the prison door and the rose. Hawthorne emphasizes the conflict between prison door and rose—symbolically between punishment and forgiveness, ugliness and beauty—that will continue through his tale. The **imagery** used to describe prison and rose provides readers with a direct contrast: the prison is the grotesque "black flower" of civilization, and the rose the "deep heart of Nature" that will pity and be kind.

Hawthorne makes setting an active force in his plot by pitting civilization against nature in the form of the prison/scaffold/town on one side and the rose/forest/wilderness on the other. The characters in the drama move between these two scenes, the two opposing forces that affect all their actions and decisions.

In other works, setting is not as overtly symbolic and rhetorical as in Hawthorne's stories and novels. In plays, for example, the details of setting are often left up to the director to fill in, and writers may provide only bare outlines of place or time. Or playwrights may specify props, the portable and detailed elements of setting, rather than specify time and place.

The details of setting in a play are often spare, leaving the director and the audience to imagine the larger contexts for the room, the street, or the forest where the action of the play might take place. Because few details are provided—*Oliver's house, Duke Frederick's court, the forest of Arden* (the setting descriptions for Shakespeare's *As You Like It*)—stage directors and set designers locate the elements and details that will convey most effectively time, place, mood, and aim. Those set elements become suggestive or symbolic, especially since the limitations of the stage make it impossible to re-create completely the actual details of a place. Looking at Tom Stoppard's setting directions in the following excerpt, you might consider how some of the details suggest that time and place will be significant in the play.

Activity

Read the stage directions for Tom Stoppard's play *The Real Thing*. Then write a paragraph speculating about how the details of setting might become important. Notice that readers aren't provided details of time or place beyond "living room." Can you infer period? Culture?

> *Living-room. Architect's drawing board, perhaps. A partly open door leads to an unseen hall and an unseen front door. One or two other doors to other rooms.*
>
> MAX *is alone, sitting in a comfortable chair, with a glass of wine and an open bottle to hand. He is using a pack of playing cards to build a pyramidical, tiered viaduct on the coffee table in front of him. He is about to add a pair of playing cards (leaning against each other to hold each other up), and the pyramid is going well. Beyond the door to the hall, the front door is heard being opened with a key. The light from there changes as the unseen front door is opened.*
>
> MAX *does not react to the opening of the door, which is more behind him than in front of him.*

Activity

Think about how you'd stage a production of a play you know well. Write directions for, or draw, a set for *Romeo and Juliet* or another play you know well. Compare your set with ones created by others in your group to see what each set has highlighted.

Summary and Scenic Narration

Setting, of course, has to do with time. The time period of the story might be used to suggest customary behaviors or attitudes that will prove to be important to the plot. The time period of *The Scarlet Letter*—seventeenth century—is significant because of what we associate with Puritan behavior in New England. We're predisposed to discover repression, judgment, humorlessness, and so on in characters' attitudes, even if those beliefs are stereotypical and prove false in the working out of the plot. Time is used for rhetorical effect in other ways, too. Time of day or year can be rhetorically significant; think of Tennessee Williams's plays, where the heat of summer becomes part of the mood of the story as well as a parallel to the characters' desires and anger.

Just as important in thinking about time is the way a writer stretches out and collapses time for effect. **Summary narration** has the narrator of the story briefly relate or sum up events so that the plot can move ahead quickly to another point: "Henry served ten years in the Army before he saw her again." **Scenic narration,** on the other hand, lets the narrator stretch out the description of a moment, sometimes for longer than it would take to accomplish in real time. Let's say the sentence above is the last sentence in a chapter. A new chapter begins, and it will use scenic narration, with one scene, one moment, dramatized for the reader.

Like all the details of setting, scenic narration and summary narration provoke different reactions in readers; they carry different rhetorical effects. Summary narration, which generalizes and summarizes events, distances the reader from the characters and from the events. Writers use summary when they want to move ahead quickly and when they want to tell readers what events mean. Scenic narration—more vivid, more playlike—allows readers to participate more directly in the moment and make more judgments about meaning for themselves.

Setting, as we've suggested, provides cultural clues that help readers understand conflicts and characters. In *The Scarlet Letter,* the prison door, the scaffold, and the forest are all setting details that suggest what this Puritan culture values and fears. One of the pleasures of reading fiction is that a reader enters another world and another culture. Entering a new world through the details of cultural setting presents one of the difficulties in reading, too, if that setting is a place or time far removed from our own.

Setting, because it's atmospheric, evokes emotional and intellectual reactions from readers. Setting helps carry thematic messages and character motivations and rationales for actions. Think about the ratio between scene and each of the other points on the pentad as you examine a piece of literature, and you'll find new perspectives from which to analyze and respond to the work you're reading.

Here are some questions to guide your consideration of setting in literary works:

1. What are the details of the physical setting? How, if at all, does setting change?

2. How are time and the passage of time used by the writer? How do they affect characters' actions and your response to them?

3. What details of culture (and time period) are reflected in setting details and in characters' actions or attitudes?

4. How does setting affect your feeling about the **mood** of the narrative? Does the atmosphere shift, and, if so, why might the writer make that shift?

5. What association do the physical objects or other setting details carry for characters or for you as a reader?

Activity

Write a paragraph or so of scenic narration that would come after the line, "Henry served ten years in the Army before he saw her again." Remember to include enough details so that your reader sees the scene rather than merely hears about it.

Activity

The landscape painting below is titled *Westward the Star of Empire Takes Its Way—Near Council Bluffs, Iowa.* Painted about 1865 by Andrew Melrose, it illuminates the setting for the westward expansion of this country. Examine the painting, and then write with your group a scene of conflict that this setting might serve as a backdrop for. Include characters if you wish, and be conscious of making them flat or round, static or dynamic.

Conflict and Plot

When listeners hear a story, they're always silently, and sometimes vocally, asking the question, "And then what happened?" As readers, we ask that question too as we read: "What's going to happen?" "What will she do?" We're propelled by the **plot,** the arrangement of events in the story. Good plots carry us along, highlighting the most important or exciting events by describing them in meaningful detail and by quickly relating in summary narration other, less significant or exciting events. Writers arrange narratives, or plot them, to keep readers asking questions. A good plot designs the particulars of the narrative to suggest

attributes and motivations of characters, to convey symbolic truths and themes, and, most important, to secure readers' involvement.

The **pace** of the plot—how quickly it moves from one event or action to another—gives writers a method for showing readers what's most significant to the characters in the story or to the message. The writer speeds up discussion or description to move to a scene of significance, where the action might slow for effect. The pace of a plot can emphasize character attitude or can create mood. "He turned the knob quietly, the tips of his fingers feeling the split in the cold metal. He closed his eyes, waiting for the sound that he was sure would follow—bare feet hitting the floor, a crash perhaps, cursing. He waited for a long time, standing there, eyes still closed. No sound." You can hear in that scene a deliberate slowing down that adds to the sense of danger or fear in the mind of the character. Careful pacing is essential for a good plot, and writers vary their pace to keep readers interested.

Writers move action forward and backward through time as well. **Flashbacks** and **flashforwards** allow writers to give past history and suggest how past events influence current actions, or how future actions will proceed from a present moment. In *A Christmas Carol*, Dickens uses both flashforwards and flashbacks in presenting the ghosts who come to call on Scrooge. The Ghost of Christmas Past is a flashback device; he shows Scrooge the scenes of his youth where he made the decisions that brought him to his miserly, and miserable, state. The Ghost of Christmas Future, a frightening emblem of death, takes Scrooge to the graveyard to gaze with horror on his own tombstone and to hear how little his acquaintances bemoan his passing.

Activity

In a novel or play you've read, find a place in the narrative where the pace changes. Write a paragraph about how the change reflects characters' attitudes or state of mind or how the change affects the meaning of the work.

Tragedy Versus Comedy

It's impossible to tell a story or to plot it without **conflict**. A character begins happy; then something happens, and he is no longer happy; maybe he dies. Or a character begins depressed; then something happens, and he becomes happy; maybe he gets married. These two scenarios represent, in their simplest forms, the way that tragedy and comedy work. And the *something* that happens between the stages of happiness and sadness, between connection and isolation, is the conflict.

In *A Christmas Carol*, Scrooge begins as a mean-spirited, rich, and lonely old bachelor with no friends and nothing good to say of anybody, but he ends as second father to Tiny Tim, reunited with his family, and a friend to all because he knows how to keep "Christmas in his heart." What has happened to change him? Dickens manipulates his story so that Scrooge faces a conflict within himself that changes the course of his actions and his life. The **plot devices** that Dickens uses are the three ghosts, who remind Scrooge of his past, force him to face his present, and foretell his gloomy future.

Romeo and Juliet carries the opposite plot line. Romeo and Juliet begin in innocence and longing. Their first encounter, at the Capulet party, is blissful. But they end in sorrow and in death. Shakespeare's plot devices include the families' feud, the bumbling priest and nurse, and the main characters' own impetuous natures and youth.

Writers use rhetoric—the decisions they make to convey their intentions most effectively and to move a reader most completely—as they determine the plot elements and the kinds of conflicts they'll pose to their characters and in their plots. The final aim of a plot—is the writer's intention to create a tragedy? comedy? lesson in humanity? lesson in injustice?—will determine the outcome of the conflicts the writer's characters engage in. You're likely familiar with the kinds of conflicts that writers use as they tell stories.

Conflict in Decision Making

In this kind of conflict, a character faces his or her own fears, flaws, and desires, and then, after a time of competing thoughts or behaviors, acts for good or ill. Psychological conflict often has characters speaking to themselves in **soliloquy** or talking to others as if they're talking to themselves. Or a narrator might enter the consciousness of the character to explain the inner conflict the character faces. The famous soliloquy that begins, "To be or not to be. That is the question," voices the psychological conflict faced by Hamlet. Should he act to avenge his father, or should he suffer in silence? If you look back at the opening passage of *The Shipping News,* you can see how the narrator describes the psychology of Quoyle, the main character, and the conflict his past presents him with.

Conflict in Relationships

Conflict is most obvious among people or groups of people whose competing interests or beliefs drive their differences to the point of war, murder, estrangement, or disagreement. **Dialogue** is a typical way to show conflict between or among people, where each person takes a competing position, and the reader makes decisions not only about who might be right but also about the reasons behind the disagreement. Descriptive scenes of battles where the narrator shows how one side outmaneuvers the other or makes tactical mistakes are useful ways of showing interpersonal or international conflict. Odysseus's many battles in the *Odyssey* with monsters, witches, gods, and men are clear examples of interpersonal conflict.

Conflict with the Elements

When characters build cities from forests, fight dragons, rescue others from flooding rivers, or face ruined harvests, they find themselves in conflict with the natural world. In some early novels and plays, characters addressed the elements directly, crying aloud to the heavens or shaking their fists and talking to the storm. They use **apostrophe**, language that addresses the natural world as if it were human. Characters can be in conflict with the heavens, marked by fate as Odysseus is, or marked by the society that surrounds them. Hester Prynne finds herself in conflict with her Puritan village in *The Scarlet Letter.* And for much of the novel she is isolated in that conflict, a lone figure whose very presence excites dismay and rebuke from the society she lives in.

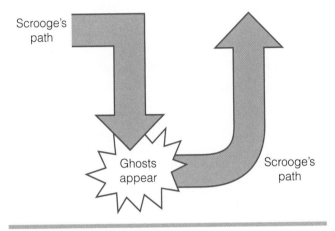

Plot line for A Christmas Carol

Activity

Choose a novel or play your class has read, and describe its plot line by drawing a picture of it and then explaining the picture you've drawn. *A Christmas Carol,* for example, might be drawn as in the graphic above and then explained by the following text.

> The character is headed toward a bad end; his views on humanity are pessimistic, and he has not met his responsibility to others. The ghosts arrive to change his mind, and he is in torment as he tries to make sense of their coming and their message. As he figures out their intention, he is persuaded to change his ways, and he sees a new path, where he develops attitudes precisely the opposite of those he began with.

Conflict and the Pentad

Burke's pentad reveals how a reader might examine the way that conflict works in a narrative. If you think of conflict as agency, the method or means for understanding actions, you can see how conflict affects the character, the action the character might take, the scene around the character, and the rationale for the character's decisions.

The following scene is from Henrik Ibsen's play *A Doll's House* (written in 1879). The scene comes at the end of the first act, where Nora Helmer has just had a conversation with Krogstad, who has helped her forge a document to save her father and has come to her in a thinly veiled blackmail attempt. This scene reveals something about Nora's husband, Torvald, and her relationship with him:

TORVALD: . . . Has anyone been here?

NORA: Here? No.

TORVALD: That is strange. I saw Krogstad going out the gate.

NORA: Did you? Oh yes, I forgot, Krogstad was here for a moment.

TORVALD: Nora, I can see from your manner that he has been here begging you to say a good word for him.

NORA: Yes.

TORVALD: And you were to appear to do it of your own accord; you were to conceal from me the fact of his having been here; didn't he beg that of you too?

NORA: Yes, Torvald, but—

TORVALD: Nora, Nora, and you would be a party to that sort of thing? To have any talk with a man like that and give him any sort of promise? And to tell me a lie into the bargain?

NORA: A lie?

TORVALD: Didn't you tell me no one had been here? [*Shakes his finger at her.*] My little songbird must never do that again. A songbird must have a clean beak to chirp with—no false notes! [*Puts his arm around her waist.*] That is so, isn't it? Yes, I am sure it is. [*Lets her go.*] We will say no more about it. How warm and snug it is here!

TORVALD: Just think how a guilty man like that has to lie and play the hypocrite with everyone, how he has to wear a mask in the presence of those near and dear to him, even before his own wife and children. And about the children—that is the most terrible part of it all, Nora.

NORA: How?

TORVALD: Because such an atmosphere of lies infects and poisons the whole life of a home. Each breath the children take in such a house is full of the germs of evil.

NORA: [*coming nearer him.*] Are you sure of that?

TORVALD: My dear, I have often seen it in the course of my life as a lawyer. Almost everyone who has gone to the bad early in life has a deceitful mother.

NORA: Why do you only say—mother?

TORVALD: It seems most commonly to be the mother's influence, though naturally a bad father's would have the same result. Every lawyer is familiar with the fact.

This Krogstad, now, has been persistently poisoning his own children with lies and dissimulation; that is why I say he has lost all moral character. [*Holds out his hands to her.*] That is why my sweet little Nora must promise me not to plead his cause. Give me your hand on it. Come, come, what is this? Give me your hand. There now, that's settled. I assure you it would be quite impossible for me to work with him; I literally feel physically ill when I am in the company of such people.

NORA: [*takes her hand out his and goes to the opposite side of the Christmas tree.*] How hot it is in here, and I have such a lot to do.

Activity

It's clear that there's a conflict between Nora and her husband. Consider the conflict as the agency in Burke's terms, and write a paragraph that explores how the conflict reveals something about the personalities of each of the characters (agency-agent), about the social and cultural scene around them (agency-scene), or about the message that either of the characters might be trying to convey through the conversation (agency-purpose).

Protagonist, Antagonist

In Ibsen's play, Nora and Torvald are the main characters, the **protagonist** and the **antagonist**. Nora, the protagonist, is the figure in the narrative whose interests the reader is most concerned about and sympathetic toward, and the author positions the protagonist in the plot so that readers understand her struggles most clearly. When she faces conflict, readers more or less side with her because we know her motivations. Nora's silliness, her hopes, and her terror at the prospect of losing everything strike a sympathetic chord in readers and viewers of the play. Torvald Helmer, the husband who misunderstands and condescends to Nora, is the antagonist because he encourages the silliness, blunts the hopes, and increases the terror. In other words, he opposes what readers (and the author) want for Nora and what she learns to want for herself.

But Torvald is also a representative of his time and place, and he plays a role assigned to him by the culture he lives in. Nora fights an antagonist greater than her husband; she's in conflict with her culture and its institutions.

Narrator: Point of View

When writers choose a narrator—the person who will tell their story—they make a rhetorical decision. Writers decide on a narrator based on how they envision the story and on how they envision readers experiencing the story. As readers, we develop emotional and intellectual relationships to events, places, and characters in the story because we view those events, places, and characters from a particular perspective. Our reaction to reading about an automobile accident—narrated, for example, by the driver of the car—will be different from our reaction to reading about it from the **point of view** of a witness standing on the corner.

First-Person Narration

Writers reveal elements of plot and character to their readers—and conceal them—by choosing to tell the story through the mind of a character *in* the story or through someone *outside* it. The first-person narrator, most often someone inside the novel, may be the main character in the story, as Huckleberry Finn is in Mark Twain's novel.

> You don't know about me without you have read a book by the name of *The Adventures of Tom Sawyer;* but that ain't no matter. That book was made by Mr. Mark Twain, and he told the truth, mainly. There was things which he stretched, but mainly he told the truth. That is nothing. I never seen anybody but lied one time or another, without it was Aunt Polly, or the widow, or maybe Mary. Aunt Polly—Tom's Aunt Polly, she is—and Mary, and the Widow Douglas is all told about in that book, which is mostly a true book, with some stretchers, as I said before.

The first-person storyteller might also be a less central character who acts as an observer of the action and of the main character, as is Jack Burden in *All the King's Men,* by Robert Penn Warren.

> "My god, folks, it's Willie!"
>
> The remark was superfluous. One look at the faces rallied around and you knew that if any citizen over the age of three didn't know that the strong-set man standing there in the Palm Beach suit was Willie Stark, that citizen was a half-wit. In the first place, all he would have to do would be to lift his eyes to the big picture high up there above the soda fountain, a picture about six times life size, which showed the same face, the big eyes, which in the picture had the suggestion of a sleepy and inward look (the eyes of the man in the Palm Beach suit didn't have that look now, but I've seen it), the pouches under the eyes and jowls beginning to sag off, and the meaty lips, which didn't sag but if you looked close were laid one on top of the other like a couple of bricks, and the tousle of hair hanging down on the not very high squarish forehead. Under the picture was the legend: *My study is the heart of the people.* In quotation marks, and signed, *Willie Stark.* I had seen that picture in a thousand places, pool halls to palaces.

Here, from Maxine Hong Kingston's *Woman Warrior,* is a final example of a first-person narrator who is a group as well as an individual character in the story. The first-person plural pronoun establishes the individual as part of a larger group identity and thus makes a rhetorical point about the narrator's position.

When we Chinese girls listened to the adults talk-story, we learned that we failed if we grew up to be but wives or slaves. We could be heroines, swordswomen. Even if she had to rage across all China, a swordswoman got even with anybody who hurt her family. Perhaps women were once so dangerous that they had to have their feet bound. It was a woman who invented white crane boxing only two hundred years ago. She was already an expert pole fighter, daughter of a teacher trained at the Shao-lin temple, where there lived an order of fighting monks. She was combing her hair one morning when a white crane alighted outside her window. She teased it with her pole, which it pushed aside with a soft brush of its wing. Amazed, she dashed outside and tried to knock the crane off its perch. It snapped her pole in two. Recognizing the presence of great power, she asked the spirit of the white crane if it would teach her to fight. It answered with a cry that white crane boxers imitate today. Later the bird returned as an old man, and he guided her boxing for many years. Thus she gave the world a new martial art.

  This was one of the tamer, more modern stories, mere introduction. My mother told others that followed swordswomen through woods and palaces for years. Night after night my mother would talk-story until we fell asleep page I couldn't tell where the stories left off and the dreams began, her voice the voice of the heroines in my sleep page and on Sundays, from noon to midnight, we went to the movies at the Confucius Church. We saw swordswomen jump over houses from a standstill; they didn't even need a running start.

As you can tell from all these examples, the first-person narrator reflects only what he or she sees or feels; readers get the "inside" view of events and of other characters from the narrator who observes and comments. With a first-person speaker, readers learn about the story from one side, and their view is therefore both subjective and intimate.

Third-Person Narration

Unlike the first-person storyteller, the third-person narrator gives readers a kind of distance on the events taking place in the story. The third-person narrator may be inside the mind of all the characters (**omniscient narration**), of one of the characters (**limited narration**), or of none of the characters (**dramatic narration**). Readers may get inside the head of one of the characters through a limited perspective or inside the head of all characters through an omniscient one, but the third-person pronoun—*he* or *she*—creates less intimacy and more seeming objectivity than does the first-person pronoun. The third-person narration suggests some outside figure observing the characters and describing their actions, even when the narration is from one character's point of view. If you look back at the opening passage to *The Shipping News* (page 197), you'll see a third-person narrator who gives the main character's thoughts and also comments on that character. Here's a passage from the opening of *Emma*, by Jane Austen.

  The real evils indeed of Emma's situation were the power of having rather too much her own way and a disposition to think a little too well of herself; these were the disadvantages which threatened to alloy her many enjoyments. The danger, however, was at present so unperceived that they did not by any means rank as misfortunes with her.

In the preceding passage, it's easy to hear a narrator who is outside and beyond the mind of any one character, who sees into the motives and flaws of those being described. The narrator is omniscient because nothing is hidden from her, and thus nothing is hidden from readers.

Activity

The five passages from novels quoted in this chapter have different kinds of narrators, three in the first person (Hong Kingston, Penn Warren, and Twain) and two in the third person (Austen and Proulx). Read the passages again, and then decide in your group what your reactions to the characters are and what you think the narrator wants readers to think or believe as he or she tells the story.

Second-Person Narration

A note on second person: Second-person narration is unusual, in part because it's hard to sustain. (Try writing a story using "you" for a page or so.) If you do find second-person narration, you will often sense tension or a feeling of immediacy as you read. Listen to this passage from John Hawkes's novel *The Lime Twig*:

> Have you ever let lodgings in the winter? Was there a bed kept waiting, a corner room kept waiting for a gentleman? And have you ever hung a cardboard in the window and, just out of view yourself, watched to see which man would stop and read the lettering on your sign, glance at the premises from roof to little sign—an awkward piece of work—then step up suddenly and hold his finger on your bell? What was it you saw from the window that made you let the bell continue ringing and the bed go empty another night? Something about the eyes? The smooth white skin between the brim of the bowler hat and the eyes?

Second-person narration is almost always connected to first-person telling. Hawkes's gothic-feeling, dreamy horror tale quickly moves into an "I-you" dialogue:

> I wouldn't advise Violet Lane—there is no telling about the beds in Violet Lane—but perhaps in Dreary Station you have already found a lodging good as mine, if you were once the gentleman or if you ever took a tea kettle from a lady's hands.

The conversation between writer and reader is made explicit in works that use the "you" overtly. You might look for that conversation in other works you read: *Catcher in the Rye*, by J. D. Salinger, uses "I-you," and you can see it in the previous excerpt from *Huckleberry Finn*. Here's one more example, from the novel *Barchester Towers* by Victorian novelist Anthony Trollope. In this passage,

Trollope stops the plot to assure his readers about the eventual fate of his heroine and to comment on the "I-you" relationship between writer and reader that he sees at the heart of reading:

> And here, perhaps, it may be allowed to the novelist to explain his views on a very important point in the art of telling tales. He ventures to reprobate that system which goes so far to violate all proper confidence between the author and his readers, by maintaining nearly to the end of the third volume a mystery as to the fate of their favorite personage. . . . Have not often the profoundest efforts of genius been used to baffle the aspirations of the reader, to raise false hopes and false fears, and to give rise to expectations which are never to be realized?
>
> . . .
>
> Our doctrine is, that the author and the reader should move along together in full confidence with each other. Let the personages of the drama undergo ever so complete a comedy of errors among themselves, but let the spectator never mistake the Syracusan for the Ephesian; otherwise he is one of the dupes, and the part of a dupe is never dignified.

Trollope's interruption, his **narrative intrusion,** establishes a clear rhetorical relationship between writer and reader—and an ethical one. Readers should have "full confidence" in writers' honor not to trick or to surprise unfairly. The real relationship, Trollope seems to indicate, is not the one between reader and character but between reader and writer. It's a bold suggestion and one that Trollope was criticized for but one that has become increasingly popular in contemporary writing. Trollope suggests that it's not plot that's the most important, and not character, but the writer-reader connection, the rhetoric of the text. Trollope's narrator is a **reliable narrator**; that is, he tells his readers as much as he knows of the characters and their actions and doesn't mislead with false clues about them or about himself. We can trust his reactions, even if they are limited.

Reliable and Unreliable Narrators

Sometimes writers choose to tell their stories through the words of an **unreliable narrator,** one who deliberately holds back information or whose judgments are unsound so that readers suspect the information the narrator gives us. Edgar Allan Poe's narrators are sometimes unreliable because they're unbalanced. In Poe's short story "The Black Cat," the narrator's first words are about his sanity and rationality: "For the most wild yet most homely narrative which I am about to pen, I neither expect nor solicit belief. Mad indeed would I be to expect it, in a case where my very senses reject their own evidence. Yet mad am I not—and very surely do I not dream." Later, the narrator's description of his morbid hatred for a cat with a strange eye that gets transferred to his wife belies the assertion. Unreliable narrators often proclaim their reliability or their logical powers; readers learn to distrust them for that very reason. An unreliable narrator strengthens the connection between the reader and the *writer*, who creates rhetorical effects that help readers see into and beyond the misinformation or silences of the unreliable narrator.

Narrators in Poems

We haven't talked much about poetry in this discussion of narrators, although the perspective from which poets describe the moments they evoke is often crucial to a reader's understanding and appreciation of the poem, especially, of course, in narrative poetry. Robert Browning's famous dramatic poems, where the narrator is a clearly defined character, show how much the teller of the tale in the poem matters. "Porphyria's Lover" describes a moment of possession, when the speaker, who has been morbidly unsure of his lover's true affection, realizes it:

> Happy and proud; at last I knew
> Porphyria worshiped me; surprise
>   Made my heart swell, and still it grew
> While I debated what to do.
> That moment she was mine, mine, fair,
>   Perfectly pure and good; I found
> A thing to do, and all her hair
>   In one long yellow string I wound
> Three times her little throat around,
> And strangled her. No pain felt she;
>   I am quite sure she felt no pain.

The poem's chilling vision is heightened by the first-person narrator, who is also the murderer. The tone of his voice might call to mind Poe, who, as just noted, also used insane but analytically insightful first-person narrators in both his poetry and fiction.

Lyric poetry, which by definition does not tell a story, or much of one, often makes use of a first-person speaker who explores a moment or a feeling memorable for the realization it evoked or the change it signaled. Although in lyric poetry, speakers may not make connections with other characters or even overt connections with readers, the perspective of the person telling about the experience is always important to the reader's ability and interest in experiencing the poem.

Here are some questions to guide your thinking about point of view in literary work:

1. Is there more than one point of view in the piece? How does the shift affect your reading?

2. How does the narrator feel about the characters in the story? What signals does the narrator give to suggest this feeling?

3. If the narrator doesn't comment much on the characters or situations or is indeed absent (as in drama), what details provide insight into the characters and their thoughts?

4. Is the narrator trustworthy or unreliable? How might you become aware of the unreliability of a narrator?

Activity

Read the following poem, by recent poet laureate Rita Dove. Then with your group decide how the speaker uses setting, character, or conflict to evoke a mood and connect with readers. It's important to know that the title refers to Rosa Parks, the southern woman who helped begin the civil-rights movement with her refusal to move to the back of the bus.

Rosa

How she sat there,
the time right inside a place
so wrong it was ready.

That trim name with
its dream of a bench
to rest on. Her sensible coat.

Doing nothing was the doing:
the clean flame of her gaze
carved by a camera flash.

How she stood up
when they bent down to retrieve
her purse. That courtesy.

Theme

The theme, or purpose or message, of a piece of literature is built from the combination of all the elements we've discussed so far. The kinds of characters and their positions in the story, the setting and atmosphere evoked by it, the conflicts described, the point of view of the story's telling—all work to give readers a sense of not just what the story is about but also what it's for. Writers and readers together create themes for the work; one reason that great literature provokes so much critical commentary is that many themes can emerge depending on who is reading, and when. Writers persuade us that they are telling some truth or giving us some insight about the real world outside the text.

Theme and the Pentad

Using Burke's pentad, you can see the relationship of theme to the individual elements in narrative. Consider, for example, the purpose-scene (theme-to-setting) ratio. Many stories, especially those with a significant conflict with the natural or social world, explore themes where setting, or scene, affects characters and meanings. In Herman Melville's novel *Moby Dick,* setting—the ocean and the whaling ship searching for the mysterious white whale—becomes almost a character. How the sailors confront the challenge of the ocean's power and changeable nature as well as the fearsome challenge of the great white whale is an important theme for Melville's work. Other ratios—purpose-act (theme to actions), purpose-agent (theme to character), or purpose-agency (theme to methods)—can each give you as a reader a way of seeing how theme develops in relationship to the individual elements in a text. Of course, it's possible to link purpose or theme to any of those elements, and that's one reason that readers find more than one theme in literary work.

Symbols

Writers use symbolic elements in their texts to help convey thematic ideas. In the play *A Raisin in the Sun*, a pot of geraniums on the windowsill tells readers how much the characters want to establish roots and to have a home without their ever saying so. In the novel *The Portrait of a Lady*, a sudden vision of people sitting together intimately tells readers about relationships that have up to that moment been hidden from them. Character names like *Mr. Gradgrind* can carry a symbolic message, just as places like the poor fishing village in *The Shipping News* or the forest in *The Scarlet Letter* might.

Symbols, like settings, can be typical, or stock; that is, whenever they are used, they carry similar associations for most readers. The Christian cross, the Statue of Liberty, a black cat, a white dove, are all stock symbols, although sometimes they're used for ironic, rather than stock, effect. Other symbols carry thematic weight only in the context of the work itself: pots of geraniums don't always mean home; a man sitting in a chair and a woman standing behind him don't always mean romantic intimacy. These elements become symbolic because the writer has placed them for rhetorical effect—to help readers perceive significance and meaning in the moment and in the work as a whole. Think of other works you've read where a gesture, an object, or a scene seemed symbolic. You were responding to the heightened sense of meaning the characters and the writer were bringing to the element or object.

Images

One of the most significant ways in which writers convey theme is through their use of language. The imagery they choose to describe characters, settings, and conflicts allows readers to experience the story in ways that suggest larger meanings for the work. Like symbols, images heighten readers' sense of the significance of the object or the moment, and foster readers' engagement with themes. "When we were small, I could catch my sisters the way they caught butterflies, capture their attention and almost make them believe that all I said was true." Dorothy Allison begins her memoir *Two or Three Things I Know For Sure* with this imagery-laden line. The analogy between catching attention and catching butterflies feels both delicate and transitory; butterflies, like stories, are insubstantial and beautiful. Readers already feel a relationship building between the narrator and her sisters that feels precious as well. And all in one small line. Indeed, the comparisons embedded in metaphors can establish tone and suggest theme through their comparisons. If you look at many of the previous examples, you'll see how writers use metaphors to suggest more than literal description might. Quoyle has "a great loaf of a body" in *The Shipping News,* and readers become ready to expect that there may be a message about how such a "loaf" might rise.

Diction

Diction, or word choice, tells readers about time, place, character, and theme. The dialect speech Twain uses in *Huckleberry Finn* differentiates characters—white from black, educated from uneducated, rich from poor. The fact that two of the dialect speakers, Jim and Huck, are the poorest, least powerful people in the story and also the most ethical ones carries a message about humanity that Twain was careful to point out. Here's an example of Huck's speech from the opening to the novel: "You don't know about me without you have read a book by the name of *The Adventures of Tom Sawyer;* but that ain't no matter. That book was made by Mr. Mark Twain, and he told the truth, mainly. There was things which he stretched, but mainly he told the truth." The use of nonstandard words and grammar as well as odd phrasing marks Huck's dialect speech, and adds to readers' understanding of Huck's character.

Syntax

The arrangement of sentences, their length and complexity, also tells us much about characters and themes. The **syntax** in *The Scarlet Letter* is complex, signaling its nineteenth-century composition. Hawthorne often uses the **periodic sentence,** holding off the full meaning of the sentence until near the end. That holding off becomes part of the plot of the story, for the narrator clearly knows the guilty secret that he keeps readers from knowing for a while and that he keeps the town from knowing for most of the novel.

The syntax helps establish theme. Short bursts of sentences, long flowing sentences, intricately designed sentences—all can give readers ideas about the narrator's position on the story being told and lead us to consider the larger meaning of what we're reading.

Consider the opening of *Daisy Miller,* the short novel by late-nineteenth-century American author Henry James: "At the little town of Vevay, in Switzerland, there is a particularly comfortable hotel. There are, indeed, many hotels, for the entertainment of the tourists is the business of the place, which, as many travelers remember, is seated upon the edge of a remarkably blue lake—a lake that it behooves every tourist to visit." Compare the complexity of that sentence construction to the opening of the short story "Me and My Baby View the Eclipse," by contemporary southern writer Lee Smith. "Sharon Shaw met her lover, Raymond Stewart, in an incident that took place in broad daylight at the Xerox machine in Stewart's Pharmacy three years ago—it *can't* be that long!" Both passages contain long sentences, but James's passage contains subordinate clauses that qualify the descriptions and delay them, while Smith's opening builds the information cumulatively with prepositional phrases that detail the information. Notice how both passages conclude with a dash, and in both cases there's some humor in the last small phrases.

A Final Word About Narrative—and About Rhetoric

All the elements of narrative work together to help readers enter the world of the texts they read, to understand that world, and to consider what that world reveals about the larger world outside the text. Writers and readers create together, communicating messages, uncovering connections and differences. Rhetoric works in narrative in many of the same ways as it operates in other genres and for other purposes, highlighting occasion and appropriateness, audiences and speakers, intentions and effects.

Activity

Read the following passage from Tom Stoppard's play *The Real Thing,* where Henry, a playwright, is arguing with his lover, Annie, about writing. Read the passage, and then choose diction, imagery, syntax, metaphor, or symbol to write about. Tell how the element you've chosen might contribute to a reader's view of the character and provide insight into the theme of the work.

> HENRY: Shut up and listen. This thing here, which looks like a wooden club, is actually several pieces of particular wood cunningly put together in a certain way so that the whole thing is sprung, like a dance floor. It's for hitting cricket balls with. If you get it right, the cricket ball will travel two hundred yards in four seconds, and all you've done is give a knock like knocking the top off a bottle of stout, and it makes a noise like a trout taking a fly. . . . [*He clucks his tongue to make the noise.*] What we're trying to do is to write cricket bats, so that when we throw up an idea and give it a little knock, it might . . . travel. . . .

As this book has attempted to illustrate, rhetoric is in large measure our cricket bat, as Henry would say—the primary tool that we use to communicate with the world around us. Becoming conscious of how rhetoric works for us as speakers, writers, listeners, and readers begins the process of becoming good rhetoricians, effective participants in the lives we live in and out of school. In the speeches, poems, textbooks, cartoons, novels, essays, assignments, and memos we read and write—in fact, in every form of communication between people—rhetoric has its everyday use.

Interchapter

7

Overview of the Major Points in Chapter 7

- The elements of literature you're familiar with are rhetorical devices, used by writers to draw out and enrich understanding by readers.
- Burke's pentad can help readers discover the significance of literary elements as they relate to other elements in the text.
- Reading literary works is like reading other kinds of writing and like experiencing life itself, with purposes and contexts available for readers to discover.

Activities and Discussion Questions Chapter 7 Use these questions and comments as guides for your own discussion and writing about these literary works.

Henry David Thoreau, "An Essay on Civil Disobedience" (published 1849)

The text appears on pages 222–237. In your group, discuss the following questions. You might use one or more of these questions as the basis for a well-organized essay or journal entry.

1. Try to create a plot line for Thoreau's essay. What happens first and next and next? What's the final outcome? How much plot does the story contain? How do you discover conflict in the story?

2. Choosing at least three images or metaphors of your own, write a character description of Thoreau. Do you find him a complex or simple (round or flat) character?

3. Which of Burke's ratios seems most important in this essay? Talk with your group to see how many different ratios your group finds important.

Eavan Boland, "It's a Woman's World" (published 1982)

The text appears on pages 238–239. In your group, discuss the following questions. You might use one or more of these questions as the basis for a well-organized essay or journal entry.

1. In your group, list the figurative language—metaphor or other imagery—you find most striking. Then talk about how the language underscores conflict in the poem.

2. Select one of Burke's ratio—scene-act or scene-agent would be useful ones—and write an analysis of the poem. Use quotations from the poem to help you. Share your analysis with your group.

3. Discuss the narrator of the poem. Is she omniscient? Limited? How does she see herself in relation to the characters she describes in the poem?

Alice Walker, "Everyday Use" (published 1973)

The text appears on pages 240–246. In your group, discuss the following questions. You might use one or more of these questions as the basis for a well-organized essay or journal entry.

1. What seems to be the central conflict in Walker's story? Find places in the story that suggest the conflict to you, and discuss those places in the text with your group. Do you find patterns or similarities in your choices?

2. What kind of narrator do you find in the story? Rewrite a paragraph or two of the story from the perspective of another kind of narrator. Then discuss with your group how your response to the story changes with a different narrator.

3. What details of setting seem especially symbolic or important to the story as a whole?

READINGS

"On the Duty of Civil Disobedience"
Henry David Thoreau

"It's a Woman's World"
Eavan Boland

"Everyday Use"
Alice Walker

Chapters 1 through 7 of this book introduce you to concepts of classical and modern rhetoric. In this section of the book, you'll find three pieces of writing reprinted in their entirety. We expect you to read the three (even if you already know them)—an essay, a poem, and a short story—at the beginning of the course in which you're using this book. We also expect you to come back and reread parts of them as you make your way through the seven main chapters of the book. In fact, at the end of each chapter, there's an interchapter waiting for you. Each interchapter will ask you to think about the concepts in the immediately preceding chapter as you focus on the essay, the poem, and the short story in this Readings section.

An Essay

Henry David Thoreau

Henry David Thoreau was born in Concord, Massachusetts, in 1817, and died there in 1862. In between, he lived a life of self-reliance on his own terms rather than society's. Indeed, one of this writer's most famous lines argues, "If a man does not keep pace with his companions, perhaps it is because he hears a different drummer. Let him step to the music which he hears, however measured or far away."

The great theme that permeates the writings of Thoreau is his life in the natural world, his quest to feel within himself the spirit of nature. He wrote his first book, A Week on the Concord and Merrimack Rivers *while living in a self-built hut at Walden Pond, where his goal was to strip away the inessential and to simplify life. There he also kept journals that formed the basis for* Walden, *which would prove to be his masterwork.*

While Thoreau was staying at the pond, the United States was involved in a war with Mexico. Because Henry David Thoreau considered the war unjust, he refused to pay a tax that he thought supported the U.S. government, and he was put in jail for a day. Two years later, he wrote the following essay, setting out his philosophy of passive resistance as a means of protest.

Henry David Thoreau
"On the Duty of Civil Disobedience"

1   I heartily accept the motto,—"That government is best which governs least"; and I should like to see it acted up to more rapidly and systematically. Carried out, it finally amounts to this, which also I believe,—"That government is best which governs not at all"; and when men are prepared for it, that will be the kind of government which they will have. Government is at best but an expedient; but most governments are usually, and all governments are sometimes, inexpedient. The objections which have been brought against a standing army, and they are many and weighty, and deserve to prevail, may also at last be brought against a standing government. The standing army is only an arm of the standing government. The government itself, which is only the mode which the people have chosen to execute their will, is equally liable to be abused and perverted before the people can act through it. Witness the present Mexican war, the work of comparatively a few individuals using the standing government as their tool; for, in the outset, the people would not have consented to this measure.

2   This American government—what is it but a tradition, though a recent one, endeavoring to transmit itself unimpaired to posterity, but each instant losing some of its integrity? It has not the vitality and force of a single living man; for a single man can bend it to his will. It is a sort of wooden gun to the people themselves. But it is not the less necessary for this; for the people must have some complicated machinery or other, and hear its din, to satisfy that idea of government which they have. Governments show thus how successfully men can be imposed on, even impose on themselves, for their own advantage. It is excellent, we must all allow. Yet this government never of itself furthered any enterprise, but by the alacrity with which it got out of its way. It does not keep the country free. It does not settle the West. It does not educate. The character inherent in the American people has done all that has been accomplished; and it would have done somewhat more, if the government had not sometimes got in its way. For government is an expedient by which men would fain succeed in letting one another alone; and, as has been said, when it is most expedient, the governed are most let alone by it. Trade and commerce, if they were not made of India *rubber*, would never manage to bounce over the obstacles

which legislators are continually putting in their way—and, if one were to judge these men wholly by the effects of their actions, and not partly by their intentions, they would deserve to be classed and punished with those mischievous persons who put obstructions on the railroads.

3   But, to speak practically and as a citizen, unlike those who call themselves no-government men, I ask for, not at once no government, but *at once* a better government. Let every man make known what kind of government would command his respect, and that will be one step toward obtaining it.

4   After all, the practical reason why, when the power is once in the hands of the people, a majority are permitted, and for a long period continue, to rule, is not because they are most likely to be in the right, nor because this seems fairest to the minority, but because they are physically the strongest. But a government in which the majority rule in all cases cannot be based on justice, even as far as men understand it. Can there not be a government in which majorities do not virtually decide right and wrong, but conscience?—in which majorities decide only those questions to which the rule of expediency is applicable? Must the citizen ever for a moment, or in the least degree, resign his conscience to the legislator? Why has every man a conscience, then? I think that we should be men first, and subjects afterward. It is not desirable to cultivate a respect for the law, so much as for the right. The only obligation which I have a right to assume is to do at any time what I think right. It is truly enough—said—that a corporation has no conscience; but a corporation of conscientious men is a corporation with a conscience. Law never made men a whit more just; and, by means of their respect for it, even the law disposed are daily made the agents of injustice. A common and natural result of an undue respect for law is, that you may see a file of soldiers, colonel, captain, corporal, privates, powder-monkeys, and all, marching in admirable order over hill and dale to the wars, against their wills, ay, against their common sense and consciences, which makes it very steep marching indeed, and produces a palpitation of the heart. They have no doubt that it is a damnable business in which they are concerned; they are all peaceably inclined. Now, what are they? Men at all? or small movable forts and magazines, at the service of some unscrupulous man in power? Visit the Navy Yard, and behold a marine, such a man as an American government can make, or such as it can make a man with its black arts—a mere shadow and reminiscence of humanity, a man laid out alive and standing, and already, as one may say, buried under arms with funeral accompaniments, though it may be

"Not a drum was heard, not a funeral note,
As his corse to the rampart we hurried;
Not a soldier discharged his farewell shot
O'er the grave where our hero we buried."

5   The mass of men serve the state thus, not as men mainly, but as machines, with their bodies. They are the standing army, and the militia, jailers, constables,

posse comitatus, etc. In most cases there is no free exercise whatever of the judgment or of the moral sense; but they put themselves on a level with wood and earth and stones; and wooden men can perhaps be manufactured that will serve the purpose as well. Such command no more respect than men of straw or a lump of dirt. They have the same sort of worth only as horses and dogs.—Yet such as these even are commonly esteemed good citizens. Others, as most legislators, politicians, lawyers, ministers, and office-holders, serve the state chiefly with their heads; and, as they rarely make any moral distinctions, they are as likely to serve the devil, without *intending* it, as God. A very few, as heroes, patriots, martyrs, reformers in the great sense, and *men,* serve the state with their consciences also, and so necessarily resist it for the most part—and they are commonly treated as enemies by it. A wise man will only be useful as a man, and will not submit to be "clay," and "stop a hole to keep the wind away," but leave that office to his dust at least:—

> "I am too high-born to be propertied, To be a secondary at control,
> Or useful serving-man and instrument
> To any sovereign state throughout the world."

6   He who gives himself entirely to his fellow-men appears to them useless and selfish; but he who gives himself partially to them is pronounced a benefactor and philanthropist.

7   How does it become a man to behave toward this American government to-day? I answer, that he cannot without disgrace be associated with it. I cannot for an instant recognize that political organization as *my* government which is *the slave's* government also.

8   All men recognize the right of revolution; that is, the right to refuse allegiance to, and to resist, the government, when its tyranny or its inefficiency are great and unendurable. But almost all say that such is not the case now. But such was the case, they think, in the Revolution of '75. If one were to tell me that this was a bad government because it taxed certain foreign commodities brought to its ports, it is most probable that I should not make an ado about it, for I can do without them. All machines have their friction—and possibly this does enough good to counterbalance the evil. At any rate, it is a great evil to make a stir about it. But when the friction comes to have its machine, and oppression and robbery are organized, I say, let us not have such a machine any longer. In other words, when a sixth of the population of a nation which has undertaken to be the refuge of liberty are slaves, and a whole country is unjustly overrun and conquered by a foreign army, and subjected to military law, I think that it is not too soon for honest men to rebel and revolutionize. What makes this duty the more urgent is the fact that the country so overrun is not our own, but ours is the invading army.

9   Paley, a common authority with many on moral questions, in his chapter on the "Duty of Submission to Civil Government," resolves all civil obligation

into expediency; and he proceeds to say that "so long as the interest of the whole society requires it, that is, so long as the established government cannot be resisted or changed without public inconveniency, it is the will of God that the established government be obeyed, and no longer"—"This principle being admitted, the justice of every particular case of resistance is reduced to a computation of the quantity of the danger and grievance on the one side, and of the probability and expense of redressing it on the other." Of this, he says, every man shall judge for himself. But Paley appears never to have contemplated those cases to which the rule of expediency does not apply, in which a people, as well as an individual, must do justice, cost what it may. If I have unjustly wrested a plank from a drowning man I must restore it to him though I drown myself. This, according to Paley, would be inconvenient. But he that would save his life, in such a case, shall lose it. This people must cease to hold slaves, and to make war on Mexico, though it cost them their existence as a people.

10   In their practice, nations agree with Paley; but does any one think that Massachusetts does exactly what is right at the present crisis?

> "A drab of state, a cloth-o'-silver slut,
> To have her train borne up, and her soul trail in the dirt."

11   Practically speaking, the opponents to a reform in Massachusetts are not a hundred thousand politicians at the South, but a hundred thousand merchants and farmers here, who are more interested in commerce and agriculture than they are in humanity, and are not prepared to do justice to the slave and to Mexico, *cost what it may*. I quarrel not with far-off foes, but with those who, near at home, co-operate with, and do the bidding of those far away, and without whom the latter would be harmless. We are accustomed to say, that the mass of men are unprepared; but improvement is slow, because the few are not materially wiser or better than the many. It is not so important that many should be as good as you, as that there be some absolute goodness. Somewhere; for that will leaven the whole lump. There are thousands who are *in opinion* opposed to slavery and to the war, who yet in effect do nothing to put an end to them; who, esteeming themselves children of Washington and Franklin, sit down with their hands in their pockets, and say that they know not what to do, and do nothing; who even postpone the question of freedom to the question of free-trade, and quietly read the prices-current along with the latest advices from Mexico, after dinner, and, it may be, fall asleep over them both. What is the price-current of an honest man and patriot to-day? They hesitate, and they regret, and sometimes they petition; but they do nothing in earnest and with effect. They will wait, well disposed, for others to remedy the evil, that they may no longer have it to regret. At most, they give only a cheap vote, and a feeble countenance and Godspeed, to the right, as it goes by them. There are nine hundred and ninety-nine patrons of virtue to one virtuous man; but it is easier to deal with the real possessor of a thing than with the temporary guardian of it.

12   All voting is a sort of gaming, like checkers or backgammon, with a slight moral tinge to it, a playing with right and wrong, with moral questions; and betting naturally accompanies it. The character of the voters is *not* staked. I cast my vote, perchance, as I think right; but I am not vitally concerned that that right should prevail. I am willing to leave it to the majority. Its obligation, therefore, never exceeds that of expediency. Even voting for *the right* is doing nothing for it. It is only expressing to men feebly your desire that it should prevail. A wise man will not leave the right to the mercy of chance, nor wish it to prevail through the power of the majority. There is but little virtue in the action of masses of men. When the majority shall at length vote for the abolition of slavery, it will be because they are indifferent to slavery, or because there is but little slavery left to be abolished by their vote. *They* will then be the only slaves. Only *his* vote can hasten the abolition of slavery who asserts his own freedom by his vote.

13   I hear of a convention to be held at Baltimore, or elsewhere, for the selection of a candidate for the Presidency, made up chiefly of editors, and men who are politicians by profession; but I think, what is it to any independent, intelligent, and respectable man what decision they may come to? Shall we not have the advantage of his wisdom and honesty, nevertheless? Can we not count upon some independent votes? Are there not many individuals in the country who do not attend conventions? But no: I find that the respectable man, so called, has immediately drifted from his position, and despairs of his country, when his country has more reason to despair of him. He forthwith adopts one of the candidates thus selected as the only *available* one, thus proving that he is *himself available* for any purposes of the demagogue. His vote is of no more worth than that of any unprincipled foreigner or hireling native, who may have been bought. Oh for a man who is a *man,* and, as my neighbor says, has a bone in his back which you cannot pass your hand through. Our statistics are at fault: the population has been returned too large. How many *men* are there to a square thousand miles in this country? Hardly one. Does not America offer any inducement for men to settle here? The American has dwindled into an Odd Fellow—one who may be known by the development of his organ of gregariousness, and a manifest lack of intellect and cheerful self-reliance; whose first and chief concern, on coming into the world, is to see that the almshouses are in good repair; and, before yet he has lawfully donned the virile garb, to collect a fund for the support of the widows and orphans that may be; who, in short, ventures to live only by the aid of the Mutual Insurance company, which has promised to bury him, decently.

14   It is not a man's duty, as a matter of course, to devote himself to the eradication of any, even the most enormous wrong—he may still properly have other concerns to engage him; but it is his duty, at least, to wash his hands of it, and, if he gives it no thought longer, not to give it practically his support. If I devote myself to other pursuits and contemplations, I must first see, at least, that I do not pursue them sitting upon another man's shoulders. I must get off him first, that he may pursue his contemplations too. See what gross inconsistency

is tolerated. I have heard some of my townsmen say, "I should like to have them order me out to help put down an insurrection of the slaves, or to March to Mexico;—see if I would go"; and yet these very men have each, directly by their allegiance, and so indirectly, at least, by their money, furnished a substitute. The soldier is applauded who refuses to serve in an unjust war by those who do not refuse to sustain the unjust government which makes the war; is applauded by those whose own act and authority he disregards and sets at naught; as if the state were penitent to that degree that it hired one to scourge it while it sinned, but not to that degree that it left off sinning for a moment. Thus, under the name of Order and Civil Government, we are all made at last to pay homage to and support our own meanness. After the first blush of sin comes its indifference; and from immoral it becomes, as it were, unmoral, and not quite unnecessary to that life which we have made.

15   The broadest and most prevalent error requires the most disinterested virtue to sustain it. The slight reproach to which the virtue of patriotism is commonly liable, the noble are most likely to incur. Those who, while they disapprove of the character and measures of a government, yield to it their allegiance and support are undoubtedly its most conscientious supporters, and so frequently the most serious obstacles to reform. Some are petitioning the State to dissolve the Union, to disregard the requisitions of the President. Why do they not dissolve it themselves—the union between themselves and the State—and refuse to pay their quota into its treasury? Do not they stand in the same relation to the State, that the State does to the Union? And have not the same reasons prevented the State from resisting the Union, which have prevented them from resisting the State?

16   How can a man be satisfied to entertain an opinion merely, and enjoy it? *Is* there any enjoyment in it, if his opinion is that he is aggrieved? If you are cheated out of a single dollar by your neighbor, you do not rest satisfied with knowing that you are cheated, or with saying that you are cheated, or even with petitioning him to pay you your due; but you take effectual steps at once to obtain the full amount, and see that you are never cheated again. Action from principle—the perception and the performance of right—changes things and relations; it is essentially revolutionary, and does not consist wholly with anything which was. It not only divides states and churches, it divides families; ay, it divides the *individual,* separating the diabolical in him from the divine.

17   Unjust laws exist; shall we be content to obey them, or shall we endeavor to amend them, and obey them until we have succeeded, or shall we transgress them at once? Men generally, under such a government as this, think that they ought to wait until they have persuaded the majority to alter them. They think that, if they should resist, the remedy would be worse than the evil. But it is the fault of the government itself that the remedy is worse than the evil. It makes it worse. Why is it not more apt to anticipate and provide for reform? Why does it not cherish its wise minority? Why does it cry and resist before it is hurt? Why does it not encourage its citizens to be on the alert to point out its faults, and *do* better than it would have them? Why does it always crucify

Christ, and excommunicate Copernicus and Luther, and pronounce Washington and Franklin rebels?

18   One would think, that a deliberate and practical denial of its authority was the only offence never contemplated by government; else, why has it not assigned its definite, its suitable and proportionate, penalty? If a man who has no property refuses but once to earn nine shillings for the State, he is put in prison for a period unlimited by any law that I know, and determined only by the discretion of those who placed him there; but if he should steal ninety times nine shillings from the State, he is soon permitted to go at large again.

19   If the injustice is part of the necessary friction of the machine of government, let it go, let it go; perchance it will wear smooth—certainly the machine will wear out. If the injustice has a spring, or a pulley, or a rope, or a crank, exclusively for itself, then perhaps you may consider whether the remedy will not be worse than the evil; but if it is of such a nature that it requires you to be the agent of injustice to another, then, I say, break the law. Let your life be a counter friction to stop the machine. What I have to do is to see, at any rate, that I do not lend myself to the wrong which I condemn.

20   As for adopting the ways which the State has provided for remedying the evil, I know not of such ways. They take too much time, and a man's life will be gone. I have other affairs to attend to. I came into this world, not chiefly to make this a good place to live in, but to live in it, be it good or bad. A man has not everything to do, but something; and because he cannot do *everything,* it is not necessary that he should do *something* wrong. It is not my business to be petitioning the Governor or the Legislature any more than it is theirs to petition me; and if they should not hear my petition, what should I do then? But in this case the State has provided no way; its very Constitution is the evil. This may seem to be harsh and stubborn and unconciliatory; but it is to treat with the utmost kindness and consideration the only spirit that can appreciate or deserves it. So is a change for the better, like birth and death which convulse the body.

21   I do not hesitate to say, that those who call themselves Abolitionists should at once effectually withdraw their support, both in person and property, from the government of Massachusetts, and not wait till they constitute a majority of one, before they suffer the right to prevail through them. I think that it is enough if they have God on their side, without waiting for that other one. Moreover, any man more right than his neighbors constitutes a majority of one already.

22   I meet this American government, or its representative, the State government, directly, and face to face, once a year—no more—in the person of its tax-gatherer; this is the only mode in which a man situated as I am necessarily meets it; and it then says distinctly, Recognize me; and the simplest, the most effectual, and, in the present posture of affairs, the indispensablest mode of treating with it on this head, of expressing your little satisfaction with and love for it, is to deny it then. My civil neighbor, the tax-gatherer, is the very man I have to deal with—for it is, after all, with men and not with parchment that

I quarrel—and he has voluntarily chosen to be an agent of the government. How shall he ever know well what he is and does as an officer of the government, or as a man, until he is obliged to consider whether he shall treat me, his neighbor, for whom he has respect, as a neighbor and well-disposed man, or as a maniac and disturber of the peace, and see if he can get over this obstruction to his neighborliness without a ruder and more impetuous thought or speech corresponding with his action? I know this well, that if one thousand, if one hundred, if ten men whom I could name—if ten *honest* men only—ay, if *one* HONEST man, in this State of Massachusetts, *ceasing to hold slaves,* were actually to withdraw from this copartnership, and be locked up in the county jail therefore, it would be the abolition of slavery in America. For it matters not how small the beginning may seem to be: what is once well done is done forever. But we love better to talk about it: that we say is our mission. Reform keeps many scores of newspapers in its service, but not one man. If my esteemed neighbor, the State's ambassador, who will devote his days to the settlement of the question of human fights in the Council Chamber, instead of being threatened with the prisons of Carolina, were to sit down the prisoner of Massachusetts, that State which is so anxious to foist the sin of slavery upon her sister—though at present she can discover only an act of inhospitality to be the ground of a quarrel with her—the Legislature would not wholly waive the subject the following winter.

23   Under a government which imprisons any unjustly, the true place for a just man is also a prison. The proper place to-day, the only place which Massachusetts has provided for her freer and less desponding spirits, is in her prisons, to be put out and locked out of the State by her own act, as they have already put themselves out by their principles. It is there that the fugitive slave, and the Mexican prisoner on parole, and the Indian come to plead the wrongs of his race, should find them; on that separate, but more free and honorable ground, where the State places those who are not *with* her, but *against* her— the only house in a slave State in which a free man can abide with honor. If any think that their influence would be lost there, and their voices no longer afflict the ear of the State, that they would not be as an enemy within its walls, they do not know by how much truth is stronger than error, nor how much more eloquently and effectively he can combat injustice who has experienced a little in his own person. Cast your whole vote, not a strip of paper merely, but your whole influence. A minority is powerless while it conforms to the majority; it is not even a minority then; but it is irresistible when it clogs by its whole weight. If the alternative is to keep all just men in prison, or give up war and slavery, the State will not hesitate which to choose. If a thousand men were not to pay their tax-bills this year, that would not be a violent and bloody measure, as it would be to pay them, and enable the State to commit violence and shed innocent blood. This is, in fact, the definition of a peaceable revolution, if any such is possible. If the tax-gatherer, or any other public officer, asks me, as one has done, "But what shall I do?" my answer is, "If you really wish to do anything, resign your office." When the subject has refused allegiance, and the officer has resigned his office, then the revolution is accomplished. But even suppose

blood should flow. Is there not a sort of blood shed when the conscience is wounded? Through this wound a man's real manhood and immortality flow out, and he bleeds to an everlasting death. I see this blood flowing now.

24   I have contemplated the imprisonment of the offender, rather than the seizure of his goods—though both will serve the same purpose—because they who assert the purest right, and consequently are most dangerous to a corrupt State, commonly have not spent much time in accumulating property. To such the State renders comparatively small service, and a slight tax is wont to appear exorbitant, particularly if they are obliged to earn it by special labor with their hands. If there were one who lived wholly without the use of money, the State itself would hesitate to demand it of him. But the rich man—not to make any invidious comparison—is always sold to the institution which makes him rich. Absolutely speaking, the more money, the less virtue; for money comes between a man and his objects, and obtains them for him; and it was certainly no great virtue to obtain it. It puts to rest many questions which he would otherwise be taxed to answer; while the only new question which it puts is the hard but superfluous one, how to spend it. Thus his moral ground is taken from under his feet. The opportunities of living are diminished in proportion as what are called the "means" are increased. The best thing a man can do for his culture when he is rich is to endeavor to carry out those schemes which he entertained when he was poor. Christ answered the Herodians according to their condition. "Show me the tribute-money," said he;—and one took a penny out of his pocket—if you use money which has the image of Caesar on it, and which he has made current and valuable that is, *if you are men of the State,* and gladly enjoy the advantages of Caesar's government, then pay him back some of his own when he demands it; "Render therefore to Caesar that which is Caesar's, and to God those things which are God's"—leaving them no wiser than before as to which was which; for they did not wish to know.

25   When I converse with the freest of my neighbors, I perceive that, whatever they may say about the magnitude and seriousness of the question, and their regard for the public tranquillity, the long and the short of the matter is, that they cannot spare the protection of the existing government, and they dread the consequences to their property and families of disobedience to it. For my own part I should not like to think that I ever rely on the protection of the State. But, if I deny the authority of the State when it presents its tax-bill, it will soon take and waste all my property, and so harass me and my children without end. This is hard. This makes it impossible for a man to live honestly, and at the same time comfortably in outward respects. It will not be worth the while to accumulate property; that would be sure to go again. You must hire or squat somewhere, and raise but a small crop, and eat that soon. You must live within yourself, and depend upon yourself always tucked up and ready for a start, and not have many affairs. A man may grow rich in Turkey even, if he will be in all respects a good subject of the Turkish government. Confucius said, "If a state is governed by the principles of reason, poverty and misery are subjects of shame; if a state is not governed by the principles of reason, riches and honors are the subjects of

shame." No: until I want the protection of Massachusetts to be extended to me in some distant Southern port, where my liberty is endangered, or until I am bent solely on building up an estate at home by peaceful enterprise, I can afford to refuse allegiance to Massachusetts, and her right to my property and life. It costs me less in every sense to incur the penalty of disobedience to the State than it would to obey. I should feel as if I were worth less in that case.

26   Some years ago, the State met me in behalf of the Church, and commanded me to pay a certain sum toward the support of a clergyman whose preaching my father attended, but never I myself. "Pay," it said, "or be locked up in the jail." I declined to pay. But, unfortunately, another man saw fit to pay it. I did not see why the schoolmaster should be taxed to support the priest, and not the priest the schoolmaster: for I was not the State's schoolmaster, but I supported myself by voluntary subscription. I did not see why the lyceum should not present its tax-bill, and have the State to back its demand, as well as the Church. However, at the request of the selectmen, I condescended to make some such statement as this in writing:—"Know all men by these presents, that I, Henry Thoreau, do not wish to be regarded as a member of any incorporated society which I have not joined." This I gave to the town clerk; and he has it. The State, having thus learned that I did not wish to be regarded as a member of that church, has never made a like demand on me since; though it said that it must adhere to its original presumption that time. If I had known how to name them, I should then have signed off in detail from all the societies which I never signed on to; but I did not know where to find a complete list.

27   I have paid no poll-tax for six years. I was put into a jail once on this account, for one night; and, as I stood considering the walls of solid stone, two or three feet thick, the door of wood and iron, a foot thick, and the iron grating which strained the light, I could not help being struck with the foolishness of that institution which treated me as if I were mere flesh and blood and bones, to be locked up. I wondered that it should have concluded at length that this was the best use it could put me to, and had never thought to avail itself of my services in some way. I saw that, if there was a wall of stone between me and my townsmen, there was a still more difficult one to climb or break through, before they could get to be as free as I was. I did not for a moment feel confined, and the walls seemed a great waste of stone and mortar. I felt as if I alone of all my townsmen had paid my tax. They plainly did not know how to treat me, but behaved like persons who are underbred. In every threat and in every compliment there was a blunder; for they thought that my chief desire was to stand the other side of that stone wall. I could not but smile to see how industriously they locked the door on my meditations, which followed them out again without let or hindrance, and they were really all that was dangerous. As they could not reach me, they had resolved to punish my body; just as boys, if they cannot come at some person against whom they have a spite, will abuse his dog. I saw that the State was half-witted, that it was timid as a tone woman with her silver spoons, and that it did not know its friends from its foes, and I lost all my remaining respect for it, and pitied it.

28   Thus the State never intentionally confronts a man's sense, intellectual or moral, but only his body, his senses. It is not armed with superior wit or honesty, but with superior physical strength. I was not born to be forced. I will breathe after my own fashion. Let us see who is the strongest. What force has a multitude? They only can force me who obey a higher law than I. They force me to become like themselves. I do not hear of *men being forced* to have this way or that by masses of men. What sort of life were that to live? When I meet a government which says to me, "Your money or your life," why should I be in haste to give it my money? It may be in a great strait, and not know what to do: I cannot help that. It must help itself, do as I do. It is not worth the while to snivel about it. I am not responsible for the successful working of the machinery of society. I am not the son of the engineer. I perceive that, when an acorn and a chestnut fall side by side, the one does not remain inert to make way for the other, but both obey their own laws, and spring and grow and flourish as best they can, till one, perchance, overshadows and destroys the other. If a plant cannot live according to its nature, it dies—and so a man.

29   The night in prison was novel and interesting enough. The prisoners in their shirt-sleeves were enjoying a chat and the evening air in the doorway, when I entered. But the jailer said, "Come, boys, it is time to lock up"; and so they dispersed, and I heard the sound of their steps returning into the hollow apartments. My room-mate was introduced to me by the jailer as "a first-rate fellow and a clever man." When the door was locked, he showed me where to hang my hat, and how he managed matters there. The rooms were whitewashed once a month; and this one, at least, was the whitest, most simply furnished, and probably the neatest apartment in the town. He naturally wanted to know where I came from, and what brought me there; and, when I had told him, I asked him in my turn how he came there, presuming him to be an honest man, of course; and, as the world goes, I believe he was. "Why," said he, "they accuse me of burning a barn; but I never did it." As near as I could discover, he had probably gone to bed in a barn when drunk, and smoked his pipe there; and so a barn was burnt. He had the reputation of being a clever man, had been there some three months waiting for his trial to come on, and would have to wait as much longer, but he was quite domesticated and contented, since he got his board for nothing, and thought that he was well treated.

30   He occupied one window, and I the other; and I saw that if one stayed there long, his principal business would be to look out the window. I had soon read all the tracts that were left there, and examined where former prisoners had broken out, and where a grate had been sawed off, and heard the history of the various occupants of that room; for I found that even here there was a history and a gossip which never circulated beyond the walls of the jail. Probably this is the only house in the town where verses are composed, which are afterward printed in a circular form, but not published. I was shown quite a long list of verses which were composed by some young men who had been detected in an attempt to escape, who avenged themselves by singing them.

31   I pumped my fellow-prisoner as dry as I could, for fear I should never see him again; but at length he showed me which was my bed, and left me to blow out the lamp.

32   It was like travelling into a far country, such as I had never expected to behold, to lie there for one night. It seemed to me that I never had heard the town-clock strike before, nor the evening sounds of the village—for we slept with the windows open, which were inside the grating. It was to see my native village in the light of the Middle Ages, and our Concord was turned into a Rhine stream, and visions of knights and castles passed before me. They were the voices of old burghers that I heard in the streets. I was an involuntary specta-tor and auditor of whatever was done and said in the kitchen of the adjacent village inn—a wholly new and rare experience to me. It was a closer view of my native town. I was fairly inside of it. I never had seen its institutions before. This is one of its peculiar institutions; for it is a shire town. I began to comprehend what its inhabitants were about.

33   In the morning, our breakfasts were put through the hole in the door, in small oblong-square tin pans, made to fit, and holding a pint of chocolate, with brown bread, and an iron spoon. When they called for the vessels again, I was green enough to return what bread I had left; but my comrade seized it, and said that I should lay that up for lunch or dinner. Soon after he was let out to work at haying in a neighboring field, whither he went every day, and would not be back till noon; so he bade me good-day, saying that he doubted if he should see me again.

34   When I came out of prison—for some one interfered, and paid that tax—I did not perceive that great changes had taken place on the common, such as he observed who went in a youth and emerged a tottering and gray-headed man; and yet a change had to my eyes come over the scene—the town, and State, and country—greater than any that mere time could effect. I saw yet more distinctly the State in which I lived. I saw to what extent the people among whom I lived could be trusted as good neighbors and friends; that their friendship was for summer weather only; that they did not greatly propose to do right; that they were a distinct race from me by their prejudices and super-stitions, as the Chinamen and Malays are; that in their sacrifices to humanity, they ran no risks, not even to their property; that after all they were not so noble but they treated the thief as he had treated them, and hoped, by a certain outward observance and a few prayers, and by walking in a particular straight though useless path from time to time, to save their souls. This may be to judge my neighbors harshly; for I believe that many of them are not aware that they have such an institution as the jail in their village.

35   It was formerly the custom in our village, when a poor debtor came out of jail, for his acquaintances to salute him, looking through their fingers, which were crossed to represent the gråting of a jail window, "How do ye do?" My neighbors did not thus salute me, but first looked at me, and then at one another, as if I had returned from a long journey. I was put into jail as I was going to the shoemaker's to get a shoe which was mended. When I was let out

the next morning, I proceeded to finish my errand, and, having put on my mended shoe, joined a huckleberry party, who were impatient to put themselves under my conduct; and in half an hour—for the horse was soon tackled—was in the midst of a huckleberry field, on one of our highest hills, two miles off, and then the State was nowhere to be seen.

36   This is the whole history of "My Prisons."

37   I have never declined paying the highway tax, because I am as desirous of being a good neighbor as I am of being a bad subject, and, as for supporting schools, I am doing my part to educate my fellow countrymen now. It is for no particular item in the tax-bill that I refuse to pay it. I simply wish to refuse allegiance to the State, to withdraw and stand aloof from it effectually. I do not care to trace the course of my dollar, if I could, till it buys a man, or a musket to shoot one with,—the dollar is innocent,—but I am concerned to trace the effects of my allegiance. In fact, I quietly declare war with the State, after my fashion, though I will still make what use and get what advantage of her I can, as is usual in such cases.

38   If others pay the tax which is demanded of me, from a sympathy with the State, they do but what they have already done in their own case, or rather they abet injustice to a greater extent than the State requires. If they pay the tax from a mistaken interest in the individual taxed, to save his property, or prevent his going to jail, it is because they have not considered wisely how far they let their private feelings interfere with the public good.

39   This, then, is my position at present. But one cannot be too much on his guard in such a case, lest his action be biased by obstinacy or an undue regard for the opinions of men. Let him see that he does only what belongs to himself and to the hour.

40   I think sometimes, Why, this people mean well; they are only ignorant; they would do better if they knew how: why give your neighbors this pain to treat you as they are not inclined to? But I think, again, This is no reason why I should do as they do, or permit others to suffer much greater pain of a different kind. Again, I sometimes say to myself, When many millions of men, without heat, without ill-will, without personal feeling of any kind, demand of you a few shillings only, without the possibility, such is their constitution, of retracting or altering their present demand, and without the possibility, on your side, of appeal to any other millions, why expose yourself to this overwhelming brute force? You do not resist cold and hunger, the winds and the waves, thus obstinately; you quietly submit to a thousand similar necessities. You do not put your head into the fire. But just in proportion as I regard this as not wholly a brute force, but partly a human force, and consider that I have relations to those millions as to so many millions of men, and not of mere brute or inanimate things, I see that appeal is possible, first and instantaneously, from them to the Maker of them, and, secondly, from them to themselves. But, if I put my head deliberately into the fire, there is no appeal to fire or to the Maker of fire, and I have only myself to blame. If I could convince myself that I have any right to be satisfied with men as they are, and to treat them accordingly, and not

according, in some respects, to my requisitions and expectations of what they and I ought to be, then, like a good Mussulman and fatalist, I should endeavor to be satisfied with things as they are, and say it is the will of God. And, above all, there is this difference between resisting this and a purely brute or natural force, that I can resist this with some effect; but I cannot expect, like Orpheus, to change the nature of the rocks and trees and beasts.

41   I do not wish to quarrel with any man or nation. I do not wish to split hairs, to make fine distinctions, or set myself up as better than my neighbors. I seek rather, I may say, even an excuse for conforming to the laws of the land. I am but too ready to conform to them. Indeed, I have reason to suspect myself on this head; and each year, as the tax-gatherer comes round, I find myself disposed to review the acts and position of the general and State governments, and the spirit of the people, to discover a pretext for conformity.

> "We must affect our country as our parents,
> And if at any time we alienate
> Our love or industry from doing it honor,
> We must respect effects and teach the soul
> Matter of conscience and religion,
> And not desire of rule or benefit."

42   I believe that the State will soon be able to take all my work of this sort out of my hands, and then I shall be no better a patriot than my fellow-countrymen. Seen from a lower point of view, the Constitution, with all its faults, is very good; the law and the courts are very respectable; even this State and this American government are, in many respects, very admirable and rare things, to be thankful for, such as a great many have described them; but seen from a point of view a little higher, they are what I have described them; seen from a higher still, and the highest, who shall say what they are, or that they are worth looking at or thinking of at all?

43   However, the government does not concern me much, and I shall bestow the fewest possible thoughts on it—It is not many moments that I live under a government, even in this world. If a man is thought-free, fancy-free, imagination-free, that which is *not* never for a long time appearing *to be* to him, unwise rulers or reformers cannot fatally interrupt him.

44   I know that most men think differently from myself; but those whose lives are by profession devoted to the study of these or kindred subjects, content me as little as any. Statesmen and legislators, standing so completely within the institution, never distinctly and nakedly behold it. They speak of moving society, but have no resting-place without it. They may be men of a certain experience and discrimination, and have no doubt invented ingenious and even useful systems, for which we sincerely thank them; but all their wit and usefulness lie within certain not very wide limits. They are wont to forget that the world is not governed by policy and expediency. Webster never goes behind government, and so cannot speak with authority about it. His words are wisdom to those

legislators who contemplate no essential reform in the existing government; but for thinkers, and those who legislate for all time, he never once glances at the subject. I know of those whose serene and wise speculations on this theme would soon reveal the limits of his mind's range and hospitality. Yet, compared with the cheap professions of most reformers, and the still cheaper wisdom and eloquence of politicians in general, his are almost the only sensible and valuable words, and we thank Heaven for him. Comparatively, he is always strong, original, and, above all, practical. Still, his quality is not wisdom, but prudence. The lawyer's truth is not truth, but consistency or a consistent expediency. Truth is always in harmony with herself, and is not concerned chiefly to reveal the justice that may consist with wrong-doing. He well deserves to be called, as he has been called, the Defender of the Constitution. There are really no blows to be given by him but defensive ones. He is not a leader, but a follower. His leaders are the men of '87. "I have never made an effort," he says, "and never propose to make an effort; I have never countenanced an effort, and never mean to countenance an effort, to disturb the arrangement as originally made, by which the various States came into the Union." Still thinking of the sanction which the Constitution gives to slavery, he says, "Because it was a part of the original compact—let it stand." Notwithstanding his special acuteness and ability, he is unable to take a fact out of its merely political relations, and behold it as it lies absolutely to be disposed of by the intellect—what, for instance, it behooves a man to do here in America to-day with regard to slavery, but ventures, or *is* driven, to make some such desperate answer as the following, while professing to speak absolutely, and as a private man—from which what new and singular code of social duties might be inferred? "The manner," says he, "in which the governments of those States where slavery exists are to regulate it is for their own consideration, under their responsibility to their constituents, to the general laws of propriety, humanity, and justice, and to God. Associations formed elsewhere, springing from a feeling of humanity, or any other cause, have nothing whatever to do with it. They have never received any encouragement from me, and they never will."

45   They who know of no purer sources of truth, who have traced up its stream no higher, stand, and wisely stand, by the Bible and the Constitution, and drink at it there with reverence and humility; but they who behold where it comes trickling into this lake or that pool, gird up their loins once more, and continue their pilgrimage toward its fountain-head.

46   No man with a genius for legislation has appeared in America. They are rare in the history of the world. There are orators, politicians, and eloquent men, by the thousand—but the speaker has not yet opened his mouth to speak who is capable of settling the much-vexed questions of the day. We love eloquence for its own sake, and not for any truth which it may utter, or any heroism it may inspire. Our legislators have not yet learned the comparative value of free-trade and of freedom, of union, and of rectitude, to a nation. They have no genius or talent for comparatively humble questions of taxation and finance, commerce and manufacturers and agriculture. If we were left solely to the

wordy wit of legislators in Congress for our guidance, uncorrected by the seasonable experience and the effectual complaints of the people, America would not long retain her rank among the nations. For eighteen hundred years, though perchance I have no right to say it, the New Testament has been written; yet where is the legislator who has wisdom and practical talent enough to avail himself of the light which it sheds on the science of legislation?

47   The authority of government, even such as I am willing to submit to—for I will cheerfully obey those who know and can do better than I, and in many things even those who neither know nor can do so well—is still an impure one: to be strictly just, it must have the sanction and consent of the governed. It can have no pure right over my person and property but what I concede to it. The progress from an absolute to a limited monarchy, from a limited monarchy to a democracy, is a progress toward a true respect for the individual. Even the Chinese philosopher was wise enough to regard the individual as the basis of the empire. Is a democracy, such as we know it, the last improvement possible in government? Is it not possible to take a step further towards recognizing and organizing the rights of man? There will never be a really free and enlightened State until the State comes to recognize the individual as a higher and independent power, from which all its own power and authority are derived, and treats him accordingly. I please myself with imagining a State at least which can afford to be just to all men, and to treat the individual with respect as a neighbor; which even would not think it inconsistent with its own repose if a few were to live aloof from it, not meddling with it, nor embraced by it, who fulfilled all the duties of neighbors and fellow-men. A State which bore this kind of fruit, and suffered it to drop off as fast as it ripened, would prepare the way for a still more perfect and glorious State, which also I have imagined, but not yet anywhere seen.

A Poem

Eavan Boland

Eavan Boland was born in Dublin, Ireland, in 1944. Her books of poetry include An Origin Like Water: Collected Poems 1967–1987 *(which includes her earlier volumes* New Territory, The War Horse, In Her Own Image, Night Feed, *and* The Journey), Against Love Poems, The Lost Land, In a Time of Violence, *and* Outside History. *Boland also wrote a volume of prose titled* Object Lessons: The Life of the Woman and the Poet in Our Time *and co-edited* The Making of a Poem: A Norton Anthology of Poetic Forms.

The winner of a Lannan Foundation Award in Poetry and an American Ireland Fund Literary Award, Boland currently is director of the creative writing program at Stanford University in California. Her writing deals with Irish culture, politics,

and religion. She also writes about relationships between the sexes and women,
the subject of this poem.

Eavan Boland
"It's a Woman's World"

Our way of life
has hardly changed
since a wheel first
whetted a knife.

5   Well, maybe flame
burns more greedily
and wheels are steadier
but we're the same

who milestone
10   our lives
with oversights—
living by the lights

of the loaf left
by the cash register,
15   the washing powder
paid for and wrapped,

the wash left wet.
Like most historic peoples
we are defined
20   by what we forget,

by what we never will be:
star-gazers,
fire-eaters.
It's our alibi

25   for all time
that as far as history goes
we were never
on the scene of the crime.

So when the king's head
30   gored its basket—
grim harvest—
we were gristing bread

or getting the recipe
for a good soup
35   to appetize
our gossip.

And it's still the same:
By night our windows
moth our children
40   to the flame

of hearth not history.
And still no page
scores the low music
of our outrage.

45   But appearances
still reassure:
That woman there,
craned to the starry mystery

is merely getting a breath
50   of evening air,
while this one here—
her mouth

a burning plume—
she's no fire-eater,
55   just my frosty neighbor
coming home.

A Short Story

Alice Walker

Alice Walker was born to African American sharecroppers in Eatonton, Georgia, in 1944. From this beginning, she went on to make her mark on American poetry, nonfiction, and fiction. In her writings, Walker explores the victories of black women over the physical and psychic violence they suffer because of racism and sexism.

Walker has won many honors, including a Pulitzer Prize and an American Book Award for The Color Purple. *Among her other heralded works have been* In Search of Our Mothers' Gardens: Womanist Prose; Meridian; The Same River Twice: Honoring the Difficult; The Temple of My Familiar; The Third Life of Grange Copeland; *and* You Can't Keep a Good Woman Down. *"Everyday Use" comes from Walker's 1973 book,* In

Love & Trouble: Stories of Black Women. *In addition to writing, Walker has spent her life working for social justice for women and minorities and teaching at the college level.*

Alice Walker
"Everyday Use"

For Your Grandmama

1   I will wait for her in the yard that Maggie and I made so clean and wavy yesterday afternoon. A yard like this is more comfortable than most people know. It is not just a yard. It is like an extended living room. When the hard clay is swept clean as a floor and the fine sand around the edges lined with tiny, irregular grooves anyone can come and sit and look up into the elm tree and wait for the breezes that never come inside the house.

2   Maggie will be nervous until after her sister goes: she will stand hopelessly in corners homely and ashamed of the burn scars down her arms and legs, eyeing her sister with a mixture of envy and awe. She thinks her sister has held life always in the palm of one hand, that "no" is a word the world never learned to say to her.

3   You've no doubt seen those TV shows where the child who has "made it" is confronted, as a surprise, by her own mother and father, tottering in weakly from backstage. (A pleasant surprise, of course: What would they do if parent and child came on the show only to curse out and insult each other?) On TV mother and child embrace and smile into each other's faces. Sometimes the mother and father weep, the child wraps them in her arms and leans across the table to tell how she would not have made it without their help. I have seen these programs.

4   Sometimes I dream a dream in which Dee and I are suddenly brought together on a TV program of this sort. Out of a dark and soft-seated limousine I am ushered into a bright room filled with many people. There I meet a smiling, gray, sporty man like Johnny Carson who shakes my hand and tells me what a fine girl I have. Then we are on the stage and Dee is embracing me with tears in her eyes. She pins on my dress a large orchid, even though she has told me once that she thinks orchids are tacky flowers.

5   In real life I am a large, big-boned woman with rough, man-working hands. In the winter I wear flannel nightgowns to bed and overalls during the day. I can kill and clean a hog as mercilessly as a man. My fat keeps me hot in zero weather. I can work all day, breaking ice to get water for washing. I can eat pork liver cooked over the open fire minutes after it comes steaming from the hog. One winter I knocked a bull calf straight in the brain between the eyes with a sledge hammer and had the meat hung up to chill before nightfall. But

of course all this does not show on television. I am the way my daughter would want me to be: a hundred pounds lighter, my skin like an uncooked barley pancake. My hair glistens in the hot bright lights. Johnny Carson has much to do to keep up with my quick and witty tongue.

6   But that is a mistake. I know even before I wake up. Who ever knew a Johnson with a quick tongue? Who can even imagine me looking a strange white man in the eye? It seems to me I have talked to them always with one foot raised in flight, with my head turned in whichever way is farthest from them. Dee, though. She would always look anyone in the eye. Hesitation was no part of her nature.

7   "How do I look, Mama?" Maggie says, showing just enough of her thin body enveloped in pink skirt and red blouse for me to know she's there, almost hidden by the door.

8   "Come out into the yard," I say.

9   Have you ever seen a lame animal, perhaps a dog run over by some careless person rich enough to own a car, sidle up to someone who is ignorant enough to be kind to him? That is the way my Maggie walks. She has been like this, chin on chest, eyes on ground, feet in shuffle, ever since the fire that burned the other house to the ground.

10   Dee is lighter than Maggie, with nicer hair and a fuller figure. She's a woman now, though sometimes I forget. How long ago was it that the other house burned? Ten, twelve years? Sometimes I can still hear the flames and feel Maggie's arm sticking to me, her hair smoking and her dress falling off her in little black papery flakes. Her eyes seemed stretched open, blazed open by the flames reflected in them. And Dee. I see her standing off under the sweet gum tree she used to dig gum out of; a look of concentration on her face as she watched the last dingy gray board of the house fall in toward the red-hot brick chimney. Why don't you do a dance around the ashes? I'd wanted to ask her. She had hated the house that much.

11   I used to think she hated Maggie, too. But that was before we raised the money, the church and me, to send her to Augusta to school. She used to read to us without pity; forcing words, lies, other folks' habits, whole lives upon us two, sitting trapped and ignorant underneath her voice. She washed us in a river of make-believe, burned us with a lot of knowledge we didn't necessarily need to know. Pressed us to her with the serious way she read, to shove us away at just the moment, like dimwits, we seemed about to understand.

12   Dee wanted nice things. A yellow organdy dress to wear to her graduation from high school; black pumps to match a green suit she'd made from an old suit somebody gave me. She was determined to stare down any disaster in her efforts. Her eyelids would not flicker for minutes at a time. Often I fought off the temptation to shake her. At sixteen she had a style of her own: and knew what style was.

13   I never had an education myself. After second grade the school was closed down. Don't ask me why: in 1927 colored asked fewer questions than they do now. Sometimes Maggie reads to me. She stumbles along good-naturedly but

can't see well. She knows she is not bright. Like good looks and money, quickness passed her by. She will marry John Thomas (who has mossy teeth in an earnest face) and then I'll be free to sit here and I guess just sing church songs to myself. Although I never was a good singer. Never could carry a tune. I was always better at a man's job. I used to love to milk till I was hoofed in the side in '49. Cows are soothing and slow and don't bother you, unless you try to milk them the wrong way.

14   I have deliberately turned my back on the house. It is three rooms, just like the one that burned, except the roof is tin; they don't make shingle roofs any more. There are no real windows, just some holes cut in the sides, like the portholes in a ship, but not round and not square, with rawhide holding the shutters up on the outside. This house is in a pasture, too, like the other one. No doubt when Dee sees it she will want to tear it down. She wrote me once that no matter where we "choose" to live, she will manage to come see us. But she will never bring her friends. Maggie and I thought about this and Maggie asked me, "Mama, when did Dee ever *have* any friends?"

15   She had a few. Furtive boys in pink shirts hanging about on washday after school. Nervous girls who never laughed. Impressed with her they worshiped the well-turned phrase, the cute shape, the scalding humor that erupted like bubbles in lye. She read to them.

16   When she was courting Jimmy T she didn't have much time to pay to us, but turned all her faultfinding power on him. He *flew* to marry a cheap gal from a family of ignorant flashy people. She hardly had time to recompose herself.

17   When she comes I will meet—but there they are!

18   Maggie attempts to make a dash for the house, in her shuffling way, but I stay her with my hand. "Come back here," I say. And she stops and tries to dig a well in the sand with her toe.

19   It is hard to see them clearly through the strong sun. But even the first glimpse of leg out of the car tells me it is Dee. Her feet were always neat-looking, as if God himself had shaped them with a certain style. From the other side of the car comes a short, stocky man. Hair is all over his head a foot long and hanging from his chin like a kinky mule tail. I hear Maggie suck in her breath. "Uhnnnh," is what it sounds like. Like when you see the wriggling end of a snake just in front of your foot on the road. "Uhnnnh."

20   Dee next. A dress down to the ground, in this hot weather. A dress so loud it hurts my eyes. There are yellows and oranges enough to throw back the light of the sun. I feel my whole face warming from the heat waves it throws out. Earrings, too, gold and hanging down to her shoulders. Bracelets dangling and making noises when she moves her arm up to shake the folds of the dress out of her armpits. The dress is loose and flows, and as she walks closer, I like it. I hear Maggie go "Uhnnnh" again. It is her sister's hair. It stands straight up like the wool on a sheep. It is black as night and around the edges are two long pigtails that rope about like small lizards disappearing behind her ears.

21   "Wa-su-zo-Tean-o!" she says, coming on in that gliding way the dress makes her move. The short stocky fellow with the hair to his navel is all grinning and

he follows up with "Asalamalakim, my mother and sister!" He moves to hug Maggie but she falls back, right up against the back of my chair. I feel her trembling there and when I look up I see the perspiration falling off her chin.

22   "Don't get up," says Dee. Since I am stout it takes something of a push. You can see me trying to move a second or two before I make it. She turns, showing white heels through her sandals, and goes back to the car. Out she peeks next with a Polaroid. She stoops down quickly and lines up picture after picture of me sitting there in front of the house with Maggie cowering behind me. She never takes a shot without making sure the house is included. When a cow comes nibbling around the edge of the yard she snaps it and me and Maggie *and* the house. Then she puts the Polaroid in the back seat of the car, and comes up and kisses me on the forehead.

23   Meanwhile Asalamalakim is going through the motions with Maggie's hand. Maggie's hand is as limp as a fish, and probably as cold, despite the sweat, and she keeps trying to pull it back. It looks like Asalamalakim wants to shake hands but wants to do it fancy. Or maybe he don't know how people shake hands. Anyhow, he soon gives up on Maggie.

24   "Well," I say. "Dee."

25   "No, Mama," she says. "Not 'Dee,' Wangero Leewanika Kemanjo!"

26   "What happened to 'Dee'?" I wanted to know.

27   "She's dead," Wangero said. "I couldn't bear it any longer being named after the people who oppress me."

28   "You know as well as me you was named after your aunt Dicie," I said. Dicie is my sister. She named Dee. We called her "Big Dee" after Dee was born.

29   "But who was *she* named after?" asked Wangero.

30   "I guess after Grandma Dee," I said.

31   "And who was she named after?" asked Wangero.

32   "Her mother," I said, and saw Wangero was getting tired. "That's about as far back as I can trace it," I said. Though, in fact, I probably could have carried it back beyond the Civil War through the branches.

33   "Well," said Asalamalakim, "there you are."

34   "Uhnnnh," I heard Maggie say.

35   "There I was not," I said, "before 'Dicie' cropped up in our family, so why should I try to trace it that far back?"

36   He just stood there grinning, looking down on me like somebody inspecting a Model A car. Every once in a while he and Wangero sent eye signals over my head.

37   "How do you pronounce this name?" I asked.

38   "You don't have to call me by it if you don't want to," said Wangero.

39   "Why shouldn't I?" I asked. "If that's what you want us to call you, we'll call you."

40   "I know it might sound awkward at first," said Wangero.

41   "I'll get used to it," I said. "Ream it out again."

42   Well, soon we got the name out of the way. Asalamalakim had a name twice as long and three times as hard. After I tripped over it two or three times he

told me to just call him Hakim-a-barber. I wanted to ask him was he a barber, but I didn't really think he was, so I didn't ask.

43   "You must belong to those beef-cattle peoples down the road," I said. They said "Asalamalakim" when they met you, too, but they didn't shake hands. Always too busy: feeding the cattle, fixing the fences, putting up salt-lick shelters, throwing down hay. When the white folks poisoned some of the herd the men stayed up all night with rifles in their hands. I walked a mile and a half just to see the sight.

44   Hakim-a-barber said, "I accept some of their doctrines, but farming and raising cattle is not my style." (They didn't tell me, and I didn't ask, whether Wangero [Dee] had really gone and married him.)

45   We sat down to eat and right away he said he didn't eat collards and pork was unclean. Wangero, though, went on through the chitlins and corn bread, the greens and everything else. She talked a blue streak over the sweet potatoes. Everything delighted her. Even the fact that we still used the benches her daddy made for the table when we couldn't afford to buy chairs.

46   "Oh, Mama!" she cried. Then turned to Hakim-a-barber. "I never knew how lovely these benches are. You can feel the rump prints," she said, running her hands underneath her and along the bench. Then she gave a sigh and her hand closed over Grandma Dee's butter dish. "That's it!" she said. "I knew there was something I wanted to ask you if I could have." She jumped up from the table and went over in the corner where the churn stood, the milk in its clabber by now. She looked at the churn and looked at it.

47   "This churn top is what I need," she said. "Didn't Uncle Buddy whittle it out of a tree you all used to have?"

48   "Yes," I said.

49   "Uh huh," she said happily. "And I want the dasher, too."

50   "Uncle Buddy whittle that, too?" asked the barber.

51   Dee (Wangero) looked up at me.

52   "Aunt Dee's first husband whittled the dash," said Maggie so low you almost couldn't hear her. "His name was Henry, but they called him Stash."

53   "Maggie's brain is like an elephant's," Wangero said, laughing. "I can use the churn top as a centerpiece for the alcove table," she said, sliding a plate over the churn, "and I'll think of something artistic to do with the dasher."

54   When she finished wrapping the dasher the handle stuck out. I took it for a moment in my hands. You didn't even have to look close to see where hands pushing the dasher up and down to make butter had left a kind of sink in the wood. In fact, there were a lot of small sinks; you could see where thumbs and fingers had sunk into the wood. It was beautiful light yellow wood, from a tree that grew in the yard where Big Dee and Stash had lived.

55   After dinner Dee (Wangero) went to the trunk at the foot of my bed and started rifling through it. Maggie hung back in the kitchen over the dishpan. Out came Wangero with two quilts. They had been pieced by Grandma Dee and then Big Dee and me had hung them on the quilt frames on the front porch and quilted them. One was in the Lone Star pattern. The other was Walk Around

the Mountain. In both of them were scraps of dresses Grandma Dee had worn fifty and more years ago. Bits and pieces of Grandpa Jarell's Paisley shirts. And one teeny faded blue piece, about the size of a penny matchbox, that was from Great Grandpa Ezra's uniform that he wore in the Civil War.

56 "Mama," Wangero said sweet as a bird. "Can I have these old quilts?"

57 I heard something fall in the kitchen, and a minute later the kitchen door slammed.

58 "Why don't you take one or two of the others?" I asked. "These old things was just done by me and Big Dee from some tops your grandma pieced before she died."

59 "No," said Wangero. "I don't want those. They are stitched around the borders by machine."

60 "That makes them last better," I said.

61 "That's not the point," said Wangero. "These are all pieces of dresses Grandma used to wear." She did all this stitching by hand. Imagine!"' She held the quilts securely in her arms, stroking them.

62 "Some of the pieces, like those lavender ones, come from old clothes her mother handed down to her," I said, moving up to touch the quilts. Dee (Wangero) moved back just enough so that I couldn't reach the quilts. They already belonged to her.

63 "Imagine!" she breathed again, clutching them closely to her bosom.

64 "The truth is," I said, "I promised to give them quilts to Maggie, for when she marries John Thomas."

65 She gasped like a bee had stung her.

66 "Maggie can't appreciate these quilts!" she said. "She'd probably be back-ward enough to put them to everyday use."

67 "I reckon she would," I said. "God knows I been saving 'em for long enough with nobody using 'em. I hope she will." I didn't want to bring up how I had offered Dee (Wangero) a quilt when she went away to college. Then she had told me they were old-fashioned, out of style.

68 "But they're *priceless!*" she was saying now, furiously; for she has a temper. "Maggie would put them on the bed and in five years they'd be in rags. Less than that!"

69 "She can always make some more," I said. "Maggie knows how to quilt."

70 Dee (Wangero) looked at me with hatred. "You just will not understand. The point is these quilts, *these* quilts!"

71 "Well," I said, stumped. "What would *you* do with them?"

72 "Hang them," she said. As if that was the only thing you *could* do with quilts.

73 Maggie by now was standing in the door. I could almost hear the sound her feet made as they scraped over each other.

74 "She can have them, Mama," she said, like somebody used to never win-ning anything, or having anything reserved for her. "I can' member Grandma Dee without the quilts."

75 I looked at her hard. She had filled her bottom lip with checkerberry snuff and it gave her face a kind of dopey, hangdog look. It was Grandma Dee and

Big Dee who taught her how to quilt herself. She stood there with her scarred hands hidden in the folds of her skirt. She looked at her sister with something like fear but she wasn't mad at her. This was Maggie's portion. This was the way she knew God to work.

76   When I looked at her like that something hit me in the top of my head and ran down to the soles of my feet. Just like when I'm in church and the spirit of God touches me and I get happy and shout. I did something I never had done before: hugged Maggie to me, then dragged her on into the room, snatched the quilts out of Miss Wangero's hands and dumped them into Maggie's lap. Maggie just sat there on my bed with her mouth open.

77   "Take one or two of the others," I said to Dee.

78   But she turned without a word and went out to Hakim-a-barber.

79   "You just don't understand," she said, as Maggie and I came out to the car.

80   "What don't I understand?" I wanted to know.

81   "Your heritage," she said. And then she turned to Maggie, kissed her, and said, "You ought to try to make something of yourself, too, Maggie. It's really a new day for us. But from the way you and Mama still live you'd never know it."

82   She put on some sunglasses that hid everything above the tip of her nose and her chin.

83   Maggie smiled; maybe at the sunglasses. But a real smile, not scared. After we watched the car dust settle I asked Maggie to bring me a dip of snuff. And then the two of us sat there just enjoying, until it was time to go in the house and go to bed.

ADDITIONAL READINGS

This group of readings extends and helps you apply the rhetorical insights you gathered as you read and reread "On the Duty of Civil Disobedience" (pages 221–237), "It's a Woman's World" (237–239), and "Everyday Use" (pages 239–246). Loosely grouped in three categories—Civil Rights and Responsibilities, Feminism and Women's Issues, and Ethnicity and Culture—the readings here invite you to consider further dimensions of ideas raised by Thoreau, Boland, and Walker.

CIVIL RIGHTS AND RESPONSIBILITIES

Bob Dylan

Bob Dylan, born in 1941 as Bob Zimmerman, changed his name in honor of the Welsh poet Dylan Thomas. He has been an important singer-songwriter in America for five decades and has been called everything from "prophetic" to "rebellious" to "entertaining." Dylan began performing almost exclusively as a folk-guitarist, writing folk ballads. In the mid-1960s, he began to use electrical instruments and the rhythms of rock and roll, later including elements of country music. Dylan continues to perform and influence popular music today.

"The Times They Are a-Changin'" became an anthem of social causes throughout the 1960s, including the American civil rights movement and opposition to America's role in the war in Vietnam.

Bob Dylan
"The Times They Are a-Changin'"

Come gather 'round people
Wherever you roam
And admit that the waters
Around you have grown
5   And accept it that soon
You'll be drenched to the bone.
If your time to you
Is worth savin'
Then you better start swimmin'
10   Or you'll sink like a stone
For the times they are a-changin'.

Come writers and critics
Who prophesize with your pen
And keep your eyes wide
15   The chance won't come again
And don't speak too soon
For the wheel's still in spin
And there's no tellin' who
That it's namin'.
20   For the loser now
Will be later to win
For the times they are a-changin'.

Come senators, congressmen
Please heed the call
25   Don't stand in the doorway
Don't block up the hall
For he that gets hurt
Will be he who has stalled
There's a battle outside
30   And it is ragin'.
It'll soon shake your windows
And rattle your walls
For the times they are a-changin'.

Come mothers and fathers
35   Throughout the land
And don't criticize
What you can't understand
Your sons and your daughters

40
Are beyond your command
Your old road is
Rapidly agin'.
Please get out of the new one
If you can't lend your hand
For the times they are a-changin'.

45
The line it is drawn
The curse it is cast
The slow one now
Will later be fast
As the present now
50
Will later be past
The order is
Rapidly fadin'.
And the first one now
Will later be last
55
For the times they are a-changin'.

Rock the Vote Web pages

Jonathan Swift

Probably the best-known prose satirist in the English language, Jonathan Swift was born in Ireland and lived from 1667 to 1745. He was famous in his day as an essayist, poet, novelist, political pamphleteer, and church figure. His novel Gulliver's Travels *is considered his masterpiece. Today, Swift is best known for the satirical essay included here. "A Modest Proposal" remains nearly timeless in its ability to both delight and warn readers about their common humanity.*

Jonathan Swift
"A Modest Proposal"

For Preventing the Children of Poor People in Ireland from Being a Burden to Their Parents or Country, and for Making Them Beneficial to the Public

1   It is a melancholy object to those who walk through this great town or travel in the country, when they see the streets, the roads, and cabin doors, crowded with beggars of the female sex, followed by three, four, or six children, all in rags and importuning every passenger for an alms. These mothers, instead of being able to work for their honest livelihood, are forced to employ all their time in strolling to beg sustenance for their helpless infants, who, as they grow up, either turn thieves for want of work, or leave their dear native country to fight for the Pretender in Spain, or sell themselves to the Barbadoes.

2   I think it is agreed by all parties that this prodigious number of children in the arms, or on the backs, or at the heels of their mothers, and frequently of their fathers, is in the present deplorable state of the Kingdom a very great additional grievance, and therefore whoever could find out a fair, cheap, and easy method of making these children sound; useful members of the commonwealth would deserve so well of the public as to have his statue set up for a preserver of the nation.

3   But my intention is very far from being confined to provide only for the children of professed beggars; it is of a much greater extent; and shall take in the whole number of infants at a certain age who are born of parents in effect as little able to support them as those who demand our charity in the streets.

4   As to my own part, having turned my thoughts for many years upon this important subject, and maturely weighed the several schemes of other projectors, I have always found them grossly mistaken in their computation. It is true, a child just dropped from its dam may be supported by her milk for a shillings, which the mother may certainly get, or the value in scraps, by her lawful occupation of begging; and it is exactly at one year old that I propose to provide for them in such a manner as instead of being a charge upon their parents or the parish, or wanting food and raiment for the rest of their lives, they shall on the contrary contribute to the feeding, and partly to the clothing, of many thousands.

5   There is likewise another great advantage in my scheme, that it will prevent those voluntary abortions, and that horrid practice of women murdering their bastard children, alas, too frequent among us, sacrificing the poor innocent babes, I doubt, more to avoid the expense than the shame, which would move tears and pity in the most savage and inhuman breast.

6   The number of souls in this kingdom being usually reckoned one million and a half, of these I calculate there may be about two hundred thousand

couple whose wives are breeders; from which number I subtract thirty thousand couples who are able to maintain their own children, although I apprehend there cannot be so many under the present distresses of the Kingdom; but this being granted, there will remain an hundred and seventy thousand breeders. I again subtract fifty thousand for those women who miscarry, or whose children die by accident or disease within the year. There only remain an hundred and twenty thousand children of poor parents annually born. The question therefore is, how this number shall be reared and provided for, which, as I have already said, under the present situation of affairs, is utterly impossible by all the methods hitherto proposed. For we can neither employ them in handicraft or agriculture; we neither build houses (I mean in the country) nor cultivate land. They can very seldom pick up a livelihood by stealing till they arrive at six years old, except where they are of towardly parts; although I confess they learn the rudiments much earlier, during which time they can however be looked upon only as probationers, as I have been informed by a principal gentleman in the county of Cavan, who protested to me that he never knew above' one or two instances under the ages of six, even in a part of the kingdom so renowned for the quickest proficiency in that art.

7   I am assured by our merchants that a boy or a girl before twelve years old is no salable commodity; and even when they come to this age they will not yield above three pounds, or three pounds and half a crown at most on the Exchange; which cannot turn to account either to the parents or the kingdom, the charge of nutriment and rags having been at least four times that value.

8   I shall now therefore humbly propose my own thoughts, which I hope will not be liable to the least objection.

9   I have been assured by a very knowing American of my acquaintance in London, that a young healthy child well nursed is at a year old a most delicious, nourishing, and wholesome food, whether stewed, roasted, baked, or boiled; and I make no doubt that it will equally serve in a fricassee or a ragout.

10   I do therefore humbly offer it to public consideration that of the hundred and twenty thousand children, already computed, twenty thousand may be reserved for breed, whereof only one fourth part to be males, which is more than we allow to sheep, black cattle, or swine; and my reason is that these children are seldom the fruits of marriage, a circumstance not much regarded by our savages, therefore one male will be sufficient to serve four females. That the remaining hundred thousand may at a year old be offered in sale to the persons of quality and fortune through the kingdom, always advising the mother to let them suck plentifully in the last month, so as to render them plump and fat for a good table. A child will make two dishes at an entertainment for friends; and when the family dines alone, the fore or hind quarter will make a reasonable dish, and seasoned with a little pepper or salt will be very good boiled on the fourth day, especially in winter.

11   I have reckoned upon a medium that a child just born will weigh twelve pounds, and in a solar year if tolerably nursed increaseth to twenty-eight pounds.

12   I grant this food will be somewhat dear, and therefore very proper for landlords, who, as they have already devoured most of the parents, seem to have the best title to the children.

13   Infant's flesh will be in season throughout the year, but more plentiful in March, and a little before and after. For we are told by a grave author, an eminent French physician, that fish being a prolific diet, there are more children born in Roman Catholic countries about nine months after Lent than at any other season; therefore, reckoning a year after Lent, the markets will be more glutted than usual, because the number of popish infants is at least three to one in this kingdom; and therefore it will have one other collateral advantage, by lessening the number of Papists among us.

14   I have already computed the charge of nursing a beggar's child (in which list I reckon all cottagers, laborers; and four fifths of the farmers) to be about two shillings per annum, rags included; and I believe no gentleman would repine to give ten shillings for the carcass of a good fat child, which, as I have said, will make four dishes of excellent nutritive meat, when he hath only some particular friend or his own family to dine with him. Thus the squire will learn to be a good landlord, and grow popular among the tenants; the mother will have eight shillings net profit, and be fit for the work till she produces another child.

15   Those who are more thrifty (as I must confess: the times require) may flay the carcass; the skin of which artificially dressed will make admirable gloves for ladies, and summer boots for fine gentlemen.

16   As to out city of Dublin, shambles may be appointed for this purpose in the most convenient parts of it, and butchers we may be assured will not be wanting; although I rather recommend buying the children alive, and dressing them hot from the knife as we do roasting pigs.

17   A very worthy person, a true lover of his country, and whose virtues I highly esteem, was lately pleased in discoursing on this matter to offer a refinement upon my scheme. He said that many gentlemen of this kingdom, having of late destroyed their deer, he conceived that the want of venison might be well supplied by the bodies of young lads and maidens, not exceeding fourteen years of age nor under twelve, so great a number of both sexes in every county being now ready to starve for want of work and service; and these to be disposed of by their parents, if alive, or otherwise by their nearest relations. But with due deference to so excellent a friend and so deserving a patriot, I cannot be altogether in his sentiments; for as to the males, my American acquaintance assured me from frequent experience that their flesh was generally tough and lean, like that of our schoolboys, by continual exercise, and their taste disagreeable; and to fatten them would not answer the charge. Then as to the females, it would, I think with humble submission, be a loss to the public, because they soon would become breeders themselves; and besides, it is not improbable that some scrupulous people might be apt to censure such a

practice (although indeed very unjustly) as a little bordering upon cruelty; which I confess, hath always been with me the strongest objection against any project, how well soever intended.

18   But in order to justify my friend, he confessed that this expedient was put into his head by the famous Psalmanazar, a native of the island Formosa, who came from thence to London above twenty years ago, and in conversation told my friend that in his country when any young person happened to be put to death, the executioner sold the carcass to persons of quality as a prime dainty; and that in his time the body of a plump girl of fifteen, who was crucified for an attempt to poison the emperor, was sold to his Imperial Majesty's prime minister of state, and other great mandarins of the court, in joints from the gibbet, at four hundred crowns. Neither indeed can I deny that if the same use were made of several plump young girls in this town, who without one single groat to their fortunes cannot stir abroad without a chair, and appear at the playhouse and assemblies in foreign fineries which they never will pay for, the kingdom would not be the worse.

19   Some persons of a desponding spirit are in great concern about that vast number of poor people who are aged, diseased, or maimed, and I have been desired to employ my thoughts what course may be taken to ease the nation of so grievous an encumbrance. But I am not in the least pain upon that matter, because it is very well known that they are every day dying and rotting by cold and famine, and filth and vermin, as fast as can be reasonably expected. And as to the younger laborers, they are now in almost as hopeful a condition. They cannot get work, and consequently pine away for want of nourishment to a degree that if at any time they are accidentally hired to common labor, they have not strength to perform it; and thus the country and themselves are happily delivered from the evils to come.

20   I have too long digressed, and therefore shall return to my subject. I think the advantages by the proposal which I have made are obvious and many, as well as of the highest importance.

21   For first, as I have already observed, it would greatly lessen the number of Papists, with whom we are yearly overrun, being the principal breeders of the nation as well as our most dangerous enemies; and who stay at home on purpose to deliver the kingdom to the Pretender, hoping to take their advantage by the absence of so many good Protestants, who have chosen rather to leave their country than stay at home and pay tithes against their conscience to an Episcopal curate.

22   Secondly, the poorer tenants will have something valuable of their own, which by law may be made liable to distress, and help to pay their landlord's rent, their corn and cattle being already seized and money a thing unknown.

23   Thirdly, whereas the maintenance of an hundred thousand children, from two years old and upwards, cannot be computed at less than ten shillings a piece per annum, the nation's stock will be thereby increased fifty thousand pounds per annum, besides the profit of a new dish introduced to the tables of all gentlemen of fortune in the kingdom who have any refinement in taste. And

the money will circulate among ourselves, the goods being entirely of our own growth and manufacture.

24   Fourthly, the constant breeders, besides the gain of eight shillings sterling per annum by the sale of their children, will be rid of the charge of maintaining them after the first year.

25   Fifthly, this, food would likewise bring great custom to taverns, where the vintners will certainly be so prudent as to procure the best receipts for dressing it to perfection, and consequently have their houses frequented by all the fine gentlemen, who justly value themselves upon their knowledge in good eating; and a skillful cook, who understands how to oblige his guests, will contrive to make it as expensive as they please.

26   Sixthly, this would be a great inducement to marriage, which all wise nations have either encouraged by rewards or enforced by laws and penalties. It would increase the care and tenderness of mothers toward their children, when they were sure of a settlement for life to the poor babes, provided in some sort by the public to their annual profit instead of expense. We should see an honest emulation among the married women, which of them could bring the fattest child to the market. Men would become as fond of their wives during the time of their pregnancy as they are now of their mares in foal, their cows in calf, or sows when they are ready to farrow; nor offer to beat or kick them (as is too frequent a practice) for fear of a miscarriage.

27   Many other advantages might be enumerated. For instance, the addition of some thousand carcasses in our exportation of barreled beef, the propagation of swine's flesh, and improvement in the art of making good bacon, so much wanted among us by the great destruction of pigs, too frequent at our tables, which are not way comparable in taste or magnificence to a well-grown, fat, yearling child, which roasted whole will make a considerable figure at a lord mayor's feast or any other public entertainment. But this and many others I omit, being studious of brevity.

28   Supposing that one thousand families in this city would be constant customers for infants' flesh, besides others who might have it at merry meetings; particularly weddings and christenings, I compute that Dublin would take off annually about twenty thousand carcasses, and the rest of the kingdom (where probably they will be sold somewhat cheaper) the remaining eighty thousand.

29   I can think of no one objection that will probably be raised against this proposal, unless it should be urged that the number of people will be thereby much lessened in the kingdom. This I freely own, and it was indeed one principal design in offering it to the world. I desire the reader will observe, that I calculate my remedy for this one individual kingdom of Ireland and for no other that ever was, is, or I think ever can be upon earth. Therefore let no man talk to me of other expedients: of taxing our absentees at five shillings a pound: of using neither clothes nor household furniture except what is of our own growth and manufacture of utterly rejecting the materials and instruments that promote foreign luxury: of curing the expensiveness of pride, vanity, idleness, and gaming in our women: of introducing a vein of a parsimony, prudence, and temperance: of learning to love our country, in the want of which we differ even from Laplanders and

the inhabitants of Topinamboo: of quitting our animosities and factions, nor acting any longer like the Jews, who were murdering one another at the very moment their city was taken: of being a little cautious not to sell our country and conscience for nothing: of teaching landlords to have at least one degree of mercy toward their tenants: lastly, of putting a spirit of honesty, industry, and skill into our shopkeepers; who, if a resolution could now be taken to buy only our native goods, would immediately unite to cheat and exact upon us in the price, the measure, and the goodness; nor could ever yet be brought to make one fair proposal of just dealing, though often and earnestly invited to it.

30   Therefore I repeat, let no man talk to me of these and the like expedients, till he hath at least some glimpse of hope that there will ever be some hearty and sincere attempt to put them in practice.

31   But as to myself, having been wearied out for many years with offering vain, idle, visionary thoughts, and at length utterly despairing of success, I fortunately fell upon this proposal, which, as it is wholly new, so it hath something solid and real, of no expense and little trouble, full in our own power, and whereby we can incur no danger in disobliging England. For this kind of commodity will not bear exportation, the flesh being of too tender a consistence to admit a long continuance in salt, although perhaps I could name a country which would be glad to eat up our whole nation without it.

32   After all, I am not so violently bent upon my own opinion as to reject any offer proposed by wise men, which shall be found equally innocent, cheap, easy, and effectual. But before something of that kind shall be advanced in contradiction to my scheme, and offering a better, I desire the author or authors will be pleased maturely to consider two points. First, as things now stand, how they will be able to find food and raiment for an hundred thousand useless mouths and backs. And secondly, there being a round million of creatures in human figure throughout this kingdom, whose sole subsistence put into a common stock would leave them in debt two millions of pounds sterling, adding those who are beggars by profession to the bulk of farmers; cottagers, and laborers, with their wives and children who are beggars in effect; I desire those politicians who dislike my overture, and may perhaps be so bold to attempt an answer, that they will first ask the parents of these mortals whether they would not at this day think it a great happiness to have been sold for food at a year old in the manner I prescribe, and thereby have avoided such a perpetual sense of misfortunes as they have since gone through by the oppression of landlords; the impossibility of paying rent without money or trade, the want of common sustenance, with neither house nor clothes to cover them from the inclemencies of the weather, and the most inevitable prospect of entailing the like or greater miseries upon their breed forever.

33   I profess, in the sincerity of my heart; that I have not the least personal interest in endeavoring to promote this necessary work, having no other motive than the public good of my country, by advancing our trade, providing for infants, relieving the poor, and giving some pleasure to the rich. I have no children by which I can propose to get a single penny; the youngest being nine years old, and my wife past childbearing.

John Donne

John Donne is one of the most influential poets of the seventeenth century. Born in London in 1572 to a Catholic family, he converted to Anglicanism and became dean of St. Paul's Cathedral in 1621. He died in 1631.

Donne's work divides into two phases: early love verses and later religious works of poetry and prose. Donne is called a metaphysical poet because of his focus on the problems of the soul as primarily intellectual rather than emotional or sensual concerns. In "Meditation 17," Donne examines the depth of human connection and its effects on individual souls.

John Donne
"Meditation 17"

Nunc lento sonitu dicunt, morieris.

1   Now this bell tolling softly for another says to me, Thou must die.

Perchance he for whom this bell tolls may be so ill as that he knows not it tolls for him; and perchance I may think myself so much better than I am, as that they who are about me and see my state may have caused it to toll for me, and I know not that. The church is catholic, universal, so are all her actions; all that she does belongs to all. When she baptizes a child, that action concerns me;
10 for that child is thereby connected to that head which is my head too, and ingrafted into that body whereof I am a member. And when she buries a man, that action concerns me; all mankind is of one author and is one volume; when one man dies, one chapter is not torn out of the book, but translated into a better language; and every chapter must be so translated. God employs several translators; some pieces are translated by age, some by sickness, some by war, some by justice: but God's hand is in every translation, and his hand shall bind up all our scattered leaves again for that library where every book shall lie open to one another. As therefore the bell that rings to a sermon calls not upon the preacher only; but upon the congregation to come, so this bell calls us all; but how much more me, who am brought so near the door by this sickness. There was a
20 contention as far as a suit (in which piety and dignity, religion and estimation, were mingled) which of the religious orders should ring to prayers first in the morning; and it was determined that they should ring first that rose earliest. If we understand aright the dignity of this bell that tolls for our evening prayer, we would be glad to make it ours by rising early, in that application, that it might be ours as well as his whose indeed it is. The bell doth toll for him that thinks it doth; and though it intermit again, yet from that minute that that occasion wrought upon him, he is united to God. Who casts not up his eye to the sun when

it rises? But who takes off his eye from a comet when that breaks out? Who bends not his ear to any bell which upon any occasion rings? But who can
30 remove it from that bell which is passing a piece of himself out of this world? No man is an island, entire of itself; every man is a piece of the continent, a part of the main. If a clod be washed away by the sea, Europe is the less, as well as if a promontory were, as well as if a manor of thy friend's or of thine own were. Any man's death diminishes me, because I am involved in mankind; and therefore never send to know for whom the bell tolls; it tolls for thee. Neither can we call this a begging of misery or a borrowing of misery, as though we were not miserable enough of ourselves but must fetch in more from the next house, in taking upon us the misery of our neighbors. Truly it were an excusable covetousness if we did; for affliction is a treasure, and scarce any man hath enough of it.
40 No man hath affliction enough that is not matured and ripened by it, and made fit for God by that affliction. If a man carry treasure in bullion, or in a wedge of gold, and have none coined into current moneys, his treasure will not defray him as he travels. Tribulation is treasure in the nature of it, but it is not current money in the use of it, except we get nearer and nearer our home, heaven, by it. Another man may be sick too, and sick to death, and this affliction may lie in his bowels as gold in a mine and be of no use to him; but this bell that tells me of his affliction digs out and applies that gold to me, if by this consideration of another's danger I take mine own into contemplation and so secure myself by making my recourse to my God, who is our only security.

Toni Morrison

Toni Morrison was born into a working-class family in Lorain, Ohio, in 1931. Concerned with the African American experience—especially, that of women—Morrison has said that her writing evokes "a question of equitable access, opening doors to all sorts of things." Her novels include The Bluest Eye, Sula, Song of Solomon, Tar Baby, Beloved, *and* Jazz. *She won the Noble Prize for Literature in 1993.*

Educated at Howard and Cornell universities, Morrison worked as an editor and has held academic positions. Her interest in myth and fantasy as well as her poetic style influences the speech she gave on accepting the Nobel Prize.

Toni Morrison
Nobel Lecture
December 7, 1993

1   "Once upon a time there was an old woman. Blind but wise." Or was it an old man? A guru, perhaps. Or a griot soothing restless children. I have heard this story, or one exactly like it, in the lore of several cultures.

2   "Once upon a time there was an old woman. Blind. Wise."

3   In the version I know the woman is the daughter of slaves, black, American, and lives alone in a small house outside of town. Her reputation for wisdom is without peer and without question. Among her people she is both the law and its transgression. The honor she is paid and the awe in which she is held reach beyond her neighborhood to places far away; to the city where the intelligence of rural prophets is the source of much amusement.

4   One day the woman is visited by some young people who seem to be bent on disproving her clairvoyance and showing her up for the fraud they believe she is. Their plan is simple: they enter her house and ask the one question the answer to which rides solely on her difference from them, a difference they regard as a profound disability; her blindness. They stand before her, and one of them says, "Old woman, I hold in my hand a bird. Tell me whether it is living or dead."

5   She does not answer, and the question is repeated. "Is the bird I am holding living or dead?"

6   Still she doesn't answer. She is blind and cannot see her visitors, let alone what is in their hands. She does not know their color, gender or homeland. She only knows their motive.

7   The old woman's silence is so long, the young people have trouble holding their laughter.

8   Finally she speaks and her voice is soft but stern. "I don't know," she says. "I don't know whether the bird you are holding is dead or alive, but what I do know is that it is in your hands. It is in your hands."

9   Her answer can be taken to mean: If it is dead, you have either found it that way or you have killed it. If it is alive, you can still kill it. Whether it is to stay alive, it is your decision. Whatever the case, it is your responsibility.

10   For parading their power and her helplessness, the young visitors are reprimanded, told they are responsible not only for the act of mockery but also for the small bundle of life sacrificed to achieve its aims. The blind woman shifts attention away from assertions of power to the instrument through which that power is exercised.

11   Speculation on what (other than its own frail body) that bird-in-the-hand might signify has always been attractive to me, but especially so now thinking, as I have been, about the work I do that has brought me to this company. So

I choose to read the bird as language and the woman as a practiced writer. She is worried about how the language she dreams in, given to her at birth, is handled, put into service, even withheld from her for certain nefarious purposes. Being a writer she thinks of language partly as a system, partly as a living thing over which one has control, but mostly as agency—as an act with consequences. So the question the children put to her: "Is it living or dead?" is not unreal because she thinks of language as susceptible to death, erasure; certainly imperiled and salvageable only by an effort of the will. She believes that if the bird in the hands of her visitors is dead the custodians are responsible for the corpse. For her a dead language is not only one no longer spoken or written, it is unyielding language content to admire its own paralysis. Like statist language, censored and censoring. Ruthless in its policing duties, it has no desire or purpose other than maintaining the free range of its own narcotic narcissism, its own exclusivity and dominance. However moribund, it is not without effect for it actively thwarts the intellect, stalls conscience, suppresses human potential. Unreceptive to interrogation, it cannot form or tolerate new ideas, shape other thoughts, tell another story, fill baffling silences. Official language smitheried to sanction ignorance and preserve privilege is a suit of armor polished to shocking glitter, a husk from which the knight departed long ago. Yet there it is: dumb, predatory, sentimental. Exciting reverence in schoolchildren, providing shelter for despots, summoning false memories of stability, harmony among the public.

12   She is convinced that when language dies, out of carelessness, disuse, indifference and absence of esteem, or killed by flat, not only she herself, but all users and makers are accountable for its demise. In her country children have bitten their tongues off and use bullets instead to iterate the voice of speechlessness, of disabled and disabling language, of language adults have abandoned altogether as a device for grappling with meaning, providing guidance, or expressing love. But she knows tongue-suicide is not only the choice of children. It is common among the Infantile heads of state and power merchants whose evacuated language leaves them with no access to what is left of their human instincts for they speak only to those who obey, or in order to force obedience.

13   The systematic looting of language can be recognized by the tendency of its users to forgo its nuanced, complex, mid-wifery properties for menace and subjugation. Oppressive language does more than represent violence; it is violence; does more than represent the limits of knowledge; It limits knowledge. Whether it is obscuring state language or the faux-language of mindless media; whether it is the proud but calcified language of the academy or the commodity driven language of science; whether it is the malign language of law-without-ethics, of language designed for the estrangement of minorities, hiding its racist plunder in its literary cheek—it must be rejected, altered and exposed. It is the language that drinks blood, laps vulnerabilities, tucks its fascist boots under crinolines of respectability and patriotism as it moves relentlessly toward the bottom line and the bottomed-out mind. Sexist language, racist language, theistic language—all are typical of the policing languages of mastery, and cannot, do not permit new knowledge to encourage the mutual exchange of ideas.

14   The old woman is keenly aware that no intellectual mercenary, nor insatiable dictator, no paid-for politician or demagogue; no counterfeit journalist would be persuaded by her thoughts. There is and will be rousing language to keep citizens armed and arming; slaughtered and slaughtering in the malls, courthouses, post offices, playgrounds, bedrooms and boulevards; stirring, memorializing language to mask the pity and waste of needless death. There will be more diplomatic language to countenance rape, torture, assassination. There is and will be more seductive, mutant language designed to throttle women, to pack their throats like paté-producing geese with their own unsayable, transgressive words; there will be more of the language of surveillance disguised as research; of politics and history calculated to render the suffering of millions mute; language glamorized to thrill the dissatisfied and bereft into assaulting their neighbors; arrogant pseudo-empirical language crafted to lock creative people into cages of inferiority and hopelessness.

15   Underneath the eloquence, the glamour, the scholarly associations, however stirring or seductive, the heart of such language is languishing, or perhaps not beating at all—if the bird is already dead.

16   She has thought about what could have been the intellectual history of any discipline if it had not insisted upon, or been forced into, the waste of time and life that rationalizations for and representations of dominance required—lethal discourses of exclusion blocking access to cognition for both the excluder and the excluded.

17   The conventional wisdom of the Tower of Babel story is that the collapse was a misfortune. That it was the distraction, or the weight of many languages that precipitated the tower's failed architecture. That one monolithic language would have expedited the building and heaven would have been reached. Whose heaven, she wonders? And what kind? Perhaps the achievement of Paradise was premature, a little hasty if no one could take the time to understand other languages, other views, other narratives period. Had they, the heaven they imagined might have been found at their feet. Complicated, demanding, yes, but a view of heaven as life; not heaven as post-life.

18   She would not want to leave her young visitors with the impression that language should be forced to stay alive merely to be. The vitality of language lies in its ability to limn the actual, imagined and possible lives of its speakers, readers, writers. Although its poise is sometimes in displacing experience it is not a substitute for it. It arcs toward the place where meaning may lie. When a President of the United States thought about the graveyard his country had become, and said. "The world will little note nor long remember what we say here. But it will never forget what they did here," his simple words are exhilarating in their life-sustaining properties because they refused to encapsulate the reality of 600,000 dead men in a cataclysmic race war. Refusing to monumentalize, disdaining the "final word," the precise "summing up," acknowledging their "poor power to add or detract," his words signal deference to the uncapturability of the life it mourns. It is the deference that moves her, that recognition that language can never live up to life once and for all. Nor should it.

Language can never "pin down" slavery, genocide, war. Nor should it yearn for arrogance to be able to do so. Its force, its felicity is in its reach toward the ineffable.

19   Be it grand or slender, burrowing, blasting, or refusing to sanctify; whether it laughs out loud or is a cry without an alphabet, the choice word, the chosen silence, unmolested language surges toward knowledge, not its destruction. But who does not know of literature banned because it is interrogative; discredited because it is critical; erased because alternate? And how many are outraged by the thought of a self-ravaged tongue?

20   Word-work is sublime, she thinks, because it is generative; it makes meaning that secures our difference, our human difference—the way in which we are like no other life.

21   We die. That may be the meaning of life. But we do language. That may be the measure of our lives.

22   "Once upon a time, . . ." visitors ask an old woman a question. Who are they, these children? What did they make of that encounter? What did they hear in those final words: "The bird is in your hands"? A sentence that gestures towards possibility or one that drops a latch? Perhaps what the children heard was "It's not my problem. I am old, female, black, blind. What wisdom I have now is in knowing I cannot help you. The future of language is yours."

23   They stand there. Suppose nothing was in their hands? Suppose the visit was only a ruse, a trick to get to be spoken to, taken seriously as they have not been before? A chance to interrupt, to violate the adult world, its miasma of discourse about them, for them, but never to them? Urgent questions are at stake, including the one they have asked: "Is the bird we hold living or dead?" Perhaps the question meant: "Could someone tell us what is life? What is death?" No trick at all; no silliness. A straightforward question worthy of the attention of a wise one. An old one. And if the old and wise who have lived life and faced death cannot describe either, who can?

24   But she does not; she keeps her secret; her good opinion of herself; her gnomic pronouncements; her art without commitment. She keeps her distance, enforces it and retreats into the singularity of isolation, in sophisticated, privileged space.

25   Nothing, no word follows her declaration of transfer. That silence is deep, deeper than the meaning available in the words she has spoken. It shivers, this silence, and the children, annoyed, fill it with language invented on the spot.

26   "Is there no speech," they ask her, "no words you can give us that helps us break through your dossier of failures? Through the education you have just given us that is no education at all because we are paying close attention to what you have done as well as to what you have said? To the barrier you have erected between generosity and wisdom?

27   "We have no bird on our hands, living or dead. We have only you and our important question. Is the nothing in our hands something you could not bear to contemplate, to even guess? Don't you remember being young when language was magic without meaning? When what you could say, could not mean?

When the invisible was what imagination strove to see? When questions and demands for answers burned so brightly you trembled with fury at not knowing?

28   "Do we have to begin consciousness with a battle heroines and heroes like you have already fought and lost leaving us with nothing in our hands except what you have imagined is there? Your answer is artful, but its artfulness embarrasses us and ought to embarrass you. Your answer is indecent in its self-congratulation. A made-for-television script that makes no sense if there is nothing in our hands.

29   "Why didn't you reach out, touch us with your soft fingers, delay the sound bite, the lesson, until you knew who we were? Did you so despise our trick, our modus operandi you could not see that we were battled about how to get your attention? We are young. Unripe. We have heard all our short lives that we have to be responsible. What could that possibly mean in the catastrophe this world has become; where, as a poet said, "nothing needs to be exposed since it is already barefaced." Our inheritance is an affront. You want us to have your old, blank eyes and see only cruelty and mediocrity. Do you think we are stupid enough to perjure ourselves again and again with the fiction of nationhood? How dare you talk to us of duty when we stand waist deep in the toxin of your past?

30   "You trivialize us and trivialize the bird that is not in our hands. Is there no context for our lives? No song, no literature, no poem full of vitamins, no history connected to experience that you can pass along to help us start strong? You are an adult. The old one, the wise one. Stop thinking about saving your face. Think of our lives and tell us your particularized world. Make up a story. Narrative is radical, creating us at the very moment it is being created. We will not blame you if your reach exceeds your grasp; if love so ignites your words they go down in flames and nothing is left but their scald. Or if, with the reticence of a surgeon's hands, your words suture only the places where blood might flow. We know you can never do it properly—once and for all. Passion is never enough; neither is skill. But try. For our sake and yours forget your name in the street; tell us what the world has been to you in the dark places and in the light. Don't tell us what to believe, what to fear. Show us belief's wide skirt and the stitch that unravels fear's caul. You, old woman, blessed with blindness, can speak the language that tells us what only language can; how to see without pictures. Language alone protects us from the scariness of things with no names. Language alone is meditation.

31   "Tell us what it is to be a woman so that we may know what it is to be a man. What moves at the margin. What it is to have no home in this place. To be set adrift from the one you knew. What it is to live at the edge of towns that cannot bear your company.

32   "Tell us about ships turned away from shorelines at Easter, placenta in a field. Tell us about a wagonload of slaves, how they sang so softly their breath was indistinguishable from the falling snow. How they knew from the hunch of the nearest shoulder that the next stop would be their last. How, with hands

prayered in their sex, they thought of heat, then sun. Lifting their faces as though it was there for the taking. Turning as though there for the taking. They stop at an inn. The driver and his mate go in with the lamp leaving them humming in the dark. The horse's void steams into the snow beneath its hooves and its hiss and melt are the envy of the freezing slaves.

33   "The Inn door opens: a girl and a boy step away from its light. They climb into the wagon bed. The body will have a gun in three years, but now he carries a lamp and a jug of warm cider. They pass it from mouth to mouth. The girl offers bread, pieces of meat and something more; a glance into the eyes of the one she serves. One helping for each man, two for each woman. And a look. They look back. The next stop will be their last. But not this one. This one is warmed."

34   It's quiet again when the children finish speaking, until the woman breaks into the silence.

35   "Finally," she says, "I trust you now. I trust you with the bird that is not in your hands because you have truly caught it. Look. How lovely it is, this thing we have done—together."

Dominic Behan

Dominic Behan wrote songs, short stories, plays, and novels in both Irish and English. He was born in Dublin in 1928 and died in Glasgow in 1989. In addition to his creative writing, Behan was a prominent socialist and Irish republican.

Behan's song describes the life of a young member of the Irish Republican Army (IRA). The IRA, an unofficial semimilitary group, was formed in the early twentieth century by Catholics in Ireland to oppose British rule in any part of Ireland. From the 1960s and into the 1990s, the IRA was involved in ongoing hostilities between Catholics and Protestants.

Dominic Behan
"Patriot Game"

Come all ye young rebels, and list while I sing,
For the love of one's country is a terrible thing.
It banishes fear with the speed of a flame,
And it makes us all part of the patriot game.

5 My name is O'Hanlon,[1] and I've just turned sixteen.
My home is in Monaghan, and where I was weaned
I learned all my life cruel England's to blame,
So now I am part of the patriot game.

9 This Ireland of ours has too long been half free.
Six counties lie under John Bull's[2] tyranny.
But still De Valera[3] is greatly to blame
For shirking his part in the patriot game.

13 They told me how Connolly[4] was shot in his chair,
His wounds from the fighting all bloody and bare.
His fine body twisted, all battered and lame
They soon made me part of the patriot game.

17 It's nearly two years since I wandered away
With the local battalion of the bold IRA,
For I read of our heroes, and wanted the same
To play out my part in the patriot game.

21 And now as I lie here, my body all holes
I think of those traitors who bargained in souls
And I wish that my rifle had given the same
To those Quislings[5] who sold out the patriot game.

---

1. **O'Hanlon**. Fergal O'Hanlon, an IRA volunteer, was killed in an attack on an English army barracks on January 1, 1957. Some sources say he was 20 at the time; some, 16 or 17.
2. **John Bull**. The term is used as a personification of England.
3. **De Valera**. Eamon de Valera (1882–1975) was an Irish politician who served several times as prime minister and then as president of Ireland.
4. **Connolly**. James Connolly (1868–1916) was an Irish socialist and rebel, who was shot by a firing squad after the Easter 1916 rebellion against England.
5. **Quisling**. Vidkun Quisling (1887–1945) was a Norwegian politician who aided the Nazis during World War II. He was later found guilty of treason and executed. His last name has become a synonym for "traitor."

Jane Addams

Jane Addams lived from 1860 to 1935, becoming one of the United States's strongest social reformers of her time, She won the Nobel Peace Prize in 1931. Hull House, the settlement house (social-welfare agency) that Addams cofounded in Chicago, served poor people in many ways—by providing day care and school for children, social gatherings for young adults, as well as job training, lectures, and medical aid to the community.

As a pragmatist and feminist, Addams worked on many issues of her day—most notably, women's rights and child labor. Although marginalized during her lifetime by academics who thought of her as a social worker rather than as a theorist, Addams is increasingly recognized as a major leader of social reform as well as social thought.

Jane Addams
"The Settlement as a Factor in the Labor Movement"
from Hull House Maps and Papers

---

1   One man or group of men sometimes reveal to their contemporaries a higher conscience by simply incorporating into the deed what has been before but a philosophic proposition. By this deed the common code of ethics is stretched to a higher point.

2   Such an act of moral significance, for instance, was John Burns's loyalty to the dockers' strike of East London. "The injury to one" did at last actually "become the concern of all"; and henceforth the man who does not share that concern drops below the standard ethics of his day. The proposition which working-men had long quoted was at last incarnated by a mechanic, who took his position so intelligently that he carried with him the best men in England, and set the public conscience. Other men became ashamed of a wrong to which before they had been easily indifferent.

3   When the social conscience, if one may use the expression, has been thus strikingly formulated, it is not so hard for others to follow. They do it weakly and stumblingly perhaps; but they yet see a glimmer of light of which the first man could not be sure, and they have a code of ethics upon which the first man was vague. They are also conscious of the backing of a large share of the community who before this expression knew not the compunction of their own hearts. A settlement accepts the ethics of its contemporaries that the sharing of the life of the poor is essential to the understanding and bettering of that life, but by its very existence it adopts this modern code somewhat formally. The

social injury of the meanest man not only becomes its concern, but by virtue of its very locality it has put itself into position to see, as no one but a neighbor can see, the stress and need of those who bear the brunt of the social injury. A settlement has not only taken a pledge towards those thus injured, but it is placed where the motive-power for the fulfillment of such a pledge is constantly renewed. Propinquity is an unceasing factor in its existence.

4   A review of the sewing-trades, as seen from a settlement, will be sufficient to illustrate this position.

5   Hull-House is situated in the midst of the sweaters' district of Chicago. The residents came to the district with the general belief that organization for working-people was a necessity. They would doubtless have said that the discovery of the power to combine was the distinguishing discovery of our time; that we are using this fore somewhat awkwardly, as men use that which is newly discovered. In social and political affairs the power to combine often works harm; but it is already operating to such an extent in commercial affairs, that the manufacturer who does not combine with others of his branch is in constant danger of failure; that a railroad cannot be successfully projected unless the interests of parallel roads are consulted; and that working-people likewise cannot be successful until they too learn skillfully to avail themselves of this power.

6   This was to the residents, as to many people, an accepted proposition, but not a working formula. It had not the driving force of a conviction. The residents have lived for five years in a neighborhood largely given over to the sewing-trades, which is an industry totally disorganized. Having observed the workers in this trade as compared to those in organized trades, they have gradually discovered that lack of organization in a trade tends to the industrial helplessness of the workers in that trade. If in all departments of social, political, and commercial life, isolation is a blunder; and results in dreariness and apathy, then in industrial affairs isolation is a social crime; for it there tends to extermination.

7   This process of extermination entails starvation and suffering, and the desperate moral disintegration which inevitably follows in their train, until the need of organization in industry gradually assumes a moral aspect. The conviction arrived at entails a social obligation.

8   No trades are so overcrowded as the sewing-trades; for the needle has ever been the refuge of the unskilled woman. The wages paid throughout the manufacture of clothing are less than those in any other trade. In order to meet the requirements of the workers' lack of skill and absence of orderly life, the work has been so subdivided that almost no skill is required after the garment leaves the cutter. It is given practically to the one who is at hand when it is ready, and who does it for the least money. This subdivision and low wage have gone so far, that the woman who does home finishing alone cannot possibly gain by it a living wage. The residents of Hull-House have carefully investigated many cases, and are ready to assert that the Italian widow who finishes the cheapest goods, although she sews from six in the morning until eleven at night, can only get enough to keep her children clothed and fed; while for her rent and fuel

she must always depend upon charity or the hospitality of her countrymen. If the American sewing-woman, supporting herself alone, lives on bread and butter and tea, she finds a Bohemian woman next door whose diet of black bread and coffee enables her to undercut. She competes with a wife who is eager to have home finishing that she may add something to the family comfort; or with a daughter who takes it that she may buy a wedding outfit.

9   The Hebrew tailor, the man with a family to support, who, but for this competition of unskilled women and girls, might earn a wage upon which a family could subsist, is obliged, in order to support them at all, to put his little children at work as soon as they can sew on buttons.

10   It does not help his industrial situation that the woman and girl who have brought it about have accepted the lower wages in order to buy comforts for an invalid child, or to add to the earnings of an aged father. The mother who sews on a gross of buttons for seven cents, in order to buy a blue ribbon with which to tie up her little daughter's hair, or the mother who finishes a dozen vests for five cents; with which to buy her children a loaf of bread, commits unwittingly a crime against her fellow-workers, although our hearts may thrill with admiration for her heroism, and ache with pity over her misery.

11   The maternal instinct and family affection is woman's most holy attribute; but if she enters industrial life, that is not enough. She must supplement her family conscience by a social and an industrial conscience. She must widen her family affection to embrace the children of the community. She is working havoc in the sewing-trades, because with the meager equipment sufficient for family life she has entered industrial life.

12   Have we any right to place before untrained women the alternative of seeing their little children suffer, or of complicating the industrial condition all the children of the community are suffering? We know of course what their decision would be. But the residents of a settlement are not put to this hard choice, although it is often difficult to urge organization when they are flying to the immediate relief of the underfed children in the neighborhood.

13   If the settlement, then, is convinced that in industrial affairs lack of organization tends to the helplessness of the isolated worker, and is a menace to the entire community, then it is bound to pledge itself to industrial organization, and to look about it for the lines upon which to work. And at this point the settlement enters into what is more technically known as the labor movement.

14   The labor movement may be called a concerted effort among the workers in all trades to obtain a more equitable distribution of the product, and to secure a more orderly existence of the laborers. How may the settlement be of value to this effort?

15   If the design of the settlement is not so much the initiation of new measures, but fraternal co-operation with all good which it finds in its neighborhood, then the most obvious line of action will be organization through the trades-unions, a movement already well established.

16   The trade-unions say to each workingman, "Associate yourself with the fellow-workers in your trade. Let your trade organization federate with the allied trades, and they, in turn, with the National and International Federation, until working-people become a solid body, ready for concerted action. It is the only possible way to prevent cuts in the rate of wages, and to regulate the hours of work. Capital is organized, and has influence with which to secure legislation in its behalf. We are scattered and feeble because we do not work together."

17   Trades-unionism, in spite of the many pits into which it has fallen, has the ring of altruism about it. It is clearly the duty of the settlement to keep it to its best ideal, and to bring into it something of the spirit which has of late characterized the unions in England. This keeping to the ideal is not so easy as the more practical work of increasing unions, although that is difficult enough. Of the two women's unions organized at Hull-House, and of the four which have regularly held their meetings there, as well as those that come to us during strikes at various times, I should venture to say only of them that it is filled with the new spirit, although they all have glimpses of it, and even during times of stress and disturbance strive for it. . . .

18   A century ago there was an irresistible impulse, an upward movement, among the mass of people to have their share in political life,—hitherto the life of the privileged. The universal franchise was demanded, not only as a holy right, but as a means of entrance into the sunshine of liberty and equality. There is a similar demand at the close of this century on the part of working-people, but this time it is for a share in the results of industry.

19   It is an impulse to come out into the sunshine of Prosperity. As the leaders of political democracy overestimated the possession of the franchise, and believed it would obtain blessings for the working-people which it has not done, so, doubtless, the leaders of the labor movement are overestimating the possession of wealth and leisure. Mazzini was the inspired prophet of the political democracy, preaching duties and responsibilities rather than rights and franchises; and we might call Arnold Toynbee the prophet of the second development when we contend that the task of the labor movement is the interpretation of democracy into industrial affairs. In that remarkable exposition called "Industry and Democracy," Toynbee sets forth the struggle between the masters and men during the industrial revolution. Two ideals in regard to the relationship between employer and employee were then developed. Carlyle represented one, pleading passionately for it. He declared that the rich mill-owner's duty did not end with the "cash nexus"; that after he had paid his men he should still cherish them in sickness, protect them in misfortune, and not dismiss them when trade was bad. In one word, he would have the rich govern and protect the poor. But the workers themselves, the mass of the people, had caught another ideal; they dreamed of a time when they should have no need of protection, but when each workman should stand by the side of his employer—the free citizen of a free state. Each workingman demanded, not class protection, but political rights. He wished to be a unit; not that he might be isolated, but that he might unite in a fuller union, first with his fellow-workers, and then with the entire people. Toynbee asks who was right, Carlyle or the people. And replies that the people were

right—"The people who, sick with hunger and deformed with toil, dreamed that democracy would bring deliverance." And democracy did save industry. It transformed disputes about wages from social feuds into business bargains. It swept away the estranging class elements of suspicion and arrogance. "It gradually did away with the feudal notion among the masters that they would deal with their men one at a time, denying to them the advantages of association." It is singular that in America, where government is founded upon the principle of representation, the capitalist should have been so slow to accord this right to workingmen; that he should refuse so steadily to treat with a "walking delegate," and so long maintain that no "outsider" could represent the men in his shop.

20   We must learn to trust our democracy, giant-like and threatening as it may appear in its uncouth strength and untried applications. When the English people were demanding the charter, the English nobility predicted that the franchise would be used to inaugurate all sorts of wild measures, to overturn long-established customs, as the capitalist now sometimes assumes that higher wages will be spent only in the saloons. In both cases there is a failure to count the sobering effect of responsibility in the education and development which attend the entrance into a wider life.

21   The effort to keep the movement to some consciousness of its historic value in the race development is perhaps no more difficult than to keep before its view the larger ethical aims. There is doubtless a tendency among the working men who reach leadership in the movement to yield to individual ambition, as there is among capitalists to regard class interests, and yield only that which must be yielded. This tendency on one side to yield to ambition, and on the other to give in to threats, may be further illustrated.

22   The poor man has proverbially been the tyrant of poor men when he has become rich. But while such a man was yet poor, his heart was closed to his fellows, and his eyes were blinded to the exploitation of them and himself, because in his heart he hoped one day to be rich, and to do the exploiting; because he secretly approved the action of his master, and said, "I would do the same if I were he."

23   Workingmen say, sometimes, that the rich will not hear the complaint of the poor until it rises into a threat, and carries a suggestion of ruin with it; that they then throw the laborers a portion of the product, to save the remainder.

24   As the tendency to warfare shows the primitive state of the labor movement, so also this division on class lines reveals its present undeveloped condition. The organization of society into huge battalions with syndicates and corporations on the side of capital, and trades-unions and federations on the side of labor, is to divide the world into two hostile camps, and to turn us back into class warfare and class limitations. All our experience tells us that no question of civilization is so simple as that, nor can we any longer settle our perplexities by mere good fighting. One is reminded of one's childish conception of life—that Right and Wrong were drawn up in battle array into two distinct armies, and that to join the army of Right and fight bravely would be to settle all problems.

25   But life itself teaches us nothing more inevitable than that right and wrong are most confusedly mixed; that the blackest wrong is by our side and within our own motives; that right does not dazzle our eyes with its radiant shining, but has to be found by exerting patience, discrimination, and impartiality. We cease to listen for the bugle note of victory our childish imagination anticipated, and learn that our finest victories are attained in the midst of self-distrust, and that the waving banner of triumph is sooner or later trailed to the dust by the weight of self-righteousness. It may be that as the labor movement grows older and riper, it will cease to divide all men so sharply into capitalists and proletarians, into exploiter and exploited.

26   We may live to remind its leaders in later years, as George Eliot has so skillfully reminded us, that the path we all like when we first set out in our youth is the path of martyrdom and endurance, where the palm branches grow; but that later we learn to take the steep highway of tolerance, just allowance, and self-blame, where there are no leafy honors to be gathered and worn. As the labor movement grows older its leaders may catch the larger ethical view which genuine experience always gives; they may have a chance to act free from the pressure of threat or ambition. They should have nothing to gain or lose save as they rise or fall with their fellows. In raising the mass, men could have a motive-power as much greater than the motive for individual success, as the force which sends the sun above the horizon is greater than the force engendered by the powder behind the rocket.

27   Is it too much to hope that as the better organized and older trades-unions are fast recognizing a solidarity of labor, and acting upon the literal notion of brotherhood, that they will later perceive the larger solidarity which includes labor and capital, and act upon the notion of universal kinship? That before this larger vision of life there can be no perception of "sides" and no "battle array"? In the light of the developed social conscience the "sympathetic strike" may be criticized, not because it is too broad, but because it is too narrow, and because the strike is but a wasteful and negative demonstration of ethical fellowship. In the summer of 1894 the Chicago unions of Russian-Jewish cloakmakers, German compositors, and Bohemian and Polish butchers struck in sympathy with the cause of the American Railway Union, whom they believed to be standing for a principle. Does an event such as this, clumsy and unsatisfactory as its results are, prefigure the time when no factory child in Chicago can be overworked and underpaid without a protest from all good citizens, capitalist and proletarian? Such a protest would be founded upon an ethical sense so strong that it would easily override business interests and class prejudices.

28   Manifestations of the labor movement are erratic and ill-timed because of the very strength of its motive power. A settlement is not affrighted nor dismayed when it sees in labor-meetings, in caucuses, and turbulent gatherings, men who are—.

"Groping for the right, with horny, calloused hands,
And staring round for God with bloodshot eyes,"

although the clumsy hands may upset some heavy pieces of convention, as a strong blindman overturns furniture, and the bloodshot eyes may be wild and fanatical. The settlement is unworthy of its calling if it is too timid or dull to interpret this groping and staring. But the settlement should be affrighted, and bestir itself to action, and when the groping is not for the right, but for the mere purpose of overturning; when the staring is not for God, but for Mammon—and there is a natural temptation towards both.

29   A settlement may well be dismayed when it sees workingmen apathetic to higher motives, and thinking only of stratagems by which to outwit the capitalists; or when workingmen justify themselves in the use of base measures, saying they have learned the lessons from the other side. Such an attitude at once turns the movement from a development into a struggle, and the sole judge left between the adversaries must in the end be force. Class interests become the governing and motive power, and the settlement can logically be of no value to either side. Its sympathies are naturally much entangled in such a struggle, but to be of value it must keep its judgment clear as to the final ethical outcome—and this requires both perceptions and training.

30   Fortunately, every action may be analyzed into its permanent and transient aspects. The transient aspect of the strike is the anger and opposition against the employer, and too often the chagrin of failure. The permanent is the binding together of the strikers in the ties of association and brotherhood, and the attainment of a more democratic relation to the employer; and it is because of a growing sense of brotherhood and of democracy in the labor movement that we see in it a growing ethical power.

31   Hence the duty of the settlement in keeping the movement from becoming in any sense a class warfare is clear. There is a temperamental bitterness among working-men which is both inherited and fostered by the conditions of their life and trade; but they cannot afford to cherish a class bitterness if the labor movement is to be held to its highest possibilities. A class working for a class, and against another class, implies that within itself there should be trades working for trades, individuals working for individuals. The universal character of the movement is gone from the start, and cannot be caught until an all-embracing ideal is accepted.

32   A recent writer has called attention to the fact that the position of the power-holding classes—capitalists, as we call them just now—is being gradually undermined by the disintegrating influence of the immense fund of altruistic-feeling with which society has become equipped; that it is within this fund of altruism that we find the motive force which is slowly enfranchising all classes and gradually insisting upon equality of condition and opportunity. If we can accept this explanation of the social and political movements of our time, then it is clear that the labor movement is at the bottom an ethical movement, and a manifestation of the orderly development of the race.

33   The settlement is pledged to insist upon the unity of life, to gather to itself the sense of righteousness to be found in its neighborhood, and as far as possible in its city; to work towards the betterment not of one kind of people or

class of people, but for the common good. The settlement believes that just as men deprived of comradeship by circumstances or law go back to the brutality from which they came, so any class or set of men deprived of the companionship of the whole, become correspondingly decivilized and crippled. No part of society can afford to get along without the others.

34　　The settlement, then, urges first, the organization of working people in order that as much leisure and orderly life as possible may be secured to them in which to carry out the higher aims of living; in the second place, it should make a constant effort to bring to bear upon the labor movement a consciousness of its historic development; and lastly, it accentuates the ultimate ethical aims of the movement.

35　　The despair of the labor movement is, as Mazzini said in another cause long ago, that we have torn the great and beautiful ensign of Democracy. Each party has snatched a rag of it, and parades it as proudly as if it were the whole flag, repudiating and not deigning to look at the others.

36　　It is this feeling of disdain to any class of men or kind of men in the community which is dangerous to the labor movement, which makes it a class-measure. It attacks its democratic character, and substitutes party enthusiasm for the irresistible force of human progress. The labor movement must include all men in its hopes. It must have the communion of universal fellowship. Any drop of gall within its cup is fatal. Any grudge treasured up against a capitalist, any desire to "get even" when the wealth has changed hands, are but the old experiences of human selfishness. All sense of injury must fall away and be absorbed in the consciousness of a common brotherhood. If to insist upon the universality of the best is the function of the settlement, nowhere is its influence more needed than in the labor movement, where there is constant temptation towards a class warfare.

Mohandas K. Gandhi

Gandhi is often referred to as Mahatma, which means "great soul." Born in 1869 in India and educated as a lawyer in England, he became the preeminent leader of Indian political reform, advocating at all times nonviolent resistance to tyranny and working toward unity between India's Muslim and Hindu communities. When he was shot and killed by a Hindu radical in 1948, he had already witnessed India's independence from Britain in 1947 but felt disappointment that his country had been partitioned into India and Pakistan.

Gandhi's "Seven Social Sins" clearly communicates the man's single-minded belief in individual freedom from tyranny. His autobiography, The Story of My Experiments with Truth, *reveals self-examination as the way to learn from our mistakes in order to rise above them. Today, Gandhi's legacy is apparent worldwide.*

Mohandas K. Gandhi
"Seven Social Sins"

Politics *without* principles

Wealth *without* work

Pleasure *without* conscience

Knowledge *without* character

Commerce *without* morality

Science *without* humanity

Worship *without* sacrifice

Sitting for Justice: Woolworth's Lunch Counter

 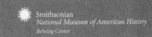

SEPARATE IS NOT EQUAL
BROWN v. BOARD OF EDUCATION

Smithsonian
National Museum of American History
Behring Center

HISTORY – REFLECTIONS – EXHIBITION – PUBLIC PROGRAMS – RESOURCES

DEFEND BROWN   REMEMBER MAY 17th

Segregated America

The Battleground

Legal Campaign

Five Communities

The Decision

 Legacy

"With All Deliberate Speed"

› Freedom Struggle

Equality for All

Changing Definitions

Communities Since Brown

Fifty Years After

Freedom Struggle
page 1 | 2 | 3

Sitting for Justice: Woolworth's Lunch Counter

On February 1, 1960, four African American college students sat down at a lunch counter at Woolworth's in Greensboro, North Carolina, and politely asked for service. Their request was refused. When asked to leave, they remained in their seats. Their passive resistance and peaceful sit-down demand helped ignite a youth-led movement to challenge racial inequality throughout the South.

Woolworth lunch counter
In Greensboro, hundreds of students, civil rights organizations, churches, and members of the community joined in a six-month-long protest. Their commitment ultimately led to the desegregation of the F. W. Woolworth lunch counter on July 25, 1960.

Greensboro first day
Ezell A. Blair, Jr. (now Jibreel Khazan), Franklin E. McCain, Joseph A. McNeil, and David L. Richmond leave the Woolworth store after the first sit-in on February 1, 1960.
(Courtesy of Greensboro *News and Record*)

Woolworth sit-in
On the second day of the Greensboro sit-in, Joseph A. McNeil and Franklin E. McCain are joined by William Smith and Clarence Henderson at the Woolworth lunch counter in Greensboro, North Carolina.
(Courtesy of Greensboro *News and Record*)

FEMINISM AND WOMEN'S ISSUES

Sojourner Truth

Sojourner Truth was born in the late eighteenth century (probably 1797) and died in 1883. In 1843, she changed her name, Isabella Van Wagener, to Sojourner Truth, a result of her decision to travel and preach about abolition. Born into slavery, bought and sold several times, Truth had escaped to freedom—along with her infant daughter—in 1826.

The fact that differing versions of her famous "Ain't I a Woman?" speech have survived underline the facts that Truth was illiterate and that others recorded her words. The first version below was recorded by Marcus Robinson and published in 1851, the year she delivered the speech at a women's rights convention; the second, by Frances Dana-Gage, appeared in 1863. Although much of Truth's life remains unclear, in spite of the publication of her Narrative of Sojourner Truth, *her strong tone and directness are unmistakable elements of her oratory style as well as her life.*

Sojourner Truth
"Ain't I a Woman?"
Two Versions

1851 Version

1   I want to say a few words about this matter.

2   I am a woman's rights. I have as much muscle as any man, and can do as much work as any man. I have plowed and reaped and husked and chopped and mowed, and can any man do more than that? I have heard much about the sexes being equal. I can carry as much as any man, and can eat as much too, if I can get it. I am as strong as any man that is now.

3   As for intellect, all I can say is, if a woman have a pint, and a man a quart—why can't she have her little pint full? You need not be afraid to give us our rights for fear we will take too much—for we can't take more than our pint'll hold.

4   The poor men seems to be all in confusion, and don't know what to do. Why children, if you have woman's rights, give it to her and you will feel better. You will have your own rights, and they won't be so much trouble.

5   I can't read, but I can hear. I have heard the bible and have learned that Eve caused man to sin. Well, if woman upset the world, do give her a chance to set it right side up again. The Lady has spoken about Jesus, how he never spurned woman from him, and she was right. When Lazarus died, Mary and

Martha came to him with faith and love and besought him to raise their brother. And Jesus wept and Lazarus came forth. And how came Jesus into the world? Through God who created him and the woman who bore him. Man, where was your part?

6   But the women are coming up blessed be God and a few of the men are coming up with them. But man is in a tight place, the poor slave is on him, woman is coming on him, he is surely between a hawk and a buzzard.

1863 Version

1   Well, children, where there is so much racket there must be something out of kilter. I think that 'twixt the negroes of the South and the women at the North, all talking about rights, the white men will be in a fix pretty soon. But what's all this here talking about?

2   That man over there says that women need to be helped into carriages, and lifted over ditches, and to have the best place everywhere. Nobody ever helps me into carriages, or over mudpuddles, or gives me any best place! And ain't I a woman? Look at me! Look at my arm! I have ploughed and planted, and gathered into barns, and no man could head me! And ain't I a woman? I could work as much and eat as much as a man—when I could get it— and bear the lash as well And ain't I a woman? I have borne thirteen children, and seen most all sold off to slavery, and when I cried out with my mother's grief, none but Jesus heard me! And ain't I a woman?

3   Then they talk about this thing in the head: what's this they call it? [member of audience whispers, "intellect"] That's it, honey. What's that got to do with women's rights or negroes' rights? If my cup won't hold but a pint, and yours holds a quart, wouldn't you be mean not to let me have my little half measure full?

4   Then that little man in black there, he says women can't have as much rights as men, 'cause Christ wasn't a woman! Where did your Christ come from? Where did your Christ come from? From God and a woman! Man had nothing to do with Him.

5   If the first woman God ever made was strong enough to turn the world upside down all alone, these women together ought to be able to turn it back, and get it right side up again! And now they is asking to do it, the men better let them.

6   Obliged to you for hearing me, and now old Sojourner ain't got nothing more to say.

Emily Dickinson

Emily Dickinson was born in 1830 and lived mostly in Amherst, Massachusetts, until her death in 1886. Although not known by the public during her life, she is now regarded as one of the most important American poets of all time.

"The Soul Selects Her Own Society" seems to carry a reclusive, even forbidding tone. But in this poem as well as in her work in general, Dickinson makes powerful observations that explore basic human problems—spirituality, love, and sexuality.

Emily Dickinson
"The Soul Selects Her Own Society"

The Soul selects her own Society—
Then—shuts the Door—
To her divine Majority—
Present no more—

5 Unmoved—she notes the Chariots—pausing—
At her low Gate—
Unmoved—an Emperor be kneeling
Upon her Mat—

I've known her—from an ample nation—
10 Choose One—
Then—close the Valves of her attention—
Like Stone—

Kate Chopin

*Kate Chopin lived from 1850 to 1904. She did not begin her publishing career until late
in her life. Known as one of the forerunners of modern feminism, Kate Chopin's novel*
The Awakening *has become one of the most well-known pieces of American literature,
with the protagonist Edna Pontellier a powerful symbol for sexual and social liberation.
In "The Story of an Hour," Chopin depicts a similar kind of female protagonist.*

Kate Chopin
"The Story of an Hour"

1   Knowing that Mrs. Mallard was afflicted with a heart trouble, great care
was taken to break to her as gently as possible the news of her husband's death.

2   It was her sister Josephine who told her, in broken sentences; veiled hints that
revealed in half concealing. Her husband's friend Richards was there, too, near her.
It was he who had been in the newspaper office when intelligence of the railroad disaster was received, with Brently Mallard's name leading the list of "killed." He had
only taken the time to assure himself of its truth by a second telegram, and had has-
tened to forestall any less careful, less tender friend in bearing the sad message.

3   She did not hear the story as many women have heard the same, with a paralyzed inability to accept its significance. She wept at once, with sudden, wild
abandonment, in her sister's arms. When the storm of grief had spent itself she
went away to her room alone. She would have no one follow her.

4   There stood, facing the open window, a comfortable, roomy armchair. Into this she sank, pressed down by a physical exhaustion that haunted her body and seemed to reach into her soul.

5   She could see in the open square before her house the tops of trees that were all aquiver with the new spring life. The delicious breath of rain was in the air. In the street below a peddler was crying his wares. The notes of a distant song which some one was singing reached her faintly, and countless sparrows were twittering in the eaves.

6   There were patches of blue sky showing here and there through the clouds that had met and piled one above the other in the west facing her window.

7   She sat with her head thrown back upon the cushion of the chair, quite motionless, except when a sob came up into her throat and shook her, as a child who has cried itself to sleep continues to sob in its dreams.

8   She was young, with a fair, calm face, whose lines bespoke repression and even a certain strength. But now there was a dull stare in her eyes, whose gaze was fixed away off yonder on one of those patches of blue sky. It was not a glance of reflection, but rather indicated a suspension of intelligent thought.

9   There was something coming to her and she was waiting for it, fearfully. What was it? She did not know; it was too subtle and elusive to name. But she felt it, creeping out of the sky, reaching toward her through the sounds, the scents, the color that filled the air.

10   Now her bosom rose and fell tumultuously. She was beginning to recognize this thing that was approaching to possess her, and she was striving to beat it back with her will—as powerless as her two white slender hands would have been.

11   When she abandoned herself a little whispered word escaped her slightly parted lips. She said it over and over under her breath: "free, free, free!" The vacant stare and the look of terror that had followed it went from her eyes. They stayed keen and bright. Her pulses beat fast, and the coursing blood warmed and relaxed every inch of her body.

12   She did not stop to ask if it were or were not a monstrous joy that held her. A clear and exalted perception enabled her to dismiss the suggestion as trivial.

13   She knew that she would weep again when she saw the kind, tender hands folded in death; the face that had never looked save with love upon her, fixed and gray and dead. But she saw beyond that bitter moment a long procession of years to come that would belong to her absolutely. And she opened and spread her arms out to them in welcome.

14   There would be no one to live for her during those coming years; she would live for herself. There would be no powerful will bending hers in that blind persistence with which men and women believe they have a right to impose a private will upon a fellow-creature. A kind intention or a cruel intention made the act seem no less a crime as she looked upon it in that brief moment of illumination.

15   And yet she had loved him—sometimes. Often she had not. What did it matter! What could love, the unsolved mystery, count for in face of this

possession of self-assertion which she suddenly recognized as the strongest impulse of her being!

16   "Free! Body and soul free!" she kept whispering.

17   Josephine was kneeling before the closed door with her lips to the keyhole, imploring for admission. "Louise, open the door! I beg; open the door—you will make yourself ill. What are you doing, Louise? For heaven's sake open the door."

18   "Go away. I am not making myself ill." No; she was drinking in a very elixir of life through that open window.

19   Her fancy was running riot along those days ahead of her. Spring days, and summer days, and all sorts of days that would be her own. She breathed a quick prayer that life might be long. It was only yesterday she had thought with a shudder that life might be long.

20   She arose at length and opened the door to her sister's importunities. There was a feverish triumph in her eyes, and she carried herself unwittingly like a goddess of Victory. She clasped her sister's waist, and together they descended the stairs. Richards stood waiting for them at the bottom.

21   Some one was opening the front door with a latchkey. It was Brently Mallard who entered, a little travel-stained, composedly carrying his grip-sack and umbrella. He had been far from the scene of accident, and did not even know there had been one. He stood amazed at Josephine's piercing cry; at Richards quick motion to screen him from the view of his wife.

22   But Richards was too late.

23   When the doctors came they said she had died of heart disease—of joy that kills.

Susan Glaspell

Susan Glaspell lived from 1876 to 1948. Her novels and plays were well known during her lifetime. She helped found the famous Provincetown (Massachusetts) Players when she moved there in 1915. In 1931, Glaspell won the Pulitzer Prize for drama. In addition to her status as an influential writer, Glaspell also worked with many important social reformers of the time.

Her play Trifles *straightforwardly depicts the actions of two separate groups—one male and one female—in the aftermath of a small-town murder. The outcome of their actions questions, even indicts, common gender practices.*

Susan Glaspell
"Trifles"

CHARACTERS

George Henderson, county attorney
Mrs. Peters
Henry Peters; sheriff
Lewis Hale, a neighboring farmer
Mrs. Hale

SCENE. *The kitchen in the now abandoned farmhouse of John Wright, a gloomy kitchen, and left without having been put in order—unwashed pans under the sink, a loaf of bread outside the bread-box, a dish-towel on the table—other signs of incompleted work. At the rear the outer door opens and the sheriff comes in followed by the County Attorney and Hale. The Sheriff and Hale are in middle life, the County Attorney is a young man; all are much bundled up and go at once to the stove. They are followed by the two women—the Sheriff's wife first; she is a slight wiry woman, a thin nervous face. Mrs. Hale is larger and would ordinarily be called more comfortable looking, but she is disturbed now and looks fearfully about as she enters. The women have come in slowly, and stand close together near the door.*

COUNTY ATTORNEY: [*Rubbing his hands.*] This feels good. Come up to the fire, ladies.

MRS. PETERS: [*After taking a step forward.*] I'm not—cold.

SHERIFF: [*Unbuttoning his overcoat and stepping away from the stove as if to mark the beginning of official business.*] Now, Mr. Hale, before we move things about, you explain to Mr. Henderson just what you saw when you came here yesterday morning.

COUNTY ATTORNEY: By the way, has anything been moved? Are things just as you left them yesterday?

SHERIFF: [*Looking about.*] It's just the same. When it dropped below zero last night, I thought I'd better send Frank out this morning to make a fire for us—no use getting pneumonia with a big case on, but I told him not to touch anything except the stove—and you know Frank.

COUNTY ATTORNEY: Somebody should have been left here yesterday.

SHERIFF: Oh—yesterday. When I had to send Frank to Morris Center for that man who went crazy—I want you to know I had my hands full yesterday. I knew you could get back from Omaha by today and as long as I went over everything here myself—

COUNTY ATTORNEY: Well, Mr. Hale, tell just what happened when you came here yesterday morning.

HALE: Harry and I and started to town with a load of potatoes. We came along the road from my place and as I got here I said, "I'm going to see if I can't get John Wright to go in with me on a party telephone." I spoke to Wright about it once before and he put me off, saying folks talked too much anyway, and all he asked was peace and quiet—I guess you know about how much he talked himself, but I thought maybe if I went to the house and talked about it before his wife, though I said to Harry that I didn't know as what his wife wanted made much difference to John—

COUNTY ATTORNEY: Let's talk about that later, Mr. Hale. I do want to talk about that, but tell now just what happened when you got to the house.

HALE: I didn't hear or see anything; I knocked at the door, and still it was all quiet inside. I knew they must be up, it was past eight o'clock. So I knocked again, and I thought I heard somebody, say, "Come in." I wasn't sure, I'm not sure yet, but I opened the door—this door [*indicating the door by which the two women are still standing*] and there in that rocker—[*pointing to it*] sat Mrs. Wright.

[*They all look at the rocker.*]

COUNTY ATTORNEY: What—was she doing?

HALE: She was rockin' back and forth. She had her apron in her hand and was kind of—pleating it.

COUNTY ATTORNEY: And how did she—look?

HALE: Well, she looked queer.

COUNTY ATTORNEY: How do you mean—queer?

HALE: Well, as if she didn't know what she was going to do next. And kind of done up.

COUNTY ATTORNEY: How did she seem to feel about your coming?

HALE: Why, I don't think she minded—one way or other. She didn't pay much attention. I said, "How do, Mrs. Wright, it's cold, ain't it?" And she said, "Is it?"—and went on kind of pleating at her apron. Well, I was surprised; she didn't ask me to come up to the stove, or to set down, but just sat there, not even looking at me, so I said, "I want to see John." And then she—laughed. I guess you would call it a laugh. I thought of Harry and the team outside, so I said a little sharp: "Can't I see John?" "No," she says, kind o' dull like. "Ain't he home?" says I. "Yes," says she, "he's home." "Then why can't I see him?" I asked her, out of patience. "'Cause he's dead," says she. *"Dead?"* says I. She just nodded her head, not getting a bit excited, but rockin' back and forth. "Why—where is he?" says I, not knowing what to say. She just pointed upstairs—like that [*himself pointing to the room above*]. I got up, with the idea of going up there. I walked from there to here—then I says, "Why, what did he die of?" "He died of a rope round his neck," says she, and just went on pleatin' at her apron. Well, I went out and called Harry. I thought I might—need help. We went upstairs and there he was lyin'—

COUNTY ATTORNEY: I think I'd rather have you go into that upstairs, where you can point it all out. Just go on now with the rest of the story.

HALE: Well, my first thought was to get that rope off. It looked . . . [*Stops, his face twitches*] . . . but Harry, he went up to him, and he said, "No, he's dead all right, and we'd better not touch anything." So we went back downstairs. She was still sitting that same way, "Has anybody been notified?" I asked. "No," says she, unconcerned. "Who did this, Mrs. Wright?" said Harry. He said it business like—and she stopped pleatin' of her apron. "I don't know," she says. "You don't *know?*" says Harry. "No," says she. "Weren't you sleepin' in the bed with him?" says Harry. "Yes," says she, "but I was on the inside." "Somebody slipped a rope round his neck and strangled him and you didn't wake up?" says Harry. "I didn't wake up," she said after him. We must 'a looked as if we didn't see how that could be, for after a minute she said, "I sleep sound." Harry was going to ask her more questions but I said maybe we ought to let her tell her story first to the coroner, or the sheriff, so Harry went fast as he could to Rivers' place, where there's a telephone.

COUNTY ATTORNEY: And what did Mrs. Wright do when she knew that you had gone for the coroner?

HALE: She moved from that chair to this one over here [*Pointing to a small chair in the corner*] and just sat there with her hands held together and looking down. I got a feeling that I ought to make some conversation, so I said I had come in to see if John wanted to put in a telephone, and at that she started to laugh, and then she stopped and looked at me—scared. [*The County Attorney, who has had his notebook out, makes a note.*] I dunno, maybe it wasn't scared. I wouldn't like to say it was. Soon Harry got back, and then Dr. Lloyd came, and you, Mr. Peters, and so I guess that's all I know that you don't.

COUNTY ATTORNEY: [*Looking around.*] I guess we'll go upstairs first—and then out to the barn and around there. [*To the Sheriff.*] You're convinced that there was nothing important here—nothing that would point to any motive.

SHERIFF: Nothing here but kitchen things.

[*The County Attorney, after again looking around the kitchen, opens the door of a cupboard closet. He gets up on a chair and looks on a shelf. Pulls his hand away, sticky.*]

COUNTY ATTORNEY: Here's a nice mess.

[*The women draw nearer.*]

MRS. PETERS: [*To the other woman.*] Oh, her fruit; it did freeze. [*To the County Attorney.*] She worried about that when it turned so cold. She said the fire'd go out and her jars would break.

SHERIFF: Well, can you beat the women! Held for murder and worryin' about her preserves.

COUNTY ATTORNEY: I guess before we're through she may have something more serious than preserves to worry about.

HALE: Well, women are used to worrying over trifles.

[*The two women move a little closer together.*]

COUNTY ATTORNEY: [*With the gallantry of a young politician.*] And yet, for all their worries, what would we do without the ladies? [*The women do not unbend. He goes to the sink, takes a dipperful of water from the pail and pouring it into a basin, washes his hands. Starts to wipe them on the roller-towel, turns it for a cleaner place.*] Dirty towels! [*Kicks his foot against the pans under the sink.*] Not much of a housekeeper, would you say, ladies?

MRS. HALE: [*Stiffly.*] There's a great deal of work to be done on a farm.

COUNTY ATTORNEY: To be sure. And yet [*With a little bow to her*] I know there are some Dickson County farmhouses which do not have such roller towels.

[*He gives it a pull to expose its full length again.*]

MRS. HALE: Those towels get dirty awful quick. Men's hands aren't always as clean as they might be.

COUNTY ATTORNEY: Ah, loyal to your sex, I see. But you and Mrs. Wright were neighbors. I suppose you were friends, too.

MRS. HALE: [*Shaking her head.*] I've not seen much of her of late years. I've not been in this house—it's more than a year.

COUNTY ATTORNEY: And why was that? You didn't like her?

MRS. HALE: I liked her all well enough. Farmers' wives have their hands full, Mr. Henderson. And then—

COUNTY ATTORNEY: Yes—?

MRS. HALE: [*Looking about.*] It never seemed a very cheerful place.

COUNTY ATTORNEY: No—it's not cheerful. I shouldn't say she had the home-making instinct.

MRS. HALE: Well, I don't know as Wright had, either.

COUNTY ATTORNEY: You mean that they didn't get on very well?

MRS. HALE: No, I don't mean anything. But I don't think a place'd be any cheer-fuller for John Wright's being in it.

COUNTY ATTORNEY: I'd like to talk more of that a little later. I want to get the lay of things upstairs now.

[*He goes to the left, where three steps lead to a stair door.*]

SHERIFF: I suppose anything Mrs. Peters does'll be all right. She was to take in some clothes for her, you know, and a few little things. We left in such a hurry yesterday.

COUNTY ATTORNEY: Yes, but I would like to see what you take, Mrs. Peters, and keep an eye out for anything that might be of use to us.

MRS. PETERS: Yes, Mr. Henderson.

[*The women listen to the men's steps on the stairs, then look about the kitchen.*]

MRS. HALE: I'd hate to have men coming into my kitchen, snooping around and criticizing.

[*She arranges the pans, under the sink, which the County Attorney had shoved out of place.*]

MRS. PETERS: Of course, it's no more than their duty.

MRS. HALE: Duty's all right, but I guess that deputy sheriff that came out to make the fire might have got a little of this on. [*Gives the roller towel a pull.*] Wish I'd thought of that sooner. Seems mean to talk about her for not having things slicked up when she had to come away in such a hurry.

MRS. PETERS: [*Who has gone to a small table in the left rear corner of the room, and lifted one end of a towel that covers a pan.*] She had bread set.

[*Stands still.*]

MRS. HALE: [*Eyes fixed on a loaf of bread beside the breadbox, which is on a low shelf at the other side of the room. Moves slowly toward it.*] She was going to put this in there. [*Picks up loaf, then abruptly drops it. In a manner of returning to familiar things.*] It's a shame about her fruit. I wonder if it's all gone. [*Gets up on the chair and looks.*] I think there's some here that's all right, Mrs. Peters. Yes—here; [*Holding it toward the window*] this is cherries, too. [*Looking again.*] I declare I believe that's the only one. [*Gets down, bottle in her hand. Goes to the sink and wipes it off on the outside.*] She'll feel awful bad after all her hard work in the hot weather. I remember the afternoon I put up my cherries last summer.

[*She puts the bottle on the big kitchen table, center of the room. With a sigh, is about to sit down in the rocking-chair. Before she is seated realizes what chair it is; with, a slow look at it, steps back. The chair, which she has touched, rocks back and forth.*]

MRS. PETERS: Well, I must get those things from the front room closet. [*She goes to the door at the right, but after looking into the other room, steps back.*] You coming with me, Mrs. Hale? You could help me carry them.

[*They go in the other room; they reappear, Mrs. Peters carrying a dress and skirt, Mrs. Hale following with a pair of shoes.*]

MRS. PETERS: My, it's cold in there.

[*She puts the clothes on the big table, and hurries to the stove.*]

MRS. HALE: [*Examining the skirt.*] Wright was close. I think maybe that's why she kept so much to herself. She didn't even belong to the Ladies Aid. I suppose she felt she couldn't do her part, and then you don't enjoy things when you feel shabby. She used to wear pretty clothes and be lively, when she was Minnie Foster, one of the town girls singing in the choir. But that—oh, that was thirty years ago. This all you was to take in?

MRS. PETERS: She said she wanted an apron. Funny thing to want, for there isn't much to get you dirty in jail, goodness knows. But I suppose just to make her feel more natural. She said they was in the top drawer in this cupboard. Yes, here. And then her little shawl that always hung behind the door. [*Opens stair door and looks.*] Yes, here it is.

[*Quickly shuts door leading upstairs.*]

MRS. HALE: [*Abruptly moving toward her.*] Mrs. Peters?

MRS. PETERS: Yes, Mrs. Hale?

MRS. HALE: Do you think she did it?

MRS. PETERS: [*In a frightened voice.*] Oh, I don't know.

MRS. HALE: Well, I don't think she did. Asking for an apron and her little shawl. Worrying about her fruit.

MRS. PETERS: [*Starts to speak, glances up, where footsteps are heard in the room above. In a low voice.*] Mr. Peters says it looks bad for her. Mr. Henderson is awful sarcastic in a speech and he'll make fun of her sayin' she didn't wake up.

MRS. HALE: Well, I guess John Wright didn't wake when they was slipping that rope under his neck.

MRS. PETERS: No, it's strange. It must have been done awful crafty and still. They say it was such a—funny way to kill a man, rigging it all up like that.

MRS. HALE: That's just what Mr. Hale said. There was a gun in the house. He says that's what he can't understand.

MRS. PETERS: Mr. Henderson said coming out that what was needed for the case was a motive; something to show anger, or—sudden feeling.

MRS. HALE: [*Who is standing by the table.*] Well, I don't see any signs of anger around here. [*She puts her hand on the dish towel which lies on the table, stands looking down at table, one half of which is clean, the other half messy.*] It's wiped to here. [*Makes a move as if to finish work, then turns and looks at loaf of bread outside the breadbox. Drops towel. In that voice of coming back to familiar things.*] Wonder how they are finding thing upstairs. I hope she had it a little more red-up up there. You know, it seems kind of sneaking. Locking her up in town and then coming out here and trying to get her own house to turn against her!

MRS. PETERS: But, Mrs. Hale, the law is the law.

MRS. HALE: I s'pose 'tis. [*Unbuttoning her coat.*] Better loosen up your things, Mrs. Peters. You won't feel them when you go out.

[*Mrs. Peters takes off her fur tippet, goes to hang it on hook at back of room, stands looking at the under part of the small corner table.*]

MRS. PETERS: She was piecing a quilt.

[*She brings the large sewing basket, and they look at the bright pieces.*]

MRS. HALE: It's log-cabin pattern. Pretty, isn't it? I wonder if she was goin' to quilt it or just knot it?

[*Footsteps have been heard coming down the stairs. The Sheriff enters followed by Hale and the County Attorney.*]

SHERIFF: They wonder if she was going to quilt it or just knot it!

[*The men laugh; the women look abashed.*]

COUNTY ATTORNEY: [*Rubbing his hands over the stove.*] Frank's fire didn't do much up there, did it? Well, let's go out to the barn and get that cleared up.

[*The men go outside.*]

MRS. HALE: [*Resentfully.*] I don't know as there's anything so strange, our takin' up our time with little things while we're waiting for them to get the evidence. [*She sits down at the big table smoothing out a block with decision.*] I don't see as it's anything to laugh about.

MRS. PETERS: [*Apologetically.*] Of course they've got awful important things on their minds.

[*Pulls up a chair and joins Mrs. Hale at the table.*]

MRS. HALE: [*Examining another block.*] Mrs. Peters, look at this one. Here, this is the one she was working on, and look at the sewing! All the rest of it has been so nice and even. And look at this! It's all over place! Why, it looks as if she didn't know what she was about!

[*After she has said this, they look at each other, then start to glance back at the door. After an instant Mrs. Hale has pulled at a knot and ripped the sewing.*]

MRS. PETERS: Oh, what are you doing, Mrs. Hale?

MRS. HALE: [*Mildly.*] Just pulling out a stitch or two that's not sewed very good. [*Threading a needle.*] Bad sewing always made me fidgety.

MRS. PETERS: [*Nervously.*] I don't think we ought to touch things.

MRS. HALE: I'll just finish up this end. [*Suddenly stopping and leaning forward.*] Mrs. Peters?

MRS. PETERS: Yes, Mrs. Hale?

MRS. HALE: What do you suppose she was so nervous about?

MRS. PETERS: Oh—I don't know. I don't know as she was nervous. I sometimes sew awful queer when I'm just tired. [*Mrs. Hale starts to say something, looks at Mrs. Peters, then goes on sewing.*] Well I must get these things wrapped up. They may be through sooner than we think. [*Putting apron and other things together.*] I wonder where I can find a piece of paper, and string.

MRS. HALE: In that cupboard, maybe.

MRS. PETERS: [*Looking in cupboard.*] Why, here's a bird-cage. [*Holds it up.*] Did she have a bird, Mrs. Hale?

MRS. HALE: Why, I don't know whether she did or not—I've not been here for so long. There was a man around last year selling canaries cheap, but I don't know as she took one; maybe she did. She used to sing real pretty herself.

MRS. PETERS: [*Glancing around.*] Seems funny to think of a bird here. But she must have had one, or why would she have a cage? I wonder what happened to it.

MRS. HALE: I s'pose maybe the cat got it.

MRS. PETERS: No, she didn't have a cat. She's got that feeling some people have about cats—being afraid of them. My cat got in her room and she was real upset and asked me to take it out.

MRS. HALE: My sister Bessie was like that. Queer, ain't it?

MRS. PETERS: [*Examining the cage.*] Why, look at this door. It's broke. One hinge is pulled apart.

MRS. HALE: [*Looking too.*] Looks as if someone must have been rough with it.

MRS. PETERS: Why, yes.

[*She brings the cage forward and puts it on the table.*]

MRS. HALE: I wish if they're going to find any evidence they'd be about it. I don't like this place.

MRS. PETERS: But I'm awful glad you came with me, Mrs. Hale. It would be lonesome for me sitting here alone.

MRS. HALE: It would, wouldn't it? [*Dropping her sewing.*] But I tell you what I do wish, Mrs. Peters. I wish I had come over sometimes when she was here. I—[*Looking around the room*]—wish I had.

MRS. PETERS: But of course you were awful busy, Mrs. Hale—your house and your children.

MRS. HALE: I could've come. I stayed away because it weren't cheerful—and that's why I ought to have come. I—I've never liked this place. Maybe because it's down in a hollow and you don't see the road. I dunno what it is, but it's a lonesome place and always was. I wish I had come over to see Minnie Foster sometimes. I can see now—

[*Shakes her head.*]

MRS. PETERS: Well, you mustn't reproach yourself, Mrs. Hale. Somehow we just don't see how it is with other folks until—something comes up.

MRS. HALE: Not having children makes less work—but it makes a quiet house, and Wright out to work all day, and no company when he did come in. Did you know John Wright, Mrs. Peters?

MRS. PETERS: Not to know him; I've seen him in town. They say he was a good man.

MRS. HALE: Yes—good; he didn't drink, and kept his word as well as most, I guess, and paid his debts. But he was a hard man, Mrs. Peters. Just to pass the time of day with him—[*Shivers.*] Like a raw wind that gets to the bone. [*Pauses, her eye falling on the cage.*] I should think she would 'a wanted a bird. But what do you suppose went wrong with it?

MRS. PETERS: I don't know, unless it got sick and died.

[*She reaches over and swings the broken door, swings it again, and both women watch it.*]

MRS. HALE: You weren't raised round here, were you? [*Mrs. Peters shakes her head.*] You didn't know—her?

MRS. PETERS: Not till they brought her yesterday.

MRS. HALE: She—come to think of it, she was kind of like a bird herself—real sweet and pretty, but kind of timid and—fluttery. How—she—did—change. [*Silence; then as if struck by a happy thought and relieved to get back to everyday things.*] Tell you what, Mrs. Peters, why don't you take the quilt in with you? It might take up her mind.

MRS. PETERS: Why, I think that's a real nice idea, Mrs. Hale. There couldn't possibly be any objection to it, could there? Now, just what would I take? I wonder if her patches are in here—and her things.

[*They look in the sewing basket.*]

MRS. HALE: Here's some red. I expect this has got sewing things in it. [*Brings out a fancy box.*] What a pretty box. Looks like something somebody would give you. Maybe her scissors are in here. [*Opens box. Suddenly puts her hand to her nose.*] Why— [*Mrs. Peters bends nearer, then turns her face away.*] There's something wrapped up in this piece of silk.

MRS. PETERS: Why, this isn't her scissors.

MRS. HALE: [*Lifting the silk.*] Oh, Mrs. Peters—it's—

[*Mrs. Peters bends closer.*]

MRS. PETERS: It's the bird.

MRS. HALE: [*Jumping up.*] But, Mrs. Peters—look at it! Its neck! Look at its neck! It's all—other side *to*

MRS. PETERS: Somebody—wrung—its—neck.

[*Their eyes meet. A look of growing comprehension, of horror. Steps are heard outside. Mrs. Hale slips box under quilt pieces, and sinks into her chair. Enter Sheriff and County Attorney. Mrs. Peters rises.*]

COUNTY ATTORYNEY: [*As one turning from serious things to little pleasantries.*] Well, ladies, have you decided whether she was going to quilt it or knot it?

MRS. PETERS: We think she was going to—knot it.

COUNTY ATTORNEY: Well, that's interesting, I'm sure. [*Seeing the bird-cage.*] Has the bird flown?

MRS. HALE: [*Putting more quilt pieces over the box.*] We think the—cat got it.

COUNTY ATTORNEY: [*Preoccupied.*] Is there a cat?

[*Mrs. Hale glances in a quick covert way at Mrs. Peters.*]

MRS. PETERS: Well, not now. They're superstitious, you know. They leave.

COUNTY ATTORNEY: [*To Sheriff Peters, continuing an interrupted conversation.*] No sign at all of anyone having come from the outside. Their own rope. Now let's go up again and go over it piece by piece. [*They start upstairs.*] It would have to have been someone who knew just the—

[*Mrs. Peters sits down. The two women sit there not looking at one another, but as if peering into something and at the same time holding back. When they talk now it is in the manner of feeling their way over strange ground, as if afraid of what they are saying, but as if they can not help saying it.*]

MRS. HALE: She liked the bird. She was going to bury it in that pretty box.

MRS. PETERS: [*In a whisper*] When I was a girl—my kitten—there was a boy took a hatchet, and before my eyes—and before I could get there—[*Covers her face an instant.*] If they hadn't held me back I would have—[*Catches herself, looks upstairs where steps are heard, falters weakly*]—hurt him.

MRS. HALE: [*With a slow look around her.*] I wonder how it would seem never to have had any children around. [*Pause.*] No, Wright wouldn't like the bird—a thing that sang. She used to sing. He killed that, too.

MRS. PETERS: [*Moving uneasily.*] We don't know who killed the bird.

MRS. HALE: I knew John Wright.

MRS. PETERS: It was an awful thing was done in this house that night, Mrs. Hale. Killing a man while he slept, slipping a rope around his neck that choked the life out of him.

MRS. HALE: His neck. Choked the life out of him.

[*Her hand goes out and rests on the bird-cage.*]

MRS. PETERS: [*With rising voice.*] We don't know who killed him. We don't *know.*

MRS. HALE: [*Her own feeling not interrupted.*] If there'd been years and years of nothing, then a bird to sing to you, it would be awful—still, after the bird was still.

MRS. PETERS: [*Something within her speaking.*] I know what stillness is. When we homesteaded in Dakota, and my first baby died— after he was two years old, and me with no other then—

MRS. HALE: [*Moving.*] How soon do you suppose they'll be through, looking for the evidence?

MRS. PETERS: I know what stillness is. [*Pulling herself back.*] The law has got to punish crime. Mrs. Hale.

MRS. HALE: [*Not as if answering that.*] I wish you'd seen Minnie Foster when she wore a white dress with blue ribbons and stood up there in the choir and sang. [*A look around the room.*] Oh, I wish I'd come over here once in a while! That was a crime! That was a crime! Who's going to punish that?

MRS. PETERS: [*Looking upstairs.*] We mustn't—*take on*.

MRS. HALE: I might have known she needed help! I know how things can be— for women, I tell you, it's queer, Mrs. Peters. We live close together and we live far apart. We all go through the same things—it's all just a different kind of the same thing. [*Brushes her eyes, noticing the bottle of fruit, reaches out for it.*] If I was you I wouldn't tell her her fruit was gone. Tell her it ain't. Tell her it's all right. Take this in to prove it to her. She—she may never know whether it was broke or not.

MRS. PETERS: [*Takes the bottle, looks about for something to wrap it in; takes petti-coat from the clothes brought from the other room, very nervously begins winding this around the bottle. In a false voice.*] My, it's a good thing the men couldn't hear us. Wouldn't they just laugh! Getting all stirred up over a little thing like a— dead canary. As if that could have anything to do with—with—wouldn't they *laugh*!

[*The men are heard coming downstairs.*]

MRS. HALE: [*Under her breath.*] Maybe they would—maybe they wouldn't.

COUNTY ATTORNEY: No, Peters, it's all perfectly clear except a reason for do-ing it. But you know juries when it comes to women. If there was some defi-nite thing. Something to show—something to make a story about—a thing that would connect up with this strange way of doing it—

[*The women's eyes meet for an instant. Enter Hale from outer door.*]

HALE: Well, I've got the team around. Pretty cold out there.

COUNTY ATTORNEY: I'm going to stay here a while by myself. [*To the sheriff.*] You can send Frank out for me, can't you? I want to go over everything. I'm not satisfied that we can't do better.

SHERIFF: Do you want to see what Mrs. Peters is going to take in?

[*The Lawyer goes to the table, picks up the apron, laughs.*]

COUNTY ATTORNEY: Oh, I guess they're not very dangerous things the ladies have picked out. [*Moves a few things about, disturbing the quilt pieces which cover the box. Steps back.*] No, Mrs. Peters doesn't need supervising. For that matter, a sheriff's wife is married to the law. Ever think of it that way, Mrs. Peters?

MRS. PETERS: Not—just that way.

SHERIFF: [*Chuckling.*] Married to the law. [*Moves toward the other room.*] I just want you to come in here a minute, George. We ought to take a look at these windows.

COUNTY ATTORNEY: [*Scoffingly.*] Oh, windows!

SHERIFF: We'll be right out, Mr. Hale.

Hale goes outside. The Sheriff follows the County Attorney into the other room. Then Mrs. Hale rises, hands tight together, looking intensely at Mrs. Peters, whose eyes make a slow turn, finally meeting Mrs. Hale's. A moment Mrs. Hale holds her; then her own eyes point the way to where the box is concealed. Suddenly Mrs. Peters throws back quilt pieces and tries to put the box in the bag she is carrying. It is too big. She opens box, starts to take bird out, cannot touch it, goes to pieces, stands there helpless. Sound of a knob turning in the other room. Mrs. Hale snatches the box and puts it in the pocket of her big coat. Enter County Attorney and Sheriff.

COUNTY ATTORNEY: [*Facetiously.*] Well, Henry, at least we found out that she was not going to quilt it. She was going to—what is it you call it, ladies?

MRS. HALE: [*Her hand against her pocket.*] We call it—knot it, Mr. Henderson.

CURTAIN

Mike Baldwin

Born in 1954, Mike Baldwin is known for his offbeat single-panel cartoon series Cornered, *which has appeared in newspapers throughout the United States and Canada. A collection of them has been published as* Don't Try Anything Funny.

Mike Baldwin
"Our Standards . . ."

"Our standards are very high. We even have high double standards."

John Everett Millais

John Everett Millais lived from 1829 to 1896. His talent as a painter was recognized early, and at the age of 11, he began to study with the British Royal Academy. He is well known for cofounding the Pre-Raphaelite Brotherhood, which aimed to reject Renaissance styles as they developed after the painter Raphael (1483–1520).

Ophelia (1852) is an example of work by the Pre-Raphaelites, whom critic John Ruskin, a friend of Millais, encouraged to "go to Nature in all singleness of heart, rejecting nothing, selecting nothing, and scorning nothing."

John Everett Millais
Ophelia

Virginia Woolf

Virginia Woolf is among the most well-known and highly respected British writers of the twentieth century. She lived from 1882 to 1941. Two of her best-known novels, Mrs. Dalloway *and* To the Lighthouse, *portray the effects of rigid social roles and isolation on human life.*

Woolf's nonfiction has become as well respected as her fiction. The piece printed here comes from A Room of One's Own, *Woolf's most famous nonfiction work, which argues that a woman must have the material resources as well as the intellectual freedom to write. (It is worth pointing out to students that only a single play written by a woman during Shakespeare's day is extant—Elizabeth Cary's* The Tragedy of Miriam, *a closet drama, meant to be read, not acted. Cary was from a privileged and wealthy family.)*

Virginia Woolf
"Shakespeare's Sister"
from Chapter 3 of A Room of One's Own

1   [I]t would have been impossible, completely and entirely, for any woman to have written the plays of Shakespeare in the age of Shakespeare. Let me imagine, since facts are so hard to come by, what would have happened had Shakespeare had a wonderfully gifted sister, called Judith, let us say. Shakespeare himself went, very probably—his mother was an heiress—to the grammar school, where he may have learnt Latin—Ovid, Virgil and Horace—and the elements of grammar and logic. He was, it is well known, a wild boy who poached rabbits, perhaps shot a deer, and had, rather sooner than he should have done, to marry a woman in the neighborhood, who bore him a child rather quicker than was right. That escapade sent him to seek his fortune in London. He had, it seemed, a taste for the theater; he began by holding horses at the stage door. Very soon he got work in the theater, became a successful actor, and lived at the hub of the universe, meeting everybody, knowing everybody, practicing his art on the boards, exercising his wits in the streets, and even getting access to the palace of the queen. Meanwhile his extraordinarily gifted sister, let us suppose, remained at home. She was as adventurous, as imaginative, as agog to see the world as he was. But she was not sent to school. She had no chance of learning grammar and logic, let alone of reading Horace and Virgil. She picked up a book now and then, one of her brother's perhaps, and read a few pages. But then her parents came in and told her to mend the stockings or mind the stew and not moon about with books and papers. They would have spoken sharply but kindly, for they were substantial people who knew the conditions of life for a woman and loved their daughter—indeed, more likely than not she was the apple of her father's eye. Perhaps she scribbled some pages up in an apple loft on the sly, but was careful to hide them or set fire to them. Soon however, before she was out of her teens, she was to be betrothed to the son of a neighboring wool-stapler. She cried out that marriage was hateful to her, and for that she was severely beaten by her father. Then he ceased to scold her. He begged her instead not to hurt him, not to shame him in this matter of her marriage. He would give her a chain of beads or a fine petticoat, he said; and there were tears in his eyes. How could she disobey him? How could she break his heart? The force of her own gift alone drove her to it. She made up a small parcel of her belongings, let herself down by a rope one summer's night and took the road to London. She was not seventeen. The birds that sang in the hedge were not more musical than she was. She had the quickest fancy, a gift like her brother's, for the tune of words. Like him, she had a taste for the theater. She stood at the stage door; she wanted to act, she said. Men laughed in her face. The manager—a fat, loose-lipped man—guffawed.

He bellowed something about poodles dancing and women acting—no woman, he said, could possibly be an actress. He hinted—you can imagine what. She could get no training in her craft. Could she even seek her dinner in a tavern or roam the streets at midnight? Yet her genius was for fiction and lusted to feed abundantly upon the lives of men and women and the study of their ways. At last—for she was very young, oddly like Shakespeare the poet in her face, with the same gray eyes and rounded brows—at last Nick Greene the actor-manager took pity on her; she found herself with child by that gentleman and so—who shall measure the heat and violence of the poet's heart when caught and tangled in a woman's body—killed herself one winter's night and lies buried at some cross-roads where the omnibuses now stop outside the Elephant and Castle.

2   That, more or less, is how the story would run, I think, if a woman in Shakespeare's day had had Shakespeare's genius. But for my part, I agree with the deceased bishop,[1] if such he was—it is unthinkable that any woman in Shakespeare's day should have had Shakespeare's genius. For genius like Shakespeare's is not born among laboring, uneducated, servile people. It was not born in England among the Saxons and the Britons. It is not born today among the working classes. How, then, could it have been born among women whose work began, according to Professor Trevelyan,[2] almost before they were out of the nursery, who were forced to it by their parents and held to it by all the power of law and custom? Yet genius of a sort must have existed among women as it must have existed among the working classes. Now and again an Emily Brontë or a Robert Burns blazes out and proves its presence. But certainly it never got itself on to paper. When, however, one reads of a witch being ducked, of a woman possessed by devils, of a wise woman selling herbs, or even of a very remarkable man who had a mother, then I think we are on the track of a lost novelist, a suppressed poet, of some mute and inglorious Jane Austen, some Emily Brontë who dashed her brains out on the moor or mopped and mowed about the highways crazed with the torture that her gift had put her to. Indeed, I would venture to guess the Anon, who wrote so many poems without signing them, was often a woman. It was a woman Edward Fitzgerald, I think, suggested who made the ballads and the folk songs, crooning them to her children, beguiling her spinning with them, or the length of the winter's night.

3   This may be true or it may be false—who can say?—but what is true in it, so it seemed to me, reviewing the story of Shakespeare's sister as I had made it is that any woman born with a great gift in the sixteenth century would certainly have gone crazed, shot herself, or ended her days in some lonely

---

1. Woolf is referring to an "old gentleman" of whom she writes earlier in the work. There she claims that he "declared that it was impossible for any woman past, present, or to come, to have the genius of Shakespeare."
2. Woolf is referring to the historian George Macaulay Trevelyan, who had written a famous one-volume history of England.

cottage outside the village, half witch, half wizard, feared and mocked at. For it needs little skill in psychology to be sure that a highly gifted girl who had tried to use her gift for poetry would have been so thwarted and hindered by other people, so tortured and pulled asunder by her own contrary instincts, that she must have lost her health and sanity to a certainty. . . .

Katha Pollitt

Katha Pollitt was born in New York City in 1949 and writes the "Subject to Debate" column in The Nation, *a weekly journal of opinion known for its liberal political stance. Pollitt has also written for other well-known periodicals and has published several books of essays. In 1983, she won a National Book Critics Circle Award for a volume of her poetry,* Antarctic Traveller.

Originally published in "Subject to Debate," the defense of contemporary feminism in the following essay is emblematic of much of Pollitt's work.

Katha Pollitt
"Girls Against Boys?"

1   I went to Radcliffe, the women's wing of Harvard, at a time when the combined undergraduate student body was fixed at four male students for every female one. I don't remember anyone worrying about the boys' social lives, or whether they would find anyone to marry—even though nationally, too, boys were more likely to go to college and to graduate than girls. When in 1975 President Derek Bok instituted equal-access admissions, nobody said, "Great idea, more marital choice for educated men!"

2   What a difference a few decades and a gender revolution make. Now, although both sexes are much more likely to go to college than forty years ago—the proportion of the population enrolled in college is 20 percentage points higher today than in 1960—girls have edged ahead of boys. Today, women make up 57 percent of undergraduates, and the gap is projected to reach 60/40 in the next few years. This year even [2006], manly Harvard admitted more girls than boys to its freshman class. So of course the big question is, Who will all those educated women marry? "Advocates for women have been so effective politically that high schools and colleges are still focusing on supposed discrimination against women," writes John Tierney in a recent *New York Times* column. "You could think of this as a victory for women's rights, but many of the victors will end up celebrating alone." If the ladies end up cuddling with their diplomas, they have only themselves—and those misguided "advocates for women"—to blame. Take that, you hyper-educated spinster, you.

3   The conservative spin on the education gender gap is that feminism has ruined school for boys. "Why would any self-respecting boy want to attend one of America's increasingly feminized universities?" asks George Gilder in *National Review*. "Most of these institutions have flounced through the last forty years fashioning a fluffy pink playpen of feminist studies and agitprop 'herstory,' taught amid a green goo of eco-motherism and anti-industrial phobia." Sounds like fun, but it doesn't sound much like West Texas A&M, Baylor, Loyola or the University of Alabama, where female students outnumber males in about the same proportion as they do at trendy Berkeley and Brown. Even Hillsdale College, the conservative academic mecca that became famous for rejecting federal funds rather than comply with government regulations against sex discrimination, has a student body that is 51 percent female. Other pundits—Michael Gurian, Kate O'Beirne, Christina Hoff Sommers—blame the culture of elementary school and high school: too many female teachers, too much sitting quietly, not enough sports and a feminist-friendly curriculum that forces boys to read—oh no!—books by women. Worse—books *about* women.

4   For the record, in middle school my daughter was assigned exactly one book by a woman: Zora Neale Hurston's *Their Eyes Were Watching God*. In high school she read three, *Mrs. Dalloway, Beloved* and *Uncle Tom's Cabin*, while required reading included male authors from Shakespeare and Fitzgerald and Sophocles to (I kid you not) James Michener and Robert Adams, author of *Watership Down*. Four books in seven years: Is that what we're arguing about here? Furthermore, I don't know where those pundits went to school, but education has always involved a lot of sitting, a lot of organizing, a lot of deadlines and a lot of work you didn't necessarily feel like doing. It's always been heavily verbal—in fact, today's textbooks are unbelievably dumbed down and visually hyped compared with fifty years ago. Conservatives talk as if boys should be taught in some kind of cross between boot camp and Treasure Island—but what kind of preparation for modern life would that be? As for the decline of gym and teams and band—activities that keep academically struggling kids, especially boys, coming to school—whose idea was it to cut those "frills" in the first place if not conservatives?

5   If the mating game worked fine when women were ignorant and helpless and breaks down when they smarten up, that certainly tells us something about marriage. But does today's dating scene really consist of women who love Woolf and men who love Grand Theft Auto? College may not create the intellectual divide elite pundits think it does. (Just spend some time looking at student life as revealed at www.facebook.com if you really want to get depressed about American universities.) For most students, it's more like trade school—they go to get credentials for employment and, because of the sexist nature of the labor market, women need those credentials more than men. Believe it or not, there are still stereotypically male jobs that pay well and don't require college degrees—plumbing, cabinetry, electrical work, computer repair, refrigeration, trucking, mining, restaurant cuisine. My daughter had two male school friends,

goods students from academically oriented families, who chose cooking school over college. Moreover, as I'll discuss in my next column, sex discrimination in employment is alive and well: Maybe boys focus less on school because they think they'll come out ahead anyway. What solid, stable jobs with a future are there for women without at least some higher ed? Heather Boushey, an economist with the Center for Economic Policy and Research, noted that women students take out more loans than their male classmates, even though a BA does less to increase their income. The sacrifice would make sense, though, if the BA made the crucial difference between respectable security and a lifetime as a waitress or a file clerk.

6   This is not to say that boys make the right choice when they blow off school, or even that it always is a choice. People's ideas about life often lag behind reality—some boys haven't gotten the message about the decline of high-paying blue-collar work, or the unlikeliness of rap or sports stardom, the way some girls haven't gotten the message that it is foolish, just really incredibly stupid, to rely on being supported by a man. Most of them, however, have read the memo about having, if not a career exactly, career skills. Their mothers, so many of them divorced and struggling, made sure of that. As for the boys, maybe they will just have to learn to learn in a room full of smart females.

Catherine Haun

Little is known about Catherine Haun. She was probably born around 1834, which makes her a young bride during the time of her travel west, which she documented in a journal. Like her husband, she was from an educated, middle-class family.

Catherine Haun
"A Woman's Trip Across the Plains in 1849"

1   Early in January of 1849 we first thought of emigrating to California. It was a period of national hard times and we being financially involved in our business interests near Clinton, Iowa, longed to go to the new El Dorado and "pick up" gold enough with which to return and pay off our debts.

2   Our discontent and restlessness were enhanced by the fact that my health was not good. Fear of my sister's having died while young of consumption, I had reason to be apprehensive on that score. The physician advised an entire change of climate thus to avoid the intense cold of Iowa, and recommended a sea voyage, but finally approved of our contemplated trip across the plains in

a "prairie schooner," for even in those days an out-of-door life was advocated as a cure for this disease. In any case, as in that of many others, my health was restored long before the end of our journey.

3   Full of the energy and enthusiasm of youth, the prospects of so hazardous an undertaking had no terror for us, indeed, as we had been married but a few months, it appealed to us as a romantic wedding tour.

4   The territory bordering upon the Mississippi River was, in those days, called "the west" and its people were accustomed to the privations and hardships of frontier life. It was mostly from their ranks that were formed the many companies of emigrants who traveled across the plains, while those who came to California from the Eastern states usually chose the less strenuous ocean voyage by way of the Isthmus of Panama or around the Horn.

5   At that time the "gold fever" was contagious and few, old or young, escaped the malady. On the streets, in the fields, in the workshops and by the fireside, golden California was the chief topic of conversation. Who were going? How was best to "fix up" the "outfit"? What to take as food and clothing? Who would stay at home to care for the farm and womenfolks? Who would take wives and children along? Advice was handed out quite free of charge and often quite free of common sense. However, as two heads are better than one, all proffered ideas helped as a means to the end. The intended adventurers diligently collected their belongings and after exchanging such articles as were not needed for others more suitable for the trip, begging, buying or borrowing what they could, with buoyant spirits started off.

6   Some half dozen families of our neighborhood joined us and probably about twenty-five persons constituted our little band.

7   Our own party consisted of six men and two women. Mr. Haun, my brother Derrick, Mr. Bowen, three young men to act as drivers, a woman cook and myself. Mr. Haun was chosen Major of the company, and as was the custom in those days, his fellow travelers ever afterwards knew him by this title. Derrick was to look after the packing and unpacking coincident to camping at night, keep tab on the commissary department and, when occasion demanded, lend a "helping hand." The latter service was expected of us all—men and women alike, was very indefinite and might mean anything from building campfires and washing dishes to fighting Indians, holding back a loaded wagon on a down grade or lifting it over boulders when climbing a mountain.

8   Mr. Bowen furnished his own saddle horse, and for his services was brought free of expense to himself. His business was to provide the wood or fuel for the campfire, hunt wild game and ride ahead with other horsemen to select a camping ground or in search of water. He proved himself invaluable and much of the time we had either buffalo antelope or deer meat, wild turkey, rabbits, prairie chickens, grouse, fish or small birds.

9   Eight strong oxen and four of the best horses on the farm were selected to draw our four wagons—two of the horses were for the saddle.

10   Two wagons were filled with merchandise which we hoped to sell at fabulous prices when we should arrive in the "land of gold." The theory of this was

good but the practice—well, we never got the goods across the first mountain. Flour ground at our own grist mill and bacon of home-curing filled the
large, four-ox wagon while another was loaded with barrels of alcohol. The
third wagon contained our household effects and provisions. The former consisted of cooking utensils, two boards nailed together, which was to serve as
our dining table, some bedding and a small tent. We had a very generous supply of provisions. All meats were either dried or salted, and vegetables and
fruit were dried, as canned goods were not common sixty years or more ago.
For luxuries we carried a gallon each of wild plum and crabapple preserves
and blackberry jam. Our groceries were wrapped in India rubber covers and
we did not lose any of them—in fact still had some when we reached
Sacramento.

11   The two-horse spring wagon was our bed-room and was driven by the
Major—on good stretches of road by myself. A hair mattress, topped off with
one of feathers and laid on the floor of the wagon with plenty of bedding made
a very comfortable bed after a hard day's travel.

12   In this wagon we had our trunk of wearing apparel, which consisted of
underclothing, a couple of blue checked gingham dresses, several large stout
aprons for general wear, one light colored for Sundays, a pink calico sunbon-
net and a white one intended for "dress up" days. My feminine vanity had also
prompted me to include, in this quasi wedding trouseau, a white cotton dress,
a black silk manteaux trimmed very fetchingly with velvet bands and fringe,
also a lace scuttle-shaped bonnet having a face wreath of tiny pink rosebuds,
and on the side of the crown nestled a cluster of the same flowers. With this
marvelous costume I had hoped to "astonish the natives" when I should make
my first appearance upon the golden streets of the mining town in which
we might locate. Should our dreams of great wealth, acquired overnight come
true it might be embarrassing not to be prepared with a suitable wardrobe for
the wife of a very rich man!

13   When we started from Iowa I wore a dark woolen dress which served me
almost constantly during the whole trip. Never without an apron and a
three-cornered kerchief, similar to those worn in those days, I presented a
comfortable, neat appearance. The wool protected me from the sun's rays and
penetrating prairie winds. Besides it economized in laundrying which was a
matter of no small importance when one considers how limited and often utterly wanting were our "wash day" conveniences. The chief requisite, water, being sometimes brought from miles away.

14   In the trunk were also a few treasures; a bible, medicines, such as quinine,
bluemass, opium, whiskey and hartshorn for snake bites and citric acid—an
antidote for scurvey. A little of the acid mixed with sugar and water and a few
drops of essence of lemon made a fine substitute for lemonade. Our matches in
a large-mouthed bottle were carefully guarded in this trunk.

15   The pockets of the canvas walls of the wagon held everyday needs and toi-
let articles, as well as small fire arms. The ready shotgun was suspended from
the hickory bows of the wagon camp. A ball of twine, an awl and buckskin

strings for mending harness, shoes, etc., were invaluable. It was more than three months before we were thoroughly equipped and on April 24th, 1849, we left our comparatively comfortable homes—and the uncomfortable creditors—for the uncertain and dangerous trip, beyond which loomed up, in our mind's eye, castles of shining gold.

16   There was still snow upon the ground and the roads were bad, but in our eagerness to be off we ventured forth. This was a mistake as had we delayed for a couple of weeks the weather would have been more settled, the roads better and much of the discouragement and hardship of the first days of travel might have been avoided.

17   Owing partly to the new order of things and partly to the saturated soil, travel was slow for our heavy-laden wagons and untried animals. We covered only ten miles the first day and both man and beast were greatly fatigued. As I look back now it seems the most tiresome day of the entire trip.

18   That night we stopped at a farm and I slept in the farm house. When I woke the next morning a strange feeling of fear at the thought of our venturesome undertaking crept over me. I was almost dazed with dread. I hurried out into the yard to be cheered by the bright sunshine, but old Sol's very brightness lent such a glamor to the peaceful, happy, restful home that my faint-heartedness was only intensified. . . . It was a restful scene—a contrast to our previous day of toil and discomfort and caused me to brake completely down with genuine homesickness and I burst out into a flood of tears. . . . I remember particularly a flock of domesticated wild geese. They craned their necks at me and seemed to encourage me to "take to the woods." Thus construing their senseless clatter I paused in my grief to recall the intense cold of the previous winter and the reputed perpetual sunshine and wealth of the promised land. Then wiping away my tears, lest they betray me to my husband, I prepared to continue my trip. I have often thought that had I confided in him he would certainly have turned back, for he, as well as the other men of the party, was disheartened and was struggling not to betray it. . . .

19   In the morning our first domestic annoyance occurred. The woman cook refused point blank to go any further. Evidently she had not been encouraged by any wild geese for she allowed her tears to be seen and furthermore her Romeo had followed her and it did not require much persuading on his part to induce her to return. Here was a dilemma! Had this episode happened on the previous morning when my stock of courage was so low and the men were all so busy with their own thoughts—our trip would have ended there.

20   Our first impulse was that we should have to return, but after a day's delay during [which] our disappointment knew no bounds, I surprised all by proposing to do the cooking, if everybody else would help. My self-reliance and the encouragement of our fellow travelers won the day and our party kept on. Having been reared in a slave state my culinary education had been neglected and I had yet to make my first cup of coffee. My offer was, however, accepted, and as quantity rather than quality was the chief requisite to satisfy our good appetites I got along very well, even though I never became an expert at turning pancakes

(slap-jacks) by tossing them into the air; a peculiarly scientific feat universally acquired by the pioneer miners of '49.

21   At the end of a month we reached Council Bluffs, having only traveled across the state of Iowa, a distance of about 350 miles every mile of which was beautifully green and well watered. We also had the advantage of camping near farm-houses and the generous supply of bread, butter, eggs and poultry greatly facilitated the cooking. Eggs were $2\frac{1}{2}$ cents a dozen—at our journey's end we paid $1 apiece—that is, when we had the dollar. Chickens were worth eight and ten cents apiece. When we reached Sacramento $10 was the ruling price and few to be had at that.

22   As Council Bluffs was the last settlement on the route we made ready for the final plunge into the wilderness by looking over our wagons and disposing of whatever we could spare. . . .

23   For the common good each party was "sized up" as it were. People insufficiently provisioned or not supplied with guns and ammunition were not desirable but, on the other hand, wagons too heavily loaded might be a hindrance. Such luxuries as rocking chairs, mirrors, washstands and corner what-nots were generally frowned down upon and when their owners insisted upon carrying them they had to be abandoned before long on the roadside and were appropriated by the Indians who were always eager to get anything that might be discarded.

24   The canvas-covered schooners were supposed to be, as nearly as possible, constructed upon the principle of the "wonderful one-horse shay." It was very essential that the animals be sturdy, whether oxen, mules or horses. Oxen were preferred as they were less liable to stampede or be stolen by Indians and for long hauls held out better and though slower they were steady and in the long run performed the journey in an equally brief time. Besides, in an emergency they could be used as beef. When possible the provisions and ammunition were protected from water and dust by heavy canvas or rubber sheets.

25   Good health, and above all, not too large a proportion of women and children was also taken into consideration. The morning starts had to be made early—always before six o'clock—and it would be hard to get children ready by that hour. Later on experience taught the mothers that in order not to delay the trains it was best to allow the smaller children to sleep in the wagons until after several hours of travel when they were taken up for the day.

26   Our caravan had a good many women and children and although we were probably longer on the journey owing to their presence—they exerted a good influence, as the men did not take such risks with Indians and thereby avoided conflict; were more alert about the care of the teams and seldom had accidents; more attention was paid to cleanliness and sanitation and, lastly but not of less importance, the meals were more regular and better cooked thus preventing much sickness and there was less waste of food.

27   Among those who formed the personnel of our train were the following families—a wonderful collection of many people with as many different dispositions and characteristics, all recognizing their mutual dependence upon each other and bound together by the single aim of "getting to California."

28   A regulation "prairie schooner" drawn by four oxen and well filled with suitable supplies, with two pack mules following on behind was the equipment of the Kenna family. There were two men, two women, a lad of fifteen years, a daughter thirteen and their half brother six weeks of age. This baby was our mascot and the youngest member of the company.
      . . .

29   One family by the name of Lemore, from Canada, consisted of man, wife and two little girls. They had only a large express wagon drawn by four mules and a meager but well chosen, supply of food and feed. A tent was strapped to one side of the wagon, a roll of bedding to the other side, baggage, bundles, pots, pans and bags of horse feed hung on behind, the effect was really grotesque. As they had already traveled half across the continent, seemed in good shape and were experienced emigrants they passed muster and were accepted. Not encumbered with useless luggage and Mr. Lamore [sic] being an expert driver his wagon did not sink into the mud or sand and got over grades and through creeks with comparative ease. He required but little help thus being a desirable member of the train.

30   Mr. West from Peoria, Ill., had another man, his wife, a son Clay about 20 years of age and his daughter, America, eighteen. Unfortunately Mr. West had gone to the extreme of providing himself with such a heavy wagon and load that they were deemed objectionable as fellow argonauts. After disposing of some of their supplies they were allowed to join us. They had four fine oxen. This wagon often got stalled in bad roads much to the annoyance of all, but as he was a wagon maker and his companion a blacksmith by trade and both were accommodating there were always ready hands to "pry the wheel out of mire."

31   A mule team from Washington, D.C., was very insufficiently provisioned . . . [by] a Southern gentlemen "unused to work. . . ." They deserted the train at Salt Lake as they could not proceed with their equipment and it was easier to embrace Mormonism than to brave the "American Desert."

32   Much in contrast to these men were four bachelors Messrs Wilson, Goodall, Fifield and Martin, who had a wagon drawn by four oxen and two milch cows following behind. The latter gave milk all the way to the sink of the Humboldt where they died, having acted as draught animals for several weeks after the oxen had perished. Many a cup of milk was given to the children of the train and the mothers tried in every way possible to express their gratitude. When these men lost all their stock and had to abandon their wagon they found that through their generosity they had made many friends. Having cast their bread, or milk, upon the waters it returned, double fold. I remember the evenings' milking was used for supper, but that milked in the morning was put into a high tin churn and the constant jostling that it got all day formed butter and delicious buttermilk by night. We all were glad to swap some of our food for a portion of these delicacies.

33   After a sufficient number of wagons and people were collected at this rendezvous we proceeded to draw up and agree upon a code of general regulations for train government and mutual protection—a necessary precaution when so many were to travel together. Each family was to be independent yet a part of

the grand unit and every man was expected to do his individual share of general work and picket duty.

34   John Brophy was selected as Colonel. He was particularly eligible having served in the Black Hawk War and as much of his life had been spent along the frontier his experience with Indians was quite exceptional.

35   Each week seven Captains were appointed to serve on "Grand Duty." They were to protect the camps and animals at night. One served each night and in case of danger gave the alarm.

36   When going into camp the "leader wagon" was turned from the road to the right, the next wagon turned to the left, the others following close after and always alternating to right and left. In this way a large circle, or corral, was formed within which the tents were pitched and the oxen herded. The horses, were picketed near by until bed time when they were tethered to the tongues of the wagons.

37   While the stock and wagons were being cared for, the tents erected and camp fires started by the side of the wagons outside the corral, the cooks busied themselves preparing the evening meal for the hungry, tired impatient travelers.

38   When the camp ground was desirable enough to warrant it we did not travel on the Sabbath.

39   Although the men were generally busy mending wagons, harness, yokes, shoeing the animals etc., and the women washed clothes, boiled a big mess of beans, to be warmed over for several meals, or perhaps mended clothes or did other household straightening up, all felt somewhat rested on Monday morning, for the change of occupation had been refreshing.

40   If we had devotional service the minister—protem—stood in the center of the corral while we all kept on with our work. There was no disrespect intended but there was little time for leisure or that the weary pilgrim could call his own.

41   When possible we rested the stock an hour at noon each day; allowing them to graze, if there was anything to graze upon or in any case they could lie down, which the fagged beasts often preferred to do as they were too tired to eat what we could give them. During the noon hour we refreshed ourselves with cold coffee and a crust of bread. Also a halt of ten minutes each hour was appreciated by all and was never a loss of time.

42   However, these respites could not always be indulged in as often the toil had to be kept up almost all day and much of the night—because of lack of water. Night work told very seriously upon the stock—they were more worn with one night's travel than they would have been by several days' work; indeed, invariably one or more poor beasts fell by the wayside—a victim of thirst and exhaustion.

43   It took us four days to organize our company of 70 wagons and 120 persons; bring our wagons and animals to the highest possible standard of preparedness; wash our clothes; soak several days' supply of food—and say good bye to civilization at Council Bluffs. Owing to the cheapness of eggs and chickens we reveled in their luxuries, carrying a big supply, ready cooked with us.

44   On May 26th we started to cross the Missouri River and our first real work affronted us. The wheels of the wagon had to be taken off and the bodies carried onto the flat-boats. They were then piled with goods and covered with heavy canvas or rubber sheets to protect the provisions from water. Sometimes two or three small wagons were taken at the same time.

45   The flat-boats were attached by a pulley to a rope stretched across the river to prevent its being carried down stream, and even so row as best the men could, it landed very far down the opposite shore and had to be towed up stream to the landing before the load could be taken off. Ropes were tied to the horns of the oxen and around the necks of the mules and horses to assist them in stemming the current as they swam the river. The women and children sat tailor fashion on the bottom of the raft. Much time and strength was thus consumed and owing to the great size of our caravan we were a week in getting across—as long a time as it takes now to go from the Pacific Coast to Chicago and return.

46   This was naturally annoying to those safely over, but we were as patient as possible under the circumstances—being fresh and good natured when we started out—but nevertheless we were convinced that our train was too large to admit of much speed even though it might be a safeguard against Indian attacks—a dread always uppermost in our minds. However, on the road some of the more slothful fell behind to augment the following company, since often only a short distance separated its different trains—a few impatient ones caught up with the caravan ahead of us, and during the first few weeks we met emigrants who had become discouraged almost before they were fairly started and were returning homeward. Indeed very few companies "stuck together" the whole trip. When we reached Sacramento not more than a dozen of our original train of 120 were with us.

47   Finally we were all safely landed upon the west side of the river, on the site on the City of Omaha, Nebraska, but there wasn't no sign [sic] of a town there then—only beautiful trees and grass. Several day's travel brought us to the Elkhorn River. . . . The bed of the river was quicksand. . . . Having once entered the water, wagons had to be rushed across to avoid sinking into the quicksand.

48   The Indians were the first that we had met and, being a novelty to most of us, we eyed them with a good deal of curiosity. One Indian girl of about fourteen years of age wept loud and incessantly for an hour or more until we women sympathizing with her in her apparent grief, gave her a few trinkets and clothes and were astonished at the efficacy of the cure.

49   The squaws carried their papooses in queer little canopied baskets suspended upon their backs by a band around their heads and across their foreheads. The infant was snugly bound, mummy-fashion with only its head free. It was here that I first saw a bit of remarkable maternal discipline, peculiar to most of the Indian tribes. The child cried whereupon the mother took it, basket and all, from her back and nursed it. It still fretted and whimpered apparently uncomfortable or ill. The mother then stood it up against a tree and dashed water in the poor little creature's face. By the time that it recovered

its breath it stopped crying. No pampered, restless urchin for the Indian household, no indeed.

50   The bucks with their bows and arrows, beaded buckskin garments and feather head gears were much in evidence and though these prairie redmen were generally friendly they were insistent beggars, often following us for miles and at mealtime disgustingly stood around and solicited food. They seldom molested us, however, but it was a case of the Indian, as well as the poor, "Ye have always with ye."

51   During the entire trip Indians were a source of anxiety, we being never sure of their friendship. Secret dread and alert watchfulness seemed always necessary for after we left the prairies they were more treacherous and numerous being in the language of the pioneer trapper: "They wus the most onsartainest vermints alive."

52   One night after we had retired, some sleeping in blankets upon the ground, some in tents, a few under the wagons and others in the wagons, Colonel Brophy gave the men a practice drill. It was impromptu and a surprise. He called: "Indians, Indians!" We were thrown into great confusion and excitement but he was gratified at the promptness and courage with which the men responded. Each immediately seized his gun and made ready for the attack. The women had been instructed to seek shelter in the wagons at such times of danger, but some screamed, others fainted, a few crawled under the wagons and those sleeping in wagons generally followed their husbands out and all of us were nearly paralyzed with fear. Fortunately, we never had occasion to put into actual use this maneuver, but the drill was quite reassuring and certainly we womenfolk would have acted braver had the alarm ever again been sounded. . . .

53   The following night brother Derrick and Mr. Bowen were sleeping as was their custom, under a wagon next to ours and it being very warm they turned their comforters down to the foot of their couch. Behold, next morning the covering was missing! It could hardly have been taken by an animal else some trace of their foot-prints and that of the dragging bedding would have been seen. The Indians with their soft moccasins and the light rapid steps and springing, long strides they take when in retreat seldom left evidence upon the ground.

54   This unwelcome call, so soon after the former theft, was anything but reassuring. It was not pleasant to know how shy, stealthy and treacherous even these *friendly* Indians were and that they kept such close watch upon our every movement both day and night.

55   The next night when we retired I had a nervous attack and was really so timid that I saw that the canvas of our wagon was snugly together; all strings and fastenings securely tied and—yes, womanlike I added pins here and there, leaving no peekholes: for I just couldn't go to sleep knowing that some bold, prying savage eye might look in at me during the night. Of course I had shut out all ventilation and during the night my husband opened the wagon cover wide enough for not only the savage eye but the whole savage himself to enter! Probably this was done as soon as I had gone to sleep.

56   Carl West was inclined to somnambulism and these annoying visits from the Indians so worked upon his mind that that night he dreamed that he was attacked by Indians and ran screaming from his wagon. He was bear footed and half clad but he ran so fast that it was all that two of his companions could do to overtake him.

57   The emigrants were often sorely tried and inconvenienced by losses more or less serious for in spite of the most alert guard it was almost impossible to see the advancing thief crawling, like a snake, on the ground up to his intended prey. . . .

58   Finally after a couple of weeks travel the distant mountains of the west came into view.

59   This was the land of the buffalo. One day a herd came in our direction like a great black cloud, a threatening moving mountain, advancing towards us very swiftly and with wild snorts, noses almost to the ground and tails flying in midair. I haven't any idea how many there were but they seemed to be innumerable and made a deafening terrible noise. As is their habit, when stampeding, they did not turn out of their course for anything. Some of our wagons were within their line of advance and in consequence one was completely demolished and two were overturned. Several persons were hurt, one child's shoulder being dislocated, but fortunately no one was killed.

60   Two of these buffaloes were shot and the humps and tongues furnished us with fine fresh meat. They happened to be buffalo cows and, in consequence, the meat was particularly good flavor and tender. It is believed that the cow can run faster than the bull. The large bone of the hind leg, after being stripped of the flesh, was buried in coals of buffalo chips and in an hour the baked marrow was served. I have never tasted such a rich, delicious food!

61   One family "jerked" some of the hump. After being cut into strips about an inch wide it was strung on ropes on the outside of the wagon cover and in two or three days was thoroughly cured. It was then packed in a bag and in the Humboldt Sink, when rations were low it came in very handy. Spite of having hung in the Alkali dust and being rather shriveled looking, it was relished for when hunger stares one in the face one isn't particular about trifles like that. . . .

62   Buffalo chips, when dry, were very useful to us as fuel. On the barren plains when we were without wood we carried empty bags and each pedestrian "picked up chips" as he, or she, walked along. Indeed we could have hardly got along without this useful animal, were always appropriating either his hump, tongue, marrowbone, tallow, skin or chips! . . .

63   The Indian is a financier of no mean ability and invariably comes out AI in a bargain. Though you may, for the time, congratulate yourself upon your own sagacity, you'll be apt to realize a little later on that you were not quite equal to the shrewd redman—had got the "short end of the deal." One of their "business tricks" was to sell horses or other necessities which were their booty acquired during an attack upon a preceeding train. When we were well along in our journey—in the Humboldt Sink—we overtook emigrants one of whom had swapped his watch with the Indians for a yoke of oxen. A few

hours afterwards he found that they had been stolen when left to rest while the owners had gone in search of water. The rightful owners established their claim and after a compromise the oxen were joint property. The watch being the profit of the middleman.

64   Trudging along within the sight of the Platte, whose waters were now almost useless to us on account of the Alkali, we one day found a post with a cross board pointing to a branch road which seemed better than the one we were on. . . . We decided to take it but before many miles suddenly found ourselves in a desolate, rough country that proved to be the edge of the "Bad Lands." I shudder yet at the thought of the ugliness and danger of the territory. Entirely destitute of vegetation the unsightly barren sandstonehills, often very high and close together formed of great boulders piled one on top of the other like glaciers, with ravines and gulches between and mighty full of crouching, treacherous Indians, they fairly swarmed and we feared that we had been purposely misled in order that they might do us harm. This, however, could not have been the case for the road often was between precipitous walls hundreds of feet high and had they cared to attack us from the heights above we could have made no effective defense. After the possible massacre had been accomplished their booty would have been our money, clothing, food and traveling paraphernalia—and worse still those of our women who had been unfortunate enough to have escaped death.

65   Unlike the Indians of the prairies and plains these mountain inhabitants did not have horses and were expert in concealing themselves, and during our entire trip we were never so apprehensive and terrified. We pushed almost recklessly forward in our endeavor to get back to the road along the river. The unevenness of the surface seemed almost like a maze, and being without a single landmark you can imagine our almost frenzied fear that we might be traveling in a circle. We made our resting stops as brief as possible and the days' work from early dawn until dark.

66   We saw nothing living but Indians, lizards and snakes. Trying, indeed, to feminine nerves. Surely Inferno can be no more horrible in formation. The pelting sun's rays reflected from the parched ground seemed a furnace heat by day and our campfires, as well as those of the Indians cast grotesque glares and terrifying shadows by night. The demon needed only horns and cloven feet to complete the soul stirring picture!

67   To add to the horrors of the surroundings one man was bitten on the ankle by a venomous snake. Although every available remedy was tried upon the wound, his limb had to be amputated with the aid of a common handsaw. Fortunately, for him, he had a good, brave wife along who helped and cheered him into health and usefulness; for it was not long before he found much that he could do and was not considered a burden, although the woman had to do a man's work as they were alone. He was of a mechanical turn, and later on helped mend wagons, yokes and harness; and when the train was "on the move" sat in the wagon, gun by his side, and repaired boots and shoes. He was one of the most cheery members of the company and told good stories and sang

at the campfire, putting to shame some of the able bodied who were given to complaining or selfishness. . . .

68   Finally after several days we got back onto the road and were entering the Black Hills Country. . . .

69   Here we also found fragments of a women's cotton dress tied to bushes and small pieces were scattered along the road. Whether this had been intended as a decoy to lead some of our men into a trap should they essay a possible rescue we did not know and the risk was too great to be taken.

70   We had not traveled many miles in the Black Hills—the beginning of the Rocky Mountains—before we realized that our loads would have to be lightened as the animals were not able to draw the heavily laden wagons over the slippery steep roads. We were obliged to sacrifice most of our merchandise that was intended for our stock in trade in California and left it by the wayside; burying the barrels of alcohol lest the Indians should drink it and frenzied thereby might follow and attack us. . . .

71   The roads were rocky and often very steep from this on to the Great Salt Lake—the distance across the Rocky Mountains. Sometimes to keep the wagons from pressing upon the animals in going down grade young pine trees were cut down and after stripping them of all but the top branches they were tied to the front and under the rear axle. The branches dragging upon the ground, or often solid rock, formed a reliable brake. Then again a rope or chain would be tied to the rear of the wagon and everyone, man, woman and child, would be pressed into service to hold the wagon back. At other times a chain or rope would be fastened to the front axle and we climbed up impossible boulders and pulled with might and main while the men pushed with herculean strength to get the loaded wagons over some barrier. The animals, owing to cramped quarters, were often led around the obstacle. Many times the greater part of the day would be consumed in this strenuous and altogether unladylike labor.

72   And oh, such pulling, pushing lugging it was! I used to pity the drivers as well as the oxen and horses—and the rest of us. The drivers of our ox teams were sturdy young men, all about twenty-two years of age who were driving for their passage to California. They were of good family connections and all became prominent citizens. One, a law student, Charles Wheeler, studied all his leisure time, and often could be seen with his open book as he walked beside his team. One, the whistler, Chester Fall, had been intended for the ministry and the third, Ralph Cushing, had run away from college.

73   The latter was the life of our party and general favorite with the entire train. I see him now, in my mind's eye, trudging along; his bright countenance and carefree air, an inspiration. The familiar tunes that he played upon his harmonica seemed to soften the groaning and creaking of the wagons and to shorten the long miles of the mountain road.

74   "Home Sweet Home," "Old Kentucky Home," "Maryland, My Maryland," "The Girl I Left Behind Me," "One More Ribber to Cross," seemed particularly appropriate and touched many a pensive heart. The strains of his ballads went straight to America West's heart even as her sweet voice as she sang at the campfire. Cupid

used as an arrow with which to pierce Ralph Cushing's manly breast. When the clumsy, heavy wagon of America's father got mired, Ralph was among the first to render assistance and towards the end of the journey when we were all enduring great hardships our young couple, lent a ray of romance by their evident regard for each other, for "All the world loves a lover." . . .

75   During the day we womenfolk visited from wagon to wagon or congenial friends spent an hour walking, ever westward, and talking over our home life back in "the states" telling of the loved ones left behind; voicing our hopes for the future in the far west and even whispering a little friendly gossip of emigrant life.

76   High teas were not popular but tatting, knitting, crocheting, exchanging recipes for cooking beans or dried apples or swapping food for the sake of variety kept us in practice of feminine occupations and diversions.

77   We did not keep late hours but when not too engrossed with fear of the red enemy or dread of impending danger we enjoyed the hour around the campfire. The menfolk lolling and smoking their pipes and guessing or maybe betting how many miles we had covered the day. We listened to readings, story telling, music and song and the day often ended in laughter and merrymaking.

78   It was the fourth of July when we reached the beautiful Laramie River. Its sparkling, pure waters were full of myriads of fish that could be caught with scarcely an effort. It was necessary to build barges to cross the river and during the enforced delay our animals rested and we had one of our periodical "house cleaning." This general systematic re-adjustment always freshened up our wagon train very much, for after a few weeks of travel things got mixed up and untidy and often wagons had to be abandoned if too worn for repairs, and generally one or more animals had died or been stolen.

79   After dinner that night it was proposed that we celebrate the day and we all heartily join[ed] in. America West was the Goddess of Liberty, Charles Wheeler was orator and Ralph Cushing acted as master of ceremonies. We sang patriotic songs, repeated what little we could of the Declaration of Independence, fired off a gun or two, and gave three cheers for the United States and California Territory in particular!

80   The young folks decorated themselves in all manner of fanciful and grotesque costumes—Indian characters being most popular. To the rollicking music of violin and Jew's harp we danced until midnight. There were Indian spectators, all bewildered by the (to them) weird war dance of the Pale Face and possibly they deemed it advisable to sharpen up their arrow heads. During the frolic when the sport was at its height a strange white woman with a little girl in her sheltering embrace rushed into the corral. She was trembling with terror, tottering with hunger. Her clothing was badly torn and her hair disheveled. The child crouched with fear and hid her face within the folds of her mother's tattered skirt. The woman could give no account of her forlorn condition but was only able to sob: "Indians," and "I have nobody nor place to go to." After she had partaken of food and was refreshed by a safe night's rest she recovered and the next day told us that her husband and sister had contracted

cholera on account of which her family consisting of husband, brother, sister, herself and two children had stayed behind their train. The sick ones died and while burying the sister the survivors were attacked by Indians, who, as she supposed, killed her brother and little son. She was obliged to flee for her life dragging with her the little five-year-old daughter.

81   She had been three days walking back to meet a train. It had been necessary, in order to avoid Indians, to conceal herself behind trees or boulders much of the time and although she had seen a train in the distance before ours she feared passing the Indians that were between the emigrants and herself. She had been obliged to go miles up the Laramie to find a place where she could get across by wading from rock to rock and the swift current had lamed her and bruised her body.

82   Raw fish that she had caught with her hands and a squirrel that she killed with a stone had been their only food. Our noise and campfire had attracted her and in desperation she braved the Indians around us and trusting to the darkness ventured to enter our camp. Martha, for that was her name, had emigrated from Wisconsin and pleaded with us to send her home; but we had now gone too far on the road to meet returning emigrants so there was no alternative for her but to accept our protection and continue on to California. When she became calm and somewhat reconciled to so long and uncertain a journey with strangers she made herself useful and loyally cast her lot with us. She assisted me with the cooking for her board; found lodgings with the woman whose husband was a cripple and in return helped the brave woman drive the ox team. Mr. & Mrs. Lamore kept her little girl with their own. . . .

83   Upon the second day of our resumed travel, still following up the North Platte, Martha spied a deserted wagon some little distance off the road which she recognized as her own. Mr. Bowen went with her to investigate, hoping to find her brother and son. The grave of her sister was still open and her clothing as well as that of her husband, who was in the wagon where he had died, were missing. The gruesome sight drove her almost mad. Mr. Bowen and she did not bury the bodies lest they might bring contagion back to us. No trace of either brother or son could be found. All supplies and the horses had been stolen by the Indians.

84   Cholera was prevalent on the plains at this time; the train preceding as well as the one following ours had one or more deaths, but fortunately we had not a single case of the disease. Often several graves together stood as silent proof of smallpox or cholera epidemic. The Indian spread the disease among themselves by digging up the bodies of the victims for the clothing. The majority of the Indians were badly pock-marked. . . .

85   Turning in a southwesterly direction we came to Fort Bridger named for the celebrated scout. It was simply a trading post for the white and Indian fur trappers. We saw a renegade white man here who having lived for years among the Indians had forgotten his native language and dressing and eating as they did, his long unkempt hair and uncouth appearance was loathsome in the extreme; it being hard to distinguish him from his brother Indians. We regarded

him with more fear and abhorrence than we did a manly buck, and his squaw and family of half-breeds as unfortunates.

86   It was with considerable apprehension that we started to traverse the treeless, alkali region of the Great Basin or Sink of the Humboldt. Our wagons were badly worn, the animals much the worse for wear; food and stock feed was getting low with no chance of replenishing the supply. During the month of transit we, like other trains, experienced the greatest privations of the whole trip. It was no unusual sight to see graves, carcasses of animals and abandoned wagons. In fact the latter furnished us with wood for the campfires as the sagebrush was scarce and unsatisfactory and buffalo chips were not as plentiful as on the plains east of the Rocky Mountains.

87   The alkali dust of this territory was suffocating, irritating our throats and clouds of it often blinded us. The mirages tantalized us; the water was unfit to drink or to use in any way; animals often perished or were so overcome by heat and exhaustion that they had to be abandoned, or in case of human hunger, the poor jaded creatures were killed and eaten. . . .

88   One of our dogs was so emaciated and exhausted that we were obliged to leave him on this desert and it said that the train following us used him for food.

89   Before leaving Bear River, knowing of the utter lack of fresh water, we cooked large quantities of bread to be used on the desert. We gave a half loaf each day to each house until the flour gave out. This was a substitute for grain.

90   Across this drear country I used to ride horseback several hours of the day which was a great relief from the continual jolting of even our spring wagon. I also walked a great deal and this lightened the wagon. One day I walked fourteen miles and was not very fatigued.

91   . . . The men seemed more tired and hungry than were the women.

92   Our only death on the journey occurred in this desert. The Canadian woman, Mrs. Lamore, suddenly sickened and died, leaving her two little girls and grief-stricken husband. We halted a day to bury her and the infant that had lived but an hour, in this weird lonely spot on God's footstool away apparently from everywhere and everybody.

93   The bodies were wrapped together in a bedcomforter and wound, quite mummified with a few yards of string that we made by tying together torn strips of a cotton dress skirt. A passage of the Bible (my own) was read; a prayer offered and "Nearer, My God to Thee" sung. Owing to the unusual surroundings the ceremony was very impressive. Every heart was touched and eyes full of tears as we lowered the body coffinless, into the grave. There was no tombstone—why should there be—the poor husband and orphans could never hope to revisit the grave, and to the world it was just one of the many hundreds that marked the trail of the argonaut.

94   This burial and one I witnessed at sea some years later made a lasting impression upon me and I always think of them when I attend a funeral; such a gruesome sensation was caused by the desolation. The immense, lonesome plain: the great fathomless ocean—how insignificant seems the human body when consigned to their cold embrace! . . . Martha and the lamented Canadian

wife had formed a fast friendship while on the plans, and the former was a faithful nurse during the latter's illness. What more natural than that the dying mother should ask her friend to continue to care for her orphan girls and to make [them] the sisters of her own daughter?

95   Years afterward when prosperity crowned Mr. Lamore's effort, the three girls were sent "back to the state" to school and Martha's daughter become the wife of a prominent United States Congressman. [Martha's little son was soon reunited with his mother, He had been traded by the Indians to some passing emigrants for a horse. In fact, the child was traveling but a few days' journey behind her in another emigrant train.]

96   . . . we reached Sacramento on November 4, 1849, just six months and ten days after leaving Clinton, Iowa; we were all in pretty good condition. . . .

97   Although very tired of tent life, many of us spent Thanksgiving and Christmas in our canvas houses. I do not remember ever having had happier holiday times. For Christmas dinner we had a grizzly bear steak for which we paid $2.50, one cabbage for $1.00 and—oh horrors—some *more* dried apples! And for a Christmas present the Sacramento river rose very high and flooded the whole town! . . . It was past the middle of January before we . . . reached Marysville—there were only a half dozen houses; all occupied at exorbitant prices. Someone was calling for the services of a lawyer to draw up a will, and my husband offered to do it for which he charged $150.00.

98   This seemed a happy omen for success, and he hung out his shingle abandoning all thought of going to the mines. As we have lived in a tent and had been on the move for nine months, traveling 2400 miles, we were glad to settle down and go housekeeping in a shed that was built in a day of lumber purchased with the first fee. The ground was given us by some gamblers who lived next door, and upon the other side. For neighbors, we had a real-live saloon. I never have received more respectful attention than I did from these neighbors.

99   Upon the whole I enjoyed the trip, spite of its hardships and dangers and the fear dread that hung as a pall over every hour. Although not so thrilling as were the experiences of many who suffered in reality what we feared, but escaped. I, like every other pioneer, love to live over again in memory those romantic months and revisit, in fancy, the scenes of the journey.

ETHNICITY AND CULTURE

William Shakespeare

William Shakespeare's name is synonymous in the English language with the best of literature. He lived from 1564 to 1616. Perhaps the American poet T. S. Eliot summed up the quality of Shakespeare's work and his towering influence best when commenting that one could spend an entire lifetime just beginning to develop an appreciation of Shakespeare. Shakespeare's plays and poetry as a whole are without an equal in English, and perhaps world, literature.

This excerpt from The Merchant of Venice *is part of Shylock's attempt at retribution. Shylock's desire to extract a* pound of flesh *as payment has become an emblem of the human propensity to overcompensate for pride.*

William Shakespeare
"Shylock's Defense"
From The Merchant of Venice, *Act III, scene 1*

SALARINO. Why, I am sure, if he forfeit thou wilt not take his flesh: what's that good for?

SHYLOCK. To bait fish withal: if it will feed nothing else, it will feed my revenge. He hath disgraced me, and hindered me half a million, laughed at my losses, mocked at my gains, scorned my nation, thwarted my bargains, cooled my friends, heated mine enemies; and what's his reason? I am a Jew. Hath not a Jew eyes? hath not a Jew hands, organs, dimensions, senses, affections, passions? fed with the same food, hurt with the same weapons, subject to the same diseases, healed by the same means, warmed and cooled by the same winter and summer, as a Christian is? If you prick us, do we not bleed? if you tickle us, do we not laugh? if you poison us, do we not die? and if you wrong us, shall we not revenge? If we are like you in the rest, we will resemble you in that. If a Jew wrong a Christian, what is his humility? Revenge. If a Christian wrong a Jew, what should his sufferance be by Christian example? Why, revenge. The villany you teach me I will execute, and it shall go hard but I will better the instruction.

James Baldwin

American author James Baldwin lived from 1924 to 1987, spending the majority of his time after 1948 away from the United States. Although published in many genres (poetry, short fiction, novels, drama, and nonfiction), Baldwin is probably best known for his 1953 autobiographical novel Go Tell It on the Mountain.

As demonstrated in "Stranger in the Village," Baldwin wrote passionately about racial issues, particularly racial issues in America. Ultimately, and perhaps notoriously, Baldwin went so far as to criticize well-known writers such as African American Richard Wright and antislavery advocate Harriet Beecher Stowe for their formulaic and stereotypical portrayal of African Americans. Today, Baldwin is revered by many well-known writers, including Toni Morrison, whose work appears on page 259 of this book.

James Baldwin
"Stranger in the Village"
from Notes of a Native Son

1   From all available evidence no black man had ever set foot in this tiny Swiss village before I came, I was told before arriving that I would probably be a "sight" for the village; I took this to mean that people of my complexion were rarely seen in Switzerland, and also that city people are always something of a "sight" outside of the city. It did not occur to me—possibly because I am an American—that there could be people anywhere who had never seen a Negro.

2   It is a fact that cannot be explained on the basis of the inaccessibility of the village. The village is very high, but it is only four hours from Milan and three hours from Lausanne. It is true that it is virtually unknown: Few people making plans for a holiday would elect to come here. On the other hand, the villagers are able, presumably, to come and go as they please—which they do to another town at the foot of the mountain, with a population of approximately five thousand, the nearest place to see a movie or go to the bank. In the village there is no movie house, no bank, no library, no theater, very few radios, one jeep, one station wagon; and, at the moment, one typewriter, mine, an invention which the woman next door to me here had never seen. There are about six hundred people living here, all Catholic—I conclude this from the fact that the Catholic church is open all year round, whereas the Protestant chapel, set off on a hill a little removed from the village, is open only in the summertime when the tourists arrive. There are four or five hotels, all closed now, and four or five *bistros,* of which, however, only two do any business during the winter. These two do not do a great deal, for life in the village seems to end around nine or ten o'clock. There are a few stores, butcher, baker, *épicerie,* a hardware store, and a money-changer—who cannot change travelers' checks, but must send them down to the bank, an operation which takes two or three days. There is something called the *Ballet Haus,* closed in the winter and used for God knows what, certainly not ballet, during the summer. There seems to be only one schoolhouse in the village, and this for the quite young children; I suppose this to mean that their older brothers and sisters at some point descend from these mountains in order to complete their education—possibly, again, to the town just below. The landscape is absolutely forbidding, mountains towering on all four sides, ice and snow as far as the eye can reach. In this white wilderness, men and women and children move all day, carrying, washing, wood, buckets of milk or water, sometimes skiing on Sunday afternoon. All week long boys and young men are to be seen shoveling snow off the rooftops, or dragging wood down from the forest in sleds.

3   The village's only real attraction, which explains the tourist season, is the hot spring water. A disquietingly high proportion of these tourists are cripples, or semi-cripples; who come year after year—from other parts of Switzerland, usually—to take the waters. This lends the village, at the height of the season, a rather terrifying air of sanctity, as though it were a lesser Lourdes. There is often something beautiful, there is always something awful, in the spectacle of a person who has lost one of his faculties, a faculty he never questioned until it was gone, and who struggles to recover it. Yet people remain people, on crutches or indeed on deathbeds; and wherever I passed, the first summer I was here, among the native villagers or among the lame, a wind passed with me—of astonishment, curiosity, amusement, and outrage. That first summer I stayed two weeks and never intended to return: But I did return in the winter, to work; the village offers, obviously, no distractions whatever and has the further advantage of being extremely cheap. Now it is winter again, a year later, and I am here again. Everyone in the village knows my name, though they scarcely ever use it, knows that I come from America—though, this, apparently, they will never really believe: black men come from Africa—and everyone knows that I am the friend of the son of a woman who was born here, and that I am staying in their chalet. But I remain as much a stranger today as I was the first day I arrived, and the children shout *Neger! Neger!* as I walk along the streets.

4   It must be admitted that in the beginning I was far too shocked to have any real reaction. In so far as I reacted at all, I reacted by trying to be pleasant—it being a great part of the American Negro's education (long before he goes to school) that he must make people "like" him. This smile-and-the-world-smiles-with-you routine worked about as well in this situation as it had in the situation for which it was designed, which is to say that it did not work at all. No one, after all, can be liked whose human weight and complexity cannot be, or has not been, admitted. My smile was simply another unheard-of phenomenon which allowed them to see my teeth—they did not, really, see my smile and I began to think that, should I take to snarling, no one would notice any difference. All of the physical characteristics of the Negro which had caused me, in America, a very different and almost forgotten pain were nothing less than miraculous—or infernal—in the eyes of the village people. Some thought my hair was the color of tar, that it had the texture of wire, or the texture of cotton. It was jocularly suggested that I might let it all grow long and make myself a winter coat. If I sat in the sun for more than five minutes some daring creature was certain to come along and gingerly put his fingers on my hair, as though he were afraid of an electric shock, or put his hand on my hand, astonished that the color did not rub off. In all of this, in which it must be conceded there was the charm of genuine wonder and in which there was certainly no element of intentional unkindness, there was yet no suggestion that I was human: I was simply a living wonder.

5   I knew that they did not mean to be unkind, and I know it now; it is necessary, nevertheless, for me to repeat this to myself each time that I walk out of the chalet. The children who shout *Neger!* have no way of knowing the echoes this sound raises in me. They are brimming with good humor and the more daring swell with pride when I stop to speak with them. Just the same, there are days when I cannot pause and smile, when I have no heart to play with them; when, indeed, I mutter sourly to myself, exactly as I muttered on the streets of a city these children have never seen, when I was no bigger than these children are now: *Your* mother *was a nigger.* Joyce is right about history being a nightmare—but it may be the nightmare from which no one *can* awaken. People are trapped in history and history is trapped in them.

6   There is a custom in the village—I am told it is repeated in many villages—of "buying" African natives for the purpose of converting them to Christianity. There stands in the church all year round a small box with a slot for money; decorated with a black figurine, and into this box the villagers drop their francs. During the *carnaval* which precedes Lent, two village children have their faces blackened—out of which bloodless darkness their blue eyes shine like ice—and fantastic horsehair wigs are placed on their blond heads; thus disguised, they solicit among the villagers for money for the missionaries in Africa. Between the box in the church and the blackened children, the village "bought" last year six or eight African natives. This was reported to me with pride by the wife of one of the *bistro* owners and I was careful to express astonishment and pleasure at the solicitude shown by the village for the souls of black folk. The *bistro* owner's wife beamed with a pleasure far more genuine than my own and seemed to feel that I might now breathe more easily concerning the souls of at least six of my kinsmen.

7   I tried not to think of these so lately baptized kinsmen, of the price paid for them, or the peculiar price they themselves would pay, and said nothing about my father, who having taken his own conversion too literally never, at bottom, forgave the white world (which he described as heathen) for having saddled him with a Christ in whom, to judge at least from their treatment of him, they themselves no longer believed. I thought of white men arriving for the first time in an African village, strangers there, as I am a stranger here, and tried to imagine the astounded populace touching their hair and marveling at the color of their skin. But there is a great difference between being the first white man to be seen by Africans and being the first black man to be seen by whites. The white man takes the astonishment as tribute, for he arrives to conquer and to convert the natives, whose inferiority in relation to himself in not even to be questioned; whereas I, without a thought of conquest, find myself among a people whose culture controls me, has even, in a sense, created me, people who have cost me more in anguish and rage than they will ever know, who yet do not even know of my existence. The astonishment with which I might have greeted them, should they have stumbled into my African village a few hundred years ago, might have rejoiced their hearts. But the astonishment with which they greet me today can only poison mine.

8   And this is so despite everything I may do to feel differently, despite my friendly conversations with the *bistro* owner's wife, despite their three-year-old son who has at last become my friend, despite the *saluts* and *bonsoirs* which I exchange with people as I walk, despite the fact that I know that no individual can be taken to task for what history is doing, or has done. I say that the culture of these people controls me—but they can scarcely be held responsible for European culture. America comes out of Europe, but these people have never seen America, nor have most of them seen more of Europe than the hamlet at the foot of their mountain. Yet they move with an authority which I shall never have; and they regard me, quite rightly, not only as a stranger in their village but as a suspect latecomer, bearing no credentials, to everything they have—however unconsciously—inherited.

9   For this village, even were it incomparably more remote and incredibly more primitive, is the West, the West onto which I have been so strangely grafted. These people cannot be, from the point of view of power, strangers anywhere in the world; they have made the modern world, in effect, even if they do not know it. The most illiterate among them is related, in a way that I am not, to Dante, Shakespeare, Michelangelo, Aeschylus, Da Vinci, Rembrandt, and Racine; the cathedral at Chartres says something to them which it cannot say to me, as indeed would New York's Empire State Building, should anyone here ever see it. Out of their hymns and dances come Beethoven and Bach. Go back a few centuries and they are in their full glory—but I am in Africa, watching the conquerors arrive.

10   The rage of the disesteemed is personally fruitless, but it is also absolutely inevitable; this rage, so generally discounted, so little understood even among the people whose daily bread it is, is one of the things that makes history. Rage can only with difficulty, and never entirely, be brought under the domination of the intelligence and is therefore not susceptible to any arguments whatever. This is a fact which ordinary representatives of the *Herrenvolk,* having never felt this rage and being unable to imagine it, quite fail to understand. Also, rage cannot be hidden, it can only be dissembled. This dissembling deludes the thoughtless, and strengthens rage and adds, to rage, contempt. There are, no doubt, as many ways of coping with the resulting complex of tensions as there are black men in the world, but no black man can hope ever to be entirely liberated from this internal warfare—rage, dissembling, and contempt having inevitably accompanied his first realization of the power of white men. What is crucial here is that, since white men represent in the black man's world so heavy a weight, white men have for black men a reality which is far from being reciprocal; and hence all black men have toward all white men an attitude which is designed, really, either to rob the white man of the jewel of his naïveté, or else to make it cost him dear.

11   The black man insists, by whatever means he finds at his disposal, that the white man cease to regard him as an exotic rarity and recognize him as a human being. This is a very charged and difficult moment, for there is a great deal of willpower involved in the white man's naïveté. Most people are not naturally

reflective any more than they are naturally malicious, and the white man prefers to keep the black man at a certain human remove because it is easier for him thus to preserve his simplicity and avoid being called to account for crimes committed by his forefathers, or his neighbors. He is inescapably aware, nevertheless, that he is in a better position in the world than black men are, nor can he quite put to death the suspicion that he is hated by black men therefore. He does not wish to be hated, neither does he wish to change places, and at this point in his uneasiness he can scarcely avoid having recourse to those legends which white men have created about black men, the most usual effect of which is that the white man finds himself enmeshed, so to speak, in his own language which describes hell, as well as the attributes which lead one to hell, as being as black as night.

12   Every legend, moreover, contains its residuum of truth, and the root function of language is to control the universe by describing it. It is of quite considerable significance that black men remain, in the imagination, and in overwhelming numbers in fact, beyond the disciplines of salvation; and this despite the fact that the West has been "buying" African natives for centuries. There is, I should hazard, an instantaneous necessity to be divorced from this so visibly unsaved stranger, in whose heart, moreover, one cannot guess what dreams of vengeance are being nourished; and, at the same time, there are few things on earth more attractive than the idea of the unspeakable liberty which is allowed the unredeemed. When, beneath the black mask, a human being begins to make himself felt one cannot escape a certain awful wonder as to what kind of human being it is. What one's imagination makes of other people is dictated, of course, by the laws of one's own personality and it is one of the ironies of black-white relations that, by means of what the white man imagines the black man to be, the black man is enabled to know who the white man is.

13   I have said, for example, that I am as much a stranger in this village today as I was the first summer I arrived, but this is not quite true. The villagers wonder less about the texture of my hair than they did then, and wonder rather more about me. And the fact that their wonder now exists on another level is reflected in their attitudes and in their eyes. There are the children who make those delightful, hilarious, sometimes astonishingly grave overtures of friendship in the unpredictable fashion of children; other children, having been taught that the devil is a black man, scream in genuine anguish as I approach. Some of the older women never pass without a friendly greeting, never pass, indeed, if it seems that they will be able to engage me in conversation; other women look down or look away or rather contemptuously smirk. Some of the men drink with me and suggest that I learn how to ski—partly, I gather, because they cannot imagine what I would look like on skis—and want to know if I am married, and ask questions about my *métier*. But some of the men have accused *le sale nègre*—behind my back—of stealing wood and there is already in the eyes of some of them that peculiar, intent, paranoiac malevolence which one sometimes surprises in the eyes of American white men when, out walking with their Sunday girl, they see a Negro male approach.

14   There is a dreadful abyss between the streets of this village and the streets of the city in which I was born, between the children who shout *Neger!* today and those who shouted *Nigger!* yesterday—the abyss is experience, the American experience. The syllable hurled behind me today expresses, above all, wonder: I am a stranger here. But I am not a stranger in America and the same syllable riding on the American air expresses the war my presence has occasioned in the American soul.

15   For this village brings home to me this fact: that there was a day, and not really a very distant day, when Americans were scarcely Americans at all but discontented Europeans, facing a great unconquered continent and strolling, say, into a marketplace and seeing black men for the first time. The shock this spectacle afforded is suggested, surely, by the promptness with which they decided that these black men were not really men but cattle. It is true that the necessity on the part of the settlers of the New World of reconciling their moral assumptions with the fact—and the necessity—of slavery enhanced immensely the charm of this idea, and it is also true that this idea expresses, with a truly American bluntness, the attitude which to varying extents all masters have had toward all slaves.

16   But between all former slaves and slave-owners and the drama which begins for Americans over three hundred years ago at Jamestown, there are at least two differences to be observed. The American Negro slave could not suppose, for one thing, as slaves in past epochs had supposed and often done, that he would ever be able to wrest the power from his master's hands. This was a supposition which the modern era, which was to bring about such vast changes in the aims and dimensions of power, put to death; it only begins, in unprecedented fashion, and with dreadful implications, to be resurrected today. But even had this supposition persisted with undiminished force, the American Negro slave could not have used it to lend his condition dignity, for the reason that this supposition rests on another: that the slave in exile yet remains related to his past, has some means—if only in memory—of revering and sustaining the forms of his former life, is able, in short, to maintain his identity.

17   This was not the case, with the American Negro slave. He is unique among the black men of the world in that his past was taken from him, almost literally, at one blow. One wonders what on earth the first slave found to say to the first dark child he bore. I am told that there are Haitians able to trace their ancestry back to African kings, but any American Negro wishing to go back so far will find his journey through time abruptly arrested by the signature on the bill of sale which served as the entrance paper for his ancestor. At the time—to say nothing of the circumstances—of the enslavement of the captive black man who was to become the American Negro, there was not the remotest possibility that he would ever take power from his master's hands. There was no reason to suppose that his situation would ever change, nor was there, shortly, anything to indicate that his situation had ever been different. It was his necessity, in the words of E. Franklin Frazier, to find a "motive for living under American culture or die." The identity of the American Negro comes out of this

extreme situation, and the evolution of this identity was a source of the most intolerable anxiety in the minds and the lives of his masters.

18   For the history of the American Negro is unique also in this: that the question of his humanity, and of his rights therefore as a human being, became a burning one for several generations of Americans, so burning a question that it ultimately became one of those used to divide the nation. It is out of this argument that the venom of the epithet *Nigger!* is derived. It is an argument which Europe has never had, and hence Europe quite sincerely fails to understand how or why the argument arose in the first place, why its effects are so frequently disastrous and always so unpredictable, why it refuses until today to be entirely settled. Europe's black possessions remained—and do remain—in Europe's colonies, at which remove they represented no threat whatever to European identity. If they posed any problem at all for the European conscience, it was a problem which remained comfortingly abstract: in effect, the black man, *as a man*, did not exist for Europe. But in America, even as a slave, he was an inescapable part of the general social fabric and no American could escape having an attitude toward him. Americans attempt until today to make an abstraction of the Negro, but the very nature of these abstractions reveals the tremendous effects the presence of the Negro has had on the American character.

19   When one considers the history of the Negro in America it is of the greatest importance to recognize that the moral beliefs of a person, or a people, are never really as tenuous as life—which is not moral—very often causes them to appear; these create for them a frame of reference and a necessary hope, the hope being that when life has done its worst they will be enabled to rise above themselves and to triumph over life. Life would scarcely be bearable if this hope did not exist. Again, even when the worst has been said, to betray a belief is not by any means to have put oneself beyond its power; the betrayal of a belief is not the same thing as ceasing to believe. If this were not so there would be no moral standards in the world at all. Yet one must also recognize that morality is based on ideas and that all ideas are dangerous—dangerous because ideas can only lead to action and where the action leads no man can say. And dangerous in this respect: that confronted with the impossibility of remaining faithful to one's beliefs, and the equal impossibility of becoming free of them, one can be driven to the most inhuman excesses. The ideas on which American beliefs are based are not, though Americans often seem to think so, ideas which originated in America. They came out of Europe. And the establishment of democracy on the American continent was scarcely as radical a break with the past as was the necessity, which Americans faced, of broadening this concept to include black men.

20   This was, literally, a hard necessity. It was impossible, for one thing, for Americans to abandon their beliefs, not only because these beliefs alone seemed able to justify the sacrifices they had endured and the blood that they had spilled, but also because these beliefs afforded them their only bulwark against a moral chaos as absolute as the physical chaos of the continent it

was their destiny to conquer. But in the situation in which Americans found themselves, these beliefs threatened an idea which, whether or not one likes to think so, is the very warp and woof of the heritage of the West, the idea of white supremacy.

21   Americans have made themselves notorious by the shrillness and the brutality with which they have insisted on this idea, but they did not invent it; and it has escaped the world's notice that those very excesses of which Americans have been guilty imply a certain, unprecedented uneasiness over the idea's life and power, if not, indeed, the idea's validity. The idea of white supremacy rests simply on the fact that white men are the creators of civilization (the present civilization, which is the only one that matters; all previous civilizations are simply "contributions" to our own) and are therefore civilization's guardians and defenders. Thus it was impossible for Americans to accept the black man as one of themselves, for to do so was to jeopardize their status as white men. But not so to accept him was to deny his human reality, his human weight and complexity, and the strain of denying the overwhelmingly undeniable forced Americans into rationalizations so fantastic that they approached the pathological.

22   At the root of the American Negro problem is the necessity of the American white man to find a way of living with the Negro in order to be able to live with himself. And the history of this problem can be reduced to the means used by Americans—lynch law and law, segregation and legal acceptance, terrorization and concession—either to come to terms with this necessity, or to find a way around it, or (most usually) to find a way of doing both these things at once. The resulting spectacle, at once foolish and dreadful, led someone to make the quite accurate observation that "the Negro-in-America is a form of insanity which overtakes white men."

23   In this long battle, a battle by no means finished, the unforeseeable effects of which will be felt by many future generations, the white man's motive was the protection of his identity; the black man was motivated by the need to establish an identity. And despite the terrorization which the Negro in America endured and endures sporadically until today, despite the cruel and totally inescapable ambivalence of his status in his country, the battle for his identity has long ago been won. He is not a visitor to the West, but a citizen there, an American as American as the Americans who despise him, the Americans who fear him, the Americans who love him—the Americans who became less than themselves, or rose to be greater than themselves by virtue of the fact that the challenge he represented was inescapable. He is perhaps the only black man in the world whose relationship to white men is more terrible, more subtle, and more meaningful than the relationship of bitter possessed to uncertain possessor. His survival depended, and his development depends, on his ability to turn his peculiar status in the Western world to his own advantage and, it may be, to the very great advantage of that world. It remains for him to fashion out of his experience that which will give sustenance, and a voice.

24   The cathedral at Chartres, I have said, says something to the people of this village which it cannot say to me; but it is important to understand that this cathedral says something to me which it cannot say to them. Perhaps they are struck by the power of the spires, the glory of the windows; but they have known God, after all, longer then I have known him, and in a different way, and I am terrified by the slippery bottomless well to be found in the crypt, down which heretics were hurled to death, and by the obscene, inescapable gargoyles jutting out of the stone and seeming to say that God and the devil can never be divorced. I doubt that the villagers think of the devil when they face a cathedral because they have never been identified with the devil. But I must accept the status which myth, if nothing else, gives me in the West before I can hope to change the myth.

25   Yet, if the American Negro has arrived at his identity by virtue of the absoluteness of his estrangement from his past, American white men still nourish the illusion that there is some means of recovering the European innocence, of returning to a state in which black men do not exist. This is one of the greatest errors Americans can make. The identity they fought so hard to protect has, by virtue of that battle, undergone a change: Americans are as unlike any other white people in the world as it is possible to be. I do not think, for example, that it is too much to suggest that the American vision of the world—which allows so little reality, generally speaking, for any of the darker forces in human life, which tends until today to paint moral issues in glaring black and white—owes a great deal to the battle waged by Americans to maintain between themselves and black men a human separation which could not be bridged. It is only now beginning to be borne in on us—very faintly, it must be admitted, very slowly, and very much against our will—that this vision of the world is dangerously inaccurate, and perfectly useless. For it protects our moral high-mindedness at the terrible expense of weakening our grasp of reality. People who shut their eyes to reality simply invite their own destruction, and anyone who insists on remaining in a state of innocence long after that innocence is dead turns himself into a monster.

26   The time has come to realize that the interracial drama acted out on the American continent has not only created a new black man, it has created a new white man, too. No road whatever will lead Americans back to the simplicity of this European village where white men still have the luxury of looking on me as a stranger. I am not, really, a stranger any longer for any American alive. One of the things that distinguishes Americans from other people is that no other people has ever been so deeply involved in the lives of black men, and vice versa. This fact faced, with all its implications, it can be seen that the history of the American Negro problem is not merely shameful, it is also something of an achievement. For even when the worst has been said, it must also be added that the perpetual challenge posed by this problem was always, somehow, perpetually met. It is precisely this black-white experience which may prove of indispensable value to us in the world we face today. This world is white no longer, and it will never be white again.

Gabriel García Márquez

Gabriel García Márquez was born in Colombia in 1927 and is best known for his novel One Hundred Years of Solitude *(1967). Truly a world-renowned figure whose influence has touched the fiction of many countries, García Márquez won the Noble Prize for Literature in 1982.*

García Márquez's fiction is marked by magical realism, a term originally applied to painting and associated with Latin American writers since the 1960s. It describes a broadly conceived notion of reality that embeds mystical elements within realistic narrative, a technique that is clearly evident "A Very Old Man with Enormous Wings." Consequently, García Márquez has said of his writing, "My most important problem was destroying the lines of demarcation that separate what seems real from what seems fantastic."

Gabriel García Márquez
"A Very Old Man with Enormous Wings"
A Tale for Children

1   On the third day of rain they had killed so many crabs inside the house that Pelayo had to cross his drenched courtyard and throw them into the sea, because the newborn child had a temperature all night and they thought it was due to the stench. The world had been sad since Tuesday. Sea and sky were a single ash-gray thing and the sands of the beach, which on March nights glimmered like powdered light, had become a stew of mud and rotten shellfish. The light was so weak at noon that when Pelayo was coming back to the house after throwing away the crabs, it was hard for him to see what it was that was moving and groaning in the rear of the courtyard. He had to go very close to see that it was an old man, a very old man, lying face down in the mud, who, in spite of his tremendous efforts, couldn't get up, impeded by his enormous wings.

2   Frightened by that nightmare, Pelayo ran to get Elisenda, his wife, who was putting compresses on the sick child, and he took her to the rear of the courtyard. They both looked at the fallen body with mute stupor. He was dressed like a ragpicker. There were only a few faded hairs left on his bald skull and very few teeth in his mouth, and his pitiful condition of a drenched great grandfather had taken away any sense of grandeur he might have had. His huge buzzard wings, dirty and half-plucked, were forever entangled in the mud. They looked at him so long and so closely that Pelayo and Elisenda very soon overcame their surprise and in the end found him familiar. Then they dared speak to him, and he answered in an incomprehensible dialect with a strong sailor's voice. That was how they skipped over the inconvenience of the wings and quite intelligently concluded that he was a lonely castaway from some foreign

ship wrecked by the storm. And yet, they called in a neighbor woman who knew everything about life and death to see him, and all she needed was one look to show them their mistake.

3   "He's an angel," she told them. "He must have been coming for the child, but the poor fellow is so old that the rain knocked him down."

4   On the following day everyone knew that a flesh-and-blood angel was held captive in Pelayo's house. Against the judgment of the wise neighbor woman, not; for whom angels in those times were the fugitive survivors of a celestial conspiracy, they did not have the heart to club him to death. Pelayo watched over him all afternoon from the kitchen, armed with his bailiff's club, and before going to bed he dragged him out of the mud and locked him up with the hens in the wire chicken coop. In the middle of the night, when the rain stopped, Pelayo and Elisenda were still killing crabs. A short time afterward the child woke up without a fever and with a desire to eat. Then they felt magnanimous and decided to put the angel on a raft with fresh water and provisions for three days and leave him to his fate on the high seas. But when they went out into the courtyard with the first light of dawn, they found the whole neighborhood in front of the chicken coop having fun with the angel, without the slightest reverence, tossing him things to eat through the openings in the wire as if he weren't a supernatural creature but a circus animal.

5   Father Gonzaga arrived before seven o'clock, alarmed at the strange news. By that time onlookers less frivolous than those at dawn had already arrived and they were making all kinds of conjectures concerning the captive's future. The simplest among them thought that he should be named mayor of the world. Others of sterner mind felt that he should be promoted to the rank of five-star general in order to win all wars. Some visionaries hoped that he could be put to stud in order to implant on earth a race of winged wise men who could take charge of the universe. But Father Gonzaga, before becoming a priest, had been a robust woodcutter. Standing by the wire, he reviewed his catechism in an instant and asked them to open the door so that he could take a close look at that pitiful man who looked more like a huge decrepit hen among the fascinated chickens. He was lying in a corner drying his open wings in the sunlight among the fruit peels and breakfast leftovers that the early risers had thrown him. Alien to the impertinences of the world, he only lifted his antiquarian eyes and murmured something in his dialect when Father Gonzaga went into the chicken coop and said good morning to him in Latin. The parish priest had his first suspicion of an imposter when he saw that he did not understand the language of God or know how to greet His ministers. Then he noticed that seen close up he was much too human: he had an unbearable smell of the outdoors, the back side of his wings was strewn with parasites and his main feathers had been mistreated by terrestrial winds, and nothing about him measured up to the proud dignity of angels. Then he came out of the chicken coop and in a brief sermon warned the curious against the risks of being ingenuous. He reminded them that the devil had the bad habit of making use of carnival tricks in order to confuse the unwary. He argued that if wings were not the essential element in

determining the difference between a hawk and an airplane, they were even less so in the recognition of angels. Nevertheless, he promised to write a letter to his bishop so that the latter would write to his primate so that the latter would write to the Supreme Pontiff in order to get the final verdict from the highest courts.

6   His prudence fell on sterile hearts. The news of the captive angel spread with such rapidity that after a few hours the courtyard had the bustle of a marketplace and they had to call in troops with fixed bayonets to disperse the mob that was about to knock the house down. Elisenda, her spine all twisted from sweeping up so much marketplace trash, then got the idea of fencing in the yard and charging five cents admission to see the angel.

7   The curious came from far away. A traveling carnival arrived with a flying acrobat who buzzed over the crowd several times, but no one paid any attention to him because his wings were not those of an angel but, rather, those of a sidereal bat. The most unfortunate invalids on earth came in search of health: a poor woman who since childhood had been counting her heartbeats and had run out of numbers; a Portuguese man who couldn't sleep because the noise of the stars disturbed him; a sleepwalker who got up at night to undo the things he had done while awake; and many others with less serious ailments. In the midst of that shipwreck disorder that made the earth tremble, Pelayo and Elisenda were happy with fatigue, for in less than a week they had crammed their rooms with money and the line of pilgrims waiting their turn to enter still reached beyond the horizon.

8   The angel was the only one who took no part in his own act. He spent his time trying to get comfortable in his borrowed nest, befuddled by the hellish heat of the oil lamps and sacramental candles that had been placed along the wire. At first they tried to make him eat some mothballs, which, according to the wisdom of the wise neighbor woman, were the food prescribed for angels. But he turned them down, just as he turned down the papal lunches that the penitents brought him, and they never found out whether it was because he was an angel or because he was an old man that in the end he ate nothing but eggplant mush. His only supernatural virtue seemed to be patience. Especially during the first days, when the hens pecked at him, searching for the stellar parasites that proliferated in his wings, and the cripples pulled out feathers to touch their defective parts with, and even the most merciful threw stones at him, trying to get him to rise so they could see him standing. The only time they succeeded in arousing him was when they burned his side with an iron for branding steers, for he had been motionless for so many hours that they thought he was dead. He awoke with a start, ranting in his hermetic language and with tears in his eyes, and he flapped his wings a couple of times, which brought on a whirlwind of chicken dung and lunar dust and a gale of panic that did not seem to be of this world. Although many thought that his reaction had been one not of rage but of pain, from then on they were careful not to annoy him, because the majority understood that his passivity was not that of a hero taking his ease but that of a cataclysm in repose.

9   Father Gonzaga held back the crowd's frivolity with formulas of maidservant inspiration while awaiting the arrival of a final judgment on the nature of the captive. But the mail from Rome showed no sense of urgency. They spent their time finding out if the prisoner had a navel, if his dialect had any connection with Aramaic, how many times he could fit on the head of a pin, or whether he wasn't just a Norwegian with wings. Those meager letters might have come and gone until the end of time if a providential event had not put an end to the priest's tribulations.

10   It so happened that during those days, among so many other carnival attractions, there arrived in town the traveling show of the woman who had been changed into a spider for having disobeyed her parents. The admission to see her was not only less than the admission to see the angel, but people were permitted to ask her all manner of questions about her absurd state and to examine her up and down so that no one would ever doubt the truth of her horror. She was a frightful tarantula the size of a ram and with the head of a sad maiden. What was most heartrending, however, was not her outlandish shape but the sincere affliction with which she recounted the details of her misfortune. While still practically a child she had sneaked out of her parents' house to go to a dance, and while she was coming back through the woods after having danced all night without permission, a fearful thunderclap rent the sky in two and through the crack came the lightning bolt of brimstone that changed her into a spider. Her only nourishment came from the meatballs that charitable souls chose to toss into her mouth. A spectacle like that, full of so much human truth and with such a fearful lesson, was bound to defeat without even trying that of a haughty angel who scarcely deigned to look at mortals. Besides, the few miracles attributed to the angel showed a certain mental disorder, like the blind man who didn't recover his sight but grew three new teeth, or the paralytic who didn't get to walk but almost won the lottery, and the leper whose sores sprouted sunflowers. Those consolation miracles, which were more like mocking fun, had already ruined the angel's reputation when the woman who had been changed into a spider finally crushed him completely. That was how Father Gonzaga was cured forever of his insomnia and Pelayo's courtyard went back to being as empty as during the time it had rained for three days and crabs walked through the bedrooms.

11   The owners of the house had no reason to lament. With the money they saved they built a two-story mansion with balconies and gardens and high netting so that crabs wouldn't get in during the winter, and with iron bars on the windows so that angels wouldn't get in. Pelayo also set up a rabbit warren close to town and gave up his job as bailiff for good, and Elisenda bought some satin pumps with high heels and many dresses of iridescent silk, the kind worn on Sunday by the most desirable women in those times. The chicken coop was the only thing that didn't receive any attention. If they washed it down with creolin and burned tears of myrrh inside it every so often, it was not in homage to the angel but to drive away the dungheap stench that still hung everywhere like a ghost and was turning the new house into an old one. At first, when the child learned to walk, they were careful that he not get too close to the chicken coop.

But then they began to lose their fears and got used to the smell, and before the child got his second teeth he'd gone inside the chicken coop to play, where the wires were falling apart. The angel was no less standoffish with him than with other mortals, but he tolerated the most ingenious infamies with the patience of a dog who had no illusions. They both came down with chicken pox at the same time. The doctor who took care of the child couldn't resist the temptation to listen to the angel's heart, and he found so much whistling in the heart and so many sounds in his kidneys that it seemed impossible for him to be alive. What surprised him most, however, was the logic of his wings. They seemed so natural on that completely human organism that he couldn't understand why other men didn't have them too.

12   When the child began school it had been some time since the sun and rain had caused the collapse of the chicken coop. The angel went dragging himself about here and there like a stray dying man. They would drive him out of the bedroom with a broom and a moment later find him in the kitchen. He seemed to be in so many places at the same time that they grew to think that he'd been duplicated, that he was reproducing himself all through the house, and the exasperated and unhinged Elisenda shouted that it was awful living in that hell full of angels. He could scarcely eat and his antiquarian eyes had also become so foggy that he went about bumping into posts. All he had left were the bare cannulae of his last feathers. Pelayo threw a blanket over him and extended him the charity of letting him sleep in the shed, and only then did they notice that he had a temperature at night, and was delirious with the tongue twisters of an old Norwegian. That was one of the few times they became alarmed, for they thought he was going to die and not even the wise neighbor woman had been able to tell them what to do with dead angels.

13   And yet he not only survived his worst winter, but seemed improved with the first sunny days. He remained motionless for several days in the farthest corner of the courtyard, where no one would see him, and at the beginning of December some large, stiff feathers began to grow on his wings, the feathers of a scarecrow which looked more like another misfortune of decrepitude. But he must have known the reason for those changes, for he was quite careful that no one should notice them, that no one should hear the sea chanteys that he sometimes sang under the stars. One morning Elisenda was cutting some bunches of onions for lunch when a wind that seemed to come from the high seas blew into the kitchen. Then she went to the window and caught the angel in his first attempts at flight. They were so clumsy that his fingernails opened a furrow in the vegetable patch and he was on the point of knocking the shed down with the ungainly flapping that slipped on the light and couldn't get a grip on the air. But he did manage to gain altitude. Elisenda let out a sigh of relief, for herself and for him, when she saw him pass over the last houses, holding himself up in some way with the risky flapping of a senile vulture. She kept watching him even when she was through cutting the onions and she kept on watching until it was no longer possible for her to see him, because then he was no longer an annoyance in her life but an imaginary dot on the horizon of the sea.

Louise Erdrich

An author of novels, poetry, children's books, and a memoir, Louise Erdrich was born in 1954 in Little Falls, Minnesota, to a German American father and a French Ojibwa mother. Erdrich attended Dartmouth College, which gained fame for its Native American studies department. She received her Master of Fine Arts from Johns Hopkins University. Then she launched a writing career that has won her the admiration of many of her contemporaries as well as many prestigious awards. She refused the distinction of an honorary doctorate from the University of Minnesota because of the university's "fighting Sioux" mascot.

In such poems as "Indian Boarding School: The Runaways," Erdrich explores the political and cultural complexities of having a mixed heritage.

Louise Erdrich
"Indian Boarding School: The Runaways"

Home's the place we head for in our sleep.
Boxcars stumbling north in dreams
don't wait for us. We catch them on the run.
The rails, old lacerations that we love,
5   shoot parallel across the face and break
just under Turtle Mountains. Riding scars
you can't get lost. Home is the place they cross.

The lame guard strikes a match and makes the dark
less tolerant. We watch through cracks in boards
10   as the land starts rolling, rolling till it hurts
to be here, cold in regulation clothes.
We know the sheriff's waiting at midrun
to take us back. His car is dumb and warm.
The highway doesn't rock, it only hums
15   like a wing of long insults. The worn-down welts
of ancient punishment lead back and forth.

All runaways wear dresses, long green ones,
the color you would think shame was. We scrub
the sidewalks down because it's shameful work.
20   Our brushes cut the stone in watered arcs
and in the soak frail outlines shiver clear
a moment, things us kids pressed on the dark
face before it hardened, place, remembering
delicate old injuries, the spines of names and leaves.

U.S. Department of Homeland Security

According to the department's Web site, one primary reason for the establishment of the department "was to provide the unifying core for the vast national network of organizations and institutions involved in efforts to secure our nation." The men and women working for the department total 180,000.

Amy Wu for the U.S. Department of Homeland Security "Border Apprehensions: 2005"

Statistics on apprehensions represent one of the few indicators available regarding illegal entry or presence in the United States. This Office of Immigration Statistics Fact Sheet provides information on recent trends in apprehensions and the gender, age, and geographic location of persons apprehended during 2005.[1]

Data for 2005 were obtained from the Enforcement Case Tracking System of U.S. Customs and Border Protection (CBP) of the Department of Homeland Security (DHS). Data for prior years were obtained from the Performance Analysis System (PAS) of DHS.

Defining Apprehensions

Apprehension statistics measure the number of foreign nationals who are caught and placed in custody for being in the United States illegally. Persons apprehended are subject to removal from the United States for violating the Immigration and Nationality Act. The relationship between apprehensions to either the number of attempted illegal entries or the number of successful illegal entries is unclear.

The vast majority of apprehensions occur near U.S. borders shortly after an illegal entry. These apprehensions are made by the Border Patrol of CBP. A much smaller number of apprehensions involve other foreign nationals illegally present in the United States. They may have entered without inspection (EWI) or entered legally but lost their legal status, for example, by overstaying the terms of their entry permit or visa. Most apprehensions made beyond U.S. borders are handled by the Investigations Office of Immigration and Customs Enforcement (ICE) of DHS.

---

1. Refers to fiscal year October 2004 through September 2005.

Apprehensions data represent events, not individuals. The total number of apprehensions during a specific time period will be greater than the total number of unique individuals apprehended since some individuals will have been apprehended more than once.

Trends

There were 1.3 million apprehensions in 2005. During the 10 year period 1996–2005, the annual number of apprehensions reached a high of 1.8 million in 2000 and a low of 1.0 million in 2003 (see Figure 1). Apprehensions made by the Border Patrol along U.S. borders represented 89 to 94 percent of all apprehensions during 1996–2005.

Demographics of Border Patrol Apprehensions

Demographic information on the characteristics of persons apprehended is presented for those apprehensions by the Border Patrol along the 8,000 miles of American international borders. The southern border with Mexico is approximately 2,000 miles. The northern border with Canada is approximately 4,000 miles. The coastal borders consist of 2,000 miles surrounding Florida and Puerto Rico.

Table 1 displays the age and country of origin of persons apprehended at the three borders during 2005. Almost all apprehensions occur at the southern border. In 2005, the southern border accounted for 98.5 percent of apprehensions. The majority (86.1 percent) of these apprehensions were Mexican nationals. More than four-fifths (81.5 percent) of persons apprehended at the southern border were male.

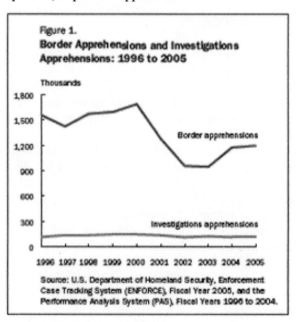

Figure 1.
Border Apprehensions and Investigations
Apprehensions: 1996 to 2005

Source: U.S. Department of Homeland Security, Enforcement Case Tracking System (ENFORCE), Fiscal Year 2005, and the Performance Analysis System (PAS), Fiscal Years 1996 to 2004.

	Border							
	Total		Southern		Northern		Coastal	
Characteristic	Number	Percent	Number	Percent	Number	Percent	Number	Percent
Gender								
Total.	1,189,108	100.0	1,171,428	100.0	7,343	100.0	10,337	100.0
Male.	969,955	81.6	955,037	81.5	6,319	86.1	8,599	83.2
Female	219,124	18.4	216,370	18.5	1,016	13.8	1,738	16.8
Unknown	29	-	21	-	8	0.1	-	-
Age								
Total.	1,189,108	100.0	1,171,428	100.0	7,343	100.0	10,337	100.0
Adult (18 over).	1,074,462	90.4	1,057,665	90.3	6,992	95.2	9,805	94.9
Juvenile (17 and under)	114,569	9.6	113,701	9.7	347	4.7	521	5.0
Unknown	77	-	62	-	4	0.1	11	0.1
Country of nationality								
Total.	1,189,108	100.0	1,171,428	100.0	7,343	100.0	10,337	100.0
Mexico	1,023,930	86.1	1,016,434	86.8	4,080	55.6	3,416	33.0
Honduras	52,760	4.4	51,889	4.4	202	2.8	669	6.5
El Salvador	39,308	3.3	39,004	3.3	100	1.4	204	2.0
Brazil.	31,072	2.6	30,843	2.6	134	1.8	95	0.9
Guatemala	22,593	1.9	21,807	1.9	233	3.2	553	5.3
Nicaragua	3,922	0.3	3,826	0.3	13	0.2	83	0.8
Cuba.	3,262	0.3	129	-	20	0.3	3,113	30.1
China	2,200	0.2	1,987	0.2	179	2.4	34	0.3
Canada	1,020	0.1	33	-	983	13.4	4	-
Other.	9,041	0.8	5,476	0.5	1,399	19.1	2,166	21.0

- Figure rounds to 0.0.
Note: Data reported as of April 13, 2006.
Source: U.S. Department of Homeland Security, Enforcement Case Tracking System (ENFORCE), Fiscal Year 2005.

Ninety percent were ages 18 and over. Eighty-seven percent were from Mexico. Other leading countries of origin included Honduras (4.4 percent), El Salvador (3.3 percent), Brazil (2.6 percent), and Guatemala (1.9 percent).

Persons apprehended at the northern and coastal borders were similar to those at the southern border with respect to gender and age. Mexico was the leading country of origin for apprehensions at the northern border (55.6 percent) and coastal borders (33.0 percent). Cuba was the next leading country (30.1 percent) for coastal border apprehensions.

For More Information

For more information about immigration and immigration statistics, visit the U.S. Department of Homeland Security Web site at http://www.dhs.gov/immigrationstatistics.

Jacob Riis

Originally from Denmark, Jacob Riis (1849–1914) became a police reporter for New York City newspapers and ultimately a photographer and social reformer. He is known both for his craft (including his innovations in flash photography) as well as his subject matter (poor, immigrant, disadvantaged New Yorkers).

As depicted in Lodgers in a Crowded Bayard Street Tenement: Five Cents a Spot, *Riis's photographs carry a strong message. Riis received criticism by those who viewed his work as exploiting the less fortunate; but whether or not Riis's work was altruistic, one cannot dismiss the strong influence of his striking images.*

Jacob Riis
Lodgers in a Crowded Bayard Street Tenement: Five Cents a Spot

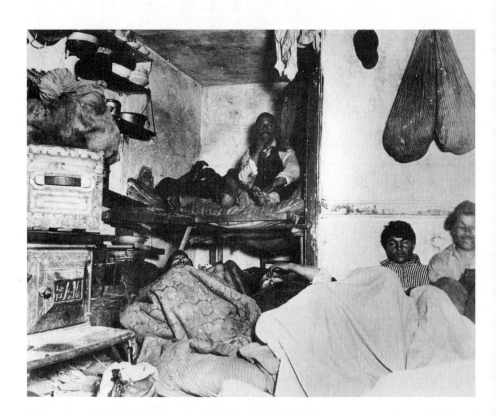

Art Spiegelman

Born in Stockholm, Sweden, in 1948 to Polish Jewish refugees, Art Speigelman grew up in New York City. He is best known for his graphic novel Maus, *which won the Pulitzer Prize in 1992.* Maus *retraces his parents' traumatic experiences during World War II.*

The excerpt from Maus *forces readers to reconsider their notions of serious art. Experiencing the horror of the holocaust through this graphic form can disorient readers. However, Spiegelman draws readers into the Nazi world by means of this juxtaposition and creates a powerful effect.*

Art Spiegelman
from Maus II. A Survivor's Tale
(And Here My Troubles Began)

A COUPLE WEEKS MORE AND THEY *WOULDN'T* HANG... IT WAS VERY NEAR TO THE END, THERE IN AUSCHWITZ.

BOOM

YOU HEAR THAT, VLADEK? THE FRONT IS NO MORE THAN 25 MILES AWAY...

IF WE CAN JUST STAY ALIVE A LITTLE BIT LONGER, THE RUSSIANS WILL BE HERE.

THIS BOY WORKED IN THE OFFICE AND KNEW RUMORS.

THE GERMANS ARE GETTING WORRIED. THE BIG SHOTS HERE ARE ALREADY RUNNING BACK INTO THE REICH.

THEY'RE PLANNING TO TAKE EVERYBODY HERE BACK TO CAMPS INSIDE GERMANY. EVERYBODY!

BUT A FEW OF US HAVE A PLAN... WE'RE NOT GOING!

YOU HAVE A FRIEND IN THE CAMP LAUNDRY. HELP US GET CIVILIAN CLOTHES AND JOIN US.

HE TOOK ME QUICK TO AN ATTIC IN ONE OF THE BLOCKS.

THIS ROOM ISN'T BEING USED ANYMORE. WHEN THE EVACUATION STARTS, THE SEVEN OF US WILL COME UP HERE TO HIDE.

WE ARRANGED THERE CLOTHING AND EVEN IDENTITY PAPERS, AND HALF EACH DAY'S BREAD WE PUT OVER HERE.

Leonard Pitts Jr.

Born in 1957 in Orange, California, Pitts won the Pulitzer Prize for distinguished commentary in 2004. His Becoming Dad: Black Men and the Journey to Fatherhood, *a best-seller in 1999, tells about Pitts's relationship with his father. "My father made our lives hell," Pitts writes. "And yet, for all that, he was one thing many other fathers were not: He was there. Present and accounted for every day. Emotionally absent, mind you. But there, at least, in body." Today, Pitts continues to write as a syndicated columnist for the* Miami Herald *and maintains a schedule of speaking engagements.*

Leonard Pitts Jr.
"The Game of Justice Is Rigged"
An Open Letter to African-American Men

1   This is an Open Letter to African-American Men.

2   I suppose I could as easily have addressed myself to the broader world, but I know how the response to that would go. Folks denying, rationalizing and arguing that facts are not truly facts.

3   That's how it always is when the subject is crime and you.

4   Earlier this week, *The Miami Herald* ran a jaw-dropping series called "Justice Withheld." It detailed the abuse of a legal procedure called a withholding of adjudication. This is a tool Florida judges can use at their discretion that allows felony offenders to avoid a conviction.

5   Receiving a withhold allows you to legally say you've never been convicted of a crime, even though a court found you guilty. There are many benefits: You retain your right to vote and hold office and you don't have to put the crime on your application for a job or a student loan.

Theory vs. Practice

6   In theory, withholds are handed out sparingly to deserving people in extenuating circumstances. The *Herald* found that in practice, they are handed out like Halloween candy.

7   Four-time losers get withholds. Rapists and car thieves get withholds. Drug dealers and batterers get withholds.

8   If you commit fraud or forgery, you've got an even chance of getting one. Abuse or molest a child and your chances are actually better than even.

9   All those folks enjoying all that judicial mercy. Guess who gets left out?

10   Yup. You.

11   Even if you commit the same crime and have the same record, a white offender is almost 50 percent more likely to get a withhold than you are. Some

folks say that's not a function of racism but of socioeconomics. Meaning that whites are more often able to afford private attorneys, less likely to have to rely on some overburdened public defender.

12   There are two answers to that. One: socioeconomics can't be disconnected from racism where black people are concerned; the disparity in black and white accumulated wealth is hardly an accident. And two: The *Herald* report shows that, even when you adjust for type of attorney, African-American defendants are still much less likely to receive withholds.

13   So I have a question for you:

14   Can we please stop being such good customers of the American injustice system? I am sick to my soul of watching shaggy-haired black boys and men in orange jumpsuits led into courtrooms to be judged for doing some stupid and heinous thing. I'm weary of the truth in that old Richard Pryor line about how he went to court looking for justice and that's what he found. Just us.

No Breaks

15   Contrary to what society has told us, to what so much of our music claims and to what too many of us have internalized, the reason isn't that we carry some kind of criminal gene. No, it's that we don't get second chances, don't have the same margin for error a white guy would. One strike, and you're out.

16   We need to recognize this. Need to make sure our sons and brothers recognize it.

17   The *Herald* report is not the first, the fifth, or even the 10th to come back with results like these, results that codify the painfully obvious: the injustice system sees no value in us, is comfortable throwing us away like so much used tissue. It doesn't give a damn about us.

18   But our children do. Our women and mothers and fathers do. So let us love them—and ourselves—enough to stay as far from that system as humanly possible. Because once you're in it, you're like a dinosaur in a tar pit. Dragged down.

19   No, it's not fair that we are held to a different standard. Say that loudly and clearly. Fight to make it right. But do not stop there.

20   You see, when you discover that a game is rigged against you, you have every right to complain that you're being cheated.

21   But a smart man does one thing more:

22   A smart man stops playing.

Glossary of Rhetorical Terms

act: In a DRAMATISTIC PENTAD created by a speaker or writer in order to invent material, the words the speaker or writer uses to describe what happened or happens in a particular situation.

aesthetic reading: Reading to experience the world of the text.

agency: In a DRAMATISTIC PENTAD created by a speaker or writer in order to invent material, the words the speaker or writer uses to describe the means by which something happened or happens in a particular situation.

agent: In a DRAMATISTIC PENTAD created by a speaker or writer in order to invent material, the words the speaker or writer uses to describe the person or persons involved in taking action in a particular situation.

aim: The goal a writer or speaker hopes to achieve with the text—for example, to clarify difficult material, to inform, to convince, to persuade. Also called INTENTION and PURPOSE.

allegory: An extended METAPHOR.

alliteration: The REPETITION of consonant sounds at the beginning or in the middle of two or more adjacent words.

allusion: A reference in a written or spoken text to another text or to some particular body of knowledge.

anadiplosis (a-nuh-duh-PLOH-suhs): The REPETITION of the last word of one clause at the beginning of the following clause.

anaphora (un-NA-fuh-ruh): The REPETITION of a group of words at the beginning of successive clauses.

anecdote: A brief narrative offered in a text to capture the AUDIENCE's attention or to support a GENERALIZATION or CLAIM.

Anglo-Saxon diction: Word choice characterized by simple, often one- or two-syllable, nouns, adjectives, and adverbs.

antagonist: The CHARACTER who opposes the interests of the protagonist.

antecedent-consequence relationship: The relationship expressed by "if . . . then" reasoning—for example, "If the Cubs sign Greg Maddux, then they will win the National League pennant."

anthimeria (an-thuh-MEER-ee-uh): One part of speech—for example, a noun—substituting for another—for example, a verb.

anticipated objection: The technique a writer or speaker uses in an argumentative text to address and answer objections, even though the audience has not had the opportunity to voice these objections.

antimetabole (an-ti-me-TA-boh-lee): The REPETITION of words in successive clauses in reverse grammatical order—for example, "You can take the boy out of the country, but you can't take the country out of the boy."

antithesis: The juxtaposition of contrasting words or ideas, often in parallel structure—for example, "Place your virtues on a pedestal; put your vices under a rock."

apologist: A person or CHARACTER who makes a case for some controversial, even contentious, position.

apology: An elaborate statement justifying some controversial, even contentious, position.

apostrophe: Type of SOLILOQUY where nature is addressed as though human.

appeal: One of three strategies for persuading AUDIENCES—LOGOS, appeal to reason; PATHOS, appeals to emotion; and ETHOS, appeals to ethics.

appeal to authority: In a text, the reference to words, action, or beliefs of a person in authority as a means of supporting a CLAIM, GENERALIZATION, or CONCLUSION.

appositive: A noun or noun phrase that follows another noun immediately and defines or amplifies its meaning.

argument: A carefully constructed, well-supported representation of how a writer sees an issue, problem, or subject.

argument by analysis: An ARGUMENT developed by breaking the subject matter into its component parts.

Aristotelian triangle: A diagram showing the relations of writer or speaker, AUDIENCE (reader or listener), and text in a RHETORICAL SITUATION.

arrangement: In a spoken or written text, the placement of ideas for effect.

assonance: The REPETITION of vowel sounds in the stressed syllables of two or more adjacent words.

assumption: An opinion, a perspective, or a belief that a writer or speaker thinks the audience holds.

asyndeton (UH-SIN-DUH-TON): The omission of conjunctions between related clauses—for example, "I came, I saw, I conquered."

attitude: In an adapted DRAMATISITIC PENTAD created by a speaker or writer in order to invent materials, the manner in which an action is carried out.

audience: The person or persons who listen to a spoken text or read a written one and are capable of responding to it.

basic topic: One of the four perspectives that Aristotle explained could be used to generate material about any subject matter: greater or less, possible and impossible, past fact, and future fact.

begging of the question: The situation that results when a writer or speaker constructs an ARGUMENT on an ASSUMPTION that the AUDIENCE does not accept.

brainstorming: Within the planning act of the WRITING PROCESS, a technique used by a writer or speaker to generate many ideas, some of which he or she will later eliminate.

canon: One of the traditional elements of rhetorical composition—INVENTION, ARRANGEMENT, STYLE, MEMORY, or DELIVERY.

casuistry: A mental exercise to discover possibilities for analysis of communication.

causal relationship (cause-and-effect relationship): The relationship expressing, "If X is the cause, then Y is the effect," or, "If Y is the effect, then X caused it"—for example, "If the state builds larger highways, then traffic congestion will just get worse because more people will move to the newly accessible regions," or, "If students plagiarize their papers, it must be because the Internet offers them such a wide array of materials from which to copy."

character: A personage in a narrative.

claim: The ultimate CONCLUSION, GENERALIZATION, or point that a SYLLOGISM or ENTHYMEME expresses. The point, backed up by support, of an ARGUMENT.

climax: The arrangement of words, phrases, or clauses in order of increasing number or importance.

climbing the ladder: A term referring to the schemes of CLIMAX and ANADIPLOSIS used together.

cloze test: A test of reading ability that requires a person to fill in missing words in a text.

common topic: One of the perspectives, derived from Aristotle's topics, used to generate material. The six common topics are definition, division, comparison, relation, circumstances, and testimony.

complex sentence: A sentence with one independent clause and one or more dependent clauses.

compound-complex sentence: A sentence with two or more independent clauses and one or more dependent clauses.

compound sentence: A sentence with two or more independent clauses.

compound subject: The construction in which two or more nouns, noun phrases, or noun clauses constitute the grammatical subject of a clause.

conclusion (of syllogism): The ultimate point or GENERALIZATION that a SYLLOGISM expresses.

confirmation: In ancient Roman oratory, the part of a speech in which the speaker or writer would offer proof or demonstration of the central idea.

conflict: The struggle of CHARACTERS with themselves, with others, or with the world around them.

connotation: The implied meaning of a word, in contrast to its directly expressed "dictionary meaning."

consulting: Seeking help for one's writing from a reader.

context: The convergence of time, place, AUDIENCE, and motivating factors in which a piece of writing or a speech is situated.

contraction: The combination of two words into one by eliminating one or more sounds and indicating the omission with an apostrophe—for example, "don't" for "do not."

contradiction: One of the types of rhetorical INVENTION included under the common topic of relationships. Contradiction urges the speaker or writer to invent an example or a proof that is counter to the main idea or ARGUMENT.

contraries: See CONTRADICTION.

data (as evidence): Facts, statistics, and examples that a speaker or writer offers in support of a CLAIM, GENERALIZATION, or CONCLUSION.

declaiming: Heightening a message by emphasizing pitch, volume, and pause and by using gestures and movements.

deductive reasoning: Reasoning that begins with a general principle and concludes with a specific instance that demonstrates the general principle.

delivery: The presentation and format of a composition.

denotation: The dictionary definition of a word, in contrast to its CONNOTATION, or implied meaning.

descriptive writing: Writing that relies on sensory IMAGES to characterize a person or place.

dialect: The describable patterns of language—grammar and vocabulary—used by a particular cultural or ethnic population.

dialogue: Conversation between and among CHARACTERS.

diction: Word choice, which is viewed on scales of formality/informality, concreteness/abstraction, Latinate derivation/Anglo-Saxon derivation, and denotative value/connotative value.

double entendre: The double (or multiple) meanings of a group of words that the speaker or writer has purposely left ambiguous.

drafting: The process by which writers get something written on paper or in a computer file so that they can develop their ideas and begin moving toward an end, the raw material for what will become the final product.

dramatic monologue: A type of poem, popular primarily in the nineteenth century, in which the speaker is delivering a monologue to an assumed group of listeners.

dramatic narration: A NARRATIVE in which the reader or viewer does not have access to the unspoken thoughts of any character.

dramatistic pentad: The INVENTION strategy, developed by Kenneth Burke, that invites a speaker or writer to create identities for the ACT, AGENT, AGENCY, SCENE, and PURPOSE in a situation. An adaptation of the pentad also calls for the speaker or writer to identify attitude in the situation.

dynamic character: One who changes during the course of the NARRATIVE.

editing: The final observation, before DELIVERY, by a writer or speaker of a composition to evaluate appropriateness and to locate missteps in the work.

effect: The emotional or psychological impact a text has on a reader or listener.

efferent reading: Reading to garner information from a text.

ellipsis: The omission of words, the meaning of which is provided by the overall context of a passage.

enthymeme (EN-thuh-meem): Logical reasoning with one premise left unstated.

epistrophe (e-PIS-truh-fee): The REPETITION of a group of words at the end of successive clauses—for example, "They saw no evil, they spoke no evil, and they heard no evil."

epithet: A word or phrase adding a characteristic to a person's name—for example, "Richard the Lion-Hearted."

ethos: The appeal of a text to the credibility and character of the speaker, writer, or narrator.

euphemism: An indirect expression of unpleasant information in such a way as to lessen its impact—for example, saying a person's position was eliminated rather than saying the person was fired.

evidence: The facts, statistics, ANECDOTES, and EXAMPLES that a speaker or writer offers in support of a CLAIM, GENERALIZATION, or CONCLUSION.

exaggeration: An overstatement; see HYPERBOLE.

example: An illustration or incident offered in support of a GENERALIZATION, CLAIM, or point.

exordium: In ancient Roman oratory, the introduction of a speech, meant to draw the AUDIENCE into the speech.

extended analogy: An extended passage arguing that if two things are similar in one or two ways, they are probably similar in other ways as well.

extended example: An EXAMPLE that is carried through several sentences or paragraphs.

fable: A NARRATIVE in which fictional CHARACTERS, often animals, take actions that have ethical or moral significance.

figurative language: Language dominated by the use of SCHEMES and TROPES.

figures of rhetoric: SCHEMES—that is, variations from typical word or sentence formation—and TROPES, which are variations from typical patterns of thought.

flashback: A part of the PLOT that moves back in time and then returns to the present.

flashforward: A part of the PLOT that jumps ahead in time and then returns to the present.

flat character: A FIGURE readily identifiable by memorable traits but not fully developed.

format: The structural elements—such as font and font size, cover page, page numbering, title and heads, bulleted and numbered lists, footnotes, end notes, and works cited/reference pages—that constitute the presentation of a written text.

freewriting: Intuitive writing strategy for generating ideas by writing without stopping.

functional part: A part of a text classified according to its function—for example, introduction, EXAMPLE, or counterargument.

generalization: A point that a speaker or writer generates on the basis of considering a number of particular EXAMPLES.

genre: A piece of writing classified by type—for example, letter, narrative, eulogy, or editorial.

heuristic: A systematic strategy or method for solving problems.

house analogy: In ancient Roman oratory, the method that speakers used to memorize their speeches, connecting the introduction to the porch of a house, the narration and partition to the front foyer, the confirmation and refutation to rooms connected to the foyer, and the conclusion to the back door.

hyperbole: An EXAGGERATION for effect.

image: A passage of text that evokes sensation or emotional intensity.

imagery: Language that evokes particular sensations or emotionally rich experiences in a reader.

implied metaphor: A METAPHOR embedded in a sentence rather than expressed directly as a sentence. For example, "His voice cascaded through the hallways" contains an implied metaphor; "His voice was a cascade of emotion" contains a direct metaphor.

inductive reasoning: Reasoning that begins by citing a number of specific instances or EXAMPLES and then shows how collectively they constitute a general principle.

inference: A CONCLUSION that a reader or listener reaches by means of his or her own thinking rather than by direct statement in a text.

intention: The goal a writer or speaker hopes to achieve with the text—for example, to clarify difficult material, to inform, to convince, or to persuade. Also called AIM and PURPOSE.

invention: The art of generating material for a text; the first of the five traditional CANONS of RHETORIC.

investigating: Carrying out activities, during the WRITING PROCESS, to locate ideas and information.

irony: Writing or speaking that implies the contrary of what is actually written or spoken.

jargon: The specialized vocabulary of a particular group.

journal: A text in which writers produce informal compositions that help them "think on paper" about TOPICS and writing projects.

journaling: The process of writing in a JOURNAL.

konnoi topoi: People's TOPICS; ordinary patterns of reasoning; also called BASIC TOPICS.

Latinate diction: Vocabulary characterized by the choice of elaborate, often complicated words derived from Latin roots.

limited narration: A NARRATIVE in which the reader or viewer has access to the unspoken thoughts of one character or partial thinking of more than one character.

litotes (LIE-toh-*tees*): UNDERSTATEMENT—for example, "Her performance ran the gamut of emotion from A to B."

logic: The art of reasoning.

logos: The appeal of a text based on the logical structure of its ARGUMENT or central ideas.

loose sentence: A sentence that adds modifying elements after the subject, verb, and complement.

major premise: See PREMISE, MAJOR.

memory: Access to information and collective knowledge for use in composition.

metaphor: An implied comparison that does not use the word *like* or *as*—for example, "His voice was a cascade of emotion"; the most important of all the TROPES.

metonymy (muh-TAH-nuh-mee): An entity referred to by one of its attributes or associations—for example, "The admissions office claims applications have risen."

minor premise: See PREMISE, MINOR.

mnemonic device: A systematic aid to MEMORY.

mood: The feeling that a text is intended to produce in the AUDIENCE.

narration: In ancient Roman oratory, the part of a speech in which the speaker provided background information on the TOPIC.

narrative: An ANECDOTE or a story offered in support of a GENERALIZATION, CLAIM, or point. Also, a function in texts accomplished when the speaker or writer tells a story.

narrative intrusion: A comment that is made directly to the reader by breaking into the forward PLOT movement.

occasion: The part of CONTEXT also referred to as time and place.

omniscient narration: A NARRATIVE in which the reader or viewer has access to the unspoken thoughts of all the CHARACTERS.

onomatopoeia: A literary device in which the sound of a word is related to its meaning—for example, "buzz" and "moan."

overstatement: See HYPERBOLE.

oxymoron: Juxtaposed words with seemingly contradictory meanings—for example, "jumbo shrimp."

pace: The speed with which a PLOT moves from one event to another.

paradox: A statement that seems untrue on the surface but is true nevertheless.

parallelism: A set of similarly structured words, phrases, or clauses that appears in a sentence or paragraph.

parenthesis: An insertion of material that interrupts the typical flow of a sentence.

partition: In ancient Roman oratory, the part of a speech where the speaker would divide the main TOPIC into parts.

pathos: The appeal of a text to the emotions or interests of the audience.

peer review: A system calling for writers to read or listen to one another's work and suggest ways to improve it.

pentad: Kenneth Burke's system for analyzing motives and actions in communication. The five points of the pentad are ACT, AGENT, AGENCY, SCENE, and PURPOSE.

people's topics: The English translation of *konnoi topoi,* the four TOPICS that Aristotle explained could be used to generate material about any subject matter; also called BASIC TOPICS.

periodic sentence: A sentence with modifying elements included before the verb and/or complement.

periphrasis (puh-RI-'frah-suhs): The substitution of an attributive word or phrase for a proper name, or the use of a proper name to suggest a personality characteristic. For example, "Pete Rose—better known as 'Charlie Hustle'—admitted his gambling problem" or "That young pop singer thinks she's a real Madonna, doesn't she?"

peroration: In ancient Roman oratory, the part of the speech in which the speaker would draw together the entire ARGUMENT and include material designed to compel the AUDIENCE to think or act in a way consonant with the central argument.

persona: The character that a writer or speaker conveys to the AUDIENCE; the plural is *personae.*

personae: Plural of *persona*.

personification: The giving of human characteristics to inanimate objects.

persuasion: The changing of people's minds or actions by language.

petitio principi: Begging of the question; disagreeing with PREMISES or reasoning.

planning: Determining appropriateness of information for AUDIENCE and for PURPOSE.

plot: Arrangement of events in a story.

plot devices: Elements of PLOT that operate to cause or resolve CONFLICTS and to provide information.

poem: Louise Rosenblatt's term for the interpretive moment when reader and text connect.

point of view: The perspective or source of a piece of writing. A first-person point of view has a narrator or speaker who refers to himself or herself as "I." A third-person point of view lacks such an "I" in its perspective. See also DRAMATIC NARRATION, LIMITED NARRATION, OMNISCIENT NARRATION.

premise, major: The first premise in a SYLLOGISM. The major premise states an irrefutable GENERALIZATION.

premise, minor: The second premise in a SYLLOGISM. The minor premise offers a particular instance of the GENERALIZATION stated in the major premise.

protagonist: The major CHARACTER in a piece of literature; the figure in the NARRATIVE whose interests the reader is most concerned about and sympathetic toward.

pun: A play on words. Types of puns include *anataclasis*, words that sound alike but behave different meanings ("The spoiled turkey meat was fowl most foul"); *paranomasia*, words alike in sound but different in meaning ("When Sybil's two boyfriends started fighting, her friends referred to it as 'The Sybil War,' or 'The War Between the Dates'"); and *syllepsis*, a word used differently in relation to two other words it governs or modifies ("Bright lights attract flies and celebrity watchers").

purpose: The goal a writer or speaker hopes to achieve with the text—for example, to clarify difficult material, to inform, to convince, and/or to persuade. Also called AIM and INTENTION. In a DRAMATISTIC PENTAD created by a speaker or writer in order to invent material, the words the speaker or writer uses to describe the reason something happened or happens in a particular situation.

ratio: Combination of two or more elements in a DRAMATISTIC PENTAD in order to invent material.

reader's repertoire: The collection of predictions and revisions a person employs when reading a text.

reading: The construction of meaning, PURPOSE, and EFFECT in a text.

reading journal: A log in which readers can trace developing reactions to what they are reading.

recursive: Referring to the moving back and forth from INVENTION to revision in the process of writing.

refutation: In ancient Roman oratory, the part of a speech in which the speaker would anticipate objections to the points being raised and counter them.

reliable narrator: A believable, trustworthy commentator on events and CHARACTERS in a story.

repertoire: A set of assumptions, skills, facts, and experience that a reader brings to a text to make meaning.

repetition: In a text, use more than once of a sound, word, phrase, or clause to emphasize meaning or achieve EFFECT.

revising: Returning to a draft to rethink, reread, and rework ideas and sentences.

rhetor: The speaker or writer who uses elements of RHETORIC effectively in oral or written text.

rhetoric: The art of analyzing all the choices involving language that a writer, speaker, reader, or listener might make in a situation so that the text becomes meaningful, purposeful, and effective; the specific features of texts, written or spoken, that cause them to be meaningful, purposeful, and effective for readers or listeners in a situation.

rhetorical choices: The particular choices a writer or speaker makes to achieve meaning, PURPOSE, or EFFECT.

rhetorical intention: Involvement and investment in and ownership of a piece of writing.

rhetorical mode: Formal patterns for organizing a text, often also used as invention devices. The traditional rhetorical modes are description, narration, exposition, and argumentation. Exposition is frequently subdivided into categories such as comparison/contrast, classification, and division.

rhetorical question: A question posed by the speaker or writer not to seek an answer but instead to affirm or deny a point simply by asking a question about it.

rhetorical situation: The convergence in a situation of exigency (the need to write), AUDIENCE, and PURPOSE.

rhetorical triangle: A diagram showing the relations of writer or speaker, reader or listener, and text in a RHETORICAL SITUATION.

Romance language: A language that is derived from Latin.

round character: A FIGURE with complexity in action and personality.

sarcasm: The use of mockery or bitter irony.

scene: In a DRAMATISTIC PENTAD created by a speaker or writer in order to invent material, the words the speaker or writer uses to describe where and when something happened or happens in a particular situation.

scenic narration: Narration in which an event or a moment of a PLOT is stretched out for dramatic effect.

scheme: An artful variation from typical formation and arrangement of words or sentences.

setting: The CONTEXT—including time and place—of a narrative.

sharing: See PEER REVIEW.

simile: A type of comparison that uses the word *like* or *as*.

simple sentence: A sentence with one independent clause and no dependent clause.

situation: See RHETORICAL SITUATION.

six-part oration: In classical RHETORIC, a speech consisting of exordium, narration, partition, confirmation, refutation, and peroration.

slang: Informal language, often considered inappropriate for formal occasions and text.

soliloquy: Dialogue in which a CHARACTER speaks aloud to himself or herself.

speaker: The person delivering a speech, or the CHARACTER assumed to be speaking a poem.

stance: A writer's or speaker's apparent attitude toward the AUDIENCE.

static character: A figure who remains the same from the beginning to the end of a NARRATIVE.

stock settings: Stereotypical time and place SETTINGS that let readers know a text's GENRE immediately.

style: The choices that writers or speakers make in language for EFFECT.

subject: One of the points on the Aristotelian or RHETORICAL TRIANGLE; the subject matter a writer or speaker is writing or speaking about.

summary narration: Narration in which a brief statement of events moves the plot quickly.

support: In a text, the material offered to make concrete or to back up a GENERALIZATION, CONCLUSION, or CLAIM.

syllogism (SIH-luh-jih-zuhm): Logical reasoning from inarguable PREMISES.

symbol: In a text, an element that stands for more than itself and, therefore, helps to convey a THEME of the text.

synecdoche (suh-NEK-duh-kee): A part of something used to refer to the whole—for example, "50 head of cattle" referring to 50 complete animals.

syntax: The order of words in a sentence.

tautology: A group of words that merely repeats the meaning already conveyed.

theme: The message conveyed by a literary work.

thesis: The main idea in a text, often the main GENERALIZATION, CONCLUSION, or CLAIM.

thesis statement: A single sentence that states a text's THESIS, usually somewhere near the beginning.

tone: The writer's or speaker's attitude toward the subject matter.

topic: The sources or "places" where writers go to discover methods for proof and strategies for presentation of ideas.

trope: An artful variation from expected modes of expression of thoughts and ideas.

understatement: Deliberate playing down of a situation in order to make a point—for example, "As the principal dancer, Joe Smith displayed only two flaws: his arms and his legs."

unity: The sense that a text is, appropriately, about only one subject and achieves one major PURPOSE or EFFECT.

unreliable narrator: An untrustworthy or a naïve commentator on events and CHARACTERS in a story.

verisimilitude: The quality of a text that reflects the truth of actual experience.

voice: The textual features, such as diction and sentence structure, that convey a writer's or speaker's persona.

writing process: The acts a writer goes through, often recursively, to complete a piece of writing: inventing, investigating, planning, drafting, consulting, revising, and editing. The book also uses the plural—writing processes— because no two writers have exactly the same set of acts in exactly the same order.

zeugma: A TROPE in which one word, usually a noun or the main verb, governs two other words not related in meaning ("He maintained a business and his innocence").

Credits

Text Credits

Page 3. From *The Washington Post*, January 16, 2001.

Page 9. From "Smelling Like a Rose", by Frank Deford, *Sports Illustrated*, August 5, 2002. Copyright © 2002 by Time, Inc. Reprinted by permission. All rights reserved.

Page 14. "How About One Study at a Time?" by Jack Anderson and Douglas Cohn, *Washington Merry-Go-Round*, February 1, 2001.

Page 41. "Corporate Sponsorship of Our Schools", by Joel Caris as appeared in *The Scrivener*. Reprinted by permission of the author.

Page 50. "The ABCs of Homeschooling" by Jodie Morse, Time.com, June 29, 2001.

Page 72. Reprinted by permission of the publisher from "On Being the Object of Property" in *The Alchemy of Race and Rights: Diary of a Law Professor* by Patricia J. Williams, pp. 223-224, Cambridge, Mass.: Harvard University Press, Copyright © 1991 by the Present and Fellows of Harvard College.

Page 87. "Testing, Testing", *The Washington Post*, May 12, 2007. © 2007, The Washington Post, reprinted with permission.

Page 101. From "My Name", *The House on Mango Street*. Copyright © 1984 by Sandra Cisneros. Published by Vintage Books, a division of Random House, Inc., and in hardcover by Alfred A. Knopf in 1994. Reprinted by permission of Susan Bergholz Literary Services, New York, NY and Lamy, NM. All rights reserved.

Page 117. "Why White People Need a Civil Rights Museum in Greensboro" by Steve Sumerford, February 4, 2001. Reprinted by permission of the author.

Page 117. Except from the speech "Is Racism Still Alive? Or Have We Overcome?" by C. Eric Lincoln, January 18, 1981, Bennett College.

Page 131. From *Wonderful Life: The Burgess Shale and the Nature of History* by Stephen Jay Gould. Copyright © 1989 by Stephen Jay Gould. Used by permission of W. W. Norton & Company, Inc.

Page 136. From Toni Morrison's 1993 Nobel Prize acceptance speech. © The Nobel Foundation. Reprinted by permission.

Page 138. From "Mother Tongue" by Amy Tan. Copyright © 1990 by Amy Tan. First appeared in *The Threepenny Review*. Reprinted by permission of the author and the Sandra Dijkstra Literary Agency.

Page 139. From "College Pressures", *Blair and Ketchum's Country Journal*, Vol. VI, No. 4, April 1979. Copyright © 1979 by William K. Zinsser. Reprinted by permission of the author.

Page 140. From *Sula* by Toni Morrison, New York: Alfred A. Knopf, Inc., 1973.

Pages 142–143. Reprinted with the permission of Simon & Schuster Adult Publishing Group from *Yellow Woman and a Beauty of the Spirit* by Leslie Marmon Silko. Copyright © 1996 by Leslie Marmon Silko.

Page 147. From *The Bridge of Beyond* by Simone Schwarz-Bart. Copyright © 1972 by Editions du Seuil. Originally published in French as *Pluie Et Vent Sur Télumée Miracle* by Editions du Seuil. English translation by Barbara Bray. Copyright © 1974 by Atheneum Publishers. Reprinted by permission of Georges Borchardt, Inc., for Editions du Seuil.

Page 275. "Freedom Struggle" from *Separate Is Not Equal: Brown v. Board of Education* online exhibition, National Museum of American History, Smithsonian Institution, Harry R. Rubenstein and Alonzo Smith, Authors. Reprinted by permission.

Page 280. "The soul selects her own society" by Emily Dickinson. Reprinted by permission of the publishers and the Trustees of Amherst College from *The Poems of Emily Dickinson*, Thomas H. Johnson, ed., Cambridge, Mass.: The Belknap Press of Harvard University Press, Copyright © 1951, 1955, 1979, 1983 by the President and Fellows of Harvard College.

Page 297. "Shakespeare's Sister" from *A Room of One's Own* by Virginia Woolf, copyright 1929 by Harcourt, Inc. and renewed 1957 by Leonard Woolf, reprinted by permission of the publisher.

Page 299. "Girls Against Boys?" by Katha Pollitt first published in *The Nation*, January 30, 2006. Reprinted by permission of the author.

Page 318. "Stranger in the Village" from *Notes of a Native Son* by James Baldwin. Copyright © 1955, renewed 1983, by James Baldwin. Reprinted by permission of Beacon Press, Boston.

Page 327. All pages from "A Very Old Man with Enormous Wings" from *Leaf Storm and Other Stories* by Gabriel Garcia Marquez. Translated by Gregory Rabassa. Copyright © 1971 by Gabriel Garcia Marquez. Reprinted by permission of HarperCollins Publishers.

Page 332. "Indian Boarding School: The Runaways" by Louise Erdrich. © 1984 by Louise Erdrich. Reprinted with permission of The Wylie Agency, Inc.

Page 339. "An Open Letter to African-American Men" by Leonard Pitts, Jr., as appeared in *Counterpunch* Magazine retrieved from http://www.counterpunch.org. © Tribune Media Services, Inc. Reprinted with permission. All rights reserved.

Pages 337–338. From *Maus II: A Survivor's Tale/and Here My Troubles Began* by Art Spiegelman, copyright © 1986, 1989, 1990, 1991 by Art Spiegelman. Used by permission of Pantheon Books, a division of Random House, Inc.

Illustration Credits

Page 1: Copyright © The New Yorker Collection, 1990. Mick Stevens from Cartoonbank.com.

Page 27: LEE Industries.

Page 28: The Advertising Archives.

Page 33: Copyright © The New Yorker Collection, 1976. George Booth from Cartoonbank.com.

Page 57: Copyright © The New Yorker Collection, 1992. Robert Weber from Cartoonbank.com.

Page 93: Copyright © The New Yorker Collection, 2004. Mick Stevens from Cartoonbank.com.

Page 125: Copyright © The New Yorker Collection. 1998. Everett Opie from Cartoonbank.com.

Page 153: PEANUTS reprinted by permission of United Feature Syndicate, Inc.

Page 182: Digital Image © The Museum of Modern Art/Licensed by SCALA / Art Resource, NY.

Page 191: PEANUTS reprinted by permission of United Feature Syndicate, Inc.

Page 204: Andrew Melrose, "Westward the Star of Empire Takes Its Way." Copyright © Post Road Gallery, Larchmont, NY, 1974.

Page 221: National Portrait Gallery, Smithsonian Institution/Art Resource, NY.

Page 237: Photo from Against Love Poetry. Photo taken by Allison Otto from Stanford Daily.

Page 239: Noah Ber/AP Images.

Page 249: © Copyright 2003. Rock the Vote.

Page 250: © Copyright 2004. Rock the Vote.

A Guide to Avoiding Plagiarism

Plagiarism is using someone else's work—words, ideas, or illustrations, published or unpublished—without giving the creator of that work sufficient credit. A serious breach of scholarly ethics, plagiarism can have severe consequences. Students risk a failing grade or disciplinary action ranging from suspension to expulsion. A record of such action can adversely affect professional opportunities in the future as well as graduate school admission.

Documentation: The Key to Avoiding Unintentional Plagiarism

It can be difficult to tell when you have unintentionally plagiarized something. The legal doctrine of **fair use** allows writers to use a limited amount of another's work in their own papers and books. However, to make sure that they are not plagiarizing that work, writers need to take care to credit the source accurately and clearly for *every* use. **Documentation** is the method writers employ to give credit to the creators of material they use. It involves providing essential information about the source of the material, which enables readers to find the material for themselves. It requires two elements: (1) a list of sources used in the paper and (2) citations in the text to items in that list. To use documentation and avoid unintentionally plagiarizing from a source, you need to know how to

- Identify sources and information that need to be documented.
- Document sources in a Works Cited list.
- Use material gathered from sources: in summary, paraphrase, and quotation.
- Create in-text references.
- Use correct grammar and punctuation to blend quotations into a paper.

Identifying Sources and Information That Need to Be Documented

Whenever you use information from **outside sources**, you need to identify the source of that material. Major outside sources include books, newspapers, magazines, government sources, radio and television programs, material from electronic databases, correspondence, films, plays, interviews, speeches, and information from Web sites. Virtually all the information you find in outside sources requires documentation. The one major exception to this guideline is that you do not have to document common knowledge. **Common knowledge** is widely known information about current events, famous people, geographical facts, or familiar history. However, when in doubt, the safest strategy is to provide documentation.

Documenting Sources in a Works Cited List

You need to choose the documentation style that is dominant in your field or required by your instructor. Take care to use only one documentation style in any one paper and to follow its documentation formats consistently. The most widely used style manuals are *MLA Handbook for Writers of Research Papers*, published by the *Modern Language Association* **(MLA)**, which is popular in the fields of English language and literature; the *Publication Manual of the American Psychological Association* **(APA)**, which is favored in the social sciences; and *The Chicago Manual of Style*, published by the **University of Chicago Press (CMS)**, which is preferred in other humanities and sometimes business. Other, more specialized style manuals are used in various fields. Certain information is included in citation formats in all styles:

- Author or other creative individual or entity
- Source of the work
- Relevant identifying numbers or letters
- Title of the work
- Publisher or distributor
- Relevant dates

Constructing a Works Cited List in MLA Style

In an actual Works Cited list, items are not listed separately by type of source. All items are alphabetized by authors' last names. When no author is given, an item can be alphabetized by title, by editor, or by the name of the sponsoring organization. MLA style spells out names in full, inverts only the first author's name, and separates elements with a period. In the MLA Works Cited list below, note the use of punctuation such as commas, colons, and angle brackets to separate and introduce material within elements.

Books

Bidart, Frank. Introduction. <u>Collected Poems</u>. By Robert Lowell. Ed. Frank Bidart and David Gewanter. New York: Farrar, Strauss and Giroux, 2003. vii–xvi.

Chernow, Ron. <u>Alexander Hamilton</u>. New York: Penguin, 2004.

Conant, Jennet. <u>109 East Palace: Robert Oppenheimer and the Secret City of Los Alamos</u>. New York: Simon, 2005.

Maupassant, Guy de. "The Necklace." Trans. Marjorie Laurie. An <u>Introduction to Fiction</u>. Ed. X. J. Kennedy and Dana Gioia. 7th ed. New York: Longman, 1999, 160–66.

—. <u>Tuxedo Park: A Wall Street Tycoon and the Secret Palace of Science That Changed the Course of World War II</u>. New York: Simon, 2002.

Periodicals

"Living on Borrowed Time." <u>Economist</u> 25 Feb.–3 Mar. 2006: 34–37.

"Restoring the Right to Vote." Editorial. <u>New York Times</u>, 10 Jan. 2006, late ed., sec. A: 24.

Spinello, Richard A. "The End of Privacy." America 4 Jan. 1997: 9–13.

Williams, N. R., M. Davey, and K. Klock-Powell. "Rising from the Ashes: Stories of Recovery, Adaptation, and Resiliency in Burn Survivors." <u>Social Work Health Care</u> 36.4 (2003): 53–77.

Zobenica, Jon. "You Might As Well Live." Rev. of <u>A Long Way Down</u> by Nick Hornby. <u>Atlantic</u> July–Aug. 2005: 148.

Electronic Sources

Glanz, William. "Colleges Offer Students Music Downloads." <u>Washington Times</u> 25 Aug. 2004. 17 Oct. 2004 http://washingtontimes.com/business/20040824-103654-1570r.htm.

Human Rights Watch. <u>Libya: A Threat to Society? Arbitrary Detention of Women and Girls for "Social Rehabilitation."</u> Feb. 2006. Index No. E1802. Human Rights Watch. 4 Mar. 2006 http://hrw.org/reports/2006/libya0206/1.htm#_Toc127869341.

McNichol, Elizabeth C., and Iris J. Lav. "State Revenues and Services Remain below Pre-Recession Levels." <u>Center on Budget Policy Priorities</u>. 6 Dec. 2005. 10 Mar. 2006 http://www.cbpp.org/12-6-05sfp2.html.

Reporters Without Borders. "Worldwide Press Freedom Index 2005." <u>Reporters Without Borders</u>. 2005. 28 Feb. 2006 http://www.rsf.org/article.php3?id_article=15331.

Using Material Gathered from Sources: Summary, Paraphrase, Quotation

You can integrate material into your paper in three ways—by summarizing, paraphrasing, and quoting. A quotation, paraphrase, or summary must be used in a manner that accurately conveys the meaning of the source.

A **summary** is a brief restatement in your own words of the source's main ideas. Summary is used to convey the general meaning of the ideas in a source, without giving specific details or examples that may appear in the original. A summary is always much shorter than the work it treats. Take care to give the essential information as clearly and succinctly as possible in your own language.

Rules to Remember

1. Write the summary using your own words.
2. Indicate clearly where the summary begins and ends.
3. Use attribution and parenthetical reference to tell the reader where the material came from.
4. Make sure your summary is an accurate restatement of the source's main ideas.
5. Check that the summary is clearly separated from your own contribution.

A **paraphrase** is a restatement, in your own words and using your own sentence structure, of specific ideas or information from a source. The chief purpose of a paraphrase is *to maintain your own writing style* throughout your paper. A paraphrase can be about as long as the original passage.

Rules to Remember

1. Use your own words and sentence structure. Do not duplicate the source's words or phrases.
2. Use quotation marks within your paraphrase to indicate words and phrases you do quote.
3. Make sure your readers know where the paraphrase begins and ends.
4. Check that your paraphrase is an accurate and objective restatement of the source's specific ideas.
5. Immediately follow your paraphrase with a parenthetical reference indicating the source.

A **quotation** reproduces an actual part of a source, word for word, to support a statement or idea, to provide an example, to advance an argument, or to add interest or color to a discussion. The length of a quotation can range from a word or a phrase to several paragraphs. In general, quote the least amount possible that gets your point across to the reader.

Rules to Remember

1. Copy the words from your source to your paper exactly as they appear in the original. Do not alter the spelling, capitalization, or punctuation of the original. If a quotation contains an obvious error, you may insert [sic], which is Latin for "so" or "thus," to show that the error is in the original.
2. Enclose short quotations (four or fewer lines of text) in quotation marks, and set off longer quotations as block quotations.
3. Immediately follow each quotation with a parenthetical reference that gives the specific source information required.

Creating In-Text References

In-text references need to supply enough information to enable a reader to find the correct source listing in the Works Cited list. To cite a source properly in the text of your report, you generally need to provide some or all of the following information for each use of the source:

- Name of the person or organization that authored the source.
- Title of the source (if there is more than one source by the same author or if no author is given).
- Page, paragraph, or line number, if the source has one.

These items can appear as an attribution in the text ("According to Smith . . . ") or in a parenthetical reference placed directly after the summary, paraphrase, or quotation. The examples that follow are in MLA style.

Using an Introductory Attribution and a Parenthetical Reference

The author, the publication, or a generalized reference can introduce source material. Remaining identifiers (title, page number) can go in the parenthetical reference at the end, as in the first sentence of the example below. If a source, such as a Web site, does not have page numbers, it may be possible to put all the necessary information into the in-text attribution, as in the second sentence of the example below.

The Economist noted that since 2004, "state tax revenues have come roaring back across the country" ("Living" 34). However, McNichol and Lav, writing for the Center on Budget and Policy Priorities, claim that recent gains are not sufficient to make up for the losses suffered.

Identifying material by an author of more than one work used in your paper

The attribution and the parenthetical reference combined must provide the title of the work, the author, and the page number of the citation.

Describing the testing of the first atom bomb, Jennet Conant says, "The test had originally been scheduled for 4:00 A.M. on July 16, when most of the surrounding population would be sound asleep and there would be the least number of witnesses" (109 East Palace 304–05).

Identifying material that the source is quoting

To use material that has been quoted in your cited source, add *qtd. in*, for "quoted in." Here, only one source by Conant is given in the Works Cited list.

The weather was worrisome, but procrastination was even more problematic. General Groves was concerned that "every hour of delay would increase the possibility of someone's attempting to sabotage the tests" (qtd. in Conant, 305).

Using Correct Grammar and Punctuation to Blend Quotations into a Paper

Quotations must blend seamlessly into the writer's original sentence, with the proper punctuation, so that the resulting sentence is neither ungrammatical nor awkward.

Using a Full-Sentence Quotation of Fewer Than Four Lines

A quotation of one or more complete sentences can be enclosed in double quotation marks and introduced with a verb, usually in the present tense and followed by a comma. Omit a period at the close of a quoted sentence, but keep any question mark or exclamation mark. Insert the parenthetical reference, then a period.

One commentator asks, "What accounts for the government's ineptitude in safeguarding our privacy rights?" (Spinello 9).
   "What accounts," Spinello asks, "for the government's ineptitude in safeguarding our privacy rights?" (9).

Introducing a Quotation with a Full Sentence

Use a colon after a full sentence that introduces a quotation.

> Spinello asks an important question: "What accounts for the government's ineptitude in safeguarding our privacy rights?" (9).

Introducing a Quotation with "That"

A single complete sentence can be introduced with a *that* construction.

> Chernow suggests that "the creation of New York's first bank was a formative moment in the city's rise as a world financial center" (199–200).

Quoting Part of a Sentence

Make sure that quoted material blends grammatically into the new sentence.

> McNichol and Lav assert that during that period, state governments were helped by "an array of fiscal gimmicks."

Using a Quotation That Contains Another Quotation

Replace the internal double quotation marks with single quotation marks.

> Lowell was "famous as a 'confessional' writer, but he scorned the term," according to Bidart (vii).

Adding Information to a Quotation

Any addition for clarity or any change for grammatical reasons should be placed in square brackets.

> In <u>109 East Palace</u>, Conant notes the timing of the first atom bomb test, "The test had originally been scheduled for 4:00 A.M. on July 16, [1945,] when most of the surrounding population would be sound asleep" (304–05).

Omitting Information from Source Sentences

Indicate an omission with ellipsis marks (three spaced dots).

> In <u>109 East Palace</u>, Conant says, "The test had originally been scheduled for 4:00 A.M. on July 16, when . . . there would be the least number of witnesses" (304–05).

Using a Quotation of More Than Four Lines

Begin a long quotation on a new line and set off the quotation by indenting it one inch from the left margin and double spacing it throughout. Do not enclose it in quotation marks. Put the parenthetical reference *after* the period at the end of the quotation.

> One international organization recently documented the repression of women's rights in Libya:

> > The government of Libya is arbitrarily detaining women and girls in "social rehabilitation" facilities, . . . locking them up indefinitely without due process. Portrayed as "protective" homes for wayward women and girls, . . . these facilities are de facto prisons . . . [where] the government routinely violates women's and girls' human rights, including those to due process, liberty, freedom of movement, personal dignity, and privacy. (Human)

Is It Plagiarism? Test Yourself on In-Text References

Read the Original Source excerpt. Can you spot the plagiarism in the examples that follow it?

Original Source

> To begin with, language is a system of communication. I make this rather obvious point because to some people nowadays it isn't obvious: they see language as above all a means of "self-expression." Of course, language is one way that we express our personal feelings and thoughts—but so, if it comes to that, are dancing, cooking and making music. Language does much more: it enables us to convey to others what we think, feel and want. Language-as-communication is the prime means of organizing the cooperative activities that enable us to accomplish as groups things we could not possibly do as individuals. Some other species also engage in cooperative activities, but these are either quite simple (as among baboons and wolves) or exceedingly stereotyped (as among bees, ants and termites). Not surprisingly, the communicative systems used by these animals are also simple or stereotypes. Language, our uniquely flexible and intricate system of communication, makes possible our equally flexible and intricate ways of coping with the world around us: in a very real sense, it is what makes us human. (Claiborne 8)

Works Cited entry:

Claiborne, Robert. <u>Our Marvelous Native Tongue: The Life and Times of the English Language</u>. New York: New York Times, 1983.

Plagiarism Example 1

One commentator makes a distinction between language used as **a means of self-expression** and **language-as-communication**. It is the latter that distinguishes human interaction from that of other species and allows humans to work cooperatively on complex tasks (8).

What's wrong? The source's name is not given, and there are no quotation marks around words taken directly from the source (in **boldface** in the example).

Plagiarism Example 2

Claiborne notes that language "is the prime means of organizing the cooperative activities." Without language, we would, consequently, not have civilization.

> *What's wrong?* The page number of the source is missing. A parenthetical reference should immediately follow the material being quoted, paraphrased, or summarized. You may omit a parenthetical reference only if the information that you have included in your attribution is sufficient to identify the source in your Works Cited list and no page number is needed.

Plagiarism Example 3

Other animals also **engage in cooperative activities**. However, these actions are not very complex. Rather they are either the very **simple** activities of, for example, **baboons and wolves** or the **stereotyped** activities of animals such as **bees, ants and termites** (Claiborne 8).

> *What's wrong?* A paraphrase should capture a specific idea from a source but must not duplicate the writer's phrases and words (in **boldface** in the example). In the example, the wording and sentence structure follow the source too closely.

Evaluating Sources

It's very important to evaluate critically every source you consult, especially sources on the Internet, where it can be difficult to separate reliable sources from questionable ones. Ask these questions to help evaluate your sources:

- Is the material relevant to your topic?
- Is the source well respected?
- Is the material accurate?
- Is the information current?
- Is the material from a primary source or a secondary source?

Avoiding Plagiarism: Note-Taking Tips

The most effective way to avoid unintentional plagiarism is to follow a systematic method of note taking and writing.

- **Keep copies of your documentation information.**   For all sources that you use, keep photocopies of the title and copyright pages and the pages with quotations you need. Highlight the relevant citation information in color. Keep these materials until you've completed your paper.

- **Quotation or paraphrase?**   Assume that all the material in your notes is direct quotation unless you indicated otherwise. Double-check any paraphrase for quoted phrases, and insert the necessary quotation marks.

- **Create the Works Cited or References list** *first.*   Before you start writing your paper, your list is a **working bibliography**, a list of possible sources to which you add source entries as you discover them. As you finalize your list, you can delete the items you decided not to use in your paper.

Source: Linda Stern, Publishing School of Continuing and Professional Studies, New York University

Index

Aims 16, 126, 157, 192
Alliteration 83
Anadiplosis 83
Anaphora 83
Antagonist 209
Anthimeria 85
Antimetabole 81
Antithesis 81
Appeals 11, 34, 100, 160, 173-176
Appositive 82
Aristotelian triad 6, 105
Arrangement 35, 58–63, 91, 94, 192,
Argument 42, 104, 136
Assonance 83
Asyndeton 82
Audience 3, 58, 94, 126, 192

Begging the question 45
Brainstorming 96–97

Canons of rhetoric 14, 34, 55, 58, 94
Character 2, 194–199
Claim 10, 35, 89, 157, 192
Climax 83
Cloze test 127–129
Common topics 89
Conflict 205–209
Connotation 79
Consulting 98–99
Context 15, 17, 34, 58, 100, 105,
    106–111
Contractions 65, 66

Delivery 35, 58, 86–87, 91, 94
Denotation 79
Dialect 78
Dialogue 163
Diction 9, 67, 73–79, 217
Drafting 97–98
Dramatic narration 211

Editing 99–100
Effect 10, 192
Ellipsis 82
Enthymeme 42–46, 88, 105, 168
Epistrophe 83
Ethos 12, 35, 169–171
Evidence 35, 157

Figurative language 65, 67,
    79–85
Freewriting 163

Genre 16, 19–21, 58–60, 126, 192
Group work 112–114

Heuristic devices 34
Hyperbole 85

Images 90, 157, 216
Intention 16, 18, 94, 103–104, 126, 135–139
Invention 14, 35, 36–51, 58, 94,
    103–104, 126
Investigating 96
Irony 85

Jargon 65, 78–29
Journalist's questions 36–39
Journals 110–111

Literacy memory 156–157
Litotes 85
Logic 9
Logos 12, 35, 166–169
Loose sentences 68–69

Memory 35, 52–53, 58, 94
Metaphor 84, 90, 162
Metonymy 84
Mnemonic devices 52

Narrative 192
Narrator 209–215

Occasion 58
Onomatopoeia 85
Oxymoron 85

Parallel structure 70–72, 80
Parenthesis 81
Passive voice 66–67
Personification 84
Pathos 12, 35, 171–173
Pentad 39–42, 89, 105, 198–199,
    215–216
Periodic sentences 68–69
Periphrasis 84
Persona 6, 11, 105, 129, 192,
Planning 96–97
Plot 204–209
Point of view 209–215
Prediction 126–130, 158–165
Pronouns 65–66
Protagonist 209
Puns 84
Purpose 16, 58, 157

Reading 157–176
Reading, aesthetic 131
Reading, efferent 131
Reader's repertoire 143–145, 157–158
Researched argument 176–187
Revising 99, 114–116, 118–122, 161–176
Rhetor 4
Rhetoric 1–92, 96, 192–218

Rhetorical analysis 87–90, 134–135,
    139–143
Rhetorical choices 2
Rhetorical questions 85, 89, 162
Rhetorical situation 18, 94
Rhetorical triangle 6–8, 11, 12, 16, 17, 130

Sarcasm 85
Scenic narration 202–204
Schemes 79–83
Sentence structure 67–68
Setting 200–202
Simile 84
Slang 78–79
Speaker 3
Stance 132
Style 35, 5863–85, 91, 94, 126
Summary narration 202–204
Syllogism 43, 88, 167
Symbols 10, 216
Synecdoche 84
Syntax 217–218
Synthesis 176–187

Theme 197–198, 215–218
Thesis statement 14, 163
Tone 9, 160, 197–198
Topics 46–51, 105
Tropes 79, 83–85

Veresimilitude 162
Voice 104, 131, 165–166

Writing process 18, 94–100